Textbook of Agriculture

About the Authors

Dr. Aashish Vivek Vaidya, presently working as Assistant Professor, Department of Horticulture, SDMVM College of Agriculture, Georai Tanda, Aurangabad, Maharashtra. He completed his Bachelor's Degree from Agriculture College, Dhule, Mahatma Phule Krishi Vidyapeeth, Rahuri, Maharashtra and Master's Degree (Horticulture - vegetable science) from Sheer-e-Kashmir University of Agricultural Sciences and Technology of Kashmir, Srinagar, J and K (India). He is awarded with Gold Medal and Certificate of Merit with 1st rank at University level, in the respective discipline. He completed his Ph.D. in Horticulture (Vegetable Science) from Post Graduate Institute, Mahatma Phule Krishi Vidyapeeth, Rahuri, Maharashtra, India. His fields of specialisation are vegetable breeding, crossing programs, producing F-1 Hybrids and Floriculture / Landscaping. He is also awarded as an INSPIRE FELLOW from Department of Science and Technology, Government of India, which is equivalent to SRF (senior research fellow) of ICAR. He has membership of different National and International Societies and has published seven full-length research papers and one Popular Article in different International Journals.

Dr. Rajan Saran presently working as Assistant Professor (Agricultural Entomology), Adhiyamaan College of Agriculture and Research, Athimugam, Krishnagiri, T.N. He completed his bachelor's degree from AC & RI, TNAU, Coimbatore, T.N. and master's degree from Sher-e-Kashmir University of Agricultural Sciences and Technology, Srinagar, J & K (India). He completed his Ph.D. in Agriculture (Entomology) from Agricultural College and Research Institute, Tamil Nadu Agricultural University, T.N. (India). His fields of specialisation are mass production of bio-control agents and hosts, DNA extraction from rice and residue estimation using HPLC and GC. He received several awards and recognitions. Dr. Rajan has membership of different national and international societies and attended many sympoisa/conferences. He has published 13 research papers/abstracts in different national and international journals.

Textbook of Agriculture

A.V . Vaidya

Assistant Professor (Horticulture)
SDM VM College of Agriculture
Georai Tanda, Aurangabad, Maharashtra

R. Saran

Assistant Professor (Agricultural Entomology)
Adhiyamaan College of Agricultural and Research
Athimugam, Krishnagiri, T.N.

2017

Educationist Press

An Imprint of

Write & Print Publications

New Delhi-110 015

Cataloging in Publication Data—DK
Courtesy: D.K. Agencies (P) Ltd. <docinfo@dkagencies.com>

Vaidya, A. V. (Ashish Vivek), author.
Textbook of agriculture / A.V. Vaidya, R. Saran.
pages cm
Includes bibliographical references and index.
ISBN 9789384649760
1. Agriculture—Textbooks. 2. Agriculture—India—Textbooks.
I. Saran, R. (Rajan), author. II. Title.

S495.V35 2017 DDC 630 23

ISBN: 978-93-84649-76-0

Publisher's note:

Every possible effort has been made to ensure that the information contained in this book is accurate at the time of going to press, and the publisher and authors/editors cannot accept responsibility for any errors or omissions, however caused. No responsibility for loss or damage occasioned to any person acting, or refraining from action, as a result of the material in this publication can be accepted by the authors/editors, the publisher or the authors/editors. The Publisher is not associated with any product or vendor mentioned in the book. The contents of this work are intended to further general scientific research, understanding and discussion only. Readers should consult with a specialist where appropriate.

Every effort has been made to trace the owners of copyright material used in this book, if any. The authors/editors and the publisher will be grateful for any omission brought to their notice for acknowledgement in the future authors/editors editions of the book.

Published by : Hitesh Mittal
For Write & Print Publications
H-13, Bali Nagar
New Delhi-110 015
Phone: 011-45635684
E-mail: info@writeandprint.com
Website: www.writeandprint.com

Laser Typesetting : Anshu Gupta
Delhi - 110 059

Printed in India

Preface

The present book is mainly intended for the agriculral courses of graduate students in the field of agriculture, and horticulture. It is clear that young students are suffering from cultural shocks to shift from their environment. Semester system of education of B.Sc.(Ag.), and B.Sc. (Horti.), students are quite dynamic for which the students are to be helped for changeover. We can identify their difficulties for comprehensation of language, non-availability of textbooks for their semester system. There is a need to use simple language. The present book titled "A Text book of Agriculture" suite to the need of students. This book is written in simple understandable language dealing with various subject matters of agriculture to keep the sylalbus od ICAR. In general, the courses dealt to the graduate students are principles of agricuture, agricultural heritage of India, principles of weed science of field crops and biofuel crops. This book has been prepared with a specific purpose of importing complete comprehensive information about agronomy and we hope that the students and readers will find this with much utility.While information in some chapters such as importance of agriculture in Indian economy, principles of crop production, cultivation of rice in India, cultivation of wheat in India, cultivation of pigeonpea, cultivation of sugarcane, cultivation of tomato, cultivation of cauliflower, cultivation of mango, cultivation of rose, weathering of rock, soil formation, major soils of India, soil erosion and its control, common farm implement, nutrient functions and deficiency symptoms, manures (FYM, compost and green manure) and fertilizers (urea, diammonium phosphate, single superphosphate and muriate of potash), structure and function and cell organelles, plant growth regulators and biotechnology, photosynthesis, respiration and transpiration, isomerism, titrimetry and volumetry, functions of carbohydrates, proteins, nucleic acids, enzymes and vitamins, major pests and diseases of rice, major pests and diseases of maize, major pests and diseases of pulses, major pest and diseases of fruits and vegetables, insect pests of crucifer vegetables, and MCQs have been included in the present edition. For those who take intelligent interest in agriculture—and their number is increasing fast-the present edition would serve as a useful book.

The book is a treasure-trove of valuable agricultural knowledge for a large audience of scientists, policy-planners, researchers, extension-workers, students, progressive farmers and other stakeholders. This expanded edition of the handbook encapsulates research information on the present science-led developments in Indian agriculture, on-going research efforts at the national level and ideas on the future needs of the agriculture.

We sure that the present book has been prepared in most simple, clear and in appropriate manner so that easy to grasp and remember, based on syllabus of most of agricultural competitive examinations with basic and current knowledge of various fields of agriculture. This book will serve as valuable text cum reference book to the graduate students of agricultural universities.

A.V . Vaidya
R. Saran

Contents

1

Importance of Agriculture in Indian Economy

INTRODUCTION

In India around 70% of the population earnsits livelihood from agriculture. It still provides livelihood to the people in our country. It fulfills the basic need of human beings and animals. It is an important source of raw material for many agro-based industries. India's geographical condition is unique for agriculture because it provides many favourable conditions. There are plain areas, fertile soil, long growing season and wide variation in climatic condition etc.

Apart from unique geographical conditions, India has been consistently making innovative efforts by using science and technology to increase production.

India is mainly an agricultural country. Agriculture is the most important occupation for most of the Indian families. In India, agriculture contributes about sixteen percent (16%) of total GDP and ten percent (10%) of total exports.

Over 60 % of India's land area is arable making it the second largest country in terms of total arable land. Agricultural products of significant economic value includes rice, wheat, potato, tomato, onion, mangoes, sugar-cane, beans, cotton, etc.

For decades, agriculture has been associated with production of essential food crops. At present, agriculture above and beyond farming includes forestry, dairy, fruit cultivation, poultry, bee keeping, mushroom, arbitrary, etc. Today, processing, marketing and distribution of crops and livestock products etc. are all acknowledged as part of current agriculture. Thus, agriculture could be referred to as the production, processing, promotion and distribution agricultural products. Agriculture plays a critical role in the entire life of a given economy. Agriculture is the backbone of economic system of a given country. In addition to providing food and raw material, agriculture also provides employment opportunities to very large percentage of population. Below are the importances of agriculture:

Source of Livelihood

The main source livelihood of many people is agriculture. Approximately 70% of the people directly rely on agriculture as a mean of living. This high percentage in agriculture is because of none development of non-agricultural activities to absorb the fast growing population. However, most people in developed countries do not engage in agriculture.

Contribution to National revenue

Agriculture is the main source of national income for most developing countries. However, for the developed countries, agriculture contributes a smaller per cent age to their national income.

Supply of Food as well as Fodder

Agricultural sector provides fodder for domestic animals .Cow provides people with milk, which is a form of protective food. Moreover, livestock also meets people's food requirements.

Significance to the International Trade

Agricultural products like sugar, tea, rice, spices, tobacco, coffee etc. constitute the major items of exports of countries that rely on agriculture. If there is smooth development practice of agriculture, imports are reduced while export increases considerably. This helps to reduce countries unfavorable balance of payments as well as saving foreign exchange. This amount may be well used to import other essential inputs, machinery, raw material, and other infrastructure that is helpful for the support of country's economic development.

Marketable Surplus

The growth of agricultural sector contributes to marketable surplus. Many people engage in manufacturing, mining as well as other non- agricultural sector as the nation develops. All these individuals rely on food production that they might meet from the nation's marketable surplus. As agricultural sector, development takes place, production increases and this leads to expansion of marketable surplus. This may be exported to other nations.

Source of Raw Material

The main source of raw materials to major industries such as cotton and jute fabric, sugar, tobacco, edible as well as non-edible oils is agriculture. Moreover, many other industries such as processing of fruits as well as vegetables and rice husking get their raw material mainly from agriculture.

Significance in Transport

Bulks of agricultural products are transported by railways and roadways from farm to factories. Mostly, internal trade is in agricultural products. Moreover, the revenue of the government, to a larger extent, relies on the success of agricultural sector.

Foreign Exchange Resources

The nation's export trade depends largely on agricultural sector. For example, agricultural commodities such as jute, tobacco, spices, oilseeds, raw cotton, tea as well as coffee accounts for approximately 18 % of the entire value of exports of a country. This demonstrates that agriculture products also continue to be important source of earning a country foreign exchange.

Economic Growth

Agriculture is the backbone of Indian economy. Though, with the growth of other sectors, the overall share of agriculture on GDP of the country has decreased. Still, Agriculture continues to play a dominant part in the overall economic scenario of India.

Source of Food for domestic consumption

Food is essential for life. We depend on agricultural outputs for our food requirements. India produces large quantity of food grains such as millets, cereals, pulses, etc. A major portion of the food-stuffs produced is consumed within the country. Our farmers works day and night to feed our population that counts over 1.21 billion.

Besides agriculture with a commercial bias, subsistence agriculture with its emphasis on the production of food for the cultivator's family is widespread. Traditionally, Agriculture is followed as the simplest method of obtaining food for the family. Agriculture in India is more a 'way of life' then a 'mode of business'.

Export

India exports excess food and agricultural products. A large proportion of India's export trade is based on the agricultural products, such as jute, tea, tobacco, coffee, spices, and sugar. It helps in increasing the foreign exchange. India is ranked seventh in terms of agricultural exports. In 2013, India exported agricultural products valuing around 39 billion dollars.

Basic occupation of millions

Agriculture is the basic occupation for majority of main-workers in India. A large number of rural women are also engaged in agriculture. According to 2001 census, over 56.6% of the main workers in India are engaged in agricultural and allied activities.

Agro-based industries

A number of industries are agro-based industries, such as jute, cotton, sugar, tobacco, etc. Raw materials for such industries are supplied from agricultural produce.

Green revolution

Green revolution began in India with an objective to give greater emphasis on Agriculture. The era of Green revolution that began in 1960s witnessed significant increase in the production of food crops. The introduction of improved methods of agriculture and high yielding varieties (HYV) seeds, mainly wheat, had resulted into remarkable improvement in agricultural outputs. The productivity of land increased tremendously giving huge economic boost to the nation.

BACKBONE OF INDIAN ECONOMY

Agriculture is considered the backbone of Indian economy. Despite the fact that in the last 6 decades of planned development era since India became a Republic, a tremendous success India has achieved in the field of industries, agriculture and allied activities of agriculture still continues to provide employment to around 65 per cent of the total workforce.

Agriculture and allied activities make the single largest contribution to GDP (Gross Domestic Product), accounting for almost 27 per cent of the total.

Agriculture supplies bulk of wage goods required by the non-agricultural sector. It provides raw materials for a large section of industries. Sugar, tea, cotton textiles, jute goods, vegetable oil, etc. industries are regularly fed by agricultural produces. Many cottage industries depend on agricultural operations. The contribution of agriculture to the nation's Forex (foreign exchange reserve) is also quite significant. Agriculture accounts for about 18 percent share of the total value of India's export. Agricultural growth has direct impact on poverty eradication.

With an objective of achieving self-sufficiency in the field of agriculture, the initiative of Green revolution were introduced during 1960s. The introduction of HYV seeds for the agriculture of wheat and other grains has given very satisfactory results. Other factors such as agricultural finance, famines, and irrigation methods were also considered. These efforts boosted the Indian economy in a great way. Thus, the importance of Agriculture in Indian economy and society can never be denied Agriculture is not only important but it also provides a base for development.

In India, the agricultural sector occupies a vital position in the overall economy of the country as would be clear from the following:

Share of Agriculture in National Income

Agriculture has got a prime role in Indian economy. Though the share of agriculture in national income has come down, still it has a substantial share in GDP. The contributory share of agriculture in Gross Domestic Product was 55.4 percent in 1950-51, 52 percent in 1960-61 and is reduced to 18.5 percent only at present. The share of the agricultural sector's capital formation in GDP has declined from 2.2 percent in the late-1999s to 1.9 per cent in 2005-06.

Important Contribution to Employment

Agriculture sector, at present, provides livelihood to 65 to 70 per cent of the total population. The sector provides employment to 58.4 per cent of country's workforce and is the single largest private sector occupation.

Important Source of Industrial Development

Various important industries in India find their raw material from agriculture sector -cotton and jute textile industries, sugar, vanaspati, etc. are directly dependent on agriculture. Handlooms, spinning oil milling, rice thrashing, etc. are various small scale and cottage industries, which are dependent on agriculture sector for their raw material. This highlights the importance of agriculture in industrial development of the nation.

Importance in International Trade

India's foreign trade is deeply associated with agriculture sector. Agriculture accounts for about 14.7 per cent of the total export earnings. Besides, goods made with the raw material of agriculture sector also contribute about 20 per cent in Indian exports. In other words, agriculture and its related goods contribute about 38 per cent in total exports of country.

In short, agriculture occupies a central place in the Indian economy. Its performance sets the pace of growth in the economy as a whole. It should, however, be noted that Indian agriculture is still in the state of backwardness, the per capita productivity in agriculture is less than in industry.

GOVERNMENT INITIATIVES

Given the importance of the agriculture sector, the Government of India, in its Budget 2016–17, planned several steps for the sustainable development of agriculture.

Budget 2016-17 proposed a slew of measures to improve agriculture and increase farmers' welfare such as 2.85 million hectares to be brought under irrigation, Rs 287,000 crore grant in aid to be given to gram panchayats and municipalities and 100 per cent village electrification targeted by May 01, 2018.

The government has already taken steps to address two major factors (soil and water) critical to improve agriculture production. Steps have been taken to improve soil fertility on a sustainable basis through the soil health card scheme and to support the organic farming scheme *'Paramparagat Krishi Vikas Yojana'*. Other steps include improved access to irrigation through *'Pradhanmantri Gram Sinchai Yojana'*; enhanced water efficiency through `Per Drop More Crop'; continued support to Mahatma Gandhi National Rural Employment Guarantee Act (MGNREGA) and the creation of a unified national agriculture market to boost the incomes of farmers.

The Government of India recognises the importance of microirrigation, watershed development and *'Pradhan Mantri Krishi Sinchai Yojana'*; thus, it allocated a sum of Rs 5,300 crore for it. It urged the states to focus on this key sector. The state governments are compelled to allocate adequate funds to develop the agriculture sector, take measures to achieve the targeted agricultural growth rate and address the problems of farmers.

The Department of Agriculture and Cooperation under the Ministry of Agriculture has inked MOUs/agreements with 52 countries including the US. In addition, the Department of Agriculture Research & Education (DARE) and the Department of Animal Husbandry, Dairying & Fisheries (DAHD&F) under the Ministry of Agriculture have signed MOUs/agreements with other countries, taking the number of partnerships with other countries to 63. These agreements would provide better agricultural facilities in areas such as research and development, capacity building, germ-plasm exchange, post-harvest management, value addition/food processing, plant protection, animal husbandry, dairy and fisheries. The agreements could help enhance bilateral trade as well.

Given the correlation between improvement in agriculture and the development of the country, the Government of India adopted several initiatives and programmes to ensure continuous growth. It allocated Rs 25,000 crore (US$ 3.67 billion) for the Rural Infrastructure Development Fund (RIFD), Rs 1,500 crore (US$ 220 million) for the long-term rural credit fund, Rs 45,000 crore (US$ 6.60 billion) for the short-term cooperative rural credit finance fund and Rs 25,000 crore (US$ 3.67 billion) for the short-term Regional rural bank (RRB) refinance fund. It also marked an ambitious target of Rs 8.5 lakh crore (US$ 124.71 billion) of agriculture credit during 2015–16.

ROAD AHEAD

The agriculture sector in India is expected to generate better momentum in the next few years due to increased investments in agricultural infrastructure such as irrigation facilities, warehousing and cold storage. Factors such as reduced transaction costs and time, improved port gate management and better fiscal incentives would contribute to the sector's growth. Furthermore, the growing use of genetically modified crops will likely improve the yield for Indian farmers.

The 12th Five-year Plan estimates the foodgrains storage capacity to expand to 35 MT. Also, a 4 per cent growth would help restructure the agriculture sector in India in the next few years.

Exchange rate used: INR1= US$ 0.0147 as of March 1, 2016

2

Principles of Crop Production

INTRODUCTION

Green plants occupy a special place among all living things on earth, the biosphere, because, uniquely, through their greenness, they connect earth to an external source of energy, the sun. They 'pack' this energy into sugars or carbohydrates (CHOs) that become the basis of all other living things, except for some chemoautotrophic organisms, principally bacteria. This puts them at first position on the food chain that includes all other organisms: humans, carnivorous and omnivorous creatures, and decomposers. The carbon-based organic compounds that plants accumulate in vegetative structures and storage organs are, directly or indirectly, food for the vast majority of organisms in the biosphere. Plants alone are independent of other organisms by fixing carbon (C) from atmospheric carbon dioxide (CO2) and producing oxygen (O2) as well as carbohydrates (CHOs). They are dependent only on mineral nutrients and water they absorb from soil for the internal chemistry of their metabolism. The unique process by which plants fix solar energy that then moves through the entire food chain until the C is returned as CO2 to the atmosphere is called photosynthesis

Humans are a part of the food chain and while our ancient ancestors collected plants and hunted animals, we now, with technological development and a large and growing population, secure our food supply and that of our domestic animals by growing plants specifically for those purposes. This essay is written to introduce this important topic of the role of crops in food supply for human existence and survival. While it is written for an agricultural audience, the general principles are relevant to all. This is true if only to counter a view, held by many urban dwellers, now comprising 50% of world population, that food originates in supermarkets.

The essay is presented in two major sections, using a structure recommended by my Australian colleague David Smith as in his book "Rain and Shine"3. First is "How plants grow". David insists we keep the basics in mind at all times using understanding of How Plants Grow as a critical backdrop to farming, which is the second part of the essay, "How we Grow Plants".

HOW PLANTS GROW?

Seed germination

Small though they often are, seeds are fascinating entities. As well as containing the 'germ' – the life package of genes/chromosomes that define the plant – they contain precursor chemicals that set growth and cell differentiation in train, and a small supply of the CHOs mentioned above. Thus, when seeds imbibe water, chemical and osmotic forces begin to operate so that embryonic cells divide and tissues of root and shoot begin to grow, recognizable in a day or two. The process is germination and seedlings can continue growth until the chemical reserves provided to them by mother plants are exhausted. The beginnings of a sense of geo-positioning in the world provided by a seed's genetic code are almost immediately obvious. First, root systems grow downwards and then shoot systems, in some species carrying the seed, grow upwards, pushing through any soil cover or litter into the atmosphere.

For individual seedlings, there are two critical steps that must be achieved before reserves are exhausted. First, emergence from the soil and expansion of seedling leaves and secondly, penetration of the developing root system into soil where it can absorb water and essential mineral nutrients. Then occurs the greatest miracle after life itself, seedling leaves turn green in the presence of sunlight by formation of chlorophyll and connect the plant to the power of the Sun. The plant is then an established properly functioning independent organism that can accumulate C-based compounds and the plant body can grow. Life on earth can now go on! These processes should be constantly on show to all children in primary school classrooms.

Continuing growth, increase in size and leaf area, requires a continuous supply of CHOs from photosynthesis in new expanding leaves and water and nutrients absorbed from soil by roots. But there is much more to growth than this, however. Plants grow by forming new organs, viz. roots, stems, seeds, and other storage organs. These processes are controlled by environmental responses that, like geotropism, come embedded in the genetic code. Thus, most plants will only flower and produce seed if conditions of temperature and day length are appropriate, and these conditions vary widely from species to species. These responses are adaptations that have evolved to ensure that, once established, development will normally lead to flowering, pollination, and seed production, thus maintaining the existence of the species. Survival of successful plants drives evolutionary adaptation. Most plants require pollination from another member of the species so the new seedling is 'after its kind' but not identical to either parent – therein lays scope for evolution – and human controlled plant breeding also.

Development and flowering

Some plants are perennial and live for a number of years, in the case of some trees, for thousands. Many are annual and germinate when conditions are suitable for growth, have a herbage producing stage, then flower and set seed, usually avoiding the season when growing is difficult - too dry, too hot, or too cold. Thus flowering is a hugely important stage in plant development. It follows changes in activity of some buds (meristems) found at ends of shoots, and in axils of leaves and branches, to form flowers rather than more leaves. These changes are mediated by chemical signals sent to these meristems, in response to temperature or changes in day length, or a combination of the two.

For example, wheat and canola respond to increasing day length, so are long-day plants that flower in Spring, though some cultivars require a chilling period (low temperature) before they can respond to increasing day length. So we have "winter" and "spring" types, suited to different sowing times depending upon the temperature regime. This terminology can be confusing, however. Winter types are always sown in Autumn, but in places where Winter is not severe, spring types can be sown also: where Winter is too severe for plant survival, however, only spring types sown in Spring can be successful.

The location of flower buds on plants is also important because it has an effect on growth strategies and thence seed production. Wheat and canola flower on terminal shoots - we call it 'determinate', field peas flower in axils - we call that 'indeterminate'. Each flowering trait has its own advantages and disadvantages. For example, determinate crops are vulnerable to unusual, isolated, periods of stress during flowering. In wheat, for example, a single stress from frost or heat can abort most flowers, so that grain yield is at best very small. In contrast, prolonged flowering of indeterminate crops means that such short stress periods of frost or heat or water shortage have less effect on seed yield. To complicate the matter further, with indeterminate plants there is significant competition for assimilates (CHOs) between growth of seed and further vegetative parts. In determinate plants, however, once seed is set the bulk of assimilate goes to seed growth. Thus, where plants are growing under resource-limiting conditions determinate plants that make a sharp transition in growth pattern at the best time - i.e. the "optimum switchover" from vegetative to reproductive growth - will yield better. By contrast in indeterminate plants, vegetative material increases as yield increases and partition of growth between vegetative and reproductive parts is not optimal for high yield.

Photosynthesis

Photosynthesis is the process of incorporating CO_2 into CHOs in chloroplasts of green leaves. Though the beginning and end points are the same, green plants, all of which have evolved from simple algae, have one of three systems of photosynthesis with different combinations of chemical steps and associated plant anatomy. The most common is the original algal C3 system (so named to recognize the chemical structure of the first product of photosynthesis), then two evolved variants called C4 or CAM, respectively. Crop plants are mainly C3 species.

All leaves have stomates (pores) through which CO_2 diffuses when photosynthesizing leaves reduce internal CO_2 below atmospheric concentration. In C3 plants, arrangement of internal cells means that movement of CO_2 into chloroplasts, where photosynthesis occurs, is slow. In C4 plants, by contrast, CO_2 is captured by an enzyme on entry and transported as C4 acids to chloroplasts in specialized cells that surround vascular traces. There, CO2 is released in high concentration and enters C3 photosynthesis. The result is that C4 plants have higher rates of photosynthesis than C3 plants. This system also works better than C3 at high temperature so, unsurprisingly, most C4 crops are found naturally in tropical and subtropical climates. For example wheat, canola and field pea are C3 plants while corn and green foxtail are C4 plants.

The third system, crassulacean acid metabolism, CAM for short, is named after a family of succulent plants, the Crassulaceae, in which it predominates. This adaptation from C3 is one of timing. Stomates are closed during day time but open at night when CO_2 enters and is concentrated in C4 acids in large succulent cells. During daytime, CO_2 is released and enters C3 photosynthesis. Photosynthetic capacity is limited by capacity for acid storage but some CAM plants also open stomates during the day and that increases photosynthesis. Pineapple is the most important CAM plant grown as a crop.

Water Relations

As we know, plants require a continuous water supply. Although a small amount is used in chemical transformations, most is lost by evaporation from wet cells inside leaves and then by diffusion through stomates to the dry atmosphere beyond, in a process known as transpiration. Stomates must open to allow CO_2 entry to support photosynthesis so transpiration is an inescapable result of plant morphology and metabolism. Plant growth is a continuing exchange with the atmosphere of water for CO_2 while plants seek to maintain water supply and turgor by extracting water from soil. The ratio of water loss:biomass gain is considerable and is in the range 800-1000:1. Since plants colonized land, evolution has presumably been seeking improvement in these processes, with limited but valuable results, such as in selection of C4 and CAM types. In CAM plants, the fact that stomates are mostly closed in daytime greatly reduces water loss so that the ratio of water loss to CO_2 gain over a daily period is much less than in C3 and also in C4 systems. Soils vary greatly in water holding capacity and plants differ significantly in rooting habit – depth, type e.g. taproots and fibrous roots - and ability to withdraw water from soil. They also vary in ability to control loss of water from leaves, owing to differences in size, shape and epidermal wax, and frequency and behavior of stomates. Control of water loss is always made at the expense of CO_2 uptake for growth.

For crops, flow of water from soil to atmosphere through plants is accompanied by direct evaporation of water from soil, particularly when the surface is wet and unprotected by foliage or mulch. This evaporation, which may consume as much of 50% of water loss in annual crops, together with transpiration through plants, is summed in the term evapotranspiration. Reduction of soil evaporation saves water for transpiration so more plant growth can be supported.

Nutrition

Plant growth is a complex of chemical reactions that requires a continuing supply of essential mineral nutrients absorbed from soil by root systems. These nutrients are required in differing amounts, depending upon their roles in plant metabolism, so it is usual to distinguish between those required in large amounts, the macronutrients (N, P, K, S, Ca, Mg) from others in smaller amounts, the micronutrients (Si, Fe, Zn, Cu, Mn, Mo, B, Ni, Co, Cl). Macronutrients occupy central roles in growth, N in photosynthesis and protein metabolism, P in energy transfers, and K in osmotic relations of cells. Micronutrients are involved in a wide range of metabolic reactions. Fe, together with Mg, are critical elements in the structure and operation of chlorophyll and hence in photosynthesis. Cu and Mn are important for N-fixing bacteria that grow symbiotically with legumes.

Many people do not recognize that plant growth is essentially an extractive process taking minerals from the soil, the exact amount varying from plant to plant, amount of growth and stage of maturity. These minerals are in the soil because of break down of the parent rock, or through deposition by dust and/or water. Each plant takes some, and under continued cropping, extraction soon exceeds any new supply. In nature, without human intervention all nutrients are returned to the system but in agriculture different amounts are extracted according to the composition of the harvested yield and its export. One interesting recent change, increasingly common in some countries for energy supply, has been harvesting of cereal straw as well as grain, leading to an additional large extraction of nutrients, notably of K. Another interesting aspect is that though nutrients are ideally available in balanced amounts required by growing plants, there can be absorption and storage for later use during the growth cycle. Thus, in annual crop plants, N for construction of grain protein, more important in legumes and oilseeds that in cereals, is mobilized from chlorophyll in senescing leaves. Thus breeding for high yield in crop plants must keep in mind this evolutionary adaptation: the more rapidly N is extracted from leaves for grain growth, the less active leaf area remains for photosynthesis and assimilate production.

Nitrogen is a very special nutrient and there has been much emphasis on it in crop research and in programs like the Green Revolution. Not only is N required in great amounts in plants but it is important through its relationship with the organic material of soil and chemical transformations by microbial activity there – and, ultimately with any sequestration of carbon in soils. The N content of decaying plant material is transformed to available, soluble, mineral form nitrate (NO_3^-) – but this is vulnerable to loss by leaching to depth as well as gaseous loss, mostly as N2 to the atmosphere. The major source of N in natural systems is from legumes that fix N2 in symbiotic relationships with bacteria, mostly in root nodules. In agriculture this source is important but is complemented by addition of N fertilizer, some mined, but mostly extracted from the atmosphere using natural gas using the Haber-Bosch industrial process.

HOW WE GROW PLANTS

This leads us to a fairly brief discussion of human intervention in the above processes. The change from hunter/gatherers to farming, even only as subsistence, was a logical one. Imagine a woman gathering food a long way from her cave sees a plant with a lot of fruit, picks some and it tastes good - better than any others she has tasted. Being a thinking person (that's what defines a human) she keeps the seed and uses her digging stick to bury it in soil nearer the cave, realizing this will mean a shorter walk to pick fruit in a year or two. The plant grows, and she is pleased. She protects her garden plants and to maintain their productivity removes others that crowd them. She and her family have noticed that faeces and urine are beneficial for plant growth, so they deposit them on the earth near plants. Here we see the beginnings of plant selection, soil cultivation, plant propagation, land clearing, and using manures, all in the cause of better production by plants and human convenience, "The beginning of agriculture".

In this way, subsistence farmers intervene in nature to grow more of the plants they like to eat or need for other uses. In the developed world, farmers grow plants that meet their economic requirements by reasons of price for product or cost of production. In this they compete for markets with other farmers, often in distant places. It is a fallacy to think that farmers simply grow the crops that are best suited to their biophysical environment. In fact, they select from plants that are sufficiently adapted to the environment (temperature, rainfall, evaporative demand) and manage them to avoid stresses that would seriously reduce yield. They do this by growing crops in sequences to make best use of biological interactions between plants of different types while also applying agrochemicals, when needed, to minimize risk of failure from low fertility and invasion by weeds, pests and diseases.

Cropping strategies

On individual farms, the sequences of crops that are grown define the cropping strategy chosen to meet economic and environmental objectives. Common features of the Prairie Zone now are sequences of cereal crops such as wheat and barley, with oil seeds such as canola and sunflower, and the legumes, field pea, lentil, and chickpea. Growing each particular crop means something different in terms of nutrient requirements, response to stresses, competitive ability with weeds, and susceptibility to herbicides applied and to their residues. Cereals are less extractive of nutrients than oilseeds or legumes and legumes fix nitrogen reducing the demand for N fertilizer. Stubble protects soil from erosion and evaporation, canola stubble inhibits root diseases of wheat, and so on.

The cropping strategy was not always like this. As in other parts of the world, prairie cropping systems are continuously evolving. The first settlers commenced with continuous cereals because that was the technology settlers brought with them. As yields declined they introduced a biennial cropping sequence with an alternate (summer) fallow. Yields increased at first but gradually fell as fertility was extracted, and there was serious soil loss by wind and water erosion during sequences of years of low rainfall. New farming techniques and machinery enabled mulch farming to protect summer fallows, but they too have largely been replaced. Research has defined the more important determinants of yield: control of weed burden and manipulation of the N cycle to optimise availability. In due course both were seen to be aspects of responses to fallowing (along with some soil moisture carryover), and it was realised the effects could be better and more economically achieved by using herbicides and N fertilizer or legume crops.

Fallowing is now restricted to low rainfall areas where its contribution to water storage is aided by herbicides rather than tillage to control weeds.

Now with continuous cropping using reduced-tillage, even no-till techniques (conservation farming), soil organic matter and structure are being restored, and costs of land management and crop establishment greatly reduced. Machinery is larger and more precise so more of the operations can be completed with near optimal timing. Standing stubble protects soil from erosion and retains snow until Spring when crops are sown. Last year's stubble means seedlings from precision-sown seed are protected during establishment as they emerge between rows of stubble. Fertilizers are applied as required and placed carefully relative to seed in appropriate quantities and formulations for most effective response. Changes to the systems continue as farmers adopt technology to adapt to changing environmental and economic conditions. The origins of change are often found in tactical variations in management as farmers seek to provide the best conditions for their crops allowing for year-to-year variability in weather and markets.

Tactical management

Measurement and technology and seasonal climate forecasts provide opportunities to better match crop performance with seasonal environmental conditions. This can either take advantage of high yield potential in some years or reduce costs when low yields are inevitable. Note we refer to cropping sequences and not "crop rotations" because that previously common term usually signified a specified, unbreakable sequence of crops. Tactical variation can start with adjustment to cropping sequence at sowing. Early or late start of season provides opportunity for change of cultivar or crop. Low content of water in the soil at sowing signals likelihood of low yield and inputs can be varied accordingly. Low nitrogen at sowing signals need for fertilizer appropriate to water supply. In-crop measurements of soil water and crop N content, or related variables of leaf colour and tiller number, can provide the basis for late fertilizer application, or equally abandonment and diversion of crops to hay or silage. Herbicide applications can be adjusted to weed counts and specific weed populations that emerge with crops. Weather and short-term climate forecasts can be combined with crop models to predict outcomes as a basis for overall management. Farmers need to consider many issues to make the decisions that determine the viability of their cropping enterprises.

Finally then, one of the great principles of crop production is that there is much more to it than adaptation to the biophysical environment in which crops grow.

Understanding the basics of plant growth is an important beginning, but successful cropping is a game of measurement and decision-making that aims to balance odds in favour of farmers. Technology and management skill are essential if farmers are to conquer the challenge of variable climatic and economic environments.

Towards 2050

There are great challenges ahead for cropping and crop production, and continuing need for new knowledge and technology. The world population that is now 7 billion is expected to rise to 9.2 billion by 2050. That introduces the challenge to increase current food production by 70% because almost 1 billion people are currently underfed.

Moreover, the challenge must be met on essentially the present cropping area of 1500 Mha because there is little opportunity for increase in the face of competition for nature conservation and other uses. This large increase in crop production can only be achieved with combinations of greater crop yields and more intensive cropping adapted to local conditions and availability of inputs. Farming systems are dynamic and continuously adapting to changing ecological, environmental and social conditions, while achieving greater production and resource-use efficiency by application of science and technology.

The word sustainability is used loosely without useful definition. In the framework used in this essay, sustainable agriculture is defined as whether society is prepared to allocate enough resources to define problems, research them to find solutions in a reasonable time frame, and ensure adaptive remediation by the farmers.

The solution to "feed and green" the world in 2050 is to support this evolution more strongly by providing farmers with necessary information, inputs, and recognition. The challenge is, however, great. Irrigation, necessary to increase cropping intensity in many areas cannot be extended much more widely than at present, and it is uncertain if the current rate of crop yield increase can be maintained. Society needs greater recognition of food-supply problems, issues of food waste generally, and overconsumption in some societies. It must be prepared to increase funding and support for agricultural research to support the competent and innovative farmers in developed nations.

3

Cultivation of Rice in India

India is one of the world's largest producers of white rice and brown rice, accounting for 20% of all world rice production. Rice is India's pre-eminent crop, and is the staple food of the people of the eastern and southern parts of the country. Production increased from 53.6 million tons in FY 1980 to 74.6 million tons in year 1990, a 39 percent increase over the decade. By year 1992, rice production had reached 181.9 kg, second in the world only to China with its 182 kg. Since 1950 the increase has been more than 350 percent. Most of this increase was the result of an increase in yields; the number of hectares increased only 0 percent during this period. Yields increased from 1,336 kilograms per hectare in FY 1980 to 1,751 kilograms per hectare in FY 1990. The per-hectare yield increased more than 262 percent between 1950 and 1992.

The country's rice production had declined to 89.14 million tonnes in 2009-10 crop year (July–June) from record 99.18 million tonnes in the previous year due to severe drought that affected almost half of the country.India could achieve a record rice production of 100 million tonnes in 2010-11 crop year on the back of better monsoon this year. The India's rice production reached to a record high of 104.32 million tonnes in 2011-2012 crop year (July–June).

Rice is one of the chief grains of India. Moreover, this country has the largest area under rice cultivation, as it is one of the principal food crops. It is in fact the dominant crop of the country. India is one of the leading producers of this crop. Rice is the basic food crop and being a tropical plant, it flourishes comfortably in hot and humid climate. Rice is mainly grown in rain fed areas that receive heavy annual rainfall. That is why it is fundamentally a kharif crop in India. It demands temperature of around 25 degree Celsius and above and rainfall of more than 100 cm. Rice is also grown through irrigation in those areas that receives comparatively less rainfall. Rice is the staple food of eastern and southern parts of India. In 2009-10, total rice production in India amounted to 89.13 million tonnes, which was much less than production of previous year, 99.18 million tonnes.

Rice can be cultivated by different methods based on the type of region. But in India, the traditional methods are still in use for harvesting rice. The fields are initially ploughed and then fertiliser is applied which typically consists of cow dung and then the field is smoothed. The seeds are transplanted by hand and then through proper irrigation, the seeds are cultivated. Rice grows on a variety of soils like silts, loams and gravels. It can also tolerate alkaline as well as acid soils. However, clayey loam is well suited to the raising of this crop. Actually the clayey soil can be easily converted into mud in which rice seedlings can be transplanted easily. Proper care has to be taken as this crop thrives if the soil remains wet and is under water during its growing years. Rice fields should be level and should have low mud walls for retaining water. In the plain areas, excessrainwater is allowed to inundate the rice fields and flow slowly. Rice raised in the well watered lowland areas is known as lowland or wet rice. In the hilly areas, slopes are cut into terraces for the cultivation of rice. Thus, the rice grown in the hilly areas is known as dry or upland rice. Interestingly, per hectare yield of upland rice is comparatively less than that of the wet rice.

The regions cultivating this crop in India is distinguished as the western coastal strip, the eastern coastal strip, covering all the primary deltas, Assam plains and surrounding low hills, foothills and Terai region- along the Himalayas and states like West Bengal, Bihar, eastern Uttar Pradesh, eastern Madhya Pradesh, northern Andhra Pradesh and Orissa. India, being a land of eternal growing season, and the deltas of Kaveri River, Krishna River, Godavari River and Mahanadi River with a thick set-up of canal irrigation, permits farmers to raise two, and in some pockets, even three crops a year. Irrigation has made even three crops a year possible. Irrigation has made it feasible even for Punjab and Haryana, known for their baked climate, to growrice. They even export their excess to other states. Punjab and Haryana grow prized rice for export purposes. The hilly terraced fields from Kashmir to Assam are idyllically suited for rice farming, with age-old hill irrigational conveniences. High yielding kinds, enhanced planting methods, promised irrigation water supply and mounting use of fertilizers have together led to beneficial and quick results. It is the rain fed area that cuts down average yields per hectare.

In some of the states like West Bengal, Assam and Orissa two crops of rice are raised in a year. Winter season in the north western India are extremely cold for rice. Rice is considered as the master crop of coastal India and in some regions of the eastern India where during the summer monsoon rainy season both high temperature and heavy rainfall provide ideal conditions for the cultivation of rice. Almost all parts of India are suitable for raising rice during the summer season provided that the water is available. Thus, rice is also raised even in those parts of western Uttar Pradesh, Punjab and Haryana where low level areas are waterlogged during the summer monsoon rainy season.

Winter rice crop is a long duration crop and summer rice crop is a short duration crop. At some places in the eastern and southern parts of India, rice crop of short duration is followed by the rice crop of long duration. Winter rice crop is raised preferably in low lying areas that remain flooded mainly during the rainy season. Autumn rice is raised in Uttar Pradesh, Maharashtra, Rajasthan, Madhya Pradesh, Punjab and Himachal Pradesh. Summer, autumn and winter rice crops are raised in West Bengal, Andhra Pradesh, Assam and Orissa. Summer rice crop is raised on a small scale and on a small area. However, winter rice crop is actually the leading rice crop accounting for a major portion of the total Hectare under rice in all seasons in the country. Moreover in the last few years, several steps in order to augment yield per hectare were taken up very seriously at all levels.Wheat is a rabbi crop in this country. India ranks fourth in the production of wheat in the world. Favorable Geographical Condition for Wheat Cultivation: In India, wheat is a winter crop. Rice requires a moderate cool climate with moderate rain. In India, it is grown in winter. It needs temperature 10 degree C to 15 degree C for its cultivation. It thrives well in an average temperature of 16-degree C. Warm and sunny weather is essential at the time of ripening. Wheat requires a rainfall of 50 cm to 100 cm during the growing season. Too much rain is injurious to the plant. On irrigated lands, a rainfall of 40 cm to 50 cm is sufficient. Light rainfall and cloudiness before the grain ripens increase the productivity. Alluvial level plains are ideal for wheat cultivation. Slightly rolling plains are also suitable. Plains should be well drained so that water cannot stand there. Wheat requires fertile alluvial soil. Clay loamy soils or even black cotton soils are suitable. Soil should retain moisture. A certain amount of lime in the soil is beneficial. Labor factors are not as important in the wheat cultivation as in the case of rice. However, labor is essential for the cultivation. The other requirements of wheat cultivation include (i) irrigation, (ii) high yielding varieties of seeds and (iii) capitals

Rice is the most important food crop of India covering about one-fourth of the total cropped area and providing food to about half of the Indian population.

This is the staple food of the people living in the eastern and the southern parts of the country, particularly in the areas having over 150 cm annual rainfall. There are about 10,000 varieties of rice in the world out of which about 4,000 are grown in India.

Rice is life for thousands of millions of people. In Asia alone, more than 2,000 million people obtain 60 to 70 per cent of their calories from rice and its products. Recognising the importance of this crop, the United Nations General Assembly declared 2004 as the "International Year of Rice" (IYR).

The theme of IYR—"Rice is life" reflects the importance of rice as a primary food source, and is drawn from an understanding that rice-based systems are essential for food security, poverty alleviation and improved livelihood.

CONDITIONS OF GROWTH

Rice is grown under varying conditions in India from 8° to 25° N latitude and from sea level to about 2,500 metre altitude. It is a tropical plant and requires high heat and high humidity for its successful growth. The temperature should be fairly high at mean monthly of 24°C. It should be 20°- 22°C at the time of sowing, 23°-25°C during growth and 25°-30°C at the harvesting time. The average annual rainfall required by rice is 150 cm.

It is the dominant crop in areas of over 200 cm annual rainfall and is still an important crop in areas of 100-200 cm rainfall. The 100 cm isohyet forms the limit of rice in rainfed areas. In areas receiving less than 100 cm annual rainfall, rice can be grown with the help of irrigation, as is done in Punjab, Haryana and western U.P. About 40 per cent of rice crop in India is raised under irrigation.

However, it is the temporal distribution of rainfall, rather than the total amount of annual rainfall which is more decisive. The rainfall should be fairly distributed throughout the year and no month should have less than 12 cm of rainfall. Lesser amount of rainfall is required as the harvesting time approaches.

The fields must be flooded under 10-12 cm deep water at the time of sowing and during early stages of growth. Therefore, the fields must be level and have low mud walls to retain water. This peculiar requirement of rice makes it primarily a crop of plain areas. Rice grown in well watered lowland plain areas is called wet or lowland rice.

In hilly areas, the hill slopes are cut into terraces for the cultivation of rice. Such a cultivation in which the hill slopes are cut into terraces is called terraced cultivation. The supply of water to the hill terraces is not as much as in the plain areas and the rice grown in hilly areas is called dry or upland rice.

Rice can be grown on a variety of soils including silts, loams and gravels and can tolerate acidic as well as alkaline soils. However, deep fertile clayey or loamy soils which can be easily puddled into mud and develop cracks on drying are considered ideal for raising this crop.

Such soil requirements make it dominantly a crop of river valleys, flood plains, deltas and coastal plains and a dominant crop there. High-level loams and lighter soils can be used for quick maturing varieties of rice. Black lava soil is also useful for rice cultivation.

Rice culture is not much suited to mechanisation and is called 'hoe-culture'. Most of the work in preparing the seed-bed, in broadcasting seeds, or in transplantation of plants from nurseries to the fields, in harvesting and in winnowing operations is done by human hand. Thus it is a labour intensive cultivation and requires large supply of cheap labour for its successful cultivation.

It is, therefore, primarily grown in areas of high population density which provide abundant labour and at the same time, offer ready market for its consumption. In most rice producing states, labour is locally available but in Punjab and Haryana, rice cultivation mainly depends upon the migrant labourers from Bihar and eastern U.P.

To sum up it can be said that rice needs plenty of heat, plenty of rain, plenty of alluvium and plenty of labour to provide plenty of food for plenty of people. There is no other food crop which is so plentiful as rice in India.

METHODS OF RICE CULTIVATION

Following methods of rice cultivation are practised in India.

Broadcasting Method

Seeds are sown broadcast by hand. This method is practised in those areas which are comparatively dry and less fertile and do not have much labour to work in the fields. It is the easiest method requiring minimum input but its yields are also minimum.

Drilling Method

Ploughing of land and sowing of seeds is done by two persons. This method is mostly confined to peninsular India.

Transplantation Method

This method is practised in areas of fertile soil, abundant rainfall and plentiful supply of labour. To begin with, seeds are sown in nursery and seedlings are prepared. After 4-5 weeks the seedlings are uprooted and planted in the field which has already been prepared for the purpose. The entire process is done by hand. It is, therefore, a very difficult method and requires heavy inputs. But at the same time it gives some of the highest yields.

Japanese Method

This method includes the use of high yielding varieties of seeds, sowing the seeds in a raised nursery-bed and transplanting the seedlings in rows so as to make weeding and fertilizing easy. It also involves the use of a heavy dose of fertilizers so that very high yields are obtained. The Japanese method of rice cultivation has been successfully adopted in the main rice producing regions of India.

Rice Cropping Seasons

Rice is grown almost throughout the year in hot and humid regions of eastern and southern parts of India where two to three crops in a year are not uncommon. But in the northern and hilly parts of the country, the winters are too cold for rice cultivation and only one crop is grown in those areas. Table 3.1 gives the period of sowing and harvesting the rice crop.

Table 3.1 Rice Cropping Seasons in India

Crop	Local name	Sowing	Harvesting	%age of area	%age of production
Autumn (Kharif)	Aus or Kar	May-June	Sept-Oct.	39.4	43.91
Winter (Rabi)	Aman, Sali or Karthika	June-July	Nov .-Dec.	54.2	48.79
Summer (Spring)	Boro or Dalua	Nov. – Dec.	March-April	6-4	7-24

Production

India is the second largest producer and consumer of rice in the world after China and accounts for 21 per cent of the world's total rice production. Assuming a normal 2015 monsoon (June to September), MY 2015/16 (October/September) rice production is forecast at 104 MMT (44 million hectares), marginally higher than last year. In MY 2014/15, higher production costs and relatively weak domestic prices created low profit margins. Nevertheless, Post expects that farmers will continue to plant rice due to expectations of prices increases in the government's MSP. Other crops are not sufficiently supported by the government's grain procurement program. Because 40 percent of the rice crop is unirrigated and depends on a good monsoon, a poor and erratic monsoon in 2015 could potentially bring down production by 10 to 12 MMT from the forecast level, while adequate and well distributed rains may further augment forecast production by 2 to 3 MMT.

MY 2014/15 rice production is estimated at 102 MMT (42.5 million hectares) on lower yields of kharif (fall planted) rice and less acreage of rabi (winter planted) rice. Despite higher kharif rice acreage, delayed plantings and erratic monsoon rains from June to August 2014 negatively affected yields in unirrigated areas. Relatively lower water levels due to below normal monsoon rains, coupled with relatively weak domestic prices, have affected planting prospects for the upcoming rabi rice crop. Latest official planting figures for the rabi season crops are significantly lower than last year (1.5 million hectares compared to 1.8 million hectares). Consequently, Post continues to estimate MY 2014/15 rice production and area at 102 MMT (kharif 89.5 MMT and rabi 13 MMT) and 42.5 million hectares (kharif 38.2 million hectares and rabi 4.3 million hectares). The government's 2nd Advance Estimate places MY 2014/15 rice production marginally higher at 103 MMT, largely on higher rabi rice production, but these estimates are subject to future revisions.

India's long-grain Indian Basmati rice is traditionally grown in Punjab, Haryana and western Uttar Pradesh. For MY 2014/15, Basmati rice production is estimated at 8.8 MMT (2.0 million hecatares), up 1.2 MMT from last year. MY 2015/16 is forecast to increase further to 9.5 MMT. Despite relatively lower Basmati prices, farmers are expected to expand area using the PUSA 1509 variety as net returns have reportedly been considerably better than other Basmati and coarse rice varieties.

Rice is the most important food crop in India, contributing more than 40 percent of total food grain production. Although about 60 percent of the rice area is irrigated, rice is predominantly a rainfed kharif season crop with most of the planting closely riding on the onset and progress of the south-west monsoon rains during June through August. However, a small rabi crop taken is grown in the states of West Bengal, Andhra Pradesh, Odisha and Tamil Nadu.

Although India's rice production shows a steady upward trend, production is subject to wider year-on-year fluctuations compared to wheat as the crop is highly dependent on monsoon rains. Expert reports that due to the intensive water and labor use in rice cultivation and diversion of agricultural land for non-agricultural use, rice cultivation area has hit a plateau (around 44 million hectares).

India's overall rice yields are well below the world average, and there are wide variations in rice productivity among the various producing states in the country. Consequently, there is scope for increasing productivity by expanding irrigation facilities and adopting technology. In 2010/11, the GOI launched an initiative to bring the Green Revolution to eastern India by promoting the Green Revolution and other improved technologies to the eastern region of the country (e.g., Bihar, Chhattisgarh, Jharkhand, eastern Uttar Pradesh, West Bengal, and Odisha). The eastern states have realized significant productivity gains in the last few years. The GOI also promotes a "System of Rice Intensification" technology in some rice growing states, which requires less water and chemical fertilizer, but the adoption of this system is relatively slow as it is highly labor intensive.

Agricultural policy makers and experts are increasingly concerned about meeting projected food demand after 2020. Surplus rice growing states like Punjab, Haryana, Uttar Pradesh, Andhra Pradesh and West Bengal, Odisha and other eastern states follow intensive rice-wheat or rice-rice cropping systems, and are facing severe environmental issues, including declining water tables, deteriorating soil health, and emergence of resistant disease/pests in the growing areas. Some state governments are promoting crop diversification to lower water intensive crops like corn, and other horticultural crops, but the higher yield and price variations in these crops discourages farmers to shift out of rice. A significant cropping shift out of rice is not imminent in the near future due to the government's continued emphasis on supporting rice-wheat production for food security and a lack of more profitable and lower risk crop rotation alternatives.

Indian rice cultivation also faces the challenge of global warming and climate change. A significant share of the rice crop is produced in the coastal regions, which are susceptible to a rise in the sea level. Climate change issues like glacier melting and aberrations in the monsoon rain patterns may also potentially affect the rice crop in the mainland.

Hybrid Rice

There are about 50 varieties of hybrid rice, most developed by private seed companies, of which about 25 are popular in the market. Most of the hybrid rice is cultivated in eastern India (e.g., eastern Uttar Pradesh, Bihar, Jharkhand, and Chhattisgarh). The National Food Security Mission set a target to plant three million hectares to hybrid rice by 2011-12. Despite sustained government efforts, area under hybrid rice is estimated at 1.8 million hectares in 2014/15, largely unchanged over the last three years. Growth of area under hybrid rice is severely hampered by (i) the inability to cater to different consumer quality preferences, (ii) low incremental yield realization, and (iii) poor milling quality over traditional varieties. Nevertheless, several private seed companies and public sector institutions are developing improved hybrid rice varieties that have higher quality and yields, which may accelerate hybrid rice adoption in the future.

Biotechnology

Efforts are also underway, mostly in the private sector, to develop transgenic rice varieties to incorporate resistance to various pests, diseases, and abiotic stresses. However, approvals and commercialization of transgenic rice are still years away. Several public sector rice research organizations are doing work on marker assisted breeding of rice for resistance to biotic and abiotic stresses and incorporating quality traits.

Conditions of Growth

Rice is grown under varying conditions in India from 8° to 25° N latitude and from sea level to about 2,500 metre altitude. It is a tropical plant and requires high heat and high humidity for its successful growth. The temperature should be fairly high at mean monthly of 24°C. It should be 20°- 22°C at the time of sowing, 23°-25°C during growth and 25°-30°C at the harvesting time. The average annual rainfall required by rice is 150 cm.

It is the dominant crop in areas of over 200 cm annual rainfall and is still an important crop in areas of 100-200 cm rainfall. The 100 cm isohyet forms the limit of rice in rainfed areas. In areas receiving less than 100 cm annual rainfall, rice can be grown with the help of irrigation, as is done in Punjab, Haryana and western U.P. About 40 per cent of rice crop in India is raised under irrigation.

However, it is the temporal distribution of rainfall, rather than the total amount of annual rainfall which is more decisive. The rainfall should be fairly distributed throughout the year and no month should have less than 12 cm of rainfall. Lesser amount of rainfall is required as the harvesting time approaches.

The fields must be flooded under 10-12 cm deep water at the time of sowing and during early stages of growth. Therefore, the fields must be level and have low mud walls to retain water. This peculiar requirement of rice makes it primarily a crop of plain areas. Rice grown in well watered lowland plain areas is called wet or lowland rice.

In hilly areas, the hill slopes are cut into terraces for the cultivation of rice. Such a cultivation in which the hill slopes are cut into terraces is called terraced cultivation. The supply of water to the hill terraces is not as much as in the plain areas and the rice grown in hilly areas is called dry or upland rice.

Rice can be grown on a variety of soils including silts, loams and gravels and can tolerate acidic as well as alkaline soils. However, deep fertile clayey or loamy soils which can be easily puddled into mud and develop cracks on drying are considered ideal for raising this crop.

Such soil requirements make it dominantly a crop of river valleys, flood plains, deltas and coastal plains and a dominant crop there. High-level loams and lighter soils can be used for quick maturing varieties of rice. Black lava soil is also useful for rice cultivation.

Rice culture is not much suited to mechanisation and is called 'hoe-culture'. Most of the work in preparing the seed-bed, in broadcasting seeds, or in transplantation of plants from nurseries to the fields, in harvesting and in winnowing operations is done by human hand. Thus it is a labour intensive cultivation and requires large supply of cheap labour for its successful cultivation.

It is, therefore, primarily grown in areas of high population density which provide abundant labour and at the same time, offer ready market for its consumption. In most rice producing states, labour is locally available but in Punjab and Haryana, rice cultivation mainly depends upon the migrant labourers from Bihar and eastern U.P.

To sum up it can be said that rice needs plenty of heat, plenty of rain, plenty of alluvium and plenty of labour to provide plenty of food for plenty of people. There is no other food crop which is so plentiful as rice in India.

Rice cultivation in India is confined to four ecosystems which are as follows.

- Irrigated
- Rainfed Upland
- Rainfed Lowland
- Flood prone.

Rice crop is extremely versatile and adaptive and as far as India is concerned it can be grown in most agro climatic zones and soil varieties. Rice can be grown at altitudes ranging from sea level to 3000metres. Heat and Humidity is a prerequisite for the rice plant The average temperature range throughout the crop cycle is between 21 to 37 degrees centigrade. Temperature, rainfall , humidity and other climatic conditions affect the plant. Rice is grown in all types of soils. Since rice cultivation requires large amounts of water and moisture ,those soils which have water retention capabilities for long periods are ideal. Clay and loam soils suit growth of rice. The following soil types are most suitable for rice cultivation.

- Alluvial soil
- Black soil
- Red soil
- Lateritic soil.

Rice is chiefly grown in the Kharif and Rabi season though there are parts of the country where it is grown in three or even four seasons. Harvesting of rice is generally undertaken upon the maturity of the grains. The paddy grains should consist of at least 20% moisture at harvest time. Harvested paddy is dried under shade to reduce the moisture content to about 14% which is the required limit for storing and milling.

Post-harvest the the problem is one of marketing the rice produced. Buyers and Sellers together create a market. Being a staple commodity the demand for rice comes from millions of consumers. In rural areas producers are also consumers and and about 57% of the production is consumed locally by the farmers and the rest is marketed.

PRPTECTION

Diseases and Pests take a heavy toll on the Rice crop every year. We can use the following classification of diseases and pests to understand the above.

- Insect Pests
- Nematode Problems
- Fungal disease
- Bacterial disease
- Viral disease

Insects Pests

Rice in India is grown in different agro-climatic zones and ecosystems. Insect pests vary according to the conditions. Insect pests are more prone to irrigated areas. Another endemic factor is the use of nitrogenous fertilizers. There are about 100 species of insect species which attack rice crops out of which about nine are considered common:

1. Stem borer	4. Leafhoppers	7. Rice bug
2. Gall midge	5. Whorl maggot	8. Rice caseworm
3. Plant hopper	6. Cutworm	9. Rice hispa

Nematode Problems

A nematode parasite affects rice plants in most agro ecological systems The losses caused due to nematodes are often difficult to investigate. These problems are often ignored by the farmers due to their unstable economic conditions. It is imperative to develop resistant varieties to reduce the incidence. Apart from causing direct damage nematodes often expose plants to disease causing pathogens thereby increasing the risk of disease infection. The average losses caused by the nematode pest is more in the developing countries than the developed ones.

Fungal Diseases

Fungal pathogens cause a number of diseases. They are about a dozen in number and their etiology has to be understood in order to manage the consequences. The following fungal diseases are worth mentioning:

1. Blast	4. Foot Rot	7. False Smut
2. Sheath Blight	5. Sheath rot	8. Bunt/kernel smut
3. Brown spot	6. Stem rot	9. Udbatta

Integrated Disease management is the best way to control the abovementioned diseases. The concern is to maintain the health of the crops. Chemical control generally dominates the IDM. Crop health surveillance is a good strategy within the IDM system. It involves a thorough monitoring system to check prevalence and severity of disease. It may be a one time activity or a regular periodical activity. Surveillance activity also help in identifying potential disease pretty early on so that corrective action may be taken.

Bacterial Disease

The etiology or the causes of bacterial disease are multifarious ranging from heavy use of nitrogenous fertilizers, uneven sowing and planting, high plant population per unit area. Although there are nine types of bacterial diseases the two most common ones are Bacterial Blight and Bacterial Leaf Streak. Bacterial blight was first observed in the coastal region of Maharashtra around the year 1951 . now the disease has spread throughout India. Within the country the losses have been huge , the quantum of loss generally depends on the stage of infection and the severity of it. The losses could range from 6 to 60% as far as grain yield is concerned. The loss is always greater when the disease strikes during the pre-emergence stage rather than the flowering and milk stages. The following management practices are generally recommended to ensure the minimization of the risk of incidence of bacterial blight disease

- Tolerant cultivars should be grown widely
- Seedlings must be raised from a disease free crop and infected seeds must be treated with antibiotics.
- Susceptible collateral hosts around rice fields have to be eradicated.
- Pruning of leaves either at the time of transplanting or afterwards must be avoided.
- Water logging wherever possible should be avoided.
- Field to field irrigation should be avoided and each field should be irrigated through a separate channel.
- Moderate levels of nitrogen and required levels of potassium have to be used.

Viral Diseases of Rice

There are roughly 21 known viral diseases of rice which occur around the world. Historically , it was Japan where a viral infection was recorded as far back as 1897. It has been noted that 1965 onwards viral diseases like tungro, grassy stunt and ragged stunt have occurred mostly in South and South-East Asia. Rice viruses are generally transmitted by insect vectors. Insects such as leafhoppers, planthoppers, aphids and beetles play a large part in transmission of virus. Out of close to thirteen viruses, about ten occur in Asia and the remaining three in Europe. The three most widespread diseases need to be briefly discussed.

Tungro Disease

It has originated in the Philippines and is known since 1940 by various names. This disease is widespread and causes serious losses in production. It has been widely reported from Indonesia, Bangladesh, Thailand , India and Malaysia.

Typical symptoms are the yellowing of leaves and severe stunting of the plant. Tungro is a composite disease caused by the combination of two distinct viruses either individually or jointly. They are the Bacciliform and Spheroid. The tungro virus is generally transmitted by the leafhopper vector. There is no transmission either through the seed or through sap inoculation.

Grassy Stunt Virus

The incidence of this virus is presently very low in India, hence its management aspects have been neglected. It was discovered in Philippines in 1962. The countries where this virus is prevalent is Ceylon, Indonesia, Thailand , Malaysia and JapanThe symptoms are quite similar to what happens in Tungro, the stunting of the plant and the paling and yellowing of leaves. In addition short , erect and pale leaves start appearing. The transmission through an insect vector such as the brown plant-hopper. Rice is the main host for this virus but infection can take place, in other words it can be transmitted to 16 oryza spp and 5 weed hosts.

Ragged Stunt Virus

It was discovered in 1976 mainly in Indonesia and Philippines Of late the incidence of this disease has been quite low and controlled but has a tendency to appear sporadically in localized areas wherever the vector insect and the virus are present. Plants affected with this virus display symptoms of stunted growth, twisting and ragging of leaves with swollen veins. Panicle emergence is late in the infected plants. It is transmitted by different species of brown plant-hopper but not through the eggs The incubation period is quite long varying from four to thirty three days. The insect is capable of long flight. Apart from rice it can infect 17 other graminaceous hosts.

Control of Rice Viral Disease

Conventional methods may not be able to control viral pathogens. Comprehensive and an integrated approach is needed. Resistant varieties, cultural control and chemical methods are used to control the virus. Time of transplanting, adjustment of planting time in low vector population period and use of insecticides are other methods of prevention of disease.

4

Cultivation of Wheat in India

Next to rice, wheat is the most important food-grain of India and is the staple food of millions of Indians, particularly in the northern and north-western parts of the country.

It is rich in proteins, vitamins and carbohydrates and provides balanced food. India is the fourth largest producer of wheat in the world after Russia, the USA and China and accounts for 8.7 per cent of the world's total production of wheat.

CONDITIONS OF GROWTH

Conditions of growth for wheat are more flexible than those of rice. In contrast to rice, wheat is a rabi crop which is sown in the beginning of winter and is harvested in the beginning of summer. The time of sowing and harvesting differs in different regions due to climatic variations.

The sowing of wheat crop normally begins in the September-October in Karnataka, Maharashtra, Andhra Pradesh, Madhya Pradesh and West Bengal; October-November in Bihar, Uttar Pradesh, Punjab, Haryana and Rajasthan and Nov.-Dee. In Himachal Pradesh and Jammu & Kashmir.

The harvesting is done in Jan.- Feb. in Karnataka, Andhra Pradesh, M.P., and in West Bengal; March-April in Punjab, Haryana, U.P. and Rajasthan and in April-May in Himachal Pradesh and J&K. The growing period is variable from one agro-climatic zone to other that effects the vegetative and reproductive period leading to differences in potential yield. The important factors affecting the productivity are seeding time and methodology, crop establishment and climatic conditions during the growing season.

Wheat is primarily a crop of mid-latitude grasslands and requires a cool climate with moderate rainfall. The ideal wheat climate has winter temperature 10° to 15°C and summer temperature varying from 21°C to 26°C. The temperature should be low at the time of sowing but as the harvesting time approaches higher temperatures are required for proper ripening of the crop. But sudden rise in temperature at the time of maturity is harmful.

Wheat thrives well in areas receiving an annual rainfall of about 75 cm. Annual rainfall of 100 cm is the highest limit of wheat cultivation. The isohyet of 100 cm marks the boundary between wheat growing areas on one hand and rice growing areas on the other.

In areas of less than 50 cm annual rainfall, irrigation is necessary for its successful growth. In fact, wheat can be grown in areas with as little as 20-25 cm annual rainfall provided proper irrigation faculties are available.

About 5 to 7 watering are required in irrigated areas depending upon the amount of rainfall. While prolonged drought, especially in rainfed areas, at the time of maturity is harmful, light drizzles and cloudiness at the time of ripening help in increasing the yield. Frost at flowering time and hail storm at the time of ripening can cause heavy damage to the wheat crop.

Although wheat can be grown in a variety of soils, well drained fertile, friable loams and clay loams are the best suited soils for wheat cultivation. It also grows well in the black soil of the Deccan plateau.

Wheat cultivation is an extensive type of farming which is highly mechanized and requires comparatively less labour. It is mainly grown in the flat alluvial plains of north India.

To sum up wheat requires a combination of factors including cool climate with moderate rainfall, flat and well drained plain areas, fertile friable loam and heavy inputs in the form of irrigation, HYV seeds, fertilizers and mechanization.

PRODUCTION

All India area, production and yield of wheat

Year	Area		Production		Yield		% Coverage under irrigation
	(million ha)	Growth rate (%)	(million t)	Growth rate (%)	(kg/ha)	Growth rate (%)	
1997-98	26.70	3.1	66.35	-4.3	2485	-7.2	85.8
1998-99	27.52	3.1	71.29	7.4	2590	4.2	85.8
1999-00	27.49	-0.1	76.37	7.1	2778	7.3	87.2
2000-01	25.73	-6.4	69.68	-8.8	2708	-2.5	88.1
2001-02	26.34	2.4	72.77	4.4	2762	2.0	87.4
2002-03	25.20	-4.3	65.76	-9.6	2610	-5.5	88.0
2003-04	26.60	5.6	72.16	9.7	2713	3.9	88.4
2004-05	26.38	-0.8	68.64	-4.9	2602	-4.1	89.4
2005-06	26.48	0.4	69.35	1.0	2619	0.7	89.6

(contd.)

Year	Area		Production		Yield		% Cover-age under irrigation
	(million ha)	Growth rate (%)	(million t)	Growth rate (%)	(kg/ha)	Growth rate (%)	
2006-07	27.99	5.7	75.81	9.3	2708	3.4	90.2
2007-08	28.04	0.2	78.57	3.6	2802	3.5	90.9
2008-09	27.75	-1.03	80.68	2.7	2907	3.7	91.3
2009-10	28.46	2.6	80.80	0.2	2839	-2.3	91.7
2010-11	29.07	2.1	86.87	7.5	2988	5.2	92.1
2011-12	29.86	2.7	94.88	9.2	3177	6.3	92.9
2012-13	30.00	0.5	93.51	-1.4	3117	-1.9	N.A.
2013-14*	31.19	4.0	95.91	2.6	3075	-1.4	N.A.
2014-15$			**88.43-102.55**				

Note : 1. The yield rates given above have been worked out on the basis of production & area figures taken in '000units,
2. N.A.: Not Available,
3. * 4th Advance estimates,
4. $ Projections are based on statistical models using past years data since 1950-51.

Source: Agricultural Statistics at a Glance, 2014, Directorate of Economics and Statistics, Ministry of Agriculture, Govt. of India (Website: http://www.dacnet.nic.in/eands).

DISTRIBUTION (2015)

India Wheat Total Distribution by Year

Market Year	Total Distribution	Unit of Measure	Growth Rate
2005	72778	(1000 MT)	-7.95 %
2006	78076	(1000 MT)	7.28 %
2007	82269	(1000 MT)	5.37 %
2008	84377	(1000 MT)	2.56 %
2009	94327	(1000 MT)	11.79 %
2010	97196	(1000 MT)	3.04 %
2011	102249	(1000 MT)	5.20 %
2012	114848	(1000 MT)	12.32 %
2013	117731	(1000 MT)	2.51 %
2014	113732	(1000 MT)	-3.40 %
2015	106640	(1000 MT)	-6.24 %

Uttar Pradesh

Uttar Pradesh is the leading player in wheat production in India and leads the front with more than 34% share of total wheat production in India. Wheat is grown in more than 96 Lakh hectares out of 168 Lakh hectares of cultivated area.

Wheat is mainly grown in three regions in Uttar Pradesh, which include Eastern Uttar Pradesh, Western Uttar Pradesh and Northern Uttar Pradesh. Out of three regions, Eastern Uttar Pradesh is the largest wheat growing region with more than 52 Lakh hectares of land under wheat cultivation.

Triticum aestivum is the specie of wheat, which is grown in Uttar Pradesh. Also, the yield of wheat production in Uttar Pradesh is more than 3,100 kg per hectare.

Production: 300.010 Lakh Metric Tonnes in 2015.

Punjab

The Land of Five Rivers, Punjab is another leading wheat producing state in the country and stand at 2nd in the list of top 10 largest wheat producing states in India 2015. Punjab has more than 40 Lakh hectares of cultivated land and out of which, wheat is grown in more than 35 Lakh hectares of land.

Punjab is a state with one of the most fertile soils in India and account for more than 18% share of total wheat production in the country, which is 2nd highest after Uttar Pradesh. The species of wheat, which are grown in Punjab are Triticum aestivum and Triticum durum.

Amritsar, Ludhiana, Faridkot, Sangrur and Patiala are some of the major wheat producing districts in Punjab. These districts collectively contribute to more than 60% of total wheat produced in the state.

Production: 164.720 Lakh Metric Tonnes in 2015.

Haryana

Haryana is the next wheat producing state, which produces more than 116 Lakh Metric Tonnes of wheat annually. Wheat is the main crop of Haryana, which is grown in more than 25 Lakh hectares out of over 35 Lakh hectares of cultivated land.

Haryana is among the states with the highest wheat productivity of more than 4 Tonnes/Hectare. *Triticum aestivum* is the specie of wheat, which is grown in districts like Rohtak, Gurgaon, Karnal and Hissar.

Production: 116.30 Lakh Metric Tonnes in 2015.

Rajasthan

Rajasthan, also known as Land of Kings is placed at 5th in the list of top 10 largest wheat producing states in India 2015. Wheat is grown in more than 24 Lakh Hectares of area in Rajasthan and accounts for more than 8% of total wheat production in India.

Triticum aestivum and *Triticum durum* are the species of wheat, which are grown in Ganganagar, Udaipur, Jaipur, Kota and Tonk district of Rajasthan. Rajasthan produces more than 72 Lakh Metric Tonnes of wheat and owns the wheat productivity of more than 2,900 kg/ha.

Production: 72.145 Lakh Metric Tonnes in 2015.

Madhya Pradesh

Madhya Pradesh also known as The Heart of India is the next leading wheat producing state, which account for more than 8.5% of total wheat production in India.

Sharbati and Durum are the famous varieties of wheat, which are produced in districts like Sehore, Hoshangabad, Vidisha, Satna, Raisen, etc. These districts have medium and deep soils, which are suitable for growing wheat.

Sharbati wheat is known for its great taste and softness and always in a great demand in different markets of the country. Wheat is grown in a large area in Madhya Pradesh with more than 43 Lakh Hectares of land under wheat cultivation. The wheat productivity of Madhya Pradesh is more than 1,700 Kg/Hectare.

Production: 76.271 Lakh Metric Tonnes in 2015.

Bihar

With Wheat Production of 40.976 Lakh Metric Tonnes, Bihar is next on this list. Bihar has more than 50 Lakh Hectares of cultivated areas and out of which, wheat is grown in over 21 Lakh hectares.

Bihar has wheat yield of more than 1,900 kg/ha and produces more than 40 Lakh Metric Tonnes of wheat. Siwan, Nalanda, Bhojpur and Begusarai are districts, which account for maximum share of wheat produced in Bihar.

Production: 40. 976 Lakh Metric Tonnes in 2015.

Others

Gujarat is the next wheat producing state and account for more than 4% of total wheat produced in the country. In Gujarat, wheat is grown in a large area, which is more than 12 Lakh hectares of land. Also, Gujarat has a good wheat productivity of more than 3 Tonnes/Hectare. *Triticum aestivum* is the wheat specie, which is grown in many districts of Gujarat that include Kheda, Mehsana, Rajkot and Bhavnagar.

Production: 40.195 Lakh Metric Tonnes in 2015.

Maharashtra is ranked 8th in the list of top 10 largest wheat producing states in India 2015. In this state, Triticum dicoccum wheat is produced, which is grown in the valleys of rivers like Godavari, Krishna and Tapi. In Maharashtra, wheat is grown in area of more than 20 Lakh hectares, which account 4.5% of the total area of the country in which wheat is cultivated.

Production: 23.010 Lakh Metric Tonnes in 2015.

Uttarakhand is in 9th place in this list, which join the league of leading wheat producers with more than 8 Lakh Metric Tonnes of wheat production every year. The area of wheat production in this state exceeds 3.7 Lakh hectares of land.

Production: 8.780 Lakh Metric Tonnes in 2015.

SOIL TREATMENT

Phosphetica culture 2.5 kg + azatobacter 2.5 kg + trycoderma powder 2.5 kg mix with 100-120 kg F.Y.M. and broadcast at the time of last ploughing.

Seed rate and its treatment

- 100kg/hact. (for normal condition)
- 120kg /hact. (for coarse size grain)
- 125 kg /hact. (for late sowing)
- 2.5 kg thiram or 2.5 kg carbendazim or 5 gram trycoderma spore @ 1kg seed.

Spacing and sowing time

- Row to row spacing should be 22.5 to 23 cm
- The late sown wheat should be sown in rows spaced 15-18 cm
- Last Dates up to which sowing would be economical are:
  1. up to 25th December - in North-West plain Zone
  2. up to 10th December - in North-East plain & Central Zone
  3. up to 30th November - in Peninsular Zone

Soaking seeds in water overnight before sowing, using higher seed rate, closer spacing, shallow sowing (2-3 cm) and spreading thin covering of FYM soon after sowing, can reduce loss caused by late sowing, The dwarf wheat should be sown only at 5-6 cm depth as they have shorter coleoptiles. Seeding depth of 8-10 cm results in poor germination and reduced yield.

Irrigation

- First at 20-25 day after sowing
- Second at 40-45 day after sowing
- Third at 60-65 day after sowing
- Forth at 80-85 day after sowing
- Fifth at 100-105 day after sowing
- Sixth at 115-120 day after sowing

Pre-emergence

As pre-emergence, only Stomp 30EC (Pendimethalin) is available which can be applied @ 3300 ml/ha (100 g a.i/ha) at 0-3 days after sowing in 500 liters of water/ ha. Care must be taken to have fine tilth for better performance of pendimethalin. It controls both grasses and broadleaved weeds.

Post-emergence

During the last 3-4 years a number of herbicides were found effective against even the resistant biotypes of Phalaris minor. Out of the four new herbicides found effective against Phalaris, two namely Sulfosulfuran and Metribuzin were effective against both grassy and non-grassy weeds, whereas clodinafop and fenoxaprop were specific to grassy weeds. Application of Metribuzin should be done carefully as this chemical is not safe at double the recommended dose. Also its application is risky if hot and windy weather prevails and rainfall occurs immediately after its spray/application.

The herbicides that are to be applied as post emergence after first irrigation at 3035 days of sowing or 2-3 leaf stage of Phalaris minor are;

Weed control

- Both Grassy and Broad Leaved
  1. Sulfosulfuran @ 25.0g a.i./ha in 250-300 liters of water /ha.
  2. Metribuzin @ 175 g a.i./ha in at least 500 liters of water /ha.
  3. A mixture of Sulfosulfuran at 25g/ha and metsulfuron methyl @ 4 g/ha in 250-300 liters water /ha.
  4. Combination of 2,4-0 and isoproturon can also be used for the control of mixed weed population in resistance free area.
- Only Grassy Weeds
  1. Clodinafop @ 400 g/ha (60g a.i./ha) in 250-300 liters of water / ha.
  2. Fenoxaprop-ethyl @ 80-120g a.i./ha in 250-300 liters of water / ha.
- Only Broadleaf Weeds
  1. 2,4-0 @ 500 g a.i./ha in 250-300 liters of water /ha.
  2. Metsulfuron methyl @ 4 g a.i. / ha 250-300 liters of water /ha.

Some Useful Hints

Do's

- spray the herbicides, both pre and post emergence, when there is sufficient moisture in the soil. S
- Spray the post-emergence herbicides when Phalaris minor is at 2-3 leaf stage.
- Spray on clear and sunny days only when the leaves are dry.
- Use only flat fan nozzle especially for Fenoxaprop.
- Remove Phalaris minor before seed setting and use as fodder.

- Ensure complete coverage of the field.

Don'ts

- Do not use Sulfosulfuran in mixed cropping system of wheat and mustard or other crops.
- Never apply these post emergence herbicides by mixing with sand, urea or soil.
- Do not mix Clodinafop and Fenoxaprop with 2,4-D

The major diseases of wheat in India are, three rusts - leaf, yellow and stem rust, Karnal bunt, foliar blights, powdery mildew and loose smut. Diseases of limited importance include head scab, foot rot and flag smut; these diseases though of lesser importance, may be important in certain pockets.

Improve varieties

- **Northern Hills Zone (NHZ)**
  1. VL-832,VL-804, HS-365, HS-240 — Irrigated/Rainfed, Medium Fertility, Timely Sown
  2. VL-829,HS-277 — Rainfed, Medium Fertility, Early Sown
  3. HS-375(Himgiri),HS-207, HS-295, HS-420 (Shivalik) — Irrigated/Rainfed, Medium Fertility, Late Sown
  4. HS375 (Himgiri), HPW42 — Very High Altitude
- **Noth Western Plains Zone (NWPZ)**
  1. HD2687,WH-147, WH-542, PBW-343, WH-896(d), PDW-233(d), UP-2338, PBW-502, Shresth (HD 2687), Aditya (HD 2781) — Irrigated, High Fertility,Timely Sown
  2. PBW-435, UP-2425, PBW-373, Raj-3765 — Irrigated, Medium Fertility, Late Sown
- **North Eastern Plain Zone (NEPZ)**
  1. PBW-443, PBW-502, HD-2733, K-9107, HD-2824 (Poorva), HUW-468, NW-1012, HUW-468, HP-1731, Poorva (HD 2824) — Irrigated,High Fertility,Timely Sown
  2. Raj-3765, HD-2643, NW-1014, NW-2036, HUW-234, HW-2045, HP-1744, DBW-14 — Irrigated, Medium Fertility, Late Sown
  3. HDR77, K8027, K8962 — Rainfed, Low Fertility, Late Sown
  4. HD-2888 — Rainfed, Timely Sown
- **Central Zone (CZ)**
  1. DL-803-3, GW-273, GW-190, Lok-1, Raj-1555, HI-8498(d), HI-8381(d) — Irrigated, High Fertility, Timely Sown

2. DL-788-2, GW-173, NI-5439, MP-4010, GW-322, Urja (HD 2864) — Irrigated, Medium Fertility, Late Sown
3. C-306, Sujata, HW-2004, HI-1500, HD-4672(d), JWS-17 — Rainfed, Low Fertility, Timely Sown

- **Peninsular Zone (PZ)**

1. DWR-195, HD-2189,DWR-1006(d), MACS-2846(d), DWR-2001(di), Raj-4037, DDK-1009(di) — Irrigated, High Fertility, Timely Sown
2. HUW-510, NIAW-34, HD-2501, HI-1977, Pusa Tripti (HD-2833) — Irrigated, Medium Fertility, Late Sown
3. A9-30-1, K-9644,NIAW-15(d), HD-2380—Rainfed, Low Fertility, Timely Sown

- **Southern Hills Zone (SHZ)**

1. HW-2044, HW-1085, NP-200(di), HW-741— Rainfed, Low Fertility, Timely Sown
2. HUW-318, HW-741, HW-517, NP-200(di), HW-1085 — Irrigated, High Fertility, Timely Sown

- **National Capital Region Delhi (NCR)**

1. HD-2851(Pusa Visesh), HD-4713(i)(d) — Irrigated, Timely Sown
2. Pusa Gold (WR-544) — Irrigated, Late Sown

Latest Release of wheat varieties

- HD-2894 (2008) — High yielding variety for NCR Delhi, with an average yield of 5.2 t/ha having a protein content of 12.9%, high gluten score, and good chapati making. It is developed by IARI New Delhi
- HD-4713 (durum) (2008) — High yielding durum variety for NCR Delhi, with an average yield of 4.71 t/ha having a protein content of 5.15%. It is resistant to brown rust under both natural and artificial conditions and is suitable for pasta products.
- Pusa Gold (WR-544)(2005) — for late sown, irrigated conditions of Delhi region, released by IARI New Delhi.
- Pusa Visesh (HD-2851) (2005) & HD-4713(d)(i) (2006) — for timely sown, irrigated conditions of Delhi region, released by IARI New Delhi
- Poorva (HD 2824) (2005) — timly sown irrigated for NEPZ region, released by IARI New Delhi
- HD-2888 (2006) — timly sown, Rainfed conditions for NEPZ region, released by IARI New Delhi
- Shresth (HD 2687)(2005), Aditya (HD 2781)(2005) — timly sown, irrigated

conditions of NWPZ region, released by IARI New Delhi

- Pusa Tripti (HD-2833)(2006) — Late sown & Irrigated conditions of PZ, released by IARI New Delhi
- Urja (HD 2864) — for late sown, irrigated conditions for CZ region, released by IARI New Delhi
- Amrta (HI 1500) — for timely sown unirrigated for central India, released by IARI Indore
- Swarna (HI 1479) — for timely sown irrigated condition for central India, released by IARI Indore
- PBW 502 — timly sown, irrigated conditions of NWPZ credited with Punjab Agriculture Univ.
- DBW 14 — late sown,irrigated conditions of NEPZ credited with Directorate of Wheat Research

Diseases

- **Leaf Rust /Brown Rust**- Puccinia recondita tritici.

Distribution: Throughout wheat growing regions of India.

Development: Pathogen over-summers in low and mid altitudes of Himalayas and Nilgiris. Primary infections develop from wind deposited urediospores in eastern Indo-gangetic plains in middle of January where it multiplies and moves westwards by March. Temperatures of 20 ± 5° C with free moisture (rain or dew) cause epidemics. Severe infection causes upto 30 percent yield losses.

Management: The presently recommended varieties in most of the wheat growing zones are rust resistant.

- **Stripe Rust /Yellow Rust-** Puccinia striiformis tritici

Distribution: Hills, foothills and plains of north western India and southern hills zone (Nilgiri hills of Tamilnadu).

Development: Spreads through air-borne urediospores, when temperature are 10¬20°C but the spread is checked above 25°C. Pathogen survives in the cool temperatures of hills (Himalayas and Nilgiris) and the primary infection takes places by middle of January in the foot hills and sub mountainous parts of north western India. Also, infection comes from across the western border, hence the probability of evolution of new races increases in this area. Yellow rust from Nilgiri hills cannot come out of the zone due to high temperatures in the Peninsular and Central India.

Management: Most of the presently recommended varieties are resistant. Major emphasis is on host resistance and cultivation of resistant varieties is the main strategy of management.

- **Stem Rust /Black Rust-** Puccinia graminis tritici

Distribution: Mainly in Peninsular and I Central India, may occur in traces in Northern India too' were the infestation comes late.

Development: Develops from air-borne urediospores, needs free moisture and temperature above 20° C for spread. It can cause severe grain losses if infection is early. The pathogen perpetuates in Nilgiri hills during off season and becomes air¬borne. If Peninsular and Central India experience rainfall during November then epidemics are severe. Late infections cause less damage in north India.

Management: The presently re¬commended varieties in most of the wheat growing zones are rust resistant, hence the old susceptible varieties be avoided.

- **Karnal Bunt-** Tilletia indica (=Neovossia indica)

Distribution: Parts of Northern Plains, especially Punjab, parts of northern Haryana, foot hills of J&K and HP., tarai area of Uttranchal, in lesser severity in Rajasthan, Bihar and UP. The states of Gujarat, Maharashtra, Karnataka and several parts of M.P. are free of KB.

Development: Seed and soil-borne; infection occurs at flowering by means of soil-borne inoculum. The degree of disease development depends upon the weather conditions prevailing during spike emergence to grain filling stage of crop. If the rains occur during the month of February in north Indian plains (disease - prone areas), the disease is likely to come with higher severity.

Management: Among the present day varieties, PBW 502 is resistant while the others show various levels of susceptibility. For management of this disease, one spray of Propiconazole (Tilt 25EC@ 0.1 %) should be given at the time of anthesis. Integration of one spray of propiconazole with one spray of bioagent fungus, Trichoderma viride (0.4% suspension) gives almost cent per cent disease control. The bioagent spray should be done before earhead emergence (Crop growth stage 31- 39 on Zadoks scale), followed by the spray of chemical at start of earhead emergence (crop growth stage 41 -49 on Zadoks scale). Two sprays of T. viride, at these two critical growth stages also give non chemical control of the disease which is almost similar to one spray of propiconazole. Chemical control should be adopted mostly in seed production plots.

- **Black Point-** Alternaria alternate

Development: Disease causes blackening of embryonic region of the seed (black point), discoloration of area beyond the embryonic region (black discoloration (Caused by Aalternata, Curvularia lunate, Epicoccum sp., Bipolaris sorokiniana, etc.) and eye-spot symptom (B. sorokiniana). The warm and humid weather at grain filling or near maturity favors this disease.

Management: This disease is of minor importance. Only when the disease percentage is high, it causes concern to the trader and the consumer. The discolored seeds are mostly shrivelled and they are separated out during processing.

- **Loose Smut-** Ustilago segatum (U. tritici)

Distribution: North Indian plains and northern hills zone.

Development: It is a seed borne disease; infection occurs during Loose Smut

flowering through wind-borne spores. The infection remains dormant inside the otherwise healthy looking seed but the plants grown from such seeds bear infected inflorescence. Infection is favored by cool, humid conditions during flowering period of the host plant.

Management: Disease can be easily controlled through seed treatment with systemic fungicides hence resistance breeding has not attracted much attention. Treat the seed with fungicides like carboxin (Vitavax 75WP @ 2.5g / kg seed), carbendazim (Bavistin 50WP @ 2.5g / kg seed), tebuconazole (Raxil 2DS @ 1.25g / kg seed) if the disease level in the seed lot is high. If it is low to moderate, treat the seed with a combination of Trichoderma viride (@4 g/ kg seed) and half the recommended dose of carboxin (Vitavax 75WP @ 1.25g / kg seed).

- **Foliar Blights-** Bipolaris sorokiniana (Spot blotch), Pyrenophora tritici repentis (leaf blotch or tan spot), Alternaria triticina (Alternaria leaf blight)

Distribution: Mainly in eastern India but also occurs in Peninsular and Central Foliar blights India. This disease complex is emerging as a problem in the north western India too.

Development: The disease requires high temperature and high humidity. This disease is more severe in late sown crop and causes substantial yield losses through formation of shrivelled grains. Most of the varieties are susceptible or moderately susceptible. The disease can be controlled through one spray of propiconazole (Tilt 25EC @ 0.1 %).

- **Powdery Mildew-** Erysiphe graminis tritici

Distribution: Mainly in the cooler areas and hilly region; foot hills and plains of north - western India and the southern hills (Nilgiris).

Development: Powdery mildew can easily be diagnosed by the white, powdery patches that form on the upper surface of leaves and stem. With age, the patches turn dull dirty white and may have small black specks embedded. This disease can spread to all aboveground parts of the plant, including earhead and awns. The disease infects plants during periods of high humidity (not necessarily rain) and cool to moderate temperatures. Low light intensity, which accompanies dry weather and a dense crop canopy favours this disease.

Management: Present day varieties are not resistant to powdery mildew. Hence, the disease severity is more in some pockets. Avoid excessively dense, stands by using adequate seed. For chemical control, one spray of propi-conazole (Tilt 25EC@ 0.1 %) on disease appearance (which usually occurs during early March in northern plains) is highly effective.

- **Head Scab-** Fusarium graminearum

Distribution: Parts of Punjab, especially in the sub mountainous regions. Bread wheat suffers lesser damage than the durum. It was first recorded in severe proportion in some parts of Punjab during 1995-96 crop season and again during 2004-05 crop season.

Development: Disease development is favoured by cool, moist weather with high humidity. Spores are produced on crop debris and reach the leaves through rain splash or wind. Apart from ear head infection, it can cause seedling blight and foot rot leading to lodging. In severe cases, it can cause shriveling of grains and low-test weights. At present, it is a disease of limited importance but has the potential to emerge as a major problem due to the production of toxins.

Management: Bread wheat are more resistant than durum. However, no resistant varieties are available. Hence, vigil is needed for this disease.

- **Cereal Cyst Nematode-** Heterodera avenae

Distribution : This nematode is found In most of the cereal growing regions of the country, especially, the dry and warmer areas of Rajasthan, Haryana and Punjab, but incidence is less in cooler climates.

Development: Larvae enter the roots near the growing point especially, at the seedling stage. Roots of infected plants become predisposed to various soil borne disease like root rots. In infected fields, the losses can be considerably enough.

Management: Most of the wheat cultivars are susceptible but some resist cyst formation. Chemical pesticides, some natural plant products and botanicals, coupled with improved cultural practices help in management of the CCN. For Rajasthan, one CCN resistant variety, CCNRV - 1 is available for the disease prone areas.

- **Seed Gall Nematode /Ear Cockle-** Anguina tritici

Distribution: It is found mainly in some parts of northern India especially the states of Bihar, Jharkhand, eastern U.P. and Chhatisgarh.

Development: These nematodes are spread through seed galls in the seed lots during planting and harvesting. Wet weather favors larval movement and infestation. The nematode invades the crown and basal stem area, finally penetrating floral primordia. This leads to formation of nematode galls in ear heads.

Management: Use of clean seed (free of galls) is the only method to prevent this disease. For removal of galls, the seed lots are floated in 2 - 5 per cent brine solution. The galls, which float on the surface, can be easily separated and destroyed away from the fields. The seed thus cleaned should be washed with fresh water and used for planting.

- **Aphids-** Sitobion avenae, Rhopalosiphum padi and various other species

Distribution: All wheat growing areas, especially in NWPZ and Peninsular India.

Development: The aphids exist in different stages, viz., winged (alates), wingless (apterous) sexual and asexual forms. The rapid spread takes place through asexual reproduction where females give rise directly to nymphs rather than eggs. Infestation usually occurs during second fortnight of January till crop maturity.

Management: When feeding in sufficient numbers, they can cause considerable damage, but under normal conditions, losses are not much. Chemical pesticides are recommended for this pest in wheat if the level of aphids per tiller crosses 10 during vegetative phase and 5 during reproductive phase. However, there is need to keep watch on this pest. The spray of imidacloprid @ 20 g a.i. per ha initially on border rows and if infestation is severe then in entire field will give good protection against this pest. Generally, natural enemies present in the field help in controlling the population of this pest.

- **Brown Wheat Mite-** Petrobia lateens

Distribution: In most of the wheat growing areas, under rainfed conditions, especially in the states of Rajasthan, Haryana and M.P. Sometimes, it is a pest in humid and warm conditions of irrigated areas also.

Development: They Brown wheat cause damage through mite infestation

sucking mouth parts. When present in large numbers, mites cause a silvery flecking on leaves. Individual mites are too small to be visible with naked eye without 'effort. These can be seen by shaking the infested leaves on a white paper.

Management: Most of the times, mites do not cause any production constraint in wheat so no management practices are required. However, there is a need to keep vigil on this pest so that it may not become important in changing cropping sequence of future.

- **Army Worm-** Mythimna separate

Distribution: Mostly in the warmer climates of central India and to some extent in northern plains.

Development & Management: The larvae are found in the cracks of soil and hide during the day but feed during night or early morning. In wet and humid weather, they may feed during day time also. They survive during summer on the subsequent crops like rice and also continue to exist in rice stubbles before wheat crop comes in the field. Recently, this pest is catching attention in the northern India under Rice-Wheat rotation and where rice stubbles / straw remain in the fields.

- **Legume Pod-borer-** Helicoverpa armigera (= Heliothis armigera)

Importance: This is a polyphagous insect that attacks various legumes as a pod border. It is seen damaging wheat ear heads at grain development stage when major hosts are not available. However, the damage is below economic threshold level.

Distribution: It is found mostly in northern and central parts of India. Wheat can serve as a bridge host for carry over of this polyphagous pest.

- **Termites-** Odontotermis obesus, Microtermis obesi

Distribution: Mainly in the northern and central India, but also in some pockets of peninsular India.

Early Symptoms of Damage: Termites attack the crop at various growth stages,

from seedlings to maturity. The severely damaged plants can be easily uprooted and look wilted and dried. In case roots are partially damaged, the plants show yellowing.

Management: For effective management, chemicals like endosulfan, chlorpyriphos and carbosulfan can be used both for seed treatment and for broadcast of treated soil in standing crop.

5

Cultivation of Pigeonpea

The pigeonpea (*Cajanus cajan*) is a perennial legume from the family Fabaceae. Since its domestication in India at least 3,500 years ago, its seeds have become a common food grain in Asia, Africa, and Latin America. It is consumed in a large scale mainly in south Asiaand is a major source of protein for the population of that subcontinent.

Today, pigeonpea is widely cultivated in all tropical and semitropical regions of both the Old and the New Worlds. Pigeon peas can be of a perennial variety, in which the crop can last three to five years (although the seed yield drops considerably after the first two years), or an annual variety more suitable for seed production.

Pigeonpea is an important legume crop of rainfed agriculture in the semiarid tropics. The Indian subcontinent, eastern Africa and Central America, in that order, are the world's three main pigeon pea-producing regions. Pigeon peas are cultivated in more than 25 tropical and subtropical countries, either as a sole crop or intermixed with cereals, such as sorghum (*Sorghum bicolor*), pearl millet (*Pennisetum glaucum*), or maize (*Zea mays*), or with other legumes, such as peanuts (*Arachis hypogaea*). Being a legume, the pigeon pea enriches soil through symbiotic nitrogen fixation.

The crop is cultivated on marginal land by resource-poor farmers, who commonly grow traditional medium- and long-duration (5-11 months) landraces. Short-duration pigeon peas (3-4 months) suitable for multiple cropping have recently been developed. Traditionally, the use of such input as fertilizers, weeding, irrigation, and pesticides is minimal, so present yield levels are low (average = 700 kg/ha). Greater attention is now being given to managing the crop because it is in high demand at remunerative prices.

Pigeon peas are very drought-resistant, so can be grown in areas with less than 650 mm annual rainfall. With the maize crop failing three out of five years in drought-prone areas of Kenya, a consortium led by the International Crops

Research Institute for the Semi-Arid Tropics (ICRISAT) aimed to promote the pigeon pea as a drought-resistant, nutritious alternative crop. Successive projects encouraged commercialization of legumes, by stimulating the growth of local seed production and agro-dealer networks for distribution and marketing. This work, which included linking producers to wholesalers, helped to increase local producer prices by 20–25% in Nairobi and Mombasa. The commercialization of the pigeon pea is now enabling farmers to buy assets, ranging from mobile phones to productive land and livestock, and is opening pathways for them to move out of poverty.

World production of pigeon peas is estimated at 4.98 million tons. About 77% of this is grown in India. Africa is the secondary centre of diversity and at present it contributes about 21% of global production with 1.05 million tons. In Africa,Malawi,Tanzania, Kenya, Mozambique and Uganda are the major producers. These days it is the most essential ingredient of animal feed used in West Africa, especially in Nigeria, where it is also grown.

John Spence, a botanist and politician from Trinidad and Tobago, developed several varieties of dwarf pigeon peas which can be harvested by machine, instead of by hand.

CLIMATE

Pigeonpea is predominantly a crop of tropical areas mainly cultivated in semi-arid regions of India. Pigeonpea can be grown between 14°N and 28°N latitude, with a temperature ranging from 26° to 30°C in the rainy season (June to October) and 17° to 22°C in the postrainy (November to March) season. The amount of daily global solar radiation varies from 400 to 430 cal cm day in the rainy season and 380-430 cal cm^{-2} day^{-1} in the postrainy season. Mean annual rainfall ranges from 600 to 1400 mm, of which 80%-90% is received in the rainy season. The length of growing season extends from 120 to 180 days. Isoclimes similar to India exist in western Africa and southern Sudan, a suitable environment for growing pigeonpea. Pigeonpea is very sensitive to low radiation at pod development, therefore flowering during the monsoon and cloudy weather, leads to poor pod formation.

SOILS

In India, pigeonpea is cultivated on Entisols, Alfisols, Enceptisols, and Vertisols. The Entisols found in the alluvial- soil belt of the Indo-Gangetic region are deep loams, slightly alkaline (pH 7.5-8.5), with about 150-200 mm available water storage capacity in 2 m of soil. The Vertisols are characterized by 40-60% clay in the surface soil horizons, pH around 8.0 with a water holding capacity between 150-300 mm, and the available water in the top 1.5-2.0 m of soil. Alfisols are neutral in reaction (pH 6.5-7.0) and relatively shallow with a low-clay content. They are often sandy loam and can retain about 100 mm available water in the root profile. Pigeonpea, being sensitive to water logging, requires a well-drained soil. It does not grow well in saline soil, but can withstand drought reasonably well. Responses to lime indicated by increase in shoot growth and nodulation, have been reported in soils with pH below 5.0 (Edwards 1981).

VARIETIES

Some of the important varieties of pigeon pea released in India for the different maturity groups.

Extra-short-duration varieties of pigeonpea released in India

UPAS-120, Pant A3, Prabhat, ICPL 87 (Pragati), ICPL 151 (Jagriti).

Short-duration varieties of pigeonpea ralaasad in India

Pusa Ageti, T21, HY2 , Pusa 84, C01.

Medium-duration varieties of pigeonpea developed in India

VHY 1, HY 3A, HY 5, AS 71-37, BDN 1, S20

Late-duration varieties of pigaonpaa ralaaaad in India

C11, Bahar, Laxmi (Kanke-3), Gwalior 3

CROPPING SYSTEMS

A cropping system is defined as a combination of crops in spaceand time. The objective of any given system should be to provide the farmer a high and sustainable level of returns. In agronomic terms, the system makes efficient use of the basic resources necessary for plant growth. Pigeon pea is grown both under sole and intercropping systems.

Sole Cropping

Early-maturing (100-120 days) genotypes are grown as a sole crop. These genotypes have a higher harvest index with an average of 34% compared to medium-maturing genotypes at 24%. Therefore, from the cropping system point of view, early-maturing genotypes are better able to 'complement' by providing an increased opportunity for a second crop. Postrainy season pigeonpea are also cultivated as a sole crop. This avoids the wet conditions associated with the rainy season, gives less incidence of pests and diseases, and makes better use of residual soil moisture. Moreover, postrainy season sole crops were found more efficient than the rainy season sole crops.

Pigeonpea Intercropping

Pigeonpea is commonly intercropped with a wide range of crops. In India, it was estimated that 80-90% of the pigeonpea were inter-cropped. Researchers grouped pigeon pea intercrops into three broad categories:

a) With cereals (sorghum, maize, pearl millet, setaria, finger millet, and rainfed rice).

b) With legumes (groundnut, cowpea, mung bean, black gram, soybean, and phaseolus bean).

c) With long-season annuals (caster, cotton, sugarcane, and cassava).

The advantages of intercrops are:

- Intercropping confers greater yield stability than sole cropping. For instance, if one crop fails or grows poorly, the other crop can produce to some extent.
- Under stress conditions, intercropping gives less yield depression than sole cropping.
- Intercropping may reduce the incidence of weeds. The poor canopy cover and slow growth of pigeonpea in the early stages makes a sole crop susceptible to weed. Therefore, a fast-growing intercrop not only gives a potential additional yield benefit, but also reduces the need for weeding.

Land Preparation

Land preparation for pigeonpea requires at least one ploughing during the dry season followed by 2 or 3 harrowings. The "summer" plowing helps in minimizing the weed flora and to conserve moisture. Well-drained soils are necessary for good root and nodule development. Contour beds or a ridge-and-furrow system are useful in preventing water logging by draining excess surface water,and in preventing soil erosion. Organic manure may be applied 2-4 weeks before sowing. In acidic soils 2-4 t ha^{-1} of lime is incorporated 3-4 weeks before sowing to neutralize the acidity. In light soils, a basal application of aldrin 5% dust @ 30 kg ha^{-1} prevents termite infestation.

SEED RATE AND SEED TREATMENT

The seeding rate of pigeonpea depends on the desired plant density for a genotype (early, medium or late), cropping system (pure crop, mixed crop, or inter crop), germination rate of seed,and mass of seed.

Seed should be own behind the plough or with the help of seed drill at a row spacing of 60-75 cm keeping 15-20 cm distance from plant to plant. A seed rate of 12-15 kg per hectare is sufficient. In mixed cropping seed rate is adjusted according to the proportion of arhar and companion crops to be grown. In the intercropping seed rate remains same as for pure crops.

Good quality and pure seed (registered or certified) of the selected variety should be used from a reliable source. Before sowing, the seed should be treated with thiram @ 1.5 g kg^{-1} of seed plus penta-chloro-nitro benzene (PCNB) [Brassicol® a.i.1.5 g kg^{-1}] seed. This will avoid seed rot and seedling blight diseases. At ICRISAT we recommend seed treatment with 3 g thiram kg^{-1} + 3 g carbendazim kg^{-1} seed.

Sowing Time

In the rainfed and dry areas pigeon pea are sown with the onset of the monsoon. Earlier sowing gives higher yields in India. When sowing extra-early and early-maturing varieties in the 1st fortnight of June, the field is available for post rainy season crops by the end of November. Therefore, sowing should not be delayed beyond June.

The sowing of medium and late-maturing varieties, under rainfed conditions, should be d o n e during June or July at the onset of the monsoon. This should be preferably before the 2nd week of July. Late sowing causes considerable reduction in yield due to photoperiodicity and excessive soil moisture stress which coincides with the reproductive growth. The postrainy season sowing in India should be done in September. In sowings later than 15 October, yields drastically decline.

Methods of Sowing

Three systems of sowings are practiced for pigeon pea. The common is flat sowing, the other methods are broadbed-and-furrow for extra-early group and ridge-and-furrow for the late maturity group. The latter two methods are useful in fields with poor surface drainage and water logging. The raised beds or ridges also provide better aeration and nodulation in comparison to the flat sown crop. Experiments at the Indian Agricultural Research Institute, New Delhi, have shown that pigeonpea sown on a ridge-and-furrow system in fields prone to water logging gave 30 % more yield compared to flat sowing (IARI 1971). At ICRISAT a broad bed and furrow system is used for sowing extra-early genotypes, and ridges-and-furrows are used for medium and late duration genotyes.

RESPONSES TO NUTRIENTS

Responses to general fertilizer applications in pigeonpea are quite meager.

Nitrogen (N): Researchers reviewed the studies in India on the pigeonpea response to N. They concluded the effect was almost negligible. However, in some situations a starter application of 20-25 kg N ha^{-1} was beneficial.

Phosphorus (P): Responses to phosphorus applications have been positive and in some cases highly significant in pigeonpea. Researchers summarized the phosphorus response studies in India.

They concluded that applications of 17-26 kg P ha^{-1} increased seed yield by 300-600 kg ha^{-1}. Responses of pigeonpea to P fertilization would not be expected in soils with more than 5 mg kg^{-1} extractable P by Olsens bicarbonate extraction; although lower values would not necessarily predict a response.

Potassium (K): Pigeonpea does not respond to potassium chloride applications unless it is grown on low available potassium soils.

***Rhizobium* inoculation**: Responses to *Rhizobium* inoculation have been inconsistent. Increases in grain yield of pigeonpea inoculated with effective *Rhizobium* ranged from 19 to 68%.

Zinc (Zn): Most of the pigeonpea cultivars are susceptible to zinc deficiency. Therefore, foliar applications of 2-4 ppm zinc as 0.5% zinc sulfate with 0.25% lime have been effective to over-come zinc deficiencies.

IRRIGATION

Pigeonpea is largely grown as a rainfed crop, however, it is well established that flower initiation and pod setting stages are the most crucial to drought stress. Therefore, irrigation at these stages usually helps the crop. The drought-stress symptoms on pigeon pea are indicated by the leaves pointing towards the sun at noon.

Excessive moisture is detrimental to pigeon pea. It promotes vegetative growth and enhances the incidence of *Phytophthora* and *Alternaria* blight. Therefore, irrigation should be given only when the crop experiences drought stress after flowering and at the pod filling stage. Responses to irrigation are more consistent in postrainy season sown pigeon pea. This crop relies on moisture stored in

the soil profile. Two or three irrigations, 1 mont h after sowing, increased seed yield by about 150-160% over the nonirrigated control at ICRISAT Center.

WEED MANAGEMENT

Pigeonpea is a slow-growing crop and mostly cultivated during the rainy season. The crop suffers from early we e d infestation. Therefore, it is necessary to keep the crop weed-free during the early growth period (4-6 weeks). The weeds can be controlled mechanically or with chemicals. A combination of chemical and mechanical control is more economical. At ICRISAT Center, it was observed that a pre emergence application of prometryn (Gesgard® or Caparol® a.i. 1.25 kg ha^{-1}) effectively controlled the initial weeds.

A hand weeding 3-4 week after sowing is required to remove the late emerging weeds. When herbicide is not applied, two or three hand weedings are required from the 1st to 6th week of crop growth. Later the crop will be able to smother t h e weeds. At ICRISAT, hand weedings were always found superior to herbicides, but the herbicides were more economical, hence preferred. The other pre emergence herbicides effective for pigeonpe a are pendimethalin (Stomp® a.i. 1.0-1.5 kg ha^{-1}) or meta chlore (Dual® a.i. 1 kg ha^{-1}). The post emergence herbicides recommended are flausifop-P butyl (Fusilate® a.i. 0.2-0.4 kg ha^{-1}) or bentazon (Basagran® a.i. 1.0 kg ha^{-1}) at 2-4 leaf stage.

DISEASES

Wilt

The most serious is wilt disease (*Fusarium udum*), favored by soil temperatures of 17°-20°C. The fungus enters the plant through the roots and may persist in soilborne stubble for a long time. The leaves of the affected plants become yellowish in colour, then drop and finally the whole plants dry out. The disease, in fact, can be diagnosed by seeing the black streaks on the wood after removing the outer epidermal strip from the major roots.

Control measure

- The only effective control measure is development of resistant cvs (e.g., 'C-ll, C-36, NP-15, NP-38, aT-17'Amar, Azad, Asha, Maruthi, BDN-1, BDN-2,NP-5).
- Rotation with tobacco and intercropping with sorghum is said to decrease the wilt problem.

6

Cultivation of Sugarcane

Sugarcane, or sugar cane, is one of the several species of tall perennial true grasses of the genus *Saccharum*, tribe Andropogoneae, native to the warm temperate to tropical regions of South Asia and Melanesia, and used for sugar production. It has stout jointed fibrous stalks that are rich in the sugar sucrose, which accumulates in the stalk internodes. The plant is two to six metres (six feet seven inches to nineteen feet eight inches) tall. All sugar cane species interbreed and the major commercial cultivars are complex hybrids. Sugarcane belongs to the grass family Poaceae, an economically important seed plant family that includes maize, wheat, rice, and sorghum and many forage crops.

Sucrose, extracted and purified in specialized mill factories, is used as raw material in human food industries or is fermented to produceethanol. Ethanol is produced on a large scale by the Brazilian sugarcane industry. Sugarcane is the world's largest crop by production quantity.[1] In 2012, The Food and Agriculture Organization (FAO) estimates it was cultivated on about 26×10^6 hectares (6.425×10^7acres), in more than 90 countries, with a worldwide harvest of 1.83×10^9 tonnes (1.80×10^9 long tons; 2.02×10^9 short tons). Brazil was the largest producer of sugar cane in the world. The next five major producers, in decreasing amounts of production, were India, China, Thailand, Pakistan and Mexico.

The world demand for sugar is the primary driver of sugarcane agriculture. Cane accounts for 80% of sugar produced; most of the rest is made from sugar beets. Sugarcane predominantly grows in the tropical and subtropical regions (sugar beets grow in colder temperate regions.) Other than sugar, products derived from sugarcane include falernum, molasses, rum, *cachaça* (a traditional spirit from Brazil), bagasse and ethanol. In some regions, people use sugarcane reeds to make pens, mats, screens, and thatch. The young unexpandedinflorescence of *tebu telor* is eaten raw, steamed or toasted, and prepared in various ways in certain island communities of Indonesia.

The Persians, followed by the Greeks, discovered the famous "reeds that produce honey without bees" in India between the 6th and 4th centuries BC. They adopted and then spread sugarcane agriculture. Merchants began to trade in sugar from India, which was considered a luxury and an expensive spice. In the 18th century AD, sugarcane plantations began in Caribbean, South American, Indian Ocean and Pacific island nations and the need for laborers became a major driver of large human migrations, including slave labor[4] andindentured servants.

SOWING OF SUGARCANE CROP

Efficient care and precautions should be taken while selecing the cuttings, treating it with chemicals at the time of planting.

a. **Selection of stem cuttings**: Sugarcane crop is propagated by stem-cutting. The upper- half-portion of the plant bears buds of high viability and are best for raising new crop. Cane setts of two or three nodes, bearing 3 or 4 vegetative buds are made from the healthy, free from insect pests and diseases, top portions of the plants after hand peeling. About 35,000 sets are required for one hectare.

b. **Sett treatment**: Cane-seed-setts are wet and sugary, therefore, while in soil, before sprouting into new plant, these are mostly damaged by insects (termites) and fungus. To avoid these losses, the sets, before planting, are dipped into 0.5% Agallol (3%), or 0.25% Aretan or Tafasan (6%) for 2-3 hours.

c. **Time of planting**: The best time of planting the sugarcane setts for spring crop is the period when the atmospheric temperature records an average of 25°C. Therefore, the time of sowing in Tamil Nadu, Andhra Pradesh, Maharashtra and Karnataka is earlier (December-January) than the time of sowing in Punjab, Haryana, Uttar Pradesh (February-March). The crop can be sown round the year. Crop planted before winter season gives less sprouting and tillers due to cold weather, during early sprouting stage.

d. **Method of sowing**: Sugarcane crop is sown by various methods, depending upon the field problems. Common methods of planting are described here.

   1. **Flat planting**: Flat planting method is mostly common in intensive sugarcane growing areas where soil-moisture is available in plenty. Sets are kept in shallow (8-10 cm) deep furrows at 75 cm apart. On an average, one viable bud per ten centimeter length in each furrow is planted (i.e. one sett/feet). The field is heavily planked. This method of sowing is popular in North India.

   2. **Furrow planting**: Furrow planting method is mostly common under low soil moisture condition. After sowing irrigation is given immediately. Sets are kept deep (10-15 cm) furrows, at 90 cm apart. On an average, a 3 budded sett/feet length is planted. Furrows are covered with 5-6 cm soil and irrigation in furrows is applied.

3. **Trench method**: Trench method of sowing sugarcane is mostly used in areas where strong winds and rainy season cause lodging of the cane i.e. in coastal areas where crop grows tall. Furrows are not made, but in place of these only trench 25 cm deep at 90 cm distance in line are made by manual labour. Fertilizers, and insecticides are mixed with soil and trenches are again filled with soil, keeping one set/trench at the depth of 5 cm. irrigation is applied only on successful sprouting.

PLANTING SEASONS OF SUGARCANE

The duration of sugarcane crop in India ranges from10-18 months. A 12 months crop is most common. Time of planting is governed by weather conditions. Sugarcane requires about 25-32° C temperature for good germination. Spring and autumn plantings are two important planting seasons.

Spring Planting

In Northern India spring planting is done in February-March while in Peninsular India it is done in January-February. Spring planted crop is known as suru in Maharashtra and eksali in Gujarat and Andhra Pradesh.

Autumn Planting

This planting is very popular in northern India. This planting is done in September-October while in Bihar and Peninsular India it is done in October-November. Autumn planting is also known as pre-seasonal planting in Maharashtra and Gujarat. The pre-seasonal crop matures in 13-15 months and supplies sugarcane in early crushing period.

Adsali Planting

In Maharashtra and Karnataka, adsali planting is done I n July-August and the crop matures in 16-18 months. Because of extended growing season, there is increase in yield as well as sugar recovery. Biggest advantage of adsali is that it passes through only one summer season. In the present scenario, area under adsali planting is declining because of less availability of irrigation water.

Late Planting

Because of wheat crop is taken on large area in rabi season in Northern and Central India, planting of sugarcane is delayed until harvesting of wheat in March-April. Research data has been proved conclusively that delay in planting causes considerable yield reduction.

SUGARCANE PLANTING METHODS

1. **Planting in flat beds**: It is very popular method on Northern India and in some parts of Maharashtra. Shallow furrows 8-10 cm deep are made.

Distance between two rows should be kept 75-90 cm. Generally 3 budded setts are used to plant in the end to end planting system. The furrow is covered by 5-7 cm of soil and field is leveled by planking.

2. **Ridge and Furrow Method**: The method is generally adopted in areas with moderate rainfall but have drainage problem. Deep furrows are opened in 'v' shape 10-15 cm deep in North India and 20 cm in Southern India.. It is also practiced in Eastern UP and in Peninsular India particular in heavy soils.

3. **Trench Method or Java method**: It is very common in Java, some coastal areas and in areas where the crop grows very tall and strong winds are blown. 'U' shape trenches are made. The depth of trench is kept 20-25 cm and line to line space is kept 75-90 cm. Setts are planted in these trenches or in small furrows prepared in the centre of trenches by end to end method.

4. **Rayungan Method**: It is the Indonesian term meaning - a developed cane shoot with single sprouted bud. A portion of field is selected for Rayungan production is left at harvesting time. The top of the cane is cut off which results auxiliary buds begin to sprout. For quick and effective sprouting fertilizer especially nitrogen in heavy dose is applied and field is irrigated. After 3-4 weeks sprouted buds are separated in single bud setts and transplanted on ridges. It is costly hence is not commonly adopted in India however is usually used for filling gap.

5. **Distant Planting Method**: It was developed at Indian Institute of Sugarcane Research (IISR) Lucknow. In this method, single budded setts are planted in nursery @20 q/ha or 18000 setts/ha. After 45-60 days single budded setts are planted in the main field at a spacing of 90cm×50cm.

6. **Pit Planting**: This method is very popular in Tillah soil in Assam and also in Kerala hilly tracts. Pits are made at the interspacing of 20-30cm in rows along the contours with row to row spacing of 75 cm, organic manure is placed at bottom of the pits. Cane setts are placed in the triangle in pits and covered with soil. This system can be used in rainhfed agriculture and very useful in conserving the soil.

7. **Skip Furrow Planting**: It is common in Odisha. It is hybrid of flat and trench method. In this method trenches are dug 45 cm apart and a gap of 90 cm is left after each two rows of cane.

8. **Sabling or Sprouting Method**: Plants are sown in fertile soil with wide spacing, shallow planting frequent irrigations and adequate fertilization. Tillers soon after they develop their own roots are separated from the mother plant and planted separately. It is very successful in Java and Cuba.

9. **Tjeblock Method**: Improved over Rayungan method because it takes care of proper availability of energy and nutrient to all the buds. Here stalks are cut off at its half length and planted vertically with node in the soil for rooting. The planted ones and the mother stalks are adequately irrigated

and fertilized. Now the upper buds of both Tjeblocks and mother cane, which sprout in due course of time, are planted by cutting them into setts, as rayungans.

10. **Bud Transplanting**: Sugarcane buds with half of its stalk can be planted in small polyphone sleeves filled with organic manure and soil and after they sprouted out, they can be transplanted in the main field. The polythene is tore at the bottom for the easy rooting. There is less mortality about 5 % only.

11. **Algin Method of Sugarcane Planting**: In this method, upper most nodes are collected while striping the canes for crushing; then it is planted in wheat field in rows after every 4 rows of wheat at 90 cm × 50 cm. The method was developed by Allahabad Agriculture Institute, Allahabad.

SUGARCANE DISEASES AND THEIR MANAGEMENT

Fungus, bacteria and virus cause diseases to sugarcane crop. These are transmitted from one plant to another and one field to another field either by original seed set or causal organism already in the soil or spores are carried by blowing wind. Some of the diseases of sugarcane crop and their suggested control measures are discussed here.

1. **Red rot disease**: This disease is caused by a fungus *Colletotrichum falcatum*: Red rod disease appears in July. Leaves start loosing colour and withering. The stalk becomes dry, wrinkled, hollow and alcoholic smell is emitted. To control disease, if a very few plants are affected then uproot these plants and burn them otherwise discord the whole of the field and do not grow this crop in the same field for at least three years. Fresh sowing should be done with seed-sets from resistant variety, dipping these in 0.25% solution of Agallol or Aretan for 2-3 minutes.

2. **Smut**: The disease is caused in April by *Ustilago scitaminea* in the form of a long, black whiplike structure at the apex of the stalk. It spreads by wind. To control the disease, if affected plants are very few, carefully cut down the apex of the plant in such a way that spores do not spread, by covering with suitable paper-bag and burn it out along with the uprooted affected plant. Otherwise discard and burn the whole field and do not grow sugarcane crop at least for three years in the same field. Fresh sowings are done with resistant varieties.

3. **Wilt**: The disease is caused by a fungus *Cephalosporium sacchari*. The crown leaves become yellow during late season and cane dries. To control the disease, if the affected plants are very i few, then uproot these and bum them otherwise discard or bum i the while field. Fresh sowings are done with resistant variety.

4. **Albino (grassy shoot)**: The disease is caused by a virus. Pale yellow narrow leaves appear in abundance. The plant look like a grass. To control the disease, if the number of the affected plants is not large, uproot and destroy

the affected clumps, otherwise discard the field. Fresh sowing is done after 3-4 years with seed-sets from resistant variety and treat sets at 54°C for 8 hours to inactivate the casual Virus.

5. **Red stripe**: The disease is caused by bacteria *Xanthomonas rubrilineans*. It appears in May. Leaves show red streaks. To control this disease, if affected plants are a few in number, then rogue out these and bum them, otherwise discard tile whole field. Fresh sowings are done with resistant variety in well drained soils.

6. **Ratoon stunting disease of sugarcane**: This disease appeared as 'Q 28 syndrome' in Australia in 1944-45 (a collection of Q28 gave better ratoon whereas another collection failed miserably, as if it was mixture of two genotypes). Initially, it was thought of viral origin but researches have conclusively demonstrated its bacterial etiology. It is caused by a fastidious xylem limited Gram positive bacterium *Leifsonia xyli* subsp. *xyli* (=*Clavibacter xyli* sub sp. *xyli*).

   In India, the presence of the disease was felt only when Prof. Chilton, who visited India as a delegate to attend IX ISSCT Congress (1956), detected it in CoS 510 at Jamnabad farm, Golagokarnath However, its presence in India was actively debated as most of the experiments conducted subsequently in India was not of affirmative nature and the nodal symptoms were elusive/ephemeral. Later on, Dr. Kisan Singh confirmed the presence of RSD from a collection of deteriorating Co 290, obtained from Jaora Sugar Mill area, Jaora (M.P.). He splited the affected canes vertically and treated one half with hot air treatment at 54⁰C for 8 hours and untreated half acted as control. This conclusively demonstrated the curing effect of heat treatment and the presence of RSD. Hereafter, a number of genotypes including the wonder cane Co 419, Co 453, Co 213, Co 312, Co 740, Co 997, CoL 9, BO 22 etc., were reported to be inflicted with the disease. Of late, it has been observed that most of the popular cane genotypes are in cultivation are carrying substantial amount of RSD bacterium. The predominant varieties of subtropical India like BO 91, Co 1148, Co 1158, Co 62399, CoH 56, CoH 72, CoJ 64, CoJ 84291, CoS 767, CoS 88216, CoS 90269, CoS 95255, CoLk 7901, CoPant 84211, CoPant 84212, CoPant 90222, CoSe 92423, etc. are in the clutch of RSD. In fact, no cane area in India is free from the RSD menace; wherever a conscious search was made, its presence was immediately become apparent. This disease is now recognized as the most important bacterial disease of sugarcane in India causing substantial loss in cane yield.

   The name 'ratoon stunting disease' is a misnomer as it is not restricted to the ratoon crop. The disease affects both plant and ratoon crops but its detrimental effect is more pronounced in the latter. In the absence of proper symptoms of the disease, diagnosis of the disease at the field level is exceedingly difficult. In some varieties/clones, pink/orange coloured vascular bundles appear at the nodes, when canes are sliced longitudinally with a sharp knife. The pin-head type symptoms appear reddish coloured on the yellowish white background of the nodal tissues. The damaging nature of the disease is not fully appreciated because the diseased plants look apparently healthy and, in most cases, healthy plants are not available for comparison. The pathogen spreads through the infected setts. Mechanical transmission by the sett cutting and harvesting implements is mainly responsible for the spread of this pathogen. As the disease cannot be detected by the external symptoms, the bacterium spreads surreptitiously defying all the barriers.

Eye Spot Disease in Sugarcane

Causal organism: *Helminthosporium sacchari*

- Usually a crop of 6 - 7 months is more susceptible to the disease.
- Fungus penetrates the host tissue either through stomata, bulliform cells or directly through the cuticle.
- Cloudy weather, high humidity with drizzle coupled with low night temperatures, wetting of leaves either through precipitation or dew greatly enhance disease development.
- Water logging, high fertility status and excess nitrogen fertilization also favour the spread of the disease.

Symptoms

Lesions first appear as small water soaked spots, darker than the surrounding tissues. The spot becomes more elongated, resembling the shape of an eye and turns straw coloured within a few days. Finally, the central portion becomes reddish brown surrounded by straw coloured tissues. Then reddish brown streaks of a runner develop extending from the lesions towards the leaf tip along the veins. Later the spots and streaks coalesce to form large patches and causes drying of leaves.

Pineapple disease in sugarcane

Causal organism: *Ceratocystis paradoxa*

- Typical disease symptoms are detected in setts after 2 - 3 weeks of planting.
- Pathogen enters the sett mainly through the cut ends and destroy the central soft portion i.e., parachymatous tissues of the internode and then damages the buds.
- Drought accelerates the damage.

Symptoms:

- Affected tissues first develop a reddish colour, which turns to brownish black at later stages.

- Cavities are formed inside the severely affected internodes.
- The presence of the fungus inside the sett prevents their rooting.
- In most cases setts decay before bud sprouts or the shoots grow to a height of 6 - 12cm. Thus, causing germination failure leading to reduced initial crop stand per unit area.
- Occasionally, the disease occurs in standing crop too due to the entry of the pathogen through stalk damaged by borers, rats or any such injuries.
- Pathogen spreads rapidly throughout the canes, foliage turns yellow, and ultimately plant withers. The diseased stalk when cut open smells like mature pineapple.

WILT DISEASE OF SUGARCANE

Causal Organism: *Cephalosporium sacchari*

- This is one of the early known diseases of sugarcane in India.
- It was first reported by Butler and Khan in 1913, from North India.
- It has been reported to cause severe damage to sugarcane crops in many parts of India. During 1965-1967 it caused severe damage to sugarcane crop in the Deccan plateau

Symptoms

- The first symptoms of the disease become apparent only when the plant has grown for about 4-5 months.
- The canes show gradual withering.
- On examination of affected clumps , the pith will be seen discoloured purple or dirty reef, with longitudinal streaks
- The leaves of affected clumps gradually turn yellow and dry up.
- A characteristic disagreeable odour is also associated with such diseased canes.
- A cottony white mycelium can also be seen in the pith region.
- Frequently this fungal disease is associated with a saprophytic bacterial growth and often the bacteria are mistaken as causal agents.

Disease Cycle

- The fungal mycelium is abundant in the infected canes.
- The hyphae are hyaline, thin walled and septate.
- They produce numerous microconidia on simple or branched, lateral or terminal hyphae, but NO macroconidia are produced.

- This is an important character which is distint from that of Fusarium. The conidia are oval to elliptical, and measure 4-12 x 2-3µm in size. They are mostly unicellular, but the ones formed later in the advanced growth of the fungus may be septate
- Conidia readily germinate to produce single germ tubes.
- The fungus is transmitted from place to place through the infected seed setts.
- When the diseased setts are planted, the eyes may fail to develop or often the shoots arising from the eyes may wilt, due to the infection spreading to the shoots.
- Root formation in such setts may be very poor. The fungus can also survive in soil as a saprophyte for 2-3 years.
- Near-neutral and alkaline soils are favoured by the fungus. The perfect stage is not known.

Control

1. The disease is controlled by selecting seed setts from disease free areas.
2. Alkaline soils may be avoided for growing the crop. The setts, selected from disease free stalk, should be dipped in organomercurial fungicide before planting.
3. Dipping the setts in 40 ppm of boron or manganese, or spraying the plants with either of these minor elements reduces the disease intensity.

Leaf scald disease in sugarcane

Causal organism: *Xanthomonas albileneans*

- It is a bacterial disease, widely spread in many countries.
- Disease is favoured by wet seasons, water stress due to drought, water logging and low temperatures.

Symptoms:

- Disease symptoms appear in two phases, the chronic and acute phases.
- In the chronic phase, "white pencil line" extending entire length of lamina reaching the margin of young leaves and stripes diffuse later resulting in leaf etiolation. Drying from tip onwards presents a scalded appearance. Different degrees of chlorosis from total albinism to interveinal chlorosis in young leaves during summer, germination of buds in acropetal manner with bushy appearance in standing cane, cut open stalks showing dark red vascular strands, prominent streaks at node invariably in the side shoots, are other prominent symptoms of chronic phase.

- In the acute phase the symptoms appear suddenly and die without any major leaf symptoms. The masking of symptoms is more common during monsoon and symptoms may appear suddenly any time during crop growth.

Grassy Shoot Disease in sugarcane

The grassy shoot disease (GSD) was first recorded by Barber(1919) from Coimbatore. GSD came into prominence when it was observed in Co 419 near Belapur (Maharashtra) in 1949. The affected plant/clump produces excessive, thin, short, lanky, albinoid tillers (grass like (no. of tillers may reach more than 100 per clump) from the base of the affected plant.

The disease is characterized by proliferation as well as premature tillering with narrow chlorotic/albinoid leaf blades. The foliage of young tillers shows different degrees of albinism from chlorotic streaks to the total albinoid plant. Generally, diseased plants raised from the infected setts do not produce millable canes and a good number of affected clump usually fail to sprout after harvest, producing gaps in the ratoons. In the affected clumps, one or two tillers may grow and give rise to full grown cane and remain green, providing nourishment to the entire clump. Such apparently healthy canes provide major source of primary inoculum for the next plant crop. In addition to primary transmission through seed cane it is transmitted (secondary transmission) through leafhopper *Deltocephalus vulgaris* in persistent way. The disease is of phytoplasmal etiology. Tetracycline group of antibiotics (250 ppm) suppress the disease symptoms. The pathogen is eliminated in diseased setts by heat therapy.

Causal organism: Phytoplasma

- It is a mycoplasamal disease.
- Primary transmission of disease is through disease infected setts.

Symptoms

- Profuse tillering with narrow chlorotic leaves giving a grass like appearance is characteristic symptom of GSD incidence.
- Very few tillers of GSD infected plants develop into canes, which are thin and produce white shoots from the side buds.

WATER MANAGEMENT PRACTICES IN SUGARCANE

Introduction

Sugarcane is the one of cash crop cultivated by majority of farmers inTamil Nadu in the irrigated and canal command areas. The crop requires more water in growth period and in the present situation the water scarcity is predominant problem in the areas of irrigated and canal command. The farmers are urged to adopt the water management practices to conserve soil moisture and to increase the water holding capacity. Keeping this in mind, a study was conducted to adoption level, advantages and constraints in adoption of water management practices in the canal command area. In India more than 70 per cent of the annual rainfall occurs during the South West monsoon period between June and September. Irrigation especially during winter months enable increased intensity of land use for cultivation. The irrigated agriculture has to expand considerably in order to increase the food production to the required level of about 400 metric tonnes by 2025.

Research methodology

Erode district was purposively selected. In order to make the study more comprehensive, the head, mid and tail reaches of LBP canal command areas were selected. The river flows through the three PWD divisions *viz.*, Sathayamanglam, Erode and Kanagayam coming under Erode district. Two blocks each at random from the head, mid and tail reaches were selected *viz.*, Sathayamanglam and Nambiyur in head reach, Perundurai and Modakuruchi in mid reach and Kanagayam and Vellakoil from the tail reach. Three villages were selected at random from each block. Thus, a total of 18 revenue villages were selected which formed the primary locale of the study.

The sample size consisted of 150 farmers, those who grow paddy, sugarcane, turmeric, banana and groundnut were considered. Fifty farmers each in head, mid and tail reach were considered based on the proportionate random sampling method..

The water management practice adoption index has been developed with a set of practices in rice, sugarcane, turmeric, banana and groundnut for assessing adoption level. One of major objectives of the study contemplated was to find out the adoption of recommended water management practices in head, mid and tail reaches of canal command area. Thirty three water management practices under the crops *viz.*, rice, sugarcane, turmeric, banana and groundnut were selected for the study.

As explained in the methodology, five principle crops namely, paddy, sugarcane, turmeric, banana and groundnut were considered for the study.

For each crop, the recommended practices were identified and the relevancy weightages were assigned based on judge's opinion. Adoption scores were further worked out. Subsequently mean adoption score were worked out for individual practices in each of the five major crops in each reach.

Six water management practices were found to be adopted by the farmers. The farmers were asked to express the merits under each water management practice in sugarcane.

The details are presented in Table1

Findings and Discussion

Table 6.1. Adoption level water management practices in sugarcane (n = 150)

Practices Merits	Alternate furrow irrigation	Skip furrow irrigation	Trash mulching	Application of compost-ed coir pith	Drip irrigation	Fertigation
Water saving	93 (62)	72 (48)	-	-	110 (73)	50 (33)
Less cost	-	-	100 (67)	-		-
Moisture conservation	100 (67)	70 (47)	140 (93)	110 (73)	-	-
Nutrient fixation	-	-	90 (60)	140 (93)	-	-
Reduction of evaporation loss	-	-	70 (47)	-	95 (63)	-
Increased soil microbial population	-	-	50 (33)	-	-	-
Reduction of run off loss	114 (76)	73 (49)	-	-	40 (27)	-
Reduction of soil temperature	-	-	33 (22)	10 (7)	-	-
Enhanced plant growth and yield	-	-	-	-	120 (80)	-
Judicious use of water	-	-	-	-	144 (96)	-
Reduced weed growth	-	-	-	-	130 (87)	-
Reduced operation and labour cost	-	-	-	-	137 (91)	-
Uninterrupted cultural operation	-	-	-	-	140 (93)	-
Improved quality of production	-	-	-	-	121 (81)	-
Application of fertilizers through irrigation water	-	-	-	-	-	52 (34)
Saving in land leveling expenses	-	-	-	-	53 (35)	-
Reduction of salinity	-	-	-	-	17 (11)	-
Less loss of Evapo transpiration	-	-	-	-	-	47 (31.33)

* Figure in parenthesis indicate percentage

Merits of water management practices adopted in sugarcane

1. **Alternative furrow irrigation** : The advantages like runoff loss (76%), moisture conservation (67%) and water saving (62%) were expressed by the majority of the respondents due to the adoption of alternate furrow irrigation.
2. **Skip furrow irrigation**: From the table1, it could be observed 49 per cent of the respondents reported that reduction of runoff (49%) followed by water saving (48%) and moisture conservation (47%) as the advantages.
3. **Trash mulching**: It is seen from the table 1that there was moisture conservation in adoption of trash mulching expressed by (93%) of respondents followed by less cost (67%), nutrient fixation (60%) and reduction of evaporation less (47%). Increased soil microbial population due to the application of trash mulching was the advantage for 33% of respondents. Reduction of soil temperature was also reported by 22% of respondents.
4. *Application of composted coir pith*: Regarding application of coir pith, nutrient fixation (93%) and moisture conservation (73%) were the advantages expressed by majority of the respondents followed by 7 per cent of the respondent reported that reduction of soil temperature as the other advantage.
5. **Drip irrigation**: It could be seen from the table 1 that advantages viz., judicious use of water (96%), uninterrupted cultural operations (93%), reduced labour cost (91%), reduced weed growth (87%), improved quality of production (81), enhanced plant growth and yield (80%), water saving (73%) and reduction of evaporation loss (63%) were reported by majority of respondents. The other advantages like saving in land levelling expenses (35%), reduction of runoff loss (27%) and reduction of salinity (11%) were also reported.
6. **Fertigation**: The fertigation is another improved micro irrigation system, where the fertilizers and nutrients are sent through irrigation water. More than one third of respondents reported that application of fertilizers through irrigation water as main advantage. Water saving (33%) and less evapo-transpiration loss (33%) were the other advantages reported.

Limitations in Adoption of Water Management Practices in Sugarcane

1. Alternate furrow irrigation and skip furrow irrigation: Marginal yield reduction (49%) and more labour requirement (57%) were the constraints experienced in adoption of alternate and skip furrow irrigation reported by one third of the respondents.
2. Trash mulching and application of coir pith:It could be observed from the table that more than one third (42%) of respondents stated that difficulty in intercultural operations and possibility of pest and diseases (20%) were

Table 6.2. Limitations in adoption of water management practices in sugarcane

Practices limitations	Alternate furrow irrigation	Skip furrow irrigation	Trash mulching	Application of compost-ed coir pith	Drip irrigation	Fertigation
Marginal yield reduction	57 (38)	74 (49)	-	-	-	-
More labour requirement	62 (41)	86 (57)	-	-	-	-
Difficulty in intercultural operations	-	-	42 (28)	-	-	-
High cost of coir pith	-	-	-	30 (20)	-	-
Accuracy of application is limited	-	-	-	-	-	37 (25)
Pressure loss in main irrigation line or booster pump	-	-	-	-	-	29 (19)
Non-suitability to small and marginal farmers	-	-	-	-	-	20 (13)
Expensive	-	-	-	-	-	33 (22)
High initial cost	-	-	-	-	62 (41)	40 (27)
Cracking and clogging of drippers	-	-	-	-	50 (33)	-
Lack of adequate technical inputs	-	-	-	-	83 (55)	-
Damage due to rats / rodents	-	-	-	-	87 (58)	-
High cost of spare parts	-	-	-	-	77 (51)	-
Difficulty in obtaining the loan	-	-	-	-	52 (35)	-
Inadequate extension and promotional activities	-	-	-	-	57 (38)	-
Salt encrustation	-	-	-	-	53 (39)	-

* Figures in parentheses indicate percentages

the constraints due to adoption of trash mulching and application of coir pith.

3. **Drip irrigation**: It is evident from the table that constraints liker lack of adequate technical inputs (55%) damage due to rats / rodents (58%) and high cost of spare parts, (51%) were experienced by respondents as major constraints in adoption of drip irrigation. Further, more than one third of respondents expressed that high initial cost (41%), salt encrustation (39%), inadequate extension or promotional activities, difficulty in getting the loan (35%) and cracking and clogging of drippers (33%) as other constraints for them.

4. **Fertigation**: Regarding fertigation, more than two-fifth of respondents reported high initial cost (27%), limited accuracy of application (25%) and expensive (22%) were the important constraints. More than 15 per cent of respondents mentioned that pressure loss in main irrigation line (19%), and non-suitability to small and marginal farmers (13%) as other constraints.

Conclusion

With respect to sugarcane, judicious use of water, uninterrupted cultural operations, nutrient fixation, moisture conservation, reduced labour cost, improved quality of production, enhanced plant growth and yield, water saving and reduced weed growth were reported as major advantages by the most of the respondents. From the agronomical point of view these are a series of functionally linked impact points in use of irrigation devices. These important points would have impressed upon the farmers for their perception.

From the above results, majority of the farmers were found to be adopting the micro-irrigation system for water management in the study area. The constraints *viz.*, marginal yield reduction, more labour requirement, lack of adequate technical inputs, damage due to rats and rodents, high cost of spare parts and high initial cost were experienced by the majority of the respondents.

7

Cultivation of Tomato

The tomato (see pronunciation) is the edible, often red berry-type fruit of the nightshade *Solanum lycopersicum*, commonly known as a tomato plant. The tomato is consumed in diverse ways, including raw, as an ingredient in many dishes, sauces, salads, and drinks. The English word tomato comes from the Spanish word, tomate, derived from the Nahuatl (Aztec language) word *tomatl*. It first appeared in print in 1595.

The tomato belongs to the nightshade family, *Solanaceae*. The species originated in Central and South America and its use as a food originated in Mexico, and spread throughout the world following the Spanish colonization of the Americas. Its many varieties are now widely grown, sometimes in greenhouses in cooler climates. The plants typically grow to 1-3 meters (3-10 ft) in height and have a weak stem that often sprawls over the ground and vines over other plants. It is a perennial in its native habitat, although often grown outdoors in temperate climates as an annual. An average common tomato weighs approximately 100 grams (4 oz). While tomatoes are botanically and scientifically the berry-type fruits of the tomato plant, they can also be considered a culinary vegetable, causing some confusion.

CULTIVATION

The tomato is botanicaly known as *Lycopersicum esculentum* belongs to the family Solanacae. The fruits are harvested as red for consumption. It has prominent place in humen food. A breif accounts on its cultivation is given below.

Varieties

Improved varieties

Arka Saurabh, Arka Vikas, Arka Ahuti, Arka Ashish, Arka Abha , Arka Alok, HS101, HS102, HS110, Hisar Arun, Hisar Lalima, Hisar Lalit, Hisar Anmol, KS.2, Narendra Tomato 1, Narendra Tomato 2, Pusa Red Plum, Pusa Early Dwarf, Pusa

Ruby, Co-1, CO 2, CO 3, S-12, Punjab Chhuhara, PKM 1, Pusa Ruby, Paiyur-1, Shakthi, SL 120, Pusa Gaurav, S 12, Pant Bahar, Pant T3, Solan Gola and Arka Meghali.

F1 hybrids

Arka Abhijit, Arka Shresta, Arka Vishal, Arka Vardan, Pusa Hybrid 1, Pusa Hybrid 2, COTH 1 Hybrid Tomato, Rashmi, Vaishali, Rupali, Naveen, Avinash 2, MTH 4, Sadabahar, Gulmohar and Sonali.

CLIMATIC REQUIREMENT

The tomato is a warm-season crop. The crop does well under an average monthly temperature of 21°C to 23°C. Temperature and light intensity affect the fruit-set, pigmentation and nutritive value of the fruit. Long dry spell and heavy rainfall both shows detrimental effect on growth and fruiting.

SOILS

The tomato grows on practically all soils from light sandy to heavy clay. Light soils are good for an early crop, while clay loam and silt-loam soils are well suited for heavy yields. Tomatoes do best in a soil that has a soil reaction from pH 6.0 to 7.0. If the soil is acidic liming is required.

SEED RATE

- For raising the seedlings in nursery bed 300 - 400 g/ha seeds are required.
- Hybrid seeds are very costly so it should be sown in plastic cups or ice cube tray, which require only 70-90 g.

TIME OF PLANTING

- Tomato is a day neutral plant so wildly it found grown in any season.
- In the northern plains three crops are taken but in frost affected area rabi crop is not fruitful. The kharif crop is transplanted in July, rabi crop in October - November and zaid crop in February months.
- In the southern plains where there is no danger of frost, The first transplanting is done in December-January, Second June-July Third in September-October depending on the irrigation facilities available.

RAISING SEEDLINGS

- Seedlings are grown before one months of transplanting raised beds of 60-100 cm width and of convenient length.
- Soil solorization of nursery bed by covering them with white transparent polythene sheet for one month should be done in hot summer months. It

will kill the disease causing organisms like fungus, bacteria, nematode as well as insects and seeds of weeds.

- For one m2 of nursery area apply 5kg well rotten FYM and 20 g of each N, P and K fertiliser, and also apply 2.5g carbofuran or 200 g of neem cake and 10-25 g tricoderma.
- While preparing the nursery beds, neem cake /castor cake/ neam leaf/ castor leaf/ pongamia leaf/ calotropis leaf has to be incorporated @ 400 g/ m^2 for protection against nematoads.
- After sowing the seeds, mulch with green leaves and irrigate with a rose-can daily in the morning. Remove the mulch immediately after germination of the seeds. Restrict irrigation one week before transplanting and irrigate heavily on the previous day of transplanting.
- Cover the nursery bed with fine nylon net to escape the damage by virus transmitting insects.

SEED TREATMENT

- To avoid damping off disease treats the seed with Tricoderma @ 5-10 g/ Kg seed or carbendazim 2g/Kg seed.
- The treated seeds are dried in shade for 30 minutes and then sown sparsely along the lines in ½ cm depth and then covered by the topsoil.

LAND PREPARATION

Land is prepared to a fine tilth by thorough ploughing or digging 2 - 3 times. At the last ploughing organic manure and 10 kg carbofuran granules or 200 kg neem cake has to be applied

MANURING

Apply well rotten farm yard manure / compost @ 20-25 t/ha at the time of land preparation and mix well with the soil. A fertilizer dose of 75:40:25 kg $N:P_2O_5:K_2O$ / ha may be given. Half the dose of nitrogen, full phosphorus and half of potash may be applied as basal before transplanting. One fourth of nitrogen and half of potash may be applied 20-30 days after planting. The remaining quantity may be applied two months after planting.

TRANSPLANTING

- The transplanting is done in small flat beds or in shallow furrow depending upon the availability of irrigation.
- In heavy soil it is usually transplanted on ridges and during the rains also it is advantageous to plant the seedlings on ridges.
- For indeterminate varieties/hybrids, the seedlings have to be staked using

bamboo sticks of two meter length or planted in broad ridge of 90 cm width and 15 cm height. The seedlings are planted in the furrows at a spacing of 30 cm and the plant is allowed to spread on the broad ridge.

SPACING

The spacing recommended for the autumn-winter crop is 75 × 60 cm and for the spring-summer crop 75 × 45 cm.

IRRIGATION

Tomatoes need very careful irrigation that is just sufficient water at the right time. It is necessary to maintain an even moisture supply. During summer season, irrigation at every 5 to 7 days interval is necessary, whereas in winter 10 to 15 days interval is sufficient. A period of drought followed by sudden heavy watering during the fruiting period may cause cracking of fruits.

WEED CONTROL

- There is need of light hoeing during first four weeks in the field which encourage the growth but also remove the weeds from the field. The surface soil is loosened by hand hoeing as soon as it is dry enough after every irrigation or shower. All weeds should also be removed in this process.
- Mulching with straw, black polythene and many other materials has been found beneficial in moisture conservation, in controlling weeds and some diseases.

PLANT PROTECTION

Insects

***Gram pod borer* (Heliothis armigera)**

It is a polyphagous, attacks most of the cultivated crops, major pest of tomato, and widely distributed throughout the country. Young larvae feed on tender foliage, while advanced stages attack the fruits. Larva bore circular holes in fruits.

***Serpentine leaf miner* (Liriomyza trifolii)**

It is a polyphagous in nature very widely distributed throughout the India. Maggot mines into the leaf and feeds on the mesophyll of the leaves making serpentine mines/galleries.

***Tobacco caterpillar* (Spotoptera litura)**

It is also polyphagous in nature, major pest of tomato, distributed widely. Freshly hatched larvae feed gregariously, scraping the leaves from ventral side, later stages, feed voraciously at night on the foliage. Larvae may also feed on fruits hollowing these out.

Root-Knot Nematode (*Meloidogyne* spp.)

This nematode has wide host range, widespread all over India, affects most of the vegetable crops, often tomato, brinjal, okra. Root-knot nematodes are small, microscopic, males are slender and females swollen. The most characteristic symptom on the root is production of root galls. Above ground symptoms are reduced growth, chlorosis of foliage, susceptibility to wilting, and reduced fruit production.

Insects Management

- Two rows of marigold for every 16 rows of tomato can be grown as a trap crop. Marigold flowers attract egg laying of H. armigera.
- Spray 5% neem seed kernel extract to kill early stages larvae.
- Placement of 15-20 bird perches (T shaped) per ha helps in inviting insectivorous birds.
- Spray NPV @ 625 LE/ha during evening hours.
- Jaggery @ 1 kg, sandovit or Teepol(100 ml) are to be mixed with NPV on need basis spary 2 ml Endosulfan, Chlorpyriphos or Quinolphos per litre of water
- Application of chopped leaves of Pongamia or Crotalaria reduces disease severity caused by nematode.
- Farmers of the Andhra Pradesh uses garlic+ chilly extract and slurry of cow dung + urine for protection against pest and diseases.

Disease

Tomato is attacked vast range of fungus, bacteria and viruses. The most common diseases are anthracnose, bacterial spot, bacterial blight, bacterial canker, buck eye rot, damping off, early blight , fusarium blight, late blight, leaf curl, mosaic, powdery mildew, rots, and septorial leaf blight. Few major disease are discussed below.

***Bacterial Wilt* (Pseudomonas solanacearum)**

Deadly disease of tomato. Wilting, stunting, yellowing of the foliage and finally collapse of the entire plant are the characteristic symptoms of the disease. The lower leaves may droop first before wilting occurs.

***Damping Off Pythium* (aphanidermatum, Rhizoctonia solani)**

Common in many parts of India, occurring in nurseries of Tomato, Tobacco, Chillies, Cabbage, Cauliflower, Brinjal and Cucurbits. Young seedlings are killed before they emerge through the soil surface or collar region of grownup plants get rotten and toppling of small plants are seen in nursery bed.

Early Blight (Alternaria solani)

Common disease of tomato occurring all over India. The characteristic leaf spots and blight first becomes visible as small, isolated, scattered pale brown spots on the leaf which later on also develop on stem and fruits. Fully developed spots are irregular, brown to dark brown in colour, and with concentric rings inside the spot. In severe attacks the entire plant may be defoliated.

Wilt (Fusarium oxysporum *f. sp.* Lycopersici)

It is a worst disease of tomato occurring all over India. First symptoms appear as chlorosis of the leaf. Soon the petiole and leaves droop and wilt. When plant roots and basal stems are split open dark brown or black discoloration of the vascular tissues may be seen.

Tomato Mosiac (Tobacco mosaic virus, Cucumber mosaic virus)

The common symptom of mosaic is mottling of the leaves. The normal green colour of the leaf is interspersed with light green to pale yellow islands of irregular patches. The edges of the leaf turn downward and are stiffer than those of a healthy leaf.

Powdery Mildew (Leveillula taurica)

A light powdery covering of the lesions may occur on the lower surface. Heavily infected leaves die but seldom drop from the plant.

Septoria Leaf Blight (Septoria lycopersici)

It is a Major disease of tomato throughout India. In young plants numerous spots appear on older leaves or on plants with poor growth. Small, circular spots are first observed as water soaked areas on the under surface of the lower leaves. As the spots enlarge, they develop dark brown marking and sunken, white or grey centres.

Rots

Black mold rot (Alternaria alternata, Stemphylium botryosum)

Sunken or slightly flattened lesions with water soaked in appearance occurs on fruits. Soon these lesion become brown to black in colour. Tomato fruits coming in contact with the soil are attacked by soil-borne fungi causing rotting of the fruits.

Disease Management

- Soil solorization or partial sterilisation of the soil by burning trash on the surface
- Seed treatment with tricoderma 5-10g or carbendazim 2g or thirum3 g/Kg seed.

- Field sanitation
- Crop rotation with non-solanaceous
- Providing better drainage, forming raised beds
- Uproot the heavily infected or virus infected plants
- Sanitation and crop rotation reduces the disease incidence
- Spraying the plants with a mixture of Streptocycline 200 ppm and Copper oxychloride 3g per litre of water gives fairly good control of the disease.

FERTILIZERS REQUIREMENTS FOR TOMATO CULTIVATION

Fertilizers

As the fruit production and quality depends upon nutrient availability and fertilizer application so balance fertilizer are applied as per requirement. The nitrogen in adequate quantity increases fruit quality, fruit size, color and taste. It also helps in increasing desirable acidic flavor. Adequate amount of potassium is also required for growth, yield and quality. Mono Ammonium Phosphate (MAP) may be used as a starter fertilizer to supply adequate phosphorus during germination and seedling stages. Calcium availability is also very important to control soil pH and nutrient availability. Sandy soils will require a higher rate of fertilizer, and more frequent applications of these fertilizers due to increased leaching of essential nutrients. The seedlings are sprayed with starter solution of micronutrient. Before planting farm yard manure @ 50 ton per hectares should be incorporated. Normally tomato crop requires 120kg Nitrogen (N), 50kg Phosphorus (P_2O_5), and 50kg Potash (K_2O). Nitrogen should be given in split doses. Half nitrogen and full P_2O_5 is given at the time of transplanting and remaining nitrogen is given after 30 days and 60 days of transplanting.

Soil and tissue analyses should be taken throughout the growing and production season to insure essential nutrients are in their proper amounts and ratios. Tissue analysis of a nutritionally sufficient plant will show the following nutrient status:

	Nitrogen	Phosphorus	Potassium	Calcium	Magnesium	Sulphur
%	4.0-5.6	0.30-0.60	3.0-4.5	1.25-3.2	0.4-0.65	0.65-1.4
ppm	Manganese	Iron	Boron	Copper	Zinc	
	30-400	30-300	20-60	5-15	30-90	

In the present situation it has been realized that the use of inorganic fertilizers should be integrated with renewable and environmental friendly organic fertilizers, crop residues and green manures.

POLYHOUSE BREEDING OF TOMATO

Introduction

Tomato, universally treated as "protective food" is being extensively grown as annual plant all over the world. In India, tomato has wider coverage in comparison to other vegetables. The leading tomato growing states are Uttar Pradesh, Karnataka, Maharashtra, Haryana, Punjab and Bihar. The area and production of tomato in our country was about 5.72 Lakh hectares and 102.60 Lakh tones respectively in 2007-08 and the development of high yielding varieties/ hybrids is making significant progress.

Tomato is a very good source of income to small and marginal farmers and contributes to the nutrition of the consumers. It is a rich source of vitamins and organic acids(healthy acids).

Tomato is a warm season crop and thrives in temperatures between 1-30^{0}C and is neither tolerant to frost, nor to waterlogged conditions. It is well fitted in different cropping systems which include cereals, grains, pulses and oilseeds.

Breeding tomato suitable for polyhouse cultivation

The introduction of protected cultivation technology in india has a time lag in relation to many countries. China has started protected cultivation technology almost at same time when India made beginning. But now China, Japan and USA are the leading countries having large area under polyhouse for horticultural crops in the world and also have developed a number of tomato varieties through ployhouse breeding.

In India the area under green/polyhouse cultivation crop is 1000 hectares, in which is mainly in Maharashtra, Uttarakhand, Karnataka and Jammu & Kashmir. The total area under polyhouse in Uttarakhand is 60-70 hectares. There appears ample scope for increasing area under low cost polyhouse in many folds in periurban areas of the Uttarakhand for production of high value vegetables during off season for taking advantage of high price of the available market in near by cities.

Tomato is high value vegetable crop for off season and main season production under polyhouses/greenhouses. The differences are observed in production and productivity in polyhouse bred tomato (350-450 tonnes/ ha) and field bred tomato (150-200 tonnes) under polyhouse condition. The average productivity of open field bred variety in field condition is 250 q/ha whereas under polyhouse condition is about 800q/ha. The average production of polyhouse bred Israeli tomato varieties under polyhouse condition at Delhi is about 2,200q/ha.The seed cost of such tomato varieties is very high, i.e. between 1.50 and 2.00 lakh/kg and grower also faces the problem of importing the seed every time. These two factors ultimately affect the cost: benefit ratio and the interest of tomato polyhouse growers.

Considering the importance and high seed cost of Israeli polyhouse bred tomato variety, a project was initiated for the first time in India by us on breeding of polyhouse tomato during 2002. By adopting appropriate selection methods and hybrid breeding procedure one pure line (PTP-1) and one hybrid (PTPH-1) have been developed. The yield potential of this newely developed pure line is about 1700 q/ha and that of F_1 hybrid 1,800 q/ha.

IMPORTANT ATTRIBUTES OF POLYHOUSE BRED TOMATO

In India polyhouse tomato breeding was started to develop the purelines (PTP 1, PTP 2, PTP 3 and PTP 4) and F1 hybrid (PTPH 1) having following traits:

1. Large fruit size (150-200g)
2. Thick pericarp (0.8-1 cm)
3. 4-5 fruits per cluster
4. Long fruiting period (8-9 months)
5. Long plant height (20-25 feets)
6. Potato leaf type
7. Ability to set fruits in wide temperature range (15-450C)
8. Resistant to fruit and shoot borer
9. Long storage life under room temperature

POLYHOUSE BRED TOMATO

1. Indeterminate, single stemmed plants
2. Medium sized bright colored fruits
3. Short internode
4. More number of fruits per plant
5. High TSS and acidity
6. Thermo-insensitivity
7. Resistance to whitefly and other important diseases and insect-pest

Fruit Characters

Characters	PBT-1	PBT-2	PBT-3	PBT-4	PBTH-1
Days to 1st flowering	43	40	43	51	41
No. of flower/cluster	10.4	9.2	8.6	6.3	7.8
No. of fruit/cluster	8.6	6.6	6.0	3.8	5.0
Fruit setting	82.6	71.7	69.76	0.30	64.10
Fruit diameter (cm)	7.74	6.04	5.28	6.30	7.86
Fruit length (cm)	5.04	5.92	5.00	5.32	6.50
Pericarp thickness	0.86	0.78	0.70	0.94	0.98
Wine length at harvesting (m)	4.90	4.92	4.40	1.95	7.00
Average fruit weight (g)	200	120	140	130	200
Yield/plant (kg)	7.40	5.13	5.75	5.06	8.50
TSS	4.2	4.2	4.5	4.5	4.7
Acidity	0.26	0.27	0.39	0.44	0.26

8

Cultivation of Cauliflower

Cauliflower is one of several vegetables in the species *Brassica oleracea*, in the family Brassicaceae. It is an annual plant that reproduces by seed. Typically, only the head (the *white curd*) is eaten. The cauliflower head is composed of a white inflorescencemeristem. Cauliflower heads resemble those in broccoli, which differs in having flower buds. *Brassica oleracea* also includes broccoli,brussels sprouts, cabbage, collard greens, and kale, though they are of different cultivar groups.

CROP VARIETY

Early kunwari, Pant gobhi 3, Pusa dipali, Pusa kataki, Pusa hybrid 2, Pusa himjyoti, Pusa synthetic, Pusasnoball 1,

LAND PREPARATION

The sandy loam to clayey loam soils which are well drained and rich in nutrients fairly deep loam soils are ideal for growing cauliflower. soil pH5.5-6.5.

CULTIVATION

Raising of nursery – the width of the bed-60 cm,15 cm high, with7-8 cm spacing of seed.Mixed FYM @ 10 kg/m^2 and seed treatment with Captan @ 3 g/kg seed.

Seed rate

450-700g/ha.

Transplanting

The seedling are ready 3-6 weeks after sowing.

Manures / fertilizers

FYM – 40-70 tonnes /ha. NPK – 150:60:50 kg/ha

AFTERCARE

Blanching – to protect the curd from direct sun light. Handweeding – should be done few days after first irrigation by hoe or khurpi. Herbicides – preplanting application of Pendimethalin (Stomp) or Fluchloralin (Basalin) @ 2.0-3.0 kg/ha.

Irrigation method: Furrow method, 5-6 irrigation are required. First- just after planting, then growth and curd formation stage.

Plant protection: Cauliflower suffers from a number of physiological disorders like Reciness, Fuzziness, Blindness, Buttoning, Browning, Whiptail etc..

Control: The planting of resistant and tolerant varieties, balanced use of fertilizer , proper seed treatment and planting at optimum time.

Harvesting: When curd are compact attain proper size and retain original colour. The plant is cut well below the curd with sharp cutting knife , sickal or khurpi.

Yield: 6-10 t/ha(early) from 25 to 30 t / ha late varieties.

CAULIFLOWER VARIETIES AND THEIR CHARACTERISTICS

Pusa Deepali: Developed at IARI, New Delhi. Recommended for Northern India particularly Delhi and Punjab. Early maturing variety, curds compact, self-blanching, white, medium sized and almost free from riceyness. Curds ready for harvest in late October. Average yield is 12 t/ha.

Early Kunwari: Recommended for Haryana, Punjab, and Delhi. Very early variety. Curds hemispherical with even surface, ready for harvesting from mid September to mid October. Average yield is 8 t/ha.

Punjab Giant-26: Main season variety. Curds solid, white, medium-sized. Ready for harvesting from mid November to December. Average yield is 17 t/ha.

Punjab Giant-35: Main season variety. Curds white, compact medium sized. Ready for harvesting from mid November to December. Average yield is 17 t/ha.

Pant Shubhra: Recommended for cultivation in Northern India. Early growing variety. Curds are compact, slightly conical and creamish white. Ready for harvest in November. Average yield is 20 t/ha.

Pusa Snowball-1: Late maturing variety. Curds very compact, medium in size and snow white in colour. Ready for harvesting from January to April. Average yield is 25-30 t/ha. Susceptible to black rot.

Sonwball-16: Ideal for cooler climates of North Indian states. Late maturing variety. Curds medium sized, solid, having attractive white colour. Ready for harvesting from January to March. Average yield is 25-30 t/ha.

Pusa Early Synthetic: Main season variety. Curds somewhat creamy white to white and compact. Ready for harvest from mid December to mid January. Average yield is 11 t/ha.

Pant Gobhi-2: Early maturing variety. Curds compact, composite and creamy white. Curds ready for harvesting from November to December. Average yield is 12 t/ha.

Pant Gobhi-3: Early maturing variety. Curds medium sized and solid white. Curds ready for harvest from October. Average yield is 10 t/ha.

Dania Kalimpong: Commonly grown in eastern parts of India. Late season variety. Curds are medium-large, compact, attractive and white. Less sensitive to fluctuations of environment. Ready for harvesting from January to April. Average yield is 25-30 t/ha.

CAULIFLOWER CROP DISEASES AND THEIR CONTROL

Stalk Rot (*Sclerotinia sclerotiorum*)

This fungus can cause serious losses in the field, in storage, and under transit and market conditions. Generally, damp weather favours the occurrence of the disease. Infections may occur on the stem at the ground level, on the leaves at their bases, or where the foliage comes in contact with the soil. The infections begin as water-soaked, circular areas, which soon become covered by white, cottony fungal growth. The affected tissue becomes soft and watery as the disease progresses. The fungus eventually colonizes the entire cabbage head and produces large, black, seedlike structures called sclerotia on the diseased tissue.

Control: The disease can be managed most successfully by combining cultural practices that discourage disease development. Planting cabbage in fields that are surrounded by dense woods will restrict air circulation and subsequently delay drying. Rows should be planted in the direction of the prevailing winds to promote free flow of air movement within the plants. Fields with a history of white mold should be planted with non-susceptible crops such as grains (corn, rye, wheat, etc.). Cabbage and other susceptible crops (cauliflower, beans, peas, etc.) should not be planted in fields where white mold has become a problem because continuous cropping of susceptible crops will result in a buildup of the fungus in the soil and increased disease incidence. Mechanical injuries to cabbage heads during harvesting operations should be avoided.

Black Rot (*Xanthomonas campestris* pv. *campestris*)

This bacterial disease is common in areas having a warm and wet climate. Plants can be infected during any growth stage and the symptoms resemble nutritional deficiencies. Infected seedlings become yellow, drop lower leaves, and may die. Leaves may be affected on only one side of a seedling. Plants infected because of contaminated seed may not develop symptoms for many weeks. The classic symptom of black rot is caused by local infection that results when bacteria enter leaves through natural openings of leaf margins. The infected tissue turns pale green-yellow and then turns brown and dies. Affected areas are usually wedge- or V-shaped. These areas enlarge as the disease progresses, and severely affected leaves may drop off. The veins in infected leaves, stems, and roots sometimes become black. The heads of the infected plants remains small and its quality is reduced making it unfit for marketing.

Control: An integrated approach is needed to manage black rot successfully. Use of black rot tolerant varieties is the best method to control the disease. Considerable reduction in disease has been observed when seeds are treated with Agrimycin-100 (100ppm) or Streptocycline (100 ppm). Planting should be done on raised beds to facilitate drainage. Cultivation in the fields where crucifers have been continuously grown during last 2 years should be avoided. Plants should be thoroughly inspected for black rot symptoms and the affected plants should be removed and destroyed.

CAULIFLOWER DISORDERS AND THEIR CONTROL

Browning

Browning is caused due to boron deficiency. Generally, the deficiency symptoms of boron are externally visible on plants after the curd formation. In early stage, the water soaked areas appear on the stem and curd surface. As the plant grows, the stem becomes hollow with water soaked tissue covering the internal walls of the cavity. In advanced stage of deficiency, brown or pink coloured areas are seen on curd surface and therefore, it is also called brown rot or red rot or browning of the curd. Sometimes the stem may become hollow even without brown areas on the curd. The affected curds are bitter in taste. The foliage colour first changes to dull green and then greenish yellow at the apical margin of the older leaves. When there is severe deficiency of boron, then leaves are under developed andsmaller. The growing point may die in young stage of plant itself.

Control: The deficiency of boron may be corrected by applying borax. The quantity of borax depends on soil type, soil pH and the extent of deficiency. In acid soil, 10- 15 kg borax/ha is sufficient while larger quantity may be required as natural and alkaline soils.

Whiptail

Whiptail disorder is caused due to deficiency of molybdenum. In young plants the deficiency symptoms are chlorosis of leaf margins and the whole leaves may turn white. The leaf blades do not develop properly. When the deficiency is severe, only the midribs develop. This condition is commonly known as 'Whiptail'. The growing point of the plant is also deformed which prevents the curd development. The deficiency of molybdenum generally occurs in acid soils when the soil pH is below 5.5.

Control: Lime application in acidic soils is done to increase the availability of molybdenum. The quantity of lime is determined by initially measuring the pH of the soil. Alternately, soil application of Sodium Molybdate (10-15 kg/ha) effectively controls the deficiency symptoms.

Buttoning

The development of small premature curds or buttons while the plants are young is known as buttoning. The button heads are exposed and the plants showing this condition have usually small poorly developed leaves. Several factors like poor nitrogen supply, planting of over-age seedlings, unfavorable climatic conditions and improper time of planting are reported to cause buttoning.

Control: Adequate supply of nitrogen and moisture for rapid vegetative growth of plant is considered important for preventing the occurrence of button plants.

CAULIFLOWER PESTS AND THEIR CONTROL

Diamondback Moth (DBM) (*Plutella xylostella*)

It is one of the most serious pests of cabbage grown under comparatively high temperature conditions. The DBM derives its name from the white markings along the back of the forewings which when folded form a diamond shaped pattern. The caterpillars are green or brownish green in colour. The adult female lays eggs on the leaves either singly or in groups. Small slender green caterpillars on emergence feed on the leaf epidermis and later make holes in the leaves. Severely affected leaves are completely skletonised. Pupation takes place in a loose mesh of silken cocoon spun by the caterpillar.

Control: Spraying the crop with Malathion (0.1%) or Profenofos (0.25-0.5 kg a.i./ha) gives excellent control of the larvae. Intercropping mustard in the cabbage crop 15 days prior to sowing and 25 days after planting cabbage was effective. As the pest preferred mustard, major pest population is attracted towards it, which can be destroyed by spraying the crop with Dichlorvos (1 ml/ litre of water).

9

Cultivation of Mango

Mango (*Mangifera indica*), the king of fruits, is grown in India for over 4000 years. More than 1,000 varieties exist today. It is grown in almost all the states. India shares about 56% of total mango production in the world. Its production has been increasing since independence in 1947, contributing 39.5% of the total fruit production of India. Andhra Pradesh tops in total production, whereas Uttar Pradesh tops area wise. Andhra Pradesh, Uttar Pradesh, Bihar, Karnataka, Maharashtra, West Bengal and Gujarat together contribute for about 82% of the total production in India. The mango is a juicy stone fruit (drupe) belonging to the genus *Mangifera*, consisting of numerous tropical fruiting trees, cultivated mostly for edible fruit. The majority of these species are found in nature as wild mangoes. They all belong to the flowering plant family Anacardiaceae. The mango is native to South Asia, from where it has been distributed worldwide to become one of the most cultivated fruits in the tropics. The center of diversity of the *Mangifera* genus is in India.

While other *Mangifera* species (e.g. horse mango, *Mangifera foetida*) are also grown on a more localized basis, *Mangifera indica*—the "common mango" or "Indian mango"—is the only mango tree commonly cultivated in many tropical and subtropical regions. It is the national fruit of India, Pakistan, and the Philippines, and the national tree of Bangladesh.

Mango trees grow up to 35-40 m (115-131 ft) tall, with a crown radius of 10 m (33 ft). The trees are long-lived, as some specimens still fruit after 300 years. In deep soil, the taproot descends to a depth of 6 m (20 ft), with profuse, wide-spreading feeder roots; the tree also sends down many anchor roots, which penetrate several feet of soil. The leaves are evergreen, alternate, simple, 15-35 cm (5.9-13.8 in) long, and 6-16 cm (2.4-6.3 in) broad; when the leaves are young they are orange-pink, rapidly changing to a dark, glossy red, then dark green as they mature. Theflowers are produced in terminal panicles 10-40 cm (3.9-15.7 in) long; each flower is small and white with five petals 5–10 mm (0.20–0.39 in) long, with a mild, sweet odor suggestive of lily of the valley. Over 400 varieties of mangoes are known, many of which ripen in summer, while some give double crop.[5] The fruit takes three to six months to ripen.

The ripe fruit varies in size and color. Cultivars are variously yellow, orange, red, or green, and carry a single flat, oblong pit that can be fibrous or hairy on the surface, and which does not separate easily from the pulp. Ripe, unpeeled mangoes give off a distinctive resinous, sweet smell. Inside the pit 1-2 mm (0.039-0.079 in) thick is a thin lining covering a single seed, 4-7 cm (1.6-2.8 in) long. The seed contains the plant embryo. Mangoes have recalcitrant seeds; they do not survive freezing and drying.

Mango can be grown on a wide variety of soils under varied climatic conditions. It can be grown from alluvial to lateritic soils except in black cotton soil having poor drainage. It grows well in soils with slightly acidic pH. It does not perform well in soils having pH beyond 7.5. Soils having good drainage are ideal for mango.

Mango is a tropical fruit, but it can be grown up to 1,100m above mean sea level. There should not be high humidity, rain or frost during flowering. The temperature between 24 and 27°C is ideal for its cultivation. Higher temperature during fruit development and maturity gives better quality fruits. The areas experiencing frequent showers and high humidity are prone to many pests and diseases. Thus it can be grown best in regions with a rainfall between 25 cm and 250cm. Regions having bright sunny days and moderate humidity during flowering are ideal for mango growing.

VARIETIES

India is the home of about 1,000 varieties. Most of them are the result of open pollination arisen as chance seedlings. However, only a few varieties are commercially cultivated throughout India (Table 1).

Mango fruits

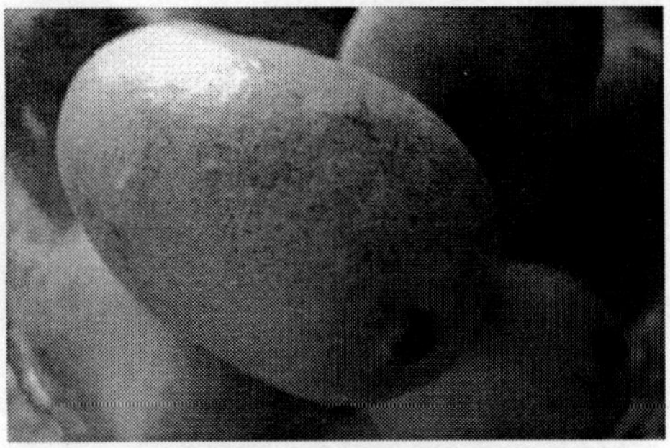

Alphonso mango

Table 9.1. Commercial mango varieties grown in different Indian states

Andhra Pradesh	Banganapalli, Suvarnarekha, Neelum and Totapuri
Bihar	Bombey Green, Chausa, Dashehari, Fazli, Gulabkhas, Kishen Bhog, Himsagar, Zardalu and Langra
Gujarat	Kesar, Alphonso, Rajapuri, Jamadar, Totapuri, Neelum, Dashehari and Langra
Haryana	Chausa, Dashehari, Langra and Fazli
Himachal Pradesh	Chausa, Dashehari and Langra
Karnataka	Alphonso, Totapuri, Banganapalli Pairi, Neelum and Mulgoa
Madhya Pradesh	Alphonso, Bombey Green, Dashehari, Fazli, Langra and Neelum
Maharashtra	Alphonso, Kesar and Pairi
Punjab	Chausa, Dashehari and Malda
Rajasthan	Bombey Green, Chausa, Dashehari and Langra
Tamil Nadu	Alphonso, Totapuri, Banganapalli and Neelum
Utter Pradesh	Bombey Green, Chausa, Dashehari and Langra
West Bengal	Fazli, Gulabkhas, Himasagar, Kishenbhog, Langra and Bombey Green

Table 9.2. State-wise availability of mango in India

State	Month
Andhra Pradesh	March to mid-August
Bihar	May-end to mid-August
Gujarat	April to July
Haryana	June to August
Himachal Pradesh	Mid-June to mid-August
Karnataka	May to July
Madhya Pradesh	Mid April to July
Maharashtra	April to July
Rajasthan	May to July
Tamil Nadu	April to August
Uttar Pradesh	Mid may to August
West Bengal	May to August

In India, mango is available from March to mid-August (Table2). The north Indian cultivars are alternate- bearer whereas south Indian ones are generally regular bearer. About 20 varieties are grown commercially. They are:

Alphonso

One of the most popular of India, it is mainly grown in Ratnagiri area of Maharashtra and to a small extent parts of south Gujarat and Karnataka. Its fruits are medium sized (250g), with attractive blush towards the basal end. Pulp is firm, fibreless with excellent orange color. It has good sugar: acid blend. Keeping quality is good. It is susceptible to spongy tissue.

Banganapalli

It is a widely cultivated, early maturing mango of south India. It is the main commercial variety of Andhra Pradesh. Its fruits are large sized, weighing on an average 350-400 g. The pulp is fibreless, firm and yellow with sweet taste. Fruits have good keeping quality.

Bombay Green

It is one of the earliest varieties of north India. Its fruits are medium- sized, weighing about 250g each. Fruits have strong and pleasant flavour. Pulp is soft and sweet.

Chausa

Late- maturing variety of south India, it matures during July or beginning of August. Fruits are large, weighing about 350g each. Fruits are bright yellow with soft and sweet pulp. It is shy bearing.

Dashehari

One of the most popular variety of north India, it is a mid-season mango. Fruits are medium sized, with pleasant flavour, sweet, firm and fibreless pulp. Stone is thin and keeping quality good.

Fazli

This is indigenous to Bihar and West Bengal. Fazli is a late maturing (August) mango. Fruits are large, with firm to soft flesh. Flavour is pleasant and pulp and pulp is sweet and fibreless. Keeping quality is good.

Gulab Khas

It is indigenous to Bihar. Regular and heavy bearer, it is mid season mango. Fruits are small to medium- sized. It has rosy flavour. Fruits are amber yellow with reddish blush towards the base and on sides. Keeping quality is good.

Himsagar

Very popular in West Bengal, it is a regular-bearing mango. Its fruits are medium-sized, having good quality. Flesh is firm, yellow, and fibreless with pleasant flavour. Keeping quality is good.

Kesar

Popular in Saurashtra region of Gujarat, Kesar is an irregular bearing mango. Fruits are medium sized. Flesh is sweet and fibreless. It has excellent sugar: acid blend. Fruits ripen to attractive apricot yellow color with red blush. It has good processing quality.

Kishenbhog

Indigenous to West Bengal, it is mid season mango. Fruits are medium to large sized, good with a pleasant flavour. There are traces of turpentine. Flesh is firm with fibres. Keeping quality is good.

Langra

An important commercial mango variety of north India, it is biennial- bearer and a mid season variety, with good quality fruits. Flesh is firm, lemon yellow in color and scarcely fibrous. It has characteristic turpentine flavour. Keeping quality is medium.

Mankurad

It is a mid-season variety, popular in Goa. Fruits are medium sized with yellow skin. Flesh is firm, cadmium yellow and fibreless. Keeping quality is good.

Neelum

A heavy yielding, late season mango in south India, it has regular bearing habit. Fruits are medium sized with good flavour. Flesh is soft, yellow and fibreless. Keeping quality is good.

Pairi

A native to coastal Maharashtra including Goa, it is an early-maturing, heavy and regular bearer mango. Fruits are medium sized with good quality. It has good flavour with sugar: acid blend. Flesh is soft, primuline-yellow and fibreless. Keeping quality is poor.

Totapuri

Widely grown in south India, Totapuri is a regular and heavy bearing mango. Fruits are medium to large with prominent sinus. Fruit quality is medium. It has a typical flavour and flat taste. Flesh is cadmium yellow and fibreless.

A number of selection / hybrids of mango have been evolved. These include Clone C-51 from Dashehari selected at the ICAR Mango Research Station, Lucknow, and an off season selection, Niranjan, selected at Parbhani. New clonal selections from Langra and Sunderja have been made at Varanasi and Rewa. A clonal selection, Paiyur 1, has been made from Neelum, in addition to few dwarf polyembryonic selections made in the north-eastern region.

As a result of systematic hybridization, several hybrids have been released. However, only a few have become commercially acceptable. Their parentage and important characteristics are given in Table 9.3. Of these, Mallika, Ratna and Arka Puneet are becoming quite popular.

Table 9.3. Mango hybrids and their characters

Hybrid	Place of research	Parentage	Importance characters
Mallika	IARI, New Delhi	Neelum x Dashehari	Regular bearers, high TSS, good color, uniform fruits, moderate keeping quality
Amrapali	IARI, New Delhi	Dashehare x Neelum	Dwarf, regular bearer, cluster. Bearing, small sized fruits, good keeping quality
Ratna	FRS, Vengurla	Neelum × Alphonso	Regular bearers, free from spongy tissue and fiblre
Sindhu	FRS, Vengurla	Ratna x Alphonso	Regular-bearer, stone thin
Arka Puneet	IIHR, Banalore	Alphonso x Banganapalli	Regular bearer, attractive skin color, medium-sized, free from spongy tissue. Good keeping quality, good sugar : acid blend

PROPAGATION

Mango is a highly heterozygous and cross pollinated crop. There are two types of mango varieties. Most of the varieties in south are polyembryonic and thus give true-to-type seedlings. In north, there are monoembryonic and need to be propagated vegetatively.

Mango is propagated on mango rootstock. For raising rootstock, the seeds of mango are sown within 4-5 weeks after extraction otherwise they lose their viability. For sowing the seeds, raised beds are prepared with a mixture of farmyard manure, red soil and sand. In some places, seeds are sown directly in polythene bags. After germination, the leaves turn green in 2-4 weeks. These seedlings are transplanted to polythene covers containing red soil, sand and farmyard manure. Addition of nitrogenous fertilizer to polythene covers after the establishment of plants helps in quick growth of seedlings. The seedlings thus raised should be used for grafting at different ages. Several methods of grafting are practiced. They are:

Inarching: It is one of the most widely practiced methods of grafting. One can get a big sized plant material for planting with over 95% success rate.

Veneer and side grafting: These can be utilized for preparing a grafted plant material or for in-situ grafting, i.e. for the rootstocks which are already planted.

Epicotyl/ stone grafting: This method is widely practiced in the Konkan region of Maharashtra. The germinated seedlings of 8-15 days old are used for grafting.

CULTIVATION

Planting

Different systems of planting like square, rectangular and hexagonal are followed at different places. However, square and rectangular systems are also popular. The spacing depends on the vigour of the variety and the cropping system. The main field is brought to fine tilth. Pits of 1mx 1m × 1m size are dug. These are exposed to sun for about 30days. Before planting, pits are filled with well rotten farmyard manure. The top and sub soil are taken out reparately while digging the pits. The grafts should be planted during rainy season. In the in situ grafting, rootstocks are planted in the main field. Then they are raised for six months to one year. Then the scions of the variety that need to be grown are taken and grafted. This is usually done when humidity is high. After grafting the scions are covered with polythene covers.

High density planting

High density planting helps increase the yield/unit area. In north India, mango Amrapali is found amenable for high density planting with a spacing of 2.5 m x 2.5. Soil drenching with paclobutrazol (2ml/tree) induces flowering during off year. It has become a commercial practice in Konkan region of Maharashtra. If coupled with pruning, it helps increase production/ unit area in Dashehari. The polyembryonic mango Vellaikolumban when used as rootstock imparts dwarfing in Alphonso.

Training and pruning

Training is an important practice during the first few years after planting. It is essential to space the branches properly and to help in intercultural operations.

Manuring and Fertilization

The nutritional requirement of mango varies with the region, soil type and age. A dose of 73g N, 18 g P_2O_5 and 68 g K_2O_5/ year of age from first to tenth year and thereafter a dose of 730gN, 180 g P_2, O_5 and 680g K_2O should be applied in two split doses during June- July and October respectively.

Spraying of zinc sulphate (0.3%) during February, March and May is recommended to correct the zinc deficiency. Spraying of Borax (0.5%) after fruit set twice at monthly intervals and 0.5% manganese sulphate after blooming corrects boron and manganese deficiencies respectively.

Organic manures and phosphatic fertilizers should be applied immediately after harvest, whereas ammonium sulphate should be given before flowering.

Intercropping

In mango, intercropping helps check weed growth and reduces nutrient losses. Intercropping black gram-wheat-mango and brinjal-onion-mango gives better monetary benefits. Besides, taking up cover crops like sun hemp, cowpea, pea and berseem help prevent soil erosion.

Irrigation

Precise water requirements for mango have not been worked out so far. The water requirements mainly depend up the age, soil type and climate. However, young plants up to two year old should be watered regularly. The newly planted grafts need about 30 liters of water every week. Irrigating grown up trees after fruit set at 10 days interval increases their yield.

HARVESTING AND POSTHARVEST MANAGEMENT

Mangoes should be harvested wit pedicel. Injury to the fruits during harvesting brings down their quality and also makes them prone to fungal attack. Several types of harvesters have been developed. These devices are simple and efficient in harvesting. Yield in mango varies with the region. However, on an average, mango yields eight tons/ha. Yield also varies with the region. The productivity of mango is higher Andhra Pradesh and Bihar. With the adoption of high density planting, its yields can easily be increased. The north Indian mangoes Langra and Dashehari are alternate bearers, whereas most of the south Indian mangoes are regular bearers. Mango Mallika and Amrapali is also comparatively regular bearer.

After harvesting, mangoes are graded according to their size. To maintain the quality, proper packaging is a must. In western region, bamboo baskets are used for packing. A basket contains 50-100 fruits. Straw is used for packing. Wooden boxes are also used in some place. However, now perforated cardboard are generally used. In these boxes either fruits are individually wrapped with tissue paper before packing or paper shavings are used for cushioning.

Minimizing the postharvest losses is one of the most important aspects. Usually green and mature mangoes are stored better than ripe ones harvested from trees. Low temperature storage, controlled atmospheric storage, use of chemical treatment for delaying ripening, irradiation heat treatment, packaging and shrink wrapping are methods to increase their shelf life. This temperature of 5°-16°C for different varieties is ideal for storing. Mangoes are highly susceptible to low temperature injury. Loss of flavour and development of undesirable softening are major symptoms of chilling injury.

Under controlled atmospheric storage, retardation of respiratory activity, delaying of softening, color development and senescence of fruits take place. Hence, this method has not been adopted in mango. The combination of waxing (3%) along with hot- water treatment results in good quality fruits with extended storage life. Individual wrapping of fruit imparts uniform color and reduces shrinkage. Hydro-cooling at 12°-15°C and holding for two weeks at 15°C followed by storage for one week at ambient temperature gives good storage life to fruits.

PHYSIOLOGICAL DISORDERS

Alternate bearing

Alternate bearing has been one of the major problems. Most of the south Indian varieties are regular-bearer, whereas north Indian ones alternate-bearer. Paclobutrazol is a promising chemical for flower induction in mango. Soil drenching with Paclobutrazol (5 g and 10g/tree) results in minimum outbreak of September to October vegetative flushes. It gives early and profuse flowering and more annual yield without affecting fruit size and quality.

Mango Malformation

It is one of the most important disorders, causing huge losses. It is a major problem in Punjab, Delhi and Uttar Pradesh. However, it has also been noticed in Gujarat, Maharashtra, Bihar, West Bengal and Odisha. Of the two types of mango malformation, vegetative malformation is more common in nursery seedlings and young plants. Floral malformation affects trees at the bearing stage. In vegetative malformation or bunchy top, compact leaves are formed in a bunch at the apex of shoot or in the leaf axil and growth of shoot let is arrested. Floral malformation directly affects the productivity. The incidence of disorder varies from variety to variety. Deblossoming alone or coupled with a spray of 200 ppm NAA lowers the number of malformed panicles significantly.

Black tip

This disorder is mainly noticed in Punjab, Uttar Pradesh, Bihar and West Bengal. The distal-end of the affected fruits turns black and become hard. These fruits ripen prematurely and become unmarketable. This disorder is caused by the smoke of brick-kilns located within a distance of 600m. Gases like carbon monoxide and carbondioxide, sulphate dioxide and acetylene cause these symptoms. It can be controlled by raising the height of the chimney of the brick kilns. Spraying borax (0.6%) at 10-14 days intervals starting from fruit set also controls it.

Clustering (Jhumka)

This malady is characterized by a cluster of fruit lets at the tip of the panicle giving an appearance of bunch tip called jhumka. These fruit lets are dark green with a deeper curve in the sinus beak region compared with normally developing fruit lets. These fruit lets grow to marble size after which their growth ceases. One of the main reasons for clustering is the adverse climate during February –March, particularly the low temperature. Most of the fruits are aborted with shriveled embryos and do not develop further, signifying the role of normal embryo growth in the development of fruits.

Spongy Tissue

It is in Alphonso mango. Fruits look normal from outside. But inside, a patch of flesh becomes spongy, yellowish and sour. This disorder has brought down the export of this variety. Inactivation of ripening enzyme due to high temperature, convective heat and postharvest exposure to sunlight are the causes. Use of sod culture and mulching are useful in reducing its incidence. Mango hybrids Ratna and Arka Puneet which have Alphonso like characters to not suffer from this malady. Harvesting mangoes when they are three-fourth matured rather than fully matured ones also reduces this malady.

MANGO DISORDERS AND THEIR CONTROL

Spongy Tissue

It is a major problem in Alphonso, where a pulp patch fails to ripen. This malady is caused due to inactivity of ripening enzymes due to high temperature, convective heat and post harvest exposure to sunlight.

Control: Use of mulching and post harvest exposure to low temperatures between 10-15 C for 10-18 hours has been useful in reducing the malady.

Mango Malformation

Malformation is widely prevalent in northern India, particularly in the states of Punjab, Delhi and western U.P. where more than 50% of the trees suffer from this malady. The malformed panicles remain unproductive and are characterized by a compact mass of male flowers, greenish in colour and stunted in growth. The main and secondary rachis is thick and short and bears flowers with relatively larger bracts, sepals and petals as compared to normal flowers. The malformed panicles remain intact on the trees for a considerable long period. The complexity of the disorder is attributed to cultural, nutritional and factors like, mites, fungal, viral, hormonal imbalance etc. The exact cause and control of the malady is yet to be established.

Control: Spraying of Planofix (200 ppm) during the first week of October followed by deblossoming at bud burst stage is recommended as a remedial measure against malformation.

Biennial Bearing

The term biennial, alternate or irregular bearing generally signifies the tendency of mango trees to bear a heavy crop in one year (On year) and very little or no crop in the succeeding year (Off year). Most of the commercial varieties of north India, namely, Dashehari, Langra and Chausa are biennial bearers, while south Indian varieties like Totapuri Red Small, Bangalora, and Neelum are known to be regular bearers. When a tree produces heavy crop in one season, it gets exhausted nutritionally and is unable to put forth new flush thereby failing to yield in the following season. The problem has been attributed to the causes like genetical, physiological, environmental and nutritional factors.

Control: For overcoming biennial bearing, deblossoming is recommended to reduce the crop load in the 'On' year so that it is balanced in the 'Off' year. Proper maintenance of orchard by way of effective control of pests and diseases and regular cultural operations may also result in better performance of the tree every year. Soil application of Paclobutrazol (PP333) or Cultar @ 4 g/tree in the month of September resulted in early flowering with higher fruit set and yield. It may be applied every year for regular fruiting, particularly in young trees. Ringing of branches is recommended as means of inducing flowering in the 'Off' year. However, Weak, stunted, unhealthy trees should not be ringed to force flowering. It involves removal of 1 cm wide ring of bark on a branch of about 15 cm thickness. Ringing stops vegetative growth and results in accumulation of carbohydrates and other metabolites in the portion of the branch above the ring, thereby creating physiological condition for flowering. Ringing should be done in August or early September, well before the time of fruit-bud differentiation.

Fruit Drop

The intensity of fruit drop varies from variety to variety. Among the commercially grown varieties, Langra is more susceptible to drop, while Dasheri is the least. The fruit drop is more or less a continuous process and can be classified into three phases, viz. (i) pinhead drop, (ii) post-setting drop and (iii) May-month drop. The fruit drop in first two phases are insignificant compared to the third phase which affects the final yield significantly and needs more attention. Embryo abortion, climatic factors, disturbed water relation, lack of nutrition, attack of disease and pest and hormonal imbalances are the major factors that lead to fruit drop.

Control: The foliar application of Alar (B-nine) @ 100 ppm or NAA 20 ppm at pea stage of fruit was found effective in controlling fruit drop in mango.

Black Tip

Black tip is a serious disorder, particularly in the cultivar Dasheri. The affected fruits become unmarketable and reduce the yield to a considerable extent. The damage to the fruit gets initiated right at marble stage with a characteristic yellowing of tissues at distal end. Gradually, the colour intensifies into brown and finally black. At this stage, further growth and development of the fruit is retarded and black ring at the tip extends towards the upper part of the fruit. Black tip disorder has generally been detected in orchards located in the vicinity of brick kilns. It has been reported that the gases like carbon monoxide, sulphur dioxide and ethylene constituting the fumes of brick kiln are known to damage growing tip of fruits and give rise to the symptoms of black tip. Apart from these factors, irrigation, condition of the tree and management practices also play important role in deciding the severity of the disorder.

Control: Planting of mango orchards in North-South direction and 5-6 km away from the brick kilns may reduce incidence of black tip to a greater extent. The incidence of black tip can also be minimized by spraying Borax (1%) or other alkaline solutions like caustic soda (0.8%) or washing soda (0.5%). The first spray of Borax should be done positively at pea stage followed by two more sprays at 15 days interval.

Clustering in Mango ('Jhumka')

A fruiting disorder, locally known as 'Jhumka', is characterised by the development of fruit lets in clusters at the tip of panicles. Such fruits cease to grow beyond pea or marble stage and drop down after a month of fruit set. Absence of sufficient population of pollinators in the orchards is the major reason. The other reasons causing the disorder are old and overcrowding of trees, indiscriminate spraying against pests and diseases, use of synthetic pyrethroids, monoculture of Dashehari and bad weather during flowering.

Control: Introduction of beehives in the orchards during flowering season for increasing the number of pollinators and restrict insecticidal sprays at full bloom to avoid killing of pollinators. Pests and diseases should be controlled in time by spraying the recommended pesticides and concentrations. Spraying of NAA (300 ppm) during October-November is recommended. The practice of monoculture of a particular variety may be avoided. Particularly in case of Dashehari, 5-6% of other varieties should be planted in new plantations.

INTEGRATED PEST MANAGEMENT FOR MANGO IN INDIA

The mango (*Mangifera indica* L.), belongs to the dicotyledonous family (Anacardiaceae), in the order Sapindales, is one of the world's most important and reputable fruits and is considered as the "King of fruits" or "Apple of tropics", probably originated from Indo Burma region and thus has prominent position among commercial fruits grown in India. Konkan region of Maharashtra is famous for a leading variety 'Alphonso', which alone occupies about 1.70 lakh hectare area under single variety. The economy of this region is mainly dependent on the mango crop. Also, Dharmapuri, Krishnagiri, Salem and Theni districts of Tamil Nadu was most famous for the production of pulpy mango varieties. The warm and humid climate of this region is most congenial for development of pests and disease. The success of mango crop is associated with how effectively pest and diseases are managed. Therefore, mango growers are very much concerned about crop protection. They indiscriminately apply whatever pesticides that is available in market. This has resulted in development of resistance to pesticides and resurgence of secondary pests like flower midge, thrips, scale insects and mealy bugs. Earlier, the infestation by mango hoppers was considered as a major problem and the plant protection measures were concentrated on these single pests. Twenty two species of mango hoppers were reported to be feeding on mango.

Out of these, only three species were economically important earlier; only *Amritodus atkinsoni* was the predominant species. However, since 1985, *Idioscopus neveosparsus* has become number one and more serious during flowering period. The nymphs and adults suck the sap from tender shoots, leaves, inflorescence and even tender fruits.

However, the infestation was more severe during flowering, causing severe flower and fruit drop. Apart from the feeding injury, they also secrete honeydew like substance which invites the problem of black sooty mould. It hinders the photosynthetic activity of the plant and deteriorates the fruit quality. Such types of fruits fetch less price in the market. Losses to the extent of 60 per cent are reported.

Now the pest scenario has changed. Apart from mango hoppers, considerable increase in midge fly, *Erosomyia indica* intensity was noticed since last decade. The blossom midge which was noticed on private orchard during 1985, is now posing serious threat in mango production. This pest was first noticed in India at Coimbatore region in 1964 and later on reported all over the country. The outbreak was observed on vegetative flush of July-August.

However, severe incidence was observed during December-January on inflorescence and as well as on vegetative shoots. Female fly lay eggs on tender shoots vegetative buds, leaf and panicle rachis. Larvae feed internally on tissues and thus develop galls. The galls finally turn black. In severe cases, affected shoots/ panicles will partially dry up. Incidence on inflorescence leads to fruit drop. Now incidence is also noticed on small fruits resulting in fruit drop.

INTEGRATED PEST MANAGEMENT FOR MANGO

Physical Method

- Removal and destruction of affected and fallen fruits due to fruit fly and fruit borer infestation
- Destruction of affected shoots due to shoot borer infestation along with larvae in young orchards.
- Remove the dead and weak branches in order to reduce the inoculum of various pathogens.
- Keep the stalks of the fruit clear by removing dried rachis, small leaves that harbor the disease and pests inoculums. Remove the unfruited panicles to avoid scratching injury to fruits, put dried leaves in between adjacent fruits.
- Ploughing/weeding or digging of the soil under tree canopy. This will expose the hibernating pupae of gall midge and other pests like fruit borer, fruit fly etc.
- Avoiding overcrowding of the laterals and foliage as it develops the favourable microclimate
- for pest and disease build up. It also prevents the penetration of the pesticide sprays, which invites the pest resurgence due to residual population. Therefore, proper thinning/centre opening should be done and trees be kept open and well aerated.

Cultural Method

- The neem products particularly Nimbicidine @ 2 ml/lit can control 50 to 60% hopper population and hence it can be used during lean periods of outbreak right from the bud burst stage and thereafter in 10 to 15 days interval, so that hopper build up will be checked without disturbing natural enemies like red ants, spiders and lace wing bugs and coccinellids which are common predators in mango garden.

Chemical Method

- For blossom protection, use 3 ml Cypermethrin 25 EC or 5ml Fenvalerate 20 EC or 9ml Decamethrin 2.8 EC or 20ml Quinalphos 25 EC or 3ml Imidacloprid 17.8 SL or 1.2 g Clothianidine 50 WDG or 1.0 g Thiomethoxam 25 WDG or 20 ml Phenthoate 50 EC or 10 ml Dimethoate 30 EC per 10 lit of water.
- **Midge** : Fenitrothion (0.05%)
- **Thirps** : Dimethoate (0.03%) or Phosalone (0.05%) if intensity is more apply Thiomethoxam 25% 2gm or Spinosad 45% 2.5 ml/10 lit.
- **Mealy bugs** : Monocrotophos (0.05%) for early outbreak and DDVP (0.05%) during advance stage of fruit development
- **Shoot borer**: Quinalphos or Monocrotophos (0.05%)
- The trees and branches when cut, invites the stem borer problem. Therefore, cut portions should be treated with pesticide and applied with Bordeaux mixture

Biological Method

- Glyricidia is a major host of mealy bugs, *Ferissia virgata* which is predominant species of mealy bugs in Konkan region. The incidence was noticed in the month of March. Therefore, the population of mealy bugs on glyricidia should be monitored form March onwards and if noticed, glyricidia stumps should be chopped off and destroyed.
- Explore the possibility of releasing, *Cryptolemus montrizerae*, a potential predator of mealy bugs during second fortnight of March as spray schedule will already be exhausted by this time and hence, there is no hurdle in establishment of predator population.

10

Cultivation of Rose

A rose is a woody perennial flowering plant of the genus *Rosa*, in the family Rosaceae, or the flower it bears. There are over a hundredspecies and thousands of cultivars. They form a group of plants that can be erect shrubs, climbing or trailing with stems that are often armed with sharp prickles. Flowers vary in size and shape and are usually large and showy, in colours ranging from white through yellows and reds. Most species are native to Asia, with smaller numbers native to Europe, North America, and northwestern Africa. Species, cultivars and hybrids are all widely grown for their beauty and often are fragrant. Roses have acquired cultural significance in many societies. Rose plants range in size from compact, miniature roses, to climbers that can reach seven meters in height. Different species hybridize easily, and this has been used in the development of the wide range of garden roses.

FLORICULTURE AND ITS SCOPE

We all know, flowers play an essential role in people's celebrations and every day lives. Weddings, graduations, funerals, Mother's Day, St. Valentine's Day, Easter and Christmas. Being a nature lover, researcher would like to share some of the interesting facts about the floriculture through this blog, with a hope that the information provided will be useful for those who are thinking of starting a business in floriculture which has tremendous opportunities in the present scenerio. And promise to keep posting about this interesting subject in future also with some more interesting facts of this business

Floriculture, or flower farming, is a discipline of horticulture concerned with the cultivation of flowering and ornamental plants for gardens and forfloristry, comprising the floral industry. The development, via plant breeding, of new varieties is a major occupation of floriculturists.

Floriculture crops include bedding plants, houseplants, flowering garden and pot plants, cut cultivated greens, and cut flowers. As distinguished from nursery crops, floriculture crops are generally herbaceous. Bedding and garden plants consist of young flowering plants (annuals and perennials) and vegetable plants. They are grown in cell packs (in flats or trays), in pots, or in hanging baskets, usually inside a controlled environment, and sold largely for gardens and landscaping. *Pelargonium* ("geraniums"), *Impatiens* ("busy lizzies"), and *Petunia* are the best-selling bedding plants. The many cultivars of *Chrysanthemum* are the major perennial garden plant in the United States.

Flowering plants are largely sold in pots for indoor use. The major flowering plants are poinsettias, orchids, florist chrysanthemums, and finished florist azaleas. Foliage plants are also sold in pots and hanging baskets for indoor and patio use, including larger specimens for office, hotel, and restaurant interiors.

Cut flowers are usually sold in bunches or as bouquets with cut foliage. The production of cut flowers is specifically known as the cut flower industry. Farming flowers and foliage employs special aspects of floriculture, such as spacing, training and pruning plants for optimal flower harvest; and post-harvest treatment such as chemical treatments, storage, preservation and packaging. In Australia and the United States some species are harvested from the wild for the cut flower market.

Floriculture is increasingly regarded as a viable diversification from the traditional field crops due to increased per unit returns and the increasing habit of "saying it with flower" during all the occasions. Though the art of growing flowers is not new to India, protected cultivation in polyhouses is relatively new in India. Enormous genetic diversity, varied agro climatic conditions and versatile human resources offer India a unique scope for diversification into new avenues which have not been explored to a greater extent. With the opening up of world market in the WTO regime, there is a free movement of floriculture products worldwide. In this context, each and every country has equal opportunity for trade in each other's territory. Globally, more than 140 countries are involved in cultivation of floricultural crops. The USA continues to be the highest consumer with more than $ 10 billion per annum, followed by Japan with more than $ 7 billion. India has better scope in the future as there is a shift in trend towards tropical flowers and this can be gainfully exploited by India with enormous amount of diversity in indigenous flora.

FLORICULTURE IN INDIA

About two decades back or so, the floriculture was just a pastime of rich people and hobby of flower lovers, but now it has opened a new vista in agri-business i,e, commercial floriculture. With the increase in buying capacity of people, the flower lovers have now started buying them from the markets to beautify their home as well as to adore some one they love simply because they don't have time and enough space to grow flowers particularly in urban areas and in metropolitan cities. Flowers, it seems, is the most wanted item in any social occasions for conveying one's status and aesthetic sense. Flower is now so indispensable that one may cancel his her birthday celebration or Yama may postpone the death of a dying person in case flowers are not available at that time. No nuptial is performed and honeymoon of a young couple is not consummated till garden fresh rose and rajanigandha or tuberose with lingering and stupefying aroma are made available.

Indian Council of Agriculture Research (ICAR) conducted a survey of assessment on the possibilities of cut flowers trade in India during 1960-62. An important conclusion was that an internal sale as RS.9.26 Crores worth flower weighing 10,460 tones grown in an area of 4000 hector. Flowers like Rose, Gladiolus, Tuberose, Chrysanthemum, Aster, Carnation, Orchids, Marigold are most popular in cut flower market all over the World.

BOTANY

The leaves are borne alternately on the stem. In most species they are 5 to 15 centimetres (2.0 to 5.9 in) long, pinnate, with (3-) 5-9 (-13) leaflets and basal stipules; the leaflets usually have a serrated margin, and often a few small prickles on the underside of the stem. Most roses aredeciduous but a few (particularly from South east Asia) are evergreen or nearly so.

The flowers of most species have five petals, with the exception of *Rosa sericea*, which usually has only four. Each petal is divided into two distinct lobes and is usually white or pink, though in a few species yellow or red. Beneath the petals are five sepals (or in the case of some *Rosa sericea*, four). These may be long enough to be visible when viewed from above and appear as green points alternating with the rounded petals. There are multiple superior ovaries that develop intoachenes. Roses are insect-pollinated in nature.

The aggregate fruit of the rose is a berry-like structure called a rose hip. Many of the domestic cultivars do not produce hips, as the flowers are so tightly petalled that they do not provide access for pollination. The hips of most species are red, but a few (e.g. *Rosa pimpinellifolia*) have dark purple to black hips. Each hip comprises an outer fleshy layer, the hypanthium, which contains 5-160 "seeds" (technically dry single-seeded fruits called achenes) embedded in a matrix of fine, but stiff, hairs.

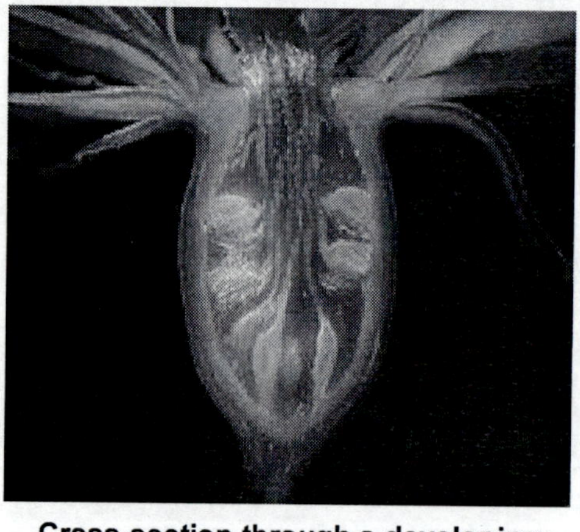

Cross-section through a developing rose hip

Exterior view of rose buds

Rose hips of some species, especially the dog rose (*Rosa canina*) and rugosa rose (*Rosa rugosa*), are very rich in vitamin C, among the richest sources of any plant. The hips are eaten by fruit-eating birds such as thrushes and waxwings, which then disperse the seeds in their droppings. Some birds, particularly finches, also eat the seeds.

The hybrid garden rose "Amber Flush"

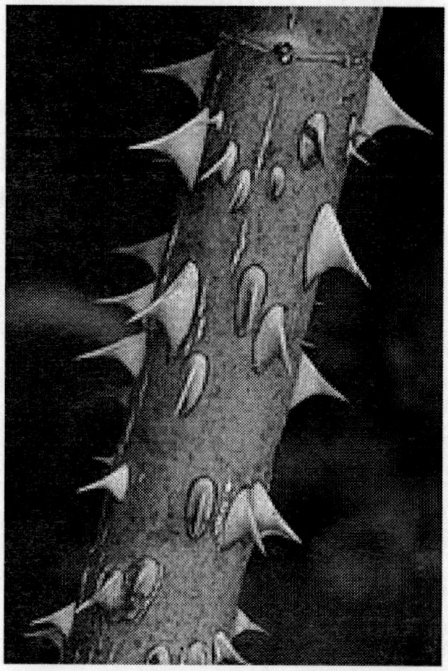

Rose thorns are actually prickles – outgrowths of the epidermis.

While the sharp objects along a rose stem are commonly called "thorns", they are technically prickles — outgrowths of the epidermis (the outer layer of tissue of the stem). (True thorns, as produced by e.g. *Citrus* or *Pyracantha*, are modified stems, which always originate at a node and which have nodes and internodes along the length of the thorn itself.) Rose prickles are typically sickle-shaped hooks, which aid the rose in hanging onto other vegetation when growing over it. Some species such as *Rosa rugosa* and *Rosa pimpinellifolia* have densely packed straight prickles, probably an adaptation to reduce browsing by animals, but also possibly an adaptation to trap wind-blown sandand so reduce erosion and protect their roots (both of these species grow naturally on coastal sand dunes). Despite the presence of prickles, roses are frequently browsed by deer. A few species of roses have only vestigial prickles that have no points.

CULTIVATION OF ROSES

Many nursery roses come with generic 'instructions' on the tag, but they're short on detail. Not all of them are localizez for our climate or conditions either. These tips are aimed mainly at the warm temperate climates common on Australia's coastline.

Soil preparation

Many parts of Australia (including most of Sydney) are plagued by clay soil. Roses don't mind clay too much. They prefer it to sandy soil and it stops them drying out in the summer heat. On the other hand, you won't get good results in clay unless you try to improve the soil.

If you're working with an existing rose garden, it's safe to rake in the following materials at the top couple of inches of the soil. For new beds, dig it through the soil:

- Gypsum (available in 5 - 25 kg bags at most nurseries). The calcium content breaks up clay in most soils.
- Blood and bone - more expensive than gypsum but includes great natural nitrogen fertiliser.
- River sand - coarse sand will break up any kind of clay.
- Compost - either home tumbled or purchased as 'soil improver'
- Cheap potting mix. Dreadful for any other purpose, but the organic matter does a great job of breaking up clay soil and the price is right. $4 a bag at Woolworths!
- Cow manure. Roses love it more than chicken based products (e.g. Dynamic Lifter) and it doesn't stink anywhere near as much.
- Mushroom compost. Same benefits as cow manure.

Sandy soils benefit from organic matter too. It aids in moisture retention. Because manures and compost release their nutrients more slowly than chemicals, they also help combat the fast leaching of minerals that happens in sandy soil.

DISEASE AND INSECT PESTS

Roses are susceptible to a number of disease and insect pests. Roses may survive without a basic pest control program, but they may not be very attractive. A pest control program starts with proper site selection, good soil preparation, good drainage, proper spacing, cultivar selection, and plant maintenance. These all foster healthy roses that are better able to withstand the pressure of disease and insects.

When selecting roses, note the resistance to disease of a particular cultivar or named variety within a class. You want to select by cultivar, not by class. All too often, many gardeners assume that shrub roses (the class) are very tolerant or resistant to disease and make their selection based solely on class. In fact, there are a number of cultivars that are very prone to severe disease injury.

Another interesting fact about diseases is that plants can have two types of resistance: phenotypic or genotypic. Phenotypic resistance is when a cultivar is resistant to a disease in one location or part of the country but not in another. Genotypic resistance is due to the presence of genes that are not affected by climate, location, or horticultural practice. That is why, when the term "resistance" is used as a blanket term and assigned to a variety or class, it may or may not apply depending on where you garden.

Diseases

Blackspot

This fungal disease can cause almost complete defoliatiation of bushes by early fall, resulting in a weakened bush on which cane die-back and cankers become severe. Blackspot is identified as circular black spots that appear on the upper surface of the leaves, starting at the bottom of the plant and moving upward. Infected leaves turn yellow and fall off prematurely. The fringed margin and black color distinguish this leaf spot from others. Infections on canes are identified as reddish-purple spots. Splashing water spreads blackspot. Infection occurs after leaves are wet for several hours, making it more serious during rainy periods. Some roses are less susceptible than others, so cultivar selection is important. The fungus overwinters in fallen leaves and stem cankers. Raking and removing these leaves as well as pruning out affected canes by spring before the buds swell may help provide some control. Avoid wetting the leaves when watering and locate plants where there is good air circulation. Fungicide spray programs need to be started as soon as new leaves appear in the spring.

Powdery Mildew

Powdery mildew is a fungus disease that affects young leaves, causing them to curl and twist and develop a purple coloration. As the disease progresses, leaves become covered with white powdery fuzz. Whereas blackspot is usually most severe on the lower part of the plant, mildew affects the top part of the plant. Mature leaves are less likely to be affected. Mildew is spread by wind and develops rapidly during periods of warm, dry days followed by cool, humid nights. Infections of mildew are actually discouraged by the presence of water on the leaves. However, keeping plants wet all night to avoid mildew provides an environment that allows other diseases to develop. Infection can be reduced through sanitation and fungicide spray programs. Prune out all dead and diseased canes to reduce initial fungus infection. Because new growth is especially susceptible, thorough coverage of new growth with fungicide is important. Plant roses in areas where they receive good air circulation and where the foliage can dry off rapidly in the early morning to prevent many types of diseases.

Stem Cankers

There are several fungi that cause cankers on roses. The different fungi can cause different-looking cankers, but they usually produce brown, oval-shaped, sunken, or shriveled areas anywhere on the cane. The cane dies, and leaves wilt from that point outward. Sometimes small black specks can be seen on the cane surface within the borders of the canker. These are fungal spore-forming structures. Cankers should be pruned out each year. Make the cut well below the affected tissue. Protect the plant from cold or freeze injury by providing adequate cover over the winter. Do not cover roses too early in the fall. When roses are mulched before the soil freezes, moisture can be trapped around the canes and this can increase the damage caused by canker disease. Keep plants vigorous with proper culture and disease control. Canker is a disease of stress. If plants are kept actively growing, they stand a better chance of avoiding cankers. There are no effective chemical controls for canker disease.

Botrytis Blight

Botrytis blight is a fungal disease that generally attacks dying tissue. It is frequently found on older flowers and other plant parts. Under certain conditions it may also attack healthy tissue. Botrytis favors moist, wet conditions, often causing the disease to attack entire flowers and produce a gray fuzzy mold. This disease is often called gray mold. Good garden sanitation and removing spent flowers often result in good control of this disease. When this is insufficient in providing adequate control, a preventative spray program may be necessary.

Mosaic

Rose mosaic is caused by a virus. Bright yellow patterns made up of wavy lines may appear on the leaves of some varieties. Other varieties may show no yellow lines, but may be stunted and weak due to virus infection. Virus-infected plants cannot be cured. Plant virus-resistant roses if possible. Try to control insects, especially aphids, since they help spread the virus. If you are pruning virus-infected plants, don't prune healthy plants unless you first disinfest your pruners. Dipping the blades in a 10 percent solution of chlorine bleach and water for 60 seconds can do this. A 25 percent concentration reduces the time needed to about 10 seconds. All infected plants should be removed and destroyed to reduce the spread of the virus to other plants.

Crown Gall

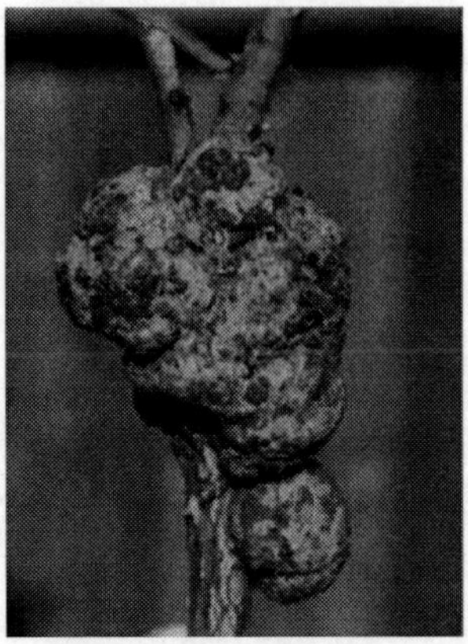

Crown gall is a bacterial disease that can survive 15-20 years in the soil. It causes irregularly shaped, rough, dark-colored masses (galls) to appear on stems near the soil line. These galls can appear as small swellings or be several inches in diameter. Severely infected plants become stunted and fail to grow properly. There are no effective controls for crown gall. Severely infected plants should be dug up and discarded and roses should not be planted in that area for at least 5 years. Avoid buying plants with suspicious swellings or gall on lower stems or crowns. However, do not confuse crown gall with normal swellings that you see as a result of the budding process. Protect plants from injury on stems during cultivation. Maintain vigor with fertilization and watering. Crown gall is not specific to roses and can affect apples, raspberries, honeysuckle, euonymus, and many vegetables. For this reason, roses should not be planted where plants susceptible to crown gall have been removed because of the disease. Galltrol-A, a non-pathogenic bacteria, has been used to prevent crown gall. It is often used as a dip on cane root roses prior to planting.

Rose Rosette

Rose rosette is becoming more common and can result in significant damage. This pathogen (not yet positively identified) is spread by an eriophid mite. Symptoms include rapid growth of shoots, development of "witches' broom," development of tufts of small, deformed reddish leaves and excessive thorniness. Plants decline over time. Because affected plants can't be cured, it is best to dig out the affected plant and destroy it. Controlling the mite has been labeled as an option but attempts at controlling it have proven inconclusive. It is very difficult to apply sprays in a timely and satisfactory way.

Insect Pests

Aphids

Aphids are very common pests. Aphids are soft-bodied insects that can be red, green, yellow, or black. They feed on very young succulent shoots, causing distortion. Aphids are often kept in check by natural predators. Alternative control measures include the use of insecticidal soaps, strong streams of water to knock them off the plant, or insecticides.

Japanese Beetles

These hard-shelled, metallic-green, black, and gold insects can cause extensive damage to roses just by their sheer numbers and voracious appetite. They prefer flowers and flower buds but will also attack foliage. Japanese beetles are difficult to control because they are strong fliers and constantly reinvade the area. Home gardeners still find that Sevin provides the best control, but it is only topical. This means that reapplication needs to be done on a regular basis to protect the foliage and flowers. Beware of Japanese beetle traps. Traps are almost too effective and will draw a great number of beetles into an area, making the problem worse. If they are used, they should be placed in areas away from the rose garden. Hand picking is also a suggested control for small numbers of beetles.

Leaf Cutter Bees

It is unusual to see the insects at work, but they make their presence known by the perfectly round holes cut near the edges of the leaves. These leaf pieces are used to make egg partitions inside their burrows. The damage they cause is strictly cosmetic and warrants no control.

Spider Mites

Mites are very tiny relatives of spiders. They can be red, black, or brown in color. Mites pierce the underside of rose leaves and suck sap, causing the leaf to turn gray or bronze. A fine web is a sign of a heavy infestation. Mites reproduce rapidly, resulting in high populations in a short time. Mites flourish in crowded, stagnant gardens. A high-pressure washing with water from a garden hose directed to the underside of the leaves every 2-3 days can manage mites. This will interrupt their life cycle. Miticides such as dicofol help in heavy infestations. Insecticidal soaps are also effective in controlling mites.

Thrips

Thrips are extremely small, brown insects usually living and feeding inside of the blooms. A deformed flower with flecked or scratched petals is usually a sign of a thrips problem. The rasping mouth parts of thrips causes this injury when they scratch the petal surface to feed. Thrips are especially attracted to yellow or light-colored roses. Some control can be achieved using materials such as orthene, malathion, or insecticidal soap, but even these often give poor results. They tend to be worse during late June, July and August when temperatures are warm.

Rose Midge

The rose midge is a tiny fly that lays eggs in the buds and shoots of roses. The larvae that develop start feeding and causes bent, mishapen or blasted flower buds and withering of the stem tips. Eventually they turn black. Control consists of pruning out buds and applying insecticide if the problem persists. Midge damage usually shows up in July. Because the larvae fall to the soil to pupate, an effective control is to place weed barrier fabric under the plants to catch the larvae and prevent them from entering the soil to pupate.

Sawfly (Rose Slug)

The common rose slug causes skeletonizing or window pane like damage to rose leaves in spring and early summer. The larvae look like caterpillars but are actually more closely related to bees and wasps. Common rose slugs are green with a light tan head and often have may hairlike bristles. Although they look like caterpillars, products with a BT are not effective because they are not larvae of moths or butterflies. Control can include hand picking and the use of horticultural oils or insecticidal soaps.

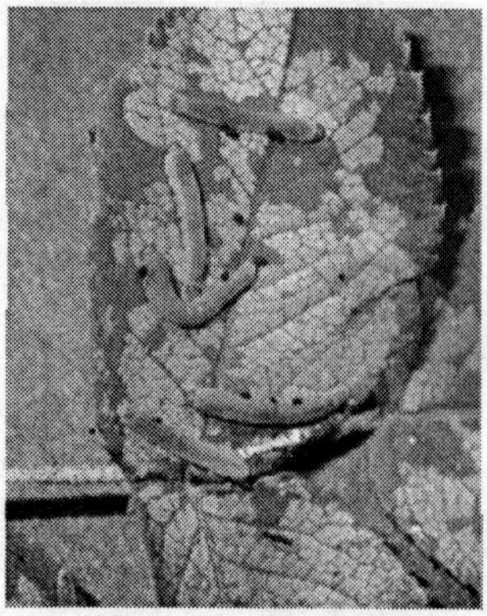

FUNGICIDE SPRAY PROGRAMS

Fungicides generally recommended for blackspot control include:

- Daconil 2787 or fungicides containing Daconil
- Phyton 27
- Mancozeb
- Funginex
- Orthenex.

Frequently used fungicides for control of powdery mildew include:

- Captan
- Daconil 2787
- Phyton 27
- Funginex
- Orthenex

Materials used in limiting botrytis are:

- Captan
- Daconil 278
- Mancozeb

As with all spray materials, follow label directions carefully for mixing and applying.

11

Weathering of Rock

Weathering is the process in which the texture and composition of rocks and minerals change after being exposed at the Earth's surface to weathering agents such as water, oxygen, organic and inorganic acids and large temperature fluctuations. These changes usually occur in place (in situ) but also continue during and after transportation. The process of weathering can be chemical or physical (mechanical).

ENVIRONMENTAL FACTORS AFFECTING RATES OF WEATHERING

The following factors can affect the rate and the amount of weathering that takes place:

1) **Rock type (what is present to be weathered)**: Different types of materials weather in different ways, thus the rate at which rocks and minerals weather depends on their composition. A rock with high amounts of stable

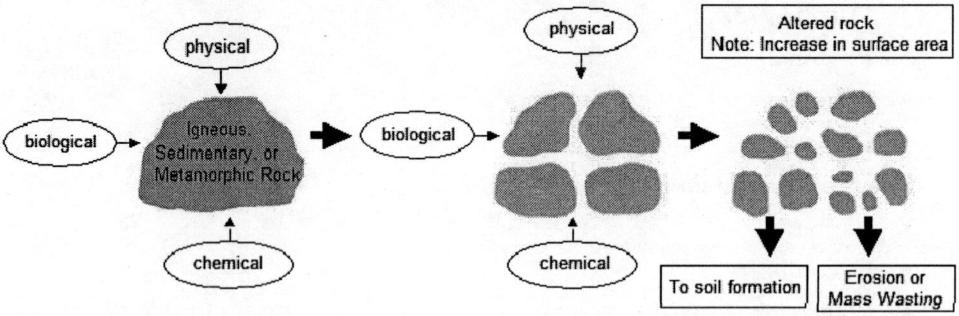

Fig. 3. A conceptual diagram showing how weathering breaks down rocks and minerals; eventually, soil formation begins in place. Erosion or mass wasting involves removal of particles offsite.

minerals like quartz-rich sandstone will be more resistant to weathering than a rock with high amounts of olivine such as basalt.

2) **Climate**: The amount of rainfall and the temperature have a significant effect on the amount and depth of weathering that takes place. The amount of rainfall helps to determine the amount of water present for weathering. The temperature governs the rate at which the weathering takes place. Areas that are cold and dry, such as Antarctica, have slow rates of chemical weathering (weathering here is mostly physical), whereas warm, moist tropical areas tend to favour chemical weathering over physical weathering, leading to greater depths of weathering.

3) **Time**: It takes a long time, relatively speaking, to develop regolith, hence the more time that has passed the more weathering that will have occurred. In areas such there are very old and stable areas called shields or cratons. Some rocks in these areas have been dated to an age of 3 800 million years and, until recently, were regarded as being the oldest in the world! Zircon crystals are now known to be the oldest minerals on Earth, dated at over 4400 million years. Here, regolith has had more than 1000 million years to develop into weathering profiles that are hundreds of metres thick. In parts of the world such as New Zealand, glaciers still cover some of the landscape

PROCESSES OF WEATHERING - INTRODUCTION

Weathering is the process of disintegration of rock from physical, chemical, and biological stresses. Weathering is influenced by temperature and moisture (climate). As rock disintegrates, it becomes more susceptible to further physical, chemical, and biological weathering due to the increase in exposed surface area. During weathering, minerals that were once bound in the rock structure are released.

The degree of weathering that occurs depends upon the resistance to weathering of the minerals in the rock, as well as the degree of the physical, chemical, and biological stresses. A rule of thumb is that minerals in rocks that are formed under high temperature and pressure tend to be less resistant to weathering, while minerals formed at low temperature and pressure are more resistant to weathering.Weathering is usually confined to the top few meters of geologic material, because physical, chemical, and biological stresses generally decrease with depth. Weathering of rocks occurs in place, but the disintegrated weathering products can be carried by water, wind, or gravity to another location (i.e., erosion or mass wasting).

Types of Weathering - Physical

Physical weathering is the weakening and subsequent disintegration of rock by physical forces. These physical forces include temperature fluctuation, abrasion, frost action (freezing and thawing), and salt crystal growth.

Temperature fluctuation can cause expansion or contraction of rock. When the temperature of rock increases, the rock expands. When the temperature of rock decreases, the rock contracts. This process of expansion and contraction is a physical stress and can crack or break rock. Abrasion of rock is caused by the friction of water, wind, or ice upon the rock. The continuous exposure to these elements slowly breaks down the exposed surface of the rock.

Frost action is the repeated cycle of ice formation and ice melt in the pore spaces and fractures of rocks causing disintegration of the rock. When water in rock pores freezes, its volume increases by about 10%. This can create a significant amount of pressure on rocks. The magnitude and extent of frost action is dependent on the frequency, duration and intensity of the freezing and thawing cycles.Salt crystal growth can cause the break-up of rock materials. Crystal growth often occurs when groundwater moves into empty pores or spaces of rock by capillary action. As the water evaporates, salt crystals grow and accumulate, putting pressure on the rock and causing it to break apart. Salt crystallization is common in drier climates.

Types of Weathering - Chemical

Chemical weathering is the weakening and subsequent disintegration of rock by chemical reactions. These reactions include oxidation, hydrolysis, and carbonation. These processes either form or destroy minerals, thus altering the nature of the rock's mineral composition. Temperature and, especially, moisture are critical for chemical weathering; chemical weathering of rock minerals generally occurs more quickly in hot, humid climatic regions.

Oxidation is the reaction of rock minerals with oxygen, thus changing the mineral composition of the rock. When minerals in rock oxidize, they become less resistant to weathering. Iron, a commonly known mineral, becomes red or rust colored when oxidized.

Carbonation is the process of rock minerals reacting with carbonic acid. Carbonic acid is formed when water combines with carbon dioxide. Carbonic acid dissolves or breaks down minerals in the rock.

$$CO_2 + H_2O \rightarrow H_2CO_3$$

(carbon dioxide + water → carbonic acid)

$$CaCO_3 + H_2CO_3 \rightarrow Ca^{2+} + 2HCO_{3-}$$

(calcite + carbonic acid → calcium + bicarbonate)

Hydrolysis is a chemical reaction caused by water. Water changes the chemical composition and size of minerals in rock, making them less resistant to weathering. Click on the video clip below to see hydrolysis of a relatively weathering resistant mineral, feldspar. When this mineral is completely hydrolyzed, clay minerals and quartz are produced and such elements as K, Ca, or Na are released.

A hydrolysis reaction of orthoclase (alkali feldspar), a common mineral found in igneous rock, yields kaolinite, silicic acid, and potassium.

$$2KAlSi_3O_8 + 2H^+ + 9H_2O \rightarrow H_4Al_2Si_2O_9 + 4H_4SiO_4 + 2K^+$$

(orthoclase + water → kaolinite + silicic acid + potassium)

Experiential Activity

- A small amount of ground calcium feldspar is placed in the mortar.
- Five drops of distilled H_2O are added (chemical weathering)
- A few drops of cresol red indicator areadded (yellow at pH < 7.2 and pink at pH = 7.8)
- Color is yellow orange
- The feldspar mixture is ground into a finer powder
- Color is now purplish red

Hydration is the absorption of water into the mineral structure. A good example of hydration is the absorption of water by anhydrite, resulting in the formation of gypsum. Hydration expands volume and also results in rock deformation.

Experiential Activity

- A small amount of limonite, $Fe_2O_3.H_2O$, is placed into a test tube.
- The tube is held with a test-tube holder just above the blue flame of a lighted Bunsen burner.
- The sample is cooled.

Note: The color change of limonite from yellow to brick red; (Reaction Fe_2O_3).

Dehydration is the removal of water from rock or mineral structures. A good example of dehydration is the removal of water from limonite, resulting in the formation of hematite.

Dehydration of limonite to hematite may be observed in the following experiential activity.

Leaching

During leaching, soluble components within the regolith are removed when they interact with water, either on the Earth's surface or underground. The soluble ions that are removed from rocks during weathering are transferred into the water and are carried away. The unpleasant taste of some groundwater can occur when components leached out of rocks become too concentrated in the water e.g. sulphate may give water the smell of rotten egg gas, and too much calcium, sodium, potassium or magnesium will cause water to become "hard", making it difficult to build up a good soapy lather in the shower! In general, the major rock-forming elements will leach in the following order (from most leachable to least leachable): Na > K > Ca> Mg > Si> Al > Fe > Ti. The last four are generally regarded as being "immobile" and will tend to stay put during weathering, but there are always exceptions.

Oxidation and reduction

In weathering, oxidation simply means the addition of oxygen to a reaction. Reduction is the removal of oxygen from a reaction. Adding oxygen forms oxides. If oxygen and water are added to minerals they form hydroxides. Minerals that contain iron are particularly susceptible and regolith may appear red or yellow accordingly because iron oxides (such as rust) are reddish and iron hydroxides yellowish. Where reduction occurs, regolith can take on a grey, green or even bluish colour.

Carbonation

This involves the reaction between minerals and carbonate or bicarbonate ions. For example, increased carbon dioxide in the air can create acid rain that contains carbonic acid. In some urban environments, these small amounts of acid in the rain are slowly dissolving buildings made of limestone and concrete. A similar process occurs where acid in water moves through the soil. The carbonic acid creates H+ ions which can be substituted for other ions within minerals, thus altering their composition and eventually causing them to break down. Acid rain is a devastating problem for those countries which depend on high sulphur coal for electricity, resulting in sulphuric acid rain!

Ferrolysis

This involves the creation of hydrogen ions (H+) by the repeated reduction (by soil-based organisms) and re-oxidation of iron. These H+ ions acidify water and are capable of dissolving clays within the regolith, releasing aluminium and other metals into groundwater toxic levels. This reaction commonly occurs in acid sulphate soil (ASS) environments in conjunction with oxidation and reduction reactions.

Types of Weathering - Biological

Biological weathering is the weakening and subsequent disintegration of rock by plants, animals and microbes.

Growing **plant roots** can exert stress or pressure on rock. Although the process is physical, the pressure is exerted by a biological process (*i.e.*, growing roots). Biological processes can also produce chemical weathering, for example where plant roots or microorganisms produce organic acids which help to dissolve minerals.

Microbial activity breaks down rock minerals by altering the rock's chemical composition, thus making it more susceptible to weathering. One example of microbial activity is lichen; lichen is fungi and algae, living together in a symbiotic relationship. Fungi release chemicals that break down rock minerals; the minerals thus released from rock are consumed by the algae. As this process continues, holes and gaps continue to develop on the rock, exposing the rock further to physical and chemical weathering.

Burrowing **animals** can move rock fragments to the surface, exposing the rock to more intense chemical, physical, and biological processes and so indirectly enhancing the process of rock weathering.

Although physical, chemical, and biological weathering are separate processes, some or all of the processes can act together in nature.

EROSION AND TRANSPORTATION BY ICE (GLACIERS)

Glaciers can form in any place where snow fall exceeds snow melt. As more and more snow accumulates it becomes more dense and is fused into ice. After accumulating for many years the thick layers of snow and ice begin to move downhill under the force of gravity and a glacier is then born.

Glaciers can be classified by their shape and size as cirque, valley, fjord and piedmont glaciers. An ice sheet is the largest type of glacier in the world. Ice sheets currently cover Greenland and Antarctica and contain 95% of all the ice existing in glaciers. If these ice sheets were to melt they would raise sea levels by almost 66 metres.

As glaciers move they carry boulders and debris that has fallen onto the surface

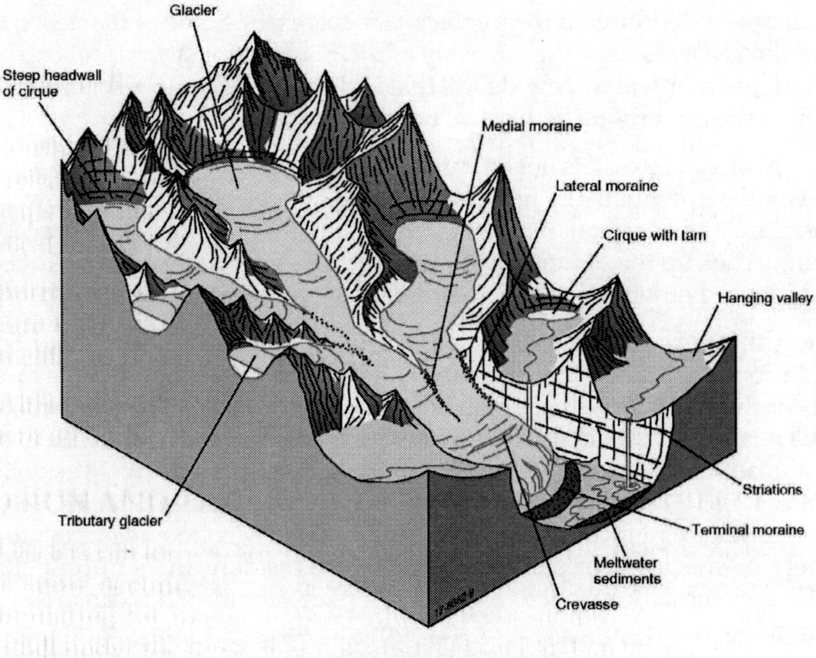

Typical features of a glacier.

of the glacier from the valley walls and move them for kilometres until they reach the face or terminus of the glacier. This may take many years, but if the position of the boulder is carefully measured, the boulder may be seen to move some several metres per year down the glacier.

Due to the sheer weight of the compacted ice and the debris present at the base of the glacier, as it moves down a valley the glacier scrapes up the materials beneath and beside it, sometimes eroding the Earth back to bare rock. A glacier can pluck out blocks of bedrock and plough the debris into piles at the face of the glacier.

Glacial striations are formed as rocks and debris underneath and sides of the glacier scrape and scratch the bedrock in a nearly parallel pattern. As larger rocks are dragged along by the glacier, glacial grooves form and are aligned to the direction of the glacial flow. Geologists are able to use these grooves and striations to determine which way former glaciers flowed.

Glaciers are renowned for the U-shaped valley they leave behind. This differs from the V-shaped valley that rivers create in their early life. A glacier is like a river of ice, but the main difference is that instead of transporting sediments, a glacier can actually cut deep into the unweathered bedrock. The transported material, including the gouged-out rock, is locked into the ice. Unlike transportation by wind and streams, glaciers are able to transport large boulders and small rocks without any degree of sorting according to size or density. As a result, sediments deposited directly by a glacier are not sorted or stratified. Underneath the glacier, fine sands and silts accumulate. These are very angular and were made from the crushing and grinding of rocks beneath the ice. As a glacier moves, the rocks and debris that accumulate can be deposited if the ice thickness decreases. Some of the debris from the base of the glacier is deposited directly as **till**. Some of the debris ends up being released into the meltwater. Any debris that is deposited by the glacier but bears no relation to the underlying bedrock is called a **moraine**.

The term 'glacial retreat' is not an entirely accurate description because a glacier always advances downhill. The term refers to the fact that the ice at the lower end of the glacier melts faster than the glacier advances, thus giving the appearance that it is retreating back up the mountain. Many glaciers today are retreating. This is one piece of evidence pointing to global warming as a real phenomenon.

Glaciers are currently retreating from the continents of North and South America, Europe, Asia and New Zealand. There has not been enough time to erase the effects of these glaciers, hence features such as striations, grooves and glacial tills are still relatively fresh. In these countries the landscape does not remain devoid of plants and animals for long and the plant community progressively establishes to its climax stage. This process is called ecological succession. The landscape is initially colonised by pioneer species that modify the environment enough for the next variety of species to replace the pioneers. This continues until a climax community is eventually founded. Establishing plant communities can modify the environment by increasing organic carbon and nitrogen concentrations and changing the soil **pH**.

In areas of recent glaciation the plant communities that develop on glacial moraines are used to determine the age of the glacial retreat. An example of glacial moraine succession in operation comes from Glacier Bay in southeastern Alaska. Since around 1750 the glaciers in this region have retreated about 100 kilometres. The pattern of glacial succession on the exposed glacial till in the region is described below:

1. Mosses, fireweed, Dryas (a hardy relative of oleander), willows (as low ground cover) and cottonwood are the first to colonise. The willows develop into communities of small shrubs, which are quickly invaded by alder (Alnus). The alder grows into dense thickets that reach up to nine metres tall. This requires about 50 years.
2. In the next 120 years the alder thicket is overrun by Sitka spruce that forms a dense forest.
3. Western hemlock and mountain hemlock invade the spruce forests. After approximately 120 years a climax community is established.
4. If the land has poor drainage, however, *Sphagnum* mosses grow on the forest floor. The moss acidifies the soil and the hemlock is unable to survive. The trees die from increased acidity, the waterlogging of the soil and the lack of oxygen around their roots. The climax vegetation in poorly drained areas is *Sphagnum* bog or **muskeg**.

12

Soil Formation, Major Soils of India, Soil Erosion and its Control

SOIL FORMATION

Some of the important factors responsible for soil formation in India are as follows:

1. Parent Material
2. Relief
3. Climate
4. Natural Vegetation!

Indian soils, like other parts of the world, reflect a combination of factors which have contributed to their formation. In Indian conditions, there is wide diversity with respect to geographical setting, physiography, climate and vegetation.

SOIL FORMATION

Consequently soils display a wide variety of physical and chemical characteristics. In India, soil formation is mainly related to the parent rock material, surface relief, climate and natural vegetation. Animals, insects and man also play an important role in soil formation.

Some of the important factors of soil formation are mentioned below:

Parent Material:

The material for soil formation is mainly derived from the rocks and is termed as the parent material by soil scientists. The parent material determines the colouration of the soil, its mineral composition and texture. India possesses a great variety of parent material which is generally categorised into following six classes:

(i) Ancient crystalline and metamorphic rocks

(ii) Cuddapah and Vindhyan rocks

(iii) Gondwana rocks

(iv) Deccan basalts

(v) Tertiary and Mesozoic sedimentary rocks of extra peninsular India

(vi) Recent and sub-recent rocks.

The surface rocks are exposed to the process of weathering and suffer decay and decomposition. In this process, the rocks are converted into fine grains and provide a base for the soil formation. The ancient crystalline and metamorphic rocks constitute greater part of the peninsular region.

These rocks are basically granites, gneisses and schists which are rich in ferromagnesian materials. Such rocks give rise to red soils on weathering. The red colour of these soils is largely due to the presence of iron oxide.

The Cuddapah and Vindhyan rocks have weathered to give calcareous and argillaceous soils. These soils are quite native. The Gondwana rocks give rise to comparatively less mature soils of more or less uniform character but of low fertility.

The Deccan traps are composed of basalt. Basalts are quite rich in titanium, magnetite, aluminium and magnesium. Consequently the weathering of these rocks has given rise to soils of darker colour. The soil derived from the Deccan trap is fertile with high moisture holding capacity and is popularly known as 'regur' or black cotton soil. The Tertiary and Mesozoic sedimentary rocks of extra peninsular India have given rise to soils with high porosity. These soils are generally immature recent ad sub recent rocks; result in alluvial soils on weathering.

The soils of the Northern Plain of India have been largely derived from the depositional work of the Himalayan Rivers. This depositional work has been continuing for thousands of years. These are alluvial fertile soils consisting of fine silts and clay.

These soils have little relation with the original rocks. On the other hand, the soils of peninsular plateau are generally coarse-grained and are closely related to the parent rocks. The peninsular soils are generally less fertile.

Relief

Relief influences the process of soil formation in many ways, the most important being the slope of land. Steep slope encourages the swift flow of water and hinders the process of soil formation. There may even be soil erosion in areas of steep slope. Chambal ravines offer an important example of soil erosion.

The areas of low relief or gentle slope generally experience deposition and have deep soils. Because of this reason, there are thick layers of fertile alluvial soils in the northern plain of India whereas the soils are generally shallow in the plateau area. The exceptions in the plateau are river basins where the soil layers are sufficiently deep. The degree of slope also largely determines the fertility of soil.

Climate

Climate is the single most important factor in soil formation. Most important climatic factors affecting soil formation are the amount and seasonal distribution of temperature and rainfall. Climate controls the type and effectiveness of weathering of the parent material, the quantity of water seeping through the soil and the type of micro-organisms present therein.

In areas of heavy rainfall and high temperature, the soils are red or lateritic. Torrential rainfall during the rainy season washes the upper soil and leaches the materials into deeper horizon. During the dry summer season the evaporation exceeds precipitation and through capillary action iron and aluminium sesquioxides are transported to the surface making the soil red.

In areas of alternate wet and dry climate, the leached material which goes deep down in the horizon is brought up and the blazing sun bakes the top soil so hard that it resembles a brick. Therefore, this soil is called lateritic which literally means brick. In arid and semi-arid regions, evaporation always exceeds precipitation. Under such circumstances, two main factors determine the nature and properties of soils. Firstly there is very little vegetation and the soils badly lack humus content.

Hence the soils are invariably of light colour. Secondly, the excess of evaporation makes soils lime accumulating. Thus they are bound to be pedocal in nature. Such soils are widely spread in the extreme western part of the country.

In cold climates of the Himalayan region, the process of vegetation decay is very low and the soils formed under such circumstances are acidic in nature. When the climatic control acts for a sufficiently long period, it reduces the differences in the parent materials. Two different parent materials may develop the same soil in the same type of climate.

Similarly, the same parent material may produce two different types of soils in two different types of climates. The crystalline granites produce laterite soil in relatively moist parts of the monsoonal region and non-laterite in drier areas.

Hot summer and low rainfall develops black soil as is found in some parts of Tamil Nadu irrespective of the parent rock. In Rajasthan, both granite and sandstone give birth to sandy soil under arid climate. This soil is poor in organic matter.

Natural Vegetation

Natural vegetation reflects the combined effects of relief and climate. The formation and development of soil is very much influenced by the growth of vegetation. The decayed leaf material adds much needed humus to soil thereby increasing its fertility. The densely forested areas contain some of the best soils in India. There is a close relationship between the vegetation types and soil types in India.

SOILS OF INDIA

Soils of India

Six Different Types of Soils Found in India are as follows:

Soil is our prime natural and economic resource. Soils in India differ in composition and structure.

Soil

Image Courtesy : images.wisegeek.com/rocky-soil.jpg

Alluvial Soils

These are formed by the deposition of sediments by rivers. They are rich in humus and very fertile. They are found in Great Northern plain, lower valleys of Narmada and Tapti and Northern Gujarat. These soils are renewed every year.

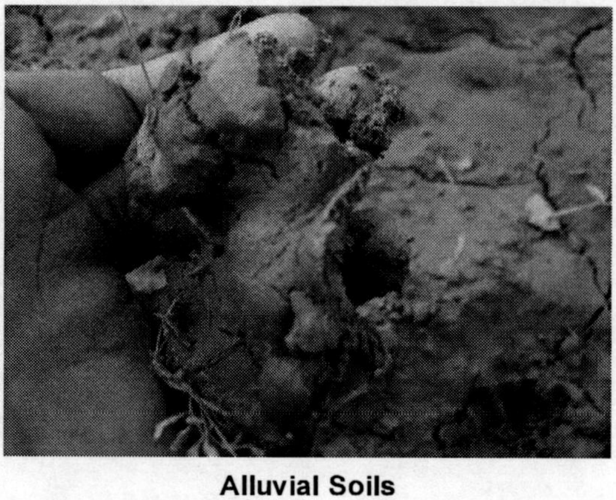

Alluvial Soils

Black Soils

These soils are made up of volcanic rocks and lava-flow. It is concentrated over Deccan Lava

Tract which includes parts of Maharashtra, Chhattisgarh, Madhya Pradesh, Gujarat, Andhra Pradesh and Tamil Nadu. It consists of Lime, Iron, Magnesium and also Potash but lacks in Phosphorus, Nitrogen and Organic matter.

Black Soils

Red Soils

These are derived from weathering of ancient metamorphic rocks of Deccan Plateau. Its redness is due to iron composition. When iron content is lower it is yellow or brown. They cover almost the whole of Tamil Nadu, Andhra Pradesh, Chhattisgarh, Karnataka, Maharashtra and parts of Odisha.

Red Soils

Laterite Soils

These soils are formed due to in-tense leaching and are well developed on the sum-mits of hills and uplands. They are commonly found in Kerala, Tamil Nadu, Maharashtra, Chhattisgarh and hilly areas of Odisha and Assam.

Laterite Soils

Mountain Soils

These soils are formed as a result of the accumulation of organic matter derived from forest growth. They are found in Himalayan region and vary in different regions according to altitude. Tea is grown in those areas which receive sufficient rainfall.

Mountain Soils

Desert Soils

In the desert regions of Rajasthan, soils are not well developed. As evaporation is in excess of rainfall, the soil has a high salt content and saline layer forms a hard crust. These soils are gen-erally sandy and deficient in organic matter.

Desert Soils

Desert Soils

In the desert regions of Rajasthan, soils are not well developed. As evaporation is in excess of rainfall, the soil has a high salt content and saline layer forms a hard crust. These soils are gen-erally sandy and deficient in organic matter.

SOIL EROSION

Soil erosion is a process of detachment and transportation of soil by natural agencies of water and wind.

Factors Influencing Soil Erosion

There are many factors which influence the process of soil erosion; these are discussed below:

Rainfall

Precipitation is the most forceful factor causing erosion.

Erosion is dependent on the amount, duration, intensity and frequency of rainfall. By the action of dashing rain drops on soil, soil granules are loosened, detached and separated into fine particles. Erosion is greater where the rainfall is not only heavy, but concentrated over short periods.

Slope of Topography

The slope accelerates erosion as it increases the velocity of the flowing water.

Vegetation

The vegetative cover protects the soil from the beating and dispersing action of the raindrops by forming a canopy over the soil surface. Vegetation also acts as a mechanical obstruction to flowing water, thus reducing its erosive potential. The plant roots help in building a better structure. They said in opening the soil and thereby accelerating water absorption and reducing surface run-off.

Tillage

The infiltration and permeability of the soil is improved by the practice of proper tillage and thereby reducing the chances of erosion. But excess tilling exposes the soil to erosion, especially by wind.

Nature of the Soil

Erodability of the soil is influenced by the nature of the soil, particularly its texture, structure, organic matter, amounts and kinds of salts present, presence of hard pan in the soil and presence of high water-table.

Soil Moisture

The presence of high water table checks the infiltration and permeability, thus allowing more flow of water on the surface, and greater erosion. At the same time, long continuous rainless periods cause loosening of soil and thus expose the soil to erosion by wind.

Wind Velocity

Stronger winds have greater erosive potential, thus wind velocity is directly proportional to intensity of erosion.

Types of Erosion by Water

Following are the types of soil erosion caused by water (Fig. 22.3).

Splash Erosion

This type of erosion occurs when the falling raindrops splash on the soil, and beat the bare soil into flowing mud.

Sheet Erosion

This occurs when soil is removed uniformly in a thin layer from the entire surface area. Movement of soil by splash erosion is the primary cause of sheet erosion.

Rill Erosion

This type of erosion takes place when the run-off water, laden with soil flowing along the slopes, forms fingerlike channels. Rill erosion is an intermediate stage between sheet erosion and gulley erosion.

Gully Erosion

As the volume of concentrated run-off increases and attains more velocity on slopes, it enlarges the rill into gullies. At an advanced stage, gullies result in ravines, which are sometimes 50 to 100 feet deep. In India ravines cover about 10 million ha.

Slip Erosion

Landslides cause slip erosion— big masses of soil and rock slip down, thus damaging the fields in the foothills and causing obstructions in communication. The effect of slip erosion is localised.

Stream Bank Erosion

Streams and rivers change their courses by cutting one bank and depositing the silt loads on the others.

During flash floods, the damage is much accelerated. The Kosi river in Bihar is reported to have changed its course westwards by 100 km within the last 100 years.

Sea Shore Erosion

This type of erosion is caused by the striking action of strong waves.

Causes of Soil Erosion

Soil erosion is also referred to as the creeping death. The causes of soil erosion are directly related to improper landuse, and are, therefore, entirely man-made.

These include the following:

Deforestation

Removal of vegetation cover has caused widespread erosion in Western Ghats, Uttar Pradesh and in Himachal Pradesh.

Faulty Cultivation Methods

For instance, in the Nilgiris, land has been opened for cultivation of tuber crops like potatoes and ginger without undertaking anti-erosive measures like terracing of slopes. Also forests on slopes have been cleared at places to make way for plantation crops. Such faulty cultivation methods have caused soil erosion—landslides are a common feature in these areas.

Shifting Cultivation:

An ecologically destructive and uneconomic cultivation method is slash and burn or shifting cultivation which is practised in hill areas of North-East,

Erosion Carried out by Action of Water

Chhotanagpur, Orissa, Madhya Pradesh and Andhra Pradesh. Vast areas have suffered erosion of soil in hill areas of North-East because of shifting cultivation.

Overgrazing

A surplus of livestock population in our country is a big strain on grasses and fodder. The tread of cattle hardens the soil and prevents new shoots from emerging. Overgrazing by goats is a serious problem in certain stretches of the Aravalis and in Punjab and Himachal hills. The goats not only pull off leaves and branches, but they also uproot grass, as opposed to sheep, which only nibble the top shoots.

Diversion in Natural Drainage Channels by Railway Embankments and Roads:

Railway tracks and roads have had to be constructed in such a manner that they are at a higher level than the surrounding area. But sometimes, road and rail embankments come in the way of natural drainage channels. This causes waterlogging on one side and water loss on the other side of embankments. All these factors contribute to erosion in one way or the other.

Lack of Proper Surface Drainage:

Because of proper drainage, waterlogging occurs in low lying areas which loosens the top-soil and makes it prone to erosion.

Denuding Forest Fires:

These fires, sometimes natural but often man-made, are very destructive. As a result of these, the forest cover is lost forever and soil is exposed to erosion.

Effects of Soil Erosion

The main effects of soil erosion are as follows:

Loss of Soil:

The top-soil is lost by erosion which is the most fertile section, having evolved over centuries of soil-forming processes. Due to formation of gullies and ravines, valuable agricultural lands are lost.

Harmful Effects of Erosion on Organic Matter and Soil Structure:

Erosion of upper layer of soil decreases the content of organic matter and as other nutrients. As a result, the soil structure gets impoverished.

Decline in Soil Capacity

When the soil is removed bodily from field, both potential and available plant food along with mineral material is carried away. As erosion progresses, the compact soil of low infiltration capacity is approached. The ability of the land to supply moisture for plant growth is reduced and the beneficial activity of micro-organisms lessened. Due to these bad effects, the yields are lowered.

Deposition of Sand and Gravel on Agricultural Lands

The wind-borne sand encroaches the arable lands and makes them unfertile. Crops are damaged due to sand storms.

Flooding of Streams

Soil erosion in catchment areas of streams due to deforestation and other destructive activities leads to silting of streams and reservoirs. This reduces the capacity of these water bodies to carry large volumes of water, as they occur during the rainy season. This way the streams are more prone to flooding. One such example is Brahmaputra river which has been exposed to siltation because of large-scale deforestation in the hills, and the floods in Brahmaputra valley have become an annual phenomenon now.

Magnitude of the Problem in India

In India, nearly 80 mHa area is exposed to the threat of soil erosion, and 43 mHa area is actually affected. In states like Madhya Pradesh. Rajasthan, Maharashtra and Punjab, upto 15 per cent of the total land suffers from soil erosion. It is reported that the annual loss of fertility by erosion is 20 times faster than what is lost by growing crops. Each year, 10,000 hectares area is exposed to erosion. Nearly 145 mHa area in India is in need of conservation measures.

SOME GLARING EXAMPLES OF SOIL EROSION

Nilgiris

Potato cultivation on steep slopes without proper terracing has caused widespread erosion here.

Gullies or Ravines

Because of gully erosion, nearly 10 mHa area is affected. These gulleys are known by different names—khars in Gujarat, Maharashtra and Karnataka; ravines in Madhya Pradesh, Uttar Pradesh and Rajasthan along Yamuna and Chambal; kotar lands in Gujarat and chos (the rainy season torrents) and landslides in Hoshiarpur in the Shivaliks.

Regions of Low and Uncertain Rainfall

Extensive regions of low and uncertain rainfall, forming parts of Punjab, Madhya Pradesh, Maharashtra, Andhra Pradesh and Karnataka, are characterised by scanty, ill-distributed and highly erosive rains, undulating topography, high wind velocity and generally shallow soils. The period of heavy downpours from August to October is the period of the heaviest erosion in these regions.

Desertification of Rajasthan

Wind erosion, coupled with loss of surface cover in the Aravallis has made the challenge of halting the march of desert in Rajasthan, one of the most vital ecological problems facing the country today.

Coastal Erosion

An extreme example of soil erosion is to be seen in sand movement from the coast in the Saurashtra region of Gujarat, where the once flourishing ports are now covered with advancing sand-dunes.

METHODS TO CHECK SOIL EROSION

These measures are a part of the overall strategy to conserve soil and water. These measures can be biological or mechanical. These are discussed below:

Biological Measures

The following are biological methods to control soil erosion:

Improving the Existing Surface Cover

This can be done by resorting to cover cropping by growing groundnut or berseem (a fodder crop) or through grasslands development by growing grasses like dub, kudzu, pans and dinanath.

Strip Cropping

This practice consists of growing erosion-permitting crops (jowar, bajra, maize) in alternate strips with erosion checking close- growing crops (grasses, pulses). The erosion checking strips check and hold the flowing water and soil.

Crop Rotation

This refers to growing of two or more different crops in sequence in a field for maintaining the soil fertility. Continuous growing of clean-cultivated crops (e.g., tobacco) causes more erosion. A good rotation should include densely planted small grains, spreading legume which may check soil erosion.

Stubble Mulching

This means leaving crop residue or vegetative litter on the land as a surface protection against erosion and for conserving moisture by favouring infiltration and reducing evaporation.

Using Organic Manures

Organic manures like cowdung, green manure, farmyard manure etc., improve the soil structure. Granular and crumby structures increase infiltration and permeability in the soil and conserve soil moisture.

Other measures include checking overgrazing, reducing surplus cattle, stopping shifting cultivation and taking preventive measures against forest fires.

Mechanical Mea sures

The mechanical measures that can be used to control erosion are as follows.

Contour Tillage

On sloping lands, all tillage operations should be done at right angles to the slope of the land. This way, each furrow intercepts the flowing water and allows it to soak into the soil.

Contour Bunding

The idea is to break the slope of the land into smaller, more level compartments by constructing mechanical structures of suitable size along contours. Each bund, thus, holds the rainwater within each compartment.

Terracing

On steeper slopes, terraces or flat platforms are constructed in steps in a series along the slope. This way water is retained on each terrace which can be used to raise crops.

Constructing Proper Drainage Channels and Plugging the Gullies:

Basin Listing

This refers to scooping out small basins at regular intervals on slopes which help in checking the run-off and in conservation of water.

Water Harvesting

This refers to trapping or channeling of water into low-lying areas. This helps in checking the run-off and also acts as a flood control measure.

Scientific Slope Management

The cropping activity on slopes should be taken up as per the nature of slope. If the slope is between 1:4 and 1:7, proper farming can be done; if more, pastures should be developed; if still more, forestry operations can be undertaken; if it is still greater, then terracing is required before any cropping activity can be done.

13

Common Farm Implement

CHAFF CUTTER

The seed casings and other inedible parts of the palnt matter harvested with cereal grains such as wheat are known as chaff. Techniques such as threshing and wind winnowing are uded to seperate chaff from the grain before use. Hay, or straw is cut short by a machine called a chaff cutter and usually fed to cattle.

LAWN MOVER

An instrument used to cut grass short to an even length is called a mower. Its used primarily to cut the lawn on sports grounds and expansive gardens. Using a mower, is a more efficient way of making the length of grass uniform.

Types of Lawn Movers

- Rotary mvers
- Riding movers
- Hover movers
- Robotic movers
- Pull movers
- Professional movers
- Edge trimmer
- Clippers

PLOUGH

Plough is used initially for soil preparation and for sowing seeds or planting developed from the pick or the spade. Initially it used to be pulled by humans and later using cattle like oxens and bullocks. Modern day ploughs are attached to tractors. The benefits of ploughing land is to turn over the top surface of the earth. It also uproots weeds growing near the crops, thereby making soil more porous and easier for later planting. The common ploughs have sets of 2 up to 5 mouldboards, but semi-mounted ploughs, the lifting of which are supplemented by a wheel about half-way along its length, can have as many as 18.

ELEVATOR

A long piece of equipment which is powered by a tractor and used to move items such as small piles of hay and to store them in a barn are known as elevators.

PUMPS AND PIPES

A pump may be defined as a mechanical device that can be used to move or carry liquids and gasses from a low pressure area to a high pressure area. The earliest form of pump is known as the 'Archimedes Screw Pump'.Pumps work by using mechanical forces to push a material either by physically lifting it or by using force of compression.

PIPES

They are usually made of polyvinyl chloride or copper and used to carry pressurized fresh water. They are usually available in straight lenghts called joints or sticks.

AGRICULTURAL IMPLEMENT

An implement or machine designed and used for ploughing, cultivation, spreading fertiliser, sowing seed, spraying, harvesting, chaff cutting or any other agricultural operation whether the implement or machine is hauled or towed by animal or mechanical power.

CHISEL PLOW

Is a common tool to get deep tillage with limited soil disruption. The main function of this plow is to loosen and aerate the soils while leaving crop residue at the top of the soil. This plow can be used to reduce the effects of compaction and to help break up plowpan and hardpan.

HARROW

A farm implement consisting of a heavy frame with sharp teeth or upright disks, used to break up and even off plowed ground.

TRACTOR

The tractor, the most frequently used machine on the farm, has two large wheels at the rear that provide the power and two smaller ones at the front for steering, with an engine in the centre. Tractors come in many sizes and have a shaft at the back that turns and provides power to other machines that it pulls. Some tractors have front-end loaders - an implement for moving feed, manure or dirt, or for lifting heavy objects like large round hay bales. The cab of the tractor protects the driver from the rain, cold, wind, dust and heat; some even have air conditioners and sound systems, just like a car. Some tractors have four wheel drive - power to the front wheels as well as the back wheels; this adds to the usefulness of the tractor and it can be used during all seasons.

CULTIVATOR

Cultivator is a farm implement for stirring and pulverizing the soil, either before planting or to remove weeds and to aerate and loosen the soil after the crop has begun to grow. The cultivator usually stirs the soil to a greater depth than does the harrow

CHISEL PLOW

Chisel Plow is a common tool to get deep tillage with limited soil disruption. The main function of this plow is to loosen and aerate the soils while leaving crop residue at the top of the soil. This plow can be used to reduce the effects of compaction and to help break up plowpan and hardpan.

HARROW

A farm implement consisting of a heavy frame with sharp teeth or upright disks, used to break up and even off plowed ground

SPIKE HARROW

The spike harrow or drag is a tillage implement for agriculture. It breaks up clods of soil that result from other tillage equipment such as the disk harrow or plough.

SEED DRILL

The seed drill is used farmers to dig the land to sow seeds in well-spaced rows at specific depths.

Rice Transplanter

Rice Transplanteris a specialized transplanter fitted to transplant rice seedlings onto puddle field.

COMBINE HARVESTER

Combine Harvester or simply combine, is a machine that harvests, threshes and cleans grain plants. The desired result is the seed (such as canola or flax) or grain (such as oats , wheat , or rye); a byproduct is loose straw , the remaining husk of the plant with all nutrients removed.

COTTON PICKER

Cotton Picker is a self-propelled machine that removes cotton lint and seed (seed-cotton) from the plant at up to six rows at a time. It uses rows of barbed spindles that rotate at high speed and remove the seed-cotton from the plant. The seed-cotton is then removed from the spindles by a counter-rotating doffer and is then blown up into a basket located on the picker

BACKHOE

Backhoe is also called a rear actor or back actor, is a piece of excavating equipment consisting of a digging bucket on the end of an articulated arm (also called a stick or dipper).

Other list are as follows :

- Rail Road Pick
- Italy Pick
- Round Eye Pick
- German Pick
- Pick Mattock
- Cutter Mattock
- Hoes
- Hoe Mattock
- Axes
- Agricultural shovels
- Agricultural Machines
- Spring Loaded Tillers
- Rigid Tillers
- Offset Disc Harrows
- Plough
- Levellers
- Rotary Tillers
- Processing Machines
- Agricultural Equipments
- Multi Crop Thresher
- Ground Nut Digger
- Automatic feeding Wheat Thresher
- Harhamba Thresher

- Paddy Thresher
- Maize Sheller
- Potato Digger
- Disc Harrow
- Seed cum Fertilizer drill
- Straw Reaper
- Zero Till Seed cum Ferti Drill
- Vegetable Seed Extractor
- Chaff Cutter
- Rotary Tiller
- Potato Planter
- Sprinklers
- Pumpsets
- Tractor
- Harvester Combine Blades
- Thrasher Blades
- Straw Reaper Blades
- Harrow Hubs Blades
- Jack Plane Blade

MODERN IMPLEMENTS AND FARM MACHINERY AND HAND TOOLS

This section is an effort to understand recent changes relating to improved agricultural vis-à-vis hand tools which may have potential impact in the creation of new livelihood opportunity in rural India. It examines the status of export-import data and also the dissemination of new technical knowledge among farmers. Further, a brief introduction to state policies relating to tools and implements is presented. A brief deliberation on standards and certification of modern implements and hand tools may help our policy planners to make country's comprehensive plan for future agri-mechanization, including creation of some new routes to job creation in rural areas. All the data used here are indicative, not exhaustive.

Introduction

Indian agriculture is as diverse as its people due to its varied agro-climatic features; it varies from the hilly and humid northeast to the plain and arid Rajasthan. Agricultural production in these diverse areas requires completely different types of farm implements (machines/tools). The land holding pattern is dominated by the small and marginal farmers (>60%). This pattern is expected to deteriorate further due to the 'laws of inheritance' common in India. This also demands different types of implements for different types of landholders, basically one type for small and marginal farmers and another for the medium and large farmers. The small and marginal farmers of India rely mostly on draught animals for their field operations, transport and agro-processing. The extent of area under the command of draught animals is estimated to be around 57%. Reduction of this area through farm mechanization with indigenous technologies would enhance the productivity of the small and marginal farmers and make them more sustainable. In subsequent issues of India S&T, specific instruments like balistic apparatus will be covered in detail.

Availability of information about new technology (NSSO, 2003)

For the rural areas, marketing of the agricultural tools is a big question. Around 40% of farmer households have problems in accessing information on modern farming technology (NSSO Report No. 499(59/33/2), 59th round, 2003). The most popular was 'other progressive farmers' with percentage of farmer households accessing information through the source as 16.7%, followed by input dealer (13.1%) and radio (13.0%).

Among various states percentage of farmer-households accessing information through 'other progressive farmers' was highest in Andhra Pradesh (34%), Gujarat (30%) and West Bengal (25%). In the case of accessing information through 'input dealers' it was highest for West Bengal (36%), Andhra Pradesh (30%) and Gujarat (24%). 'Radio' was highest in Jammu & Kashmir (36%), then Kerala (31%) and Assam (29%). The report also indicated that the two most popular sources, namely 'other progressive farmers' and 'input dealer' were contacted by the farmer households mainly on 'need basis' or 'seasonally'.

Observation: In rural areas, dissemination of information regarding new advanced agricultural tools is mainly dispersed through progressive farmers to others, whereas the intervention of KVKs, extension workers, Government demonstrations is less effective. It affects the proper diffusion of technical knowledge. There is an urgent need to focus on information dissemination for spreading technical knowledge.

Credit and Finance for Farmers

After getting information about the new equipment the next important thing is to get the credit to buy the tools because our farmers have low purchasing capacity. The Government provides incentives to farmers for modernization of agriculture which are linked to crop specific programmes operated by state governments. State governments may need to strengthen their extension machinery for providing information to the farmers. Agricultural Policy resolution includes special emphasis for input support to poor farmers with small land holdings and especially for those in eastern, hilly regions, rain fed and drought prone areas. According to the report from NABARD, GoI set a target of Rs.1,75,000 crore credit flow to agriculture for 2006-07 against which disbursements by all agencies stood at Rs.2,03,296 crore, exceeding the target by 16 per cent. Commercial banks, cooperative banks and RRBs disbursed Rs.1, 40, 382 crore, Rs.42, 480 crore and Rs.20,434 crore achieving 118, 104 and 136 per cent of the targets, respectively. During the year, 83.50 lakh new farmers were brought under the institutional fold, 74.70 lakh fresh KCCs issued, 631 agri-clinics financed, debt relief of Rs.4,873.37 crore and Rs.673.90 crore provided to farmers in distress and in arrears, respectively. An amount of Rs. 460.06 crore to small/marginal farmers under one time settlement scheme was provided by banks. Banks also extended loans to the extent of Rs.73.41 crore to 27,810 farmers, to redeem their debts availed from informal sources. In some of the cases the subsidy is also available for the agricultural equipments. Agricultural equipments, namely tractor, power tiller, power threshers, sprinklers, drip irrigation sets, self propelled reapers, rotavators etc. are available on subsidy under Central Sector Plan Schemes. The subsidy is available to the farmers @ 25% of the cost of equipment subject to certain ceiling limits.

Observation: Very recently Govt. of India released a debt waiver scheme in 2008 for the welfare of poor farmers. This may have provided short term relief to the small and marginal farmers. But for long term gain we need to focus on capacity building of these farmers to sustain in adverse conditions with more credit solutions.

Major farm machinery training and testing institutes in India

The Farm Machinery Training & Testing Institutes (FMTTI) at Budni (M.P.), Hissar (Haryana), Garladinne (A.P.) and Bishwanath Chariali (Assam) established by the Government of India have been playing a vital role in promoting agricultural mechanization.

The types of tests undertaken by FMTTIs are as under:

Commercial Tests for establishing performance characteristics of machines which are ready for commercial production. The following types of commercial tests are undertaken: Initial Commercial Tests on indigenous or imported proto-type machines ready for commercial production. Batch Test on machines, which have already undergone Initial Commercial Test and/or are being manufactured commercially in the country. Test in accordance with OECD Standard Test Code shall be undertaken on machines on the specific request of the manufacturer/applicant, exclusively for export purposes.

Confidential Tests are done for providing confidential information on the performance of machines, whether ready for commercial production or not, or to provide any special data that may be required by the manufacturer/applicant.

Standards: For wider acceptability and safety of equipments, various Indian Standards applicable for testing of different types of equipment have been published by the Bureau of Indian Standards (BIS). These are available at BIS headquarter at New Delhi and its regional offices at Kolkata, Chandigarh, Chennai, and Mumbai.

Observation: The number of central farm machinery testing and training centre is small compared to the agricultural area of India. To cover up the vast pool of farmers, the outreach of the testing facilities needs broaden, may be through creation of more centres. In fact, another gateway of job creation in rural India is by imparting training to some nodal rural persons about standards and giving them rights to certify the rural unorganized small agri-machinery and tools on reasonable payment basis. In this way we may think of including the large unorganized hand tool and agri-machinery industry into our organized system with proper safety measures and global acceptance.

Usage of Agricultural Implements in rural India (NSSO)

Even today, majority of Indian farmers have the tendency to use wooden plough rather than iron plough. On an average, 46 households are using wooden plough and 14 households are using iron plough in rural India per 100 households.

In case of draught power also, use of carts outnumber the use of the mechanized tractor trolley. Further, it is apparent that intervention for mechanization of farm implements for marginal and small land holders is negligible in comparison to the large farmers. Total revenue earned from agricultural implements is less than one per cent.

AGRICULTURAL EQUIPMENT MARKET

Agriculture equipment market in India is dominated by private players like Mahindra & Mahindra (M&M), TAFE, Escorts and PTL (Tractor manufactures association). These players not only do well in national market but also in international market.

The number of tractors per million hectares of gross cropped area is also increasing. Other advanced agricultural equipments taken together also show a similar increasing trend in their numbers during the same period. If we follow the World agricultural equipment market for the year 2006, we observe that India holds only 10% of the world agri-equipment market which is equivalent to $6.6 billion.

Export-Import data for Agri-machinery

The following graphs show the export-import trends for soil machinery, dairy and milking machines and for the tractors over last 12 years. It is based on the values (in 1000 US$) of the particular item imported or exported as reported in FAOSTAT. These trends show the revenue generation pattern through the export of agriculture machinery.

Observation: More focus on R&D is needed to develop new mechanized agri-machinery that may help us to reduce import dependency especially in dairy and milking machinery sector.

14

Nutrient Functions and Deficiency Symptoms

Plants, like all other living things, need food for their growth and development. Plants require 16 essential elements. Carbon, hydrogen, and oxygen are derived from the atmosphere and soil water. The remaining 13 essential elements (nitrogen, phosphorus, potassium, calcium, magnesium, sulfur, iron, zinc, manganese, copper, boron, molybdenum, and chlorine) are supplied either from soil minerals and soil organic matter or by organic or inorganic fertilizers.

For plants to utilize these nutrients efficiently, light, heat, and water must be adequately supplied. Cultural practices and control of diseases and insects also play important roles in crop production.

Each type of plant is unique and has an optimum nutrient range as well as a minimum requirement level. Below this minimum level, plants start to show nutrient deficiency symptoms. Excessive nutrient uptake can also cause poor growth because of toxicity. Therefore, the proper amount of application and the placement of nutrients is important.

Soil and plant tissue tests have been developed to assess the nutrient content of both the soil and plants. By analyzing this information, plant scientists can determine the nutrient need of a given plant in a given soil. In addition to the levels of plant-available nutrients in soils, the soil pH plays an important role in nutrient availability and elemental toxicity.

This chapter describes the essential nutrients, the chemical forms in which they are available to plants, their function in plants, symptoms of their deficiencies, and recommended nutrient levels in plant tissues of selected crops.

NITROGEN

symbol: N; available to plants as nitrate (NO_3^-) , and ammonium (NH_4^+) ions.

Nutrient functions

- N is biologically combined with C, H, O, and S to create amino acids, which are the building blocks of proteins. Amino acids are used in forming protoplasm, the site for cell division and thus for plant growth and development.
- Since all plant enzymes are made of proteins, N is needed for all of the enzymatic reactions in a plant.
- N is a major part of the chlorophyll molecule and is therefore necessary for photosynthesis.
- N is a necessary component of several vitamins.
- N improves the quality and quantity of dry matter in leafy vegetables and protein in grain crops.

Deficiency symptoms

- Stunted growth may occur because of reduction in cell division.

Nitrogen deficient soybean; lower leaves turn uniformly pale green, then yellow.

Severe nitrogen deficiency in citrus

Nitrogen deficient potato plant (left) is chlorotic; plant at right is normal.

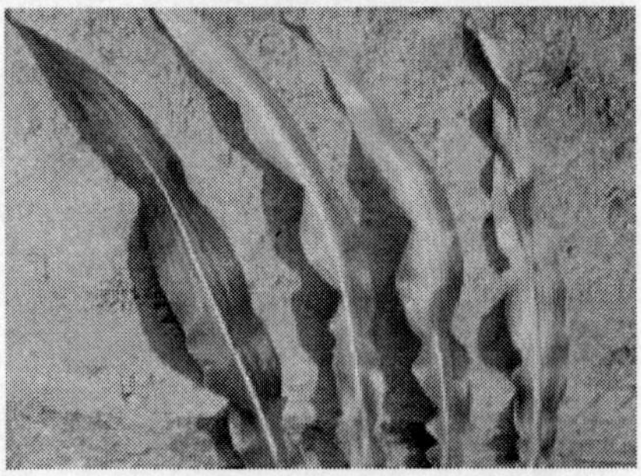

Nitrogen deficient corn; yellowing proceeds down the midrib of older leaves.

- Pale green to light yellow color (chlorosis) appearing first on older leaves, usually starting at the tips. Depending on the severity of deficiency, the chlorosis could result in the death and/or dropping of the older leaves. This is caused by the translocation of N from the older to the younger tissues.
- Reduced N lowers the protein content of seeds and vegetative parts. In severe cases, flowering is greatly reduced.
- N deficiency causes early maturity in some crops, which results in a significant reduction in yield and quality.

PHOSPHORUS

symbol: P; available to plants as orthophosphate ions (HPO_4^{2-}, $H_2PO_4^-$).

Nutrient functions

- In photosynthesis and respiration, P plays a major role in energy storage and transfer as ADP and ATP (adenosine di- and triphosphate) and DPN and TPN (di- and triphosphopyridine nucleotide).
- P is part of the RNA and DNA structures, which are the major components of genetic information.
- Seeds have the highest concentration of P in a mature plant, and P is required in large quantities in young cells, such as shoots and root tips, where metabolism is high and cell division is rapid.
- P aids in root development, flower initiation, and seed and fruit development.
- P has been shown to reduce disease incidence in some plants and has been found to improve the quality of certain crops.

Deficiency symptoms

- Because P is needed in large quantities during the early stages of cell division, the initial overall symptom is slow, weak, and stunted growth.

Phosphorus deficient sugarbeet plants are stunted, with dark green leaves.

Phosphorus deficient corn; lower leaves become reddish-purple.

- P is relatively mobile in plants and can be transferred to sites of new growth, causing symptoms of dark to blue-green coloration to appear on older leaves of some plants. Under severe deficiency, purpling of leaves and stems may appear.
- Lack of P can cause delayed maturity and poor seed and fruit development.

POTASSIUM

symbol: K; available to plants as the ion K^+

Nutrient functions

- Unlike N and P, K does not form any vital organic compounds in the plant. However, the presence of K is vital for plant growth because K is known to be an enzyme activator that promotes metabolism.
- K assists in regulating the plant's use of water by controlling the opening and closing of leaf stomates, where water is released to cool the plant.
- In photosynthesis, K has the role of maintaining the balance of electrical charges at the site of ATP production.
- K promotes the translocation of photosythates (sugars) for plant growth or storage in fruits or roots.
- Through its role assisting ATP production, K is involved in protein synthesis.
- K has been shown to improve disease resistance in plants, improve the size of grains and seeds, and improve the quality of fruits and vegetables.

Deficiency symptoms

- The most common symptom is chlorosis along the edges of leaves (leaf margin scorching). This occurs first in older leaves, because K is very mobile in the plant.

Potassium deficient banana; older leaves become chlorotic, then necrotic, and the tip of the midrib bends downward.

Potassium deficient corn; margins of older leaves become chlorotic and necrotic.

- Because K is needed in photosynthesis and the synthesis of proteins, plants lacking K will have slow and stunted growth.
- In some crops, stems are weak and lodging is common if K is deficient.
- The size of seeds and fruits and the quantity of their production is reduced.

CALCIUM

symbol: Ca; available to plants as the ion Ca_2^+

Nutrient functions

- Ca has a major role in the formation of the cell wall membrane and its plasticity, affecting normal cell division by maintaining cell integrity and membrane permeability.
- Ca is an activator of several enzyme systems in protein synthesis and carbohydrate transfer.
- Ca combines with anions including organic acids, sulfates, and phosphates. It acts as a detoxifying agent by neutralizing organic acids in plants.
- Ca is essential for seed production in peanuts.
- Ca indirectly assists in improving crop yields by reducing soil acidity when soils are limed.

Deficiency symptoms

- Ca is not mobile and is not translocated in the plant, so symptoms first appear on the younger leaves and leaf tips. The growing tips of roots and leaves turn brown and die.
- Ca deficiency is not often observed in plants because secondary effects of high acidity resulting from soil calcium deficiency usually limit growth, precluding expressions of Ca deficiency symptoms.

Calcium deficient celery; young leaves are necrotic and the growing point dies.

Calcium deficient bean leaves have chlorotic and necrotic spots.

- Without adequate Ca, which in the form of calcium pectate is needed to form rigid cell walls, newly emerging leaves may stick together at the margins, which causes tearing as the leaves expand and unfurl. This may also cause the stem structure to be weakened.
- In some crops, younger leaves may be cupped and crinkled, with the terminal bud deteriorating.
- Buds and blossoms fall prematurely in some crops.

MAGNESIUM

symbol: Mg; available to plants as the ion Mg_2^+

Nutrient functions

- The predominant role of Mg is as a major constituent of the chlorophyll molecule, and it is therefore actively involved in photosynthesis.
- Mg is a co-factor in several enzymatic reactions that activate the phosphorylation processes.
- Mg is required to stabilize ribosome particles and also helps stabilize the structure of nucleic acids.
- Mg assists the movement of sugars within a plant.

Deficiency symptoms

- Because Mg is a mobile element and part of the chlorophyll molecule, the deficiency symptom of interveinal chlorosis first appears in older leaves. Leaf tissue between the veins may be yellowish, bronze, or reddish, while the leaf veins remain green. Corn leaves appear yellow-striped with green veins, while crops such as potatoes, tomatoes, soybeans, and cabbage show orange-yellow color with green veins.

Magnesium deficient corn; interveinal chlorosis of older leaves.

Magnesium deficient tomato; interveinal chlorosis of older leaves.

- In severe cases, symptoms may appear on younger leaves and cause premature leaf drop.
- Symptoms occur most frequently in acid soils and soils receiving high amounts of K fertilizer or Ca.

SULFUR

symbol: S; available to plants as the sulfate ion, SO_4^{2-}

Nutrient functions

- S is essential in forming plant proteins because it is a constituent of certain amino acids.
- It is actively involved in metabolism of the B vitamins biotin and thiamine and co-enzyme A.
- S aids in seed production, chlorophyll formation, nodule formation in legumes, and stabilizing protein structure.

Deficiency symptoms

- Younger leaves are chlorotic with evenly, lightly colored veins. In some plants (e.g., citrus) the older leaves may show symptoms first. However, deficiency is not commonly found in most plants.
- Growth rate is retarded and maturity is delayed.
- Plant stems are stiff, thin, and woody.
- Symptoms may be similar to N deficiency and are most often found in sandy soils that are low in organic matter and receive moderate to heavy rainfall.

Sulfur deficient macadamia; young leaves are chlorotic.

Sulfur deficient tomato; young leaves are uniformly chlorotic.

BORON

Symbol: B. Available to plants as borate, H_3BO_3

Nutrient functions

- B is necessary in the synthesis of one of the bases for RNA formation and in cellular activities.
- B has been shown to promote root growth.
- B is essential for pollen germination and growth of the pollen tube.
- B has been associated with lignin synthesis, activities of certain enzymes, seed and cell wall formation, and sugar transport.

Deficiency symptoms

- Generally, B deficiency causes stunted growth, first showing symptoms on the growing point and younger leaves. The leaves tend to be thickened and may curl and become brittle.
- In many crops, the symptoms are well defined and crop-specific, such as:
  - peanuts: hollow hearts
  - celery: crooked and cracked stem
  - beets: black hearts
  - papaya: distorted and lumpy fruit
  - carnation: splitting of calyx
  - Chinese cabbage: midribs crack, turn brown
  - cabbage, broccoli, and cauliflower: pith in hollow stem

Boron deficient radish plants are stunted, with distorted leaves.

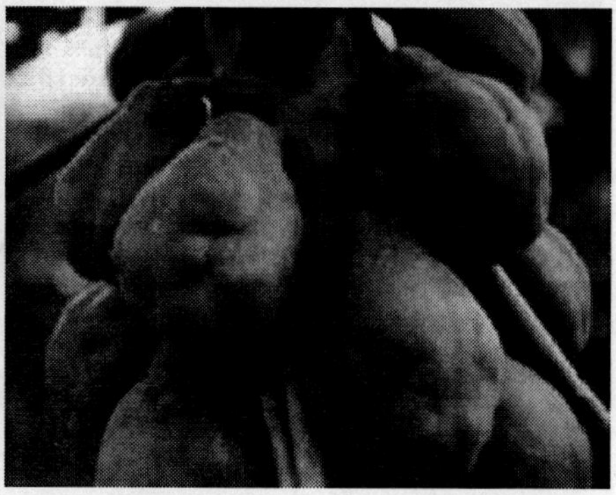

Boron deficient papaya fruits develop bumps.

COPPER

symbol: Cu; available to plants as the ion Cu^{++}

Nutrient functions

- Cu is essential in several plant enzyme systems involved in photosynthesis.
- Cu is part of the chloroplast protein plastocyanin, which forms part of the electron transport chain.
- Cu may have a role in the synthesis and/or stability of chlorophyll and other plant pigments.

Deficiency symptoms

- Reduced growth, distortion of the younger leaves, and possible necrosis of the apical meristem.
- In trees, multiple sprouts occur at growing points, resulting in a bushy appearance. Young leaves become bleached, and eventually there is defoliation and dieback of twigs.
- In forage grasses, young leaf tips and growing points are affected first. The plant is stunted and chlorotic.

Copper deficient corn leaf tips bend and droop.

Copper deficient tomato leaves are stunted and deformed.

CHLORINE

symbol: Cl; available to plants as the chloride ion, Cl^-

Nutrient functions

- Cl is essential in photosynthesis, where it is involved in the evolution of oxygen.
- Cl increases cell osmotic pressure and the water content of plant tissues.
- Cl is found in many bacteria and fungi.

Chlorine deficient tomato; leaf edges roll upward.

Chlorine deficient sugarbeet; young leaves are chlorotic.

- Cl reduces the severity of certain fungal diseases, e.g., take-all disease of wheat.

Deficiency symptoms

- Chlorosis of younger leaves and wilting of the plant.
- Deficiency seldom occurs because Cl is found in the atmosphere and rainwater.

IRON

symbol: Fe; available to plants as Fe_2^+, Fe_3^+

Nutrient functions

- Fe is essential in the heme enzyme system in plant metabolism (photosynthesis and respiration). The enzymes involved include catalase, peroxidase, cytochrome oxidase, and other cytochromes.

Iron deficient macademia; young leaves have interveinal chlorosis

Iron deficient gardenia; young leaves have interveinal chlorosis.

- Fe is part of protein ferredoxin and is required in nitrate and sulfate reductions.
- Fe is essential in the synthesis and maintenance of chlorophyll in plants.
- Fe has been strongly associated with protein metabolism.

Deficiency symptoms

- Interveinal chlorosis in younger leaves. The youngest leaves maybe white, because Fe, like Mg, is involved in chlorophyll production.
- Usually observed in alkaline or over-limed soils.

MANGANESE

symbol: Mn; available to plants as Mn_2^+, Mn_3^+

Nutrient functions

Manganese deficient soybean; young leaves have interveinal chlorosis.

- Mn primarily functions as part of the plant enzyme system, activating several metabolic functions. It is a constituent of pyruvate carboxylase.
- Mn is involved in the oxidation-reduction process in photosynthesis.
- Mn is necessary in Photosystem II, where it participates in photolysis.
- Mn activates indole acetic acid oxidase, which then oxidizes indole acetic acid in plants.

Deficiency symptoms

- Symptoms first appear as chlorosis in young tissues. Unlike Fe chlorosis symptoms, in dicots Mn chlorosis shows up as tiny yellow spots.
- In monocots, greenish-grey specks appear at the lower base of younger leaves. The specks may eventually become yellowish to yellow-orange.
- In legumes, necrotic areas develop on the cotyledons, a symptom known as marsh spots.

MOLYBDENUM

symbol: Mo; available to plants as molybdate, MoO_4

Nutrient functions

- Mo is a necessary component of two major enzymes in plants, nitrate reductase and nitrogenase, which are required for normal assimilation of N.

Molybdenum deficient onion leaves show wilting and dieback.

Molybdenum deficient grapefruit leaves have interveinal chlorosis.

- Mo is required by some soil microorganisms for nitrogen fixation in soils.

Deficiency symptoms

- Deficiency symptoms resemble those of N because the function of Mo is to assimilate N in the plant. Older and middle leaves become chlorotic, and the leaf margins roll inwards.
- In contrast to N deficiency, necrotic spots appear at the leaf margins because of nitrate accumulation.
- Deficient plants are stunted, and flower formation may be restricted.
- Mo deficiency can be common in nitrogen-fixing legumes.

ZINC

symbol: Zn; available to plants as Zn^{++}

Nutrient functions

- Zn is required in the synthesis of tryptophan, which in turn is necessary for the formation of indole acetic acid in plants.
- Zn is an essential component of several metallo-enzymes in plants (variety dehydorgenases) and therefore is necessary for several different function in plant metabolism.
- The enzyme carbonic anhydrase is specifically activated by Zn.
- Zn has a role in RNA and protein synthesis.

Deficiency symptoms

- Interveinal chlorosis occurs on younger leaves, similar to Fe deficiency. However, Zn deficiency is more defined, appearing as banding at the basal part of the leaf, whereas Fe deficiency results in interveinal chlorosis along the entire length of the leaf.

- In vegetable crops, color change appears in the younger leaves first. The new leaves are usually abnormally small, mottled, and chlorotic.
- In citrus, irregular interveinal chlorosis occurs with small, pointed, mottled leaves. Fruit formation is significantly reduced.
- In legumes, stunted growth with interveinal chlorosis appears on the older, lower leaves. Dead tissue drops out of the chlorotic spots.

Zinc deficient mango shoots have shortened internodes, resulting in leaf rosetting.

Zinc deficient avocado; young leaves have interveinal chlorosis.

15

Manures (FYM, Compost and Green Manure) and Fertilizers (Urea, Diammonium Phosphate, Single Superphosphate and Muriate of Potash)

MANURE

Organic manures are natural products used by farmers to enhanced sustainable crop production. There are a number of organic manures like farm yard manure, green manures, compost prepared from crop residues and other farm wastes, vermicompost, oil cakes, and biological wastes - animal bones, slaughter house refuse.

Manures are plant and animal wastes that are used as sources of plant nutrients. They release nutrients after their decomposition. The art of collecting and using wastes from animal, human and vegetable sources for improving crop productivity is as old as agriculture. Manures are the organic materials derived from animal, human and plant residues which contain plant nutrients in complex organic forms. Naturally occurring or synthetic chemicals containing plant nutrients are called fertilizers. Manures with low nutrient, content per unit quantity have longer residual effect besides improving soil physical properties compared to fertilizer with high nutrient content. Major sources of manures are:

1. Cattle shed wastes-dung, urine and slurry from biogas plants
2. Human habitation wastes-night soil, human urine, town refuse, sewage, sludge and sullage
3. Poultry Jitter, droppings of sheep and goat
4. Slaughterhouse wastes-bone meal, meat meal, blood meal, horn and hoof meal, Fish wastes
5. Byproducts of agro industries-oil cakes, bagasse and press mud, fruit and vegetable processing wastes etc

6. Crop wastes-sugarcane trash, stubbles and other related material
7. Water hyacinth, weeds and tank silt, and
8. Green manure crops and green leaf manuring material

Manures can also be grouped, into bulky organic manures and concentrated organic manures based on concentration of the nutrients.

BENEFITS OF ORGANIC MANURES

- Organic manures increase the organic matter in the soil.
- Organic matter in turn releases the plant food in available form for the use of crops.
- Organic manures should not be seen only as carriers of plant food.
- These manures also enable a soil to hold more water and also help to improve the drainage in clay soils.
- They provide organic acids that help to dissolve soil nutrients and make them available for the plants.

TYPES OF ORGANIC MANURES

1. Farm yard manure (FYM)
2. Green manures
3. Crop residues
4. Compost
5. Home compost
6. Concentrated organic manures

Nutritional Status of FYM	(%)
Nitrogen	0.5000
Phosphorus	0.2500
Potassium	0.4000
Calcium	0.0800
Sulfur	0.0200
Zinc	0.0040
Copper	0.0003
Manganese	0.0070
Iron	0.4500

Farm yard Manure

- Farm yard Manure is prepared basically using cow dung, cow urine, waste straw and other dairy wastes.
- It is highly useful and some of its properties are
  - FYM is rich in nutrients
  - When cow dung and urine are mixed, a balanced nutrition is made available to the plants.
  - Availability of Potassium and Phosphorus from FYM is similar to that from inorganic sources.
  - Application of FYM improves soil fertility.

Green Manures

- India has changed from a region of food scarcity to food sufficiency by increased fertilizer use with subsidized prices, but use of organic manures including green manure, declined substantially.

- Inorganic fertilizers are becoming more expensive, therefore sustainability of soil productivity has become a question.
- Hence, alternate sources to supplement inorganic fertilizers are thought.
- Green manuring are low cost and effective technology in minimizing cost of fertilizers and safeguarding productivity.

Crop Residues

- Crop residues are the non-economic plant parts that are left in the field after harvest.
- The harvest refuses include straws, stubble, Stover and haulms of different crops.
- Crop remains are also from thrashing sheds or that are discarded during crop processing.
- This process includes wastes like groundnut shell, oil cakes, rice husks and cobs of maize, sorghum and cumbu.
- The greatest potential as a biomass resource appears to be from the field residues of sorghum, maize, soybean, cotton, sugarcane etc.
- These residues will contribute 1.0 lakh ton of nitrogen, 0.5 lakh ton of phosphorus and 2.0 lakh tons of potassium.
- How ever crop residues need composting before being used as manure.

Compost

- Compost is a rich source of organic matter.
- Soil organic matter plays an important role in sustaining soil fertility, and hence in sustainable agricultural production.
- In addition to being a source of plant nutrient, it improves the physico-chemical and biological properties of the soil.

Importance of Composting

- Final weight of compost is very less.
- Composting temperature kill pathogen, weed seeds and seeds.
- Saleable product
- Improves manure handling
- Reduces the risk of pollution
- Volume reduction of waste. During composting number of wastes from several sources are blended together.

- Composting temperature kills pathogen, weed seeds and seeds.
- Matured compost comes into equilibrium with the soil.
- Excellent soil conditioner.

Vermi-Compost

- Vermicompost is an organic manure (bio-fertilizer) produced as the vermicast by earth worm feeding on biological waste material; plant residues.
- This compost is an odorless, clean, organic material containing adequate quantities of N, P, K and several micronutrients essential for plant growth.
- Vermicompost is a preferred nutrient source for organic farming.
- It is eco-friendly, non-toxic, consumes low energy input for composting and is a recycled biological product.
- The process allows for the safe conversion of waste into a valuable nutrient rich humus fertilizer - Vermicompost.

Home Compost

Concentrated Organic Manures

- Edible oil cakes which can be safely fed to livestock; e.g.: Groundnut cake, Coconut cake etc.,
- Non edible oil cakes which are not fit for feeding livestock; e.g.: Castor cake, Neem cake, Mahua cake etc.,
- Both edible and non-edible oil cakes can be used as manures.
- However, edible oil cakes are fed to cattle and non-edible oil cakes are used as manures especially for horticultural crops.
- Nutrients present in oil cakes, after mineralization, are made available to crops 7 to 10 days after application.

BULKY ORGANIC MANURES

Bulky organic manures contain small percentage of nutrients and they are applied in large quantities. Farmyard manure (FYM), compost and green-manure are the most important and widely used bulky organic manures. Use of bulky organic manures has several advantages:

- They supply plant nutrients including micronutrients
- They improve soil physical properties like structure, water holding capacity etc.,
- They increase the availability of nutrients

- Carbon dioxide released during decomposition acts as a CO2 fertilizer and
- Plant parasitic nematodes and fungi are controlled to some extent by altering the balance of microorganisms in the soil.

FARMYARD MANURE

Farmyard manure refers to the decomposed mixture of dung and urine of farm animals along with litter and left over material from roughages or fodder fed to the cattle. On an average well decomposed farmyard manure contains 0.5 per cent N, 0.2 per cent P_2O_5 and 0.5 per cent K_2O.The present method of preparing farmyard manure by the farmers is defective. Urine, which is wasted, contains one per cent nitrogen and 1.35 per cent potassium. Nitrogen present in urine is mostly in the form of urea which is subjected to volatilization losses. Even during storage, nutrients are lost due to leaching and volatilization. However, it is practically impossible to avoid losses altogether, but can be reduced by following improved method of preparation of farmyard manure. Trenches of size 6 m to 7.5 m length, 1.5 m to 2.0 m width and 1.0 m deep are dug.

All available litter and refuse is mixed with soil and spread in the shed so as to absorb urine. The next morning, urine soaked refuse along with dung is collected and placed in the trench. A section of the trench from one end should be taken up for filling with daily collection. When the section is filled up to a height of 45 cm to 60 cm above the ground level, the top of the heap is made into a dome and plastered with cow dung earth slurry. The process is continued and when the first trench is completely filled, second trench is prepared.

The manure becomes ready for use in about four to five months after plastering. If urine is not collected in the bedding, it can be collected along with washings of the cattle shed in a cemented pit from which it is later added to the farmyard manure pit. Chemical preservatives can also be used to reduce losses and enrich farmyard manure. The commonly used chemicals are gypsum and superphosphate. Gypsum is spread in the cattle shed which absorbs urine and prevents volatilization loss of urea present in the urine and also adds calcium and sulphur. Superphosphate also acts similarly in reducing losses and also increases phosphorus content.

Partially rotten farmyard manure has to be applied three to four weeks before sowing while well rotten manure can be applied immediately before sowing. Generally 10 to 20 t/ha is applied, but more than 20 t/ha is applied to fodder grasses and vegetables. In such cases farmyard manure should be applied at least 15 days in advance to avoid immobilization of nitrogen. The existing practice of leaving manure in small heaps scattered in the field for a very long period leads toloss of nutrients. These losses can be reduced by spreading the manure and incorporating by ploughing immediately after application.

Vegetable crops like potato, tomato, sweet-potato, carrot, raddish, onion etc., respond well to the farmyard manure. The other responsive crops are sugarcane, rice, napier grass and orchard crops like oranges, banana, mango and plantation crop like coconut.

The entire amount of nutrients present in farmyard manure is not available immediately. About 30 per cent of nitrogen, 60 to 70 per cent of phosphorus and 70 per cent of potassium are available to the first crop.

Sheep and Goat Manure

The droppings of sheep and goats contain higher nutrients than farmyard manure and compost. On an average, the manure contains 3 per cent N, 1 per cent P_2O_5 and 2 per cent K_2O. It is applied to the field in two ways. The sweeping of sheep or goat sheds are placed in pits for decomposition and it is applied later to the field. The nutrients present in the urine are *wasted* in this method. The second method is sheep penning, wherein sheep and goats are kept overnight in the field and urine and fecal matter added to the soil is incorporated to a shallow depth by working blade harrow or cultivator or cultivator.

Poultry Manure

The excreta of birds ferment very quickly. If left exposed, 50 percent of its nitrogen is lost within 30 days. Poultry manure contains higher nitrogen and phosphorus compared to other bulky organic manures. The average nutrient content is 3.03 per cent N; 2.63 per cent P_2O_5 and 1.4 per cent K_2O.

Concentrated organic manures

Concentrated organic manures have higher nutrient content than bulky organic manure. The important concentrated organic manures are oilcakes, blood meal, fish manure etc. These are also known as organic nitrogen fertilizer. Before their organic nitrogen is used by the crops, it is converted through bacterial action into readily usable ammoniacal nitrogen and nitrate nitrogen. These organic fertilizers are, therefore, relatively slow acting, but they supply available nitrogen for a longer period.

OIL CAKES

After oil is extracted from oilseeds, the remaining solid portion is dried as cake which can, be used as manure. The oil cakes are of two types:

- Edible oil cakes which can be safely fed to livestock; e.g.: Groundnut cake, Coconut cake etc., and
- Non edible oil cakes which are not fit for feeding livestock; e.g.: Castor cake, Neem cake, Mahua cake etc.,

Both edible and non-edible oil cakes can be used as manures. However, edible oil cakes are fed to cattle and non-edible oil cakes are used as manures especially for horticultural crops. Nutrients present in oil cakes, after mineralization, are made

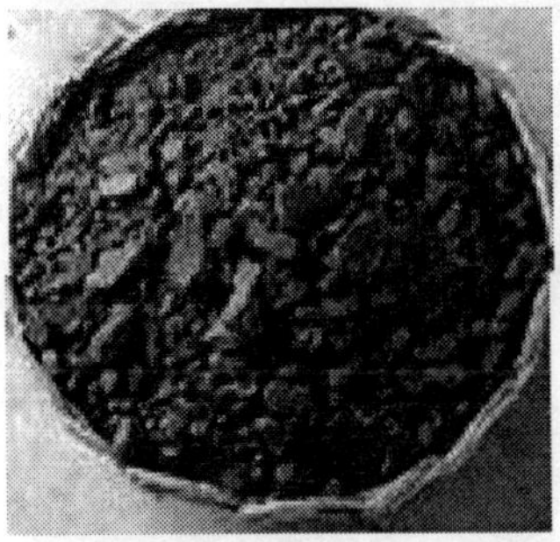

Jatropha oil cakes

Pongamia oil cakes

Cotton seed oil cakes

available to crops 7 to 10 days after application. Oilcakes need to be well powdered before application for even distribution and quicker decomposition.

The average nutrient content of different oil-cakes is presented in the following table.

Average nutrient content of oil cakes

Oil-cakes	Nutrient content (%)		
	N	P_2O_5	K_2O
Non edible oil-cakes			
Castor cake	4.3	1.8	1.3
Cotton seed cake (undecorticated)	3.9	1.8	1.6
Karanj cake	3.9	0.9	1.2
Mahua cake	2.5	0.8	1.2
Safflower cake (undecorticated)	4.9	1.4	1.2
Edible oil-cakes			
Coconut cake	3.0	1.9	1.8
Cotton seed cake (decorticated)	6.4	2.9	2.2
Groundnut cake	7.3	1.5	1.3
Linseed cake	4.9	1.4	1.3
Niger cake	4.7	1.8	1.3
Rape seed cake	5.2	1.8	1.2
Safflower cake (decorticated)	7.9	2.2	1.9
Sesamum cake	6.2	2.0	1.2

OTHER CONCENTRATED ORGANIC MANURES

Blood meal when dried and powdered can be used as manure. The meat of dead animals is dried and converted into meat meal which is a good source of nitrogen. Average nutrient content of animal based concentrated organic manures is given as follows.

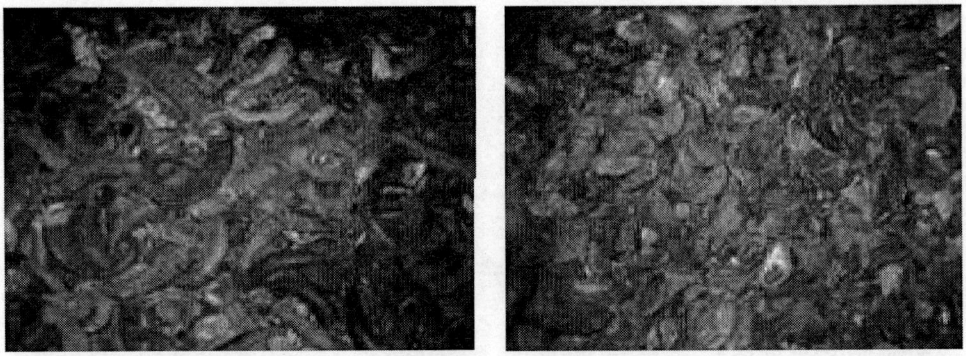

Horn and hoof meal

Raw bone meal

Crushed bone meal

Animal based concentrated organic manures

Average nutrient content of animal based concentrated organic manures

Organic manures	Nutrient content (%)		
	N	P_2O_5	K_2O
Blood meal	10-12	1-2	1.0
Meat meal	10.5	2.5	0.5
Fish meal	4-10	3-9	0.3-1.5
Horn and Hoof meal	13	-	-
Raw bone meal	3-4	20-25	-
Steamed bone meal	1-2	25-30	-

Many prefixes such as mineral, inorganic, or chemical are often used to describe fertilizers and these are used interchangeably.

Fertilizer grade is an expression referring to the legal guarantee of the available plant nutrients expressed as a percentage by weight in a fertilizer, e.g. a 12-32-16 grade of NPK complex fertilizer indicates the presence of 12 % nitrogen (N), 32 %

phosphorous (P_2O_5) and 16 %potash (K_2O). On a fertilizer bag, the NPK content is always written in the sequence N, P_2O_5, K_2O.

Fertilizers are classified as

- **Straight fertilizers:** These contain one of the 3 major nutrients N, P or K.
- **Compound /complex fertilizers:** These contain at least two out of the three major nutrients.

Plants need nutrients for healthy growth. These nutrients are available to plants through water-soluble minerals from the ground. If these nutrients deplete from the soil, they can be supplemented by applying organic manures like farmyard manure, green manure, leaf mould, oil cake, earth worm compost, fish / bone meal, sheep droppings and poultry litter. Alternatively the nutrients can be supplied to plants by applying inorganic fertilizers, which are also called as chemical fertilizers. The nutrients are divided in two groups, namely – macro nutrients and micro nutrients. The plants need macro nutrients in larger quantity than the micro nutrients. Macro nutrients are nitrogen, phosphorus and potassium (N = nitrogen, P = phosphorus, K = potassium). Calcium, magnesium, iron, and sulphur are micro nutrients. There are some other nutrients, which are needed by plants in very minute quantities. Such nutrients are called as 'Trace elements'. Zinc, manganese, copper and boron are the trace elements.

Chemical Fertilizers

Chemical fertilizers are water soluble minerals. So, as soon as they are applied to plants and water given, they dissolve in water and are absorbed by the plants. Thus, a slight overdose of a chemical fertilizer could damage the plant or may even kill it. Due to their water solubility, the chemical fertilizers are easily washed out of soil. This too makes them unavailable to plants. When used with caution and along with organic manures, chemical fertilizers can give good results.

- **Symptoms of Nitrogen Deficiency (Chlorosis)** : Nitrogen encourages growth of chlorophyll and proteins. This helps plants to produce more food. Due to nitrogen deficiency plants get stunted, leaves turn yellowish. Normally lower leaves turn yellow first.
- **Symptoms of Phosphorus Deficiency :** Phosphorus encourages healthy growth of cells. It also helps in fruit and seed formation. Stunted growth of stems, leaves and roots is due to deficiency of this nutrient. Twiggy branches and poor fruit and seed formation is a symptom of phosphorus deficiency.
- **Symptoms of Potassium Deficiency :** Potassium helps in protein formation. It also helps in photosynthesis and in transportation of food. Plants get vigour and resistance to diseases because of potassium. Due to potassium deficiency edges of leaves turn dry and yellowish. Leaves get wrinkled and turn downwards. New shoots start drying.

Fertilizer for flowering and fruiting plants

Super phosphate – 4 kg. Ammonium sulphate – 750 grams, Potassium nitrate – 1.5 kg. Potassium sulphate – 2 kg. Magnesium sulphate – 500 grams, Iron sulphate – 125 grams. 1 level tablespoon of this fertilizer should be applied to a potted rose or fruit plant, once a month. The fertilizer should be applied in a trench dug around the edge of the pot. After putting fertilizer in the circular tench, cover it with soil and feed water.

Except for Super phosphate mix all the ingedients and powder them, Mix Super phosphate in the above and store in airtight container. Note that Potassiu nitrate shoild not be powdered seperately; as on impact it can explode.

NPK Contents Of Various Manures and Fertlizers

Type of manure / fertilizer	Nitrogen %	Phosphorus %	Potassium %
Organic Manures			
Farmyard manure	0.3 to 0.4	0.1 to 0.2	0.1 to 0.3
Sheep/goat droppings	0.5 to 0.7	0.4 to 0.6	0.3 to 1.0
Poultry litter	1.0 to 1.8	1.4 to 1.8	0.8 to 0.9
Cattle urine	0.9 to 1.2	—	0.5 to 1.0
Bone meal	3.5	22.0	—
Fish meal	4.0	3.9	0.3
Sesbania aculeata	0.62	0.15	0.5
Sunn hemp	0.75	0.12	0.5
Castor cake	4.0	2.0	1.0
Neem cake	5.2	1.0	1.4
Simple Chemical Fertlizers			
Ammonium sulphate	20	—	—
Ammonium chloride	25	—	—
Ammonium nitrate	18	—	—
Potassium nitrate	15	—	—
Urea	46	—	—
Single super phosphate	—	16	—
Triple super phosphate	—	45	—
Muriate of potash	—	—	50 to 60
Potassium sulphate	—	—	50
Compound Chemical Fertilizers			
Diammonium phosphate (DAP)	18	46	—
Ammonium phosphate	11	48	—
Potassium ammonium chloride	13	—	22
NPK 15:15:15 (Suphala)	15	15	15

Foliar fertilizer

Mix together Urea – 500 grams, Diammonium hydrogen phosphate – 500 grams and Dipotassium hydrogen phosphate – 500 grams and store in air tight container. 3 grams of above mixture is to be diluted in 1 litre of water and sprayed on all parts of plants; particularly undersides of the leaves.

Foliar micro-nutrient

Zinc sulphate – 100 grams, Copper sulphate – 100 grams, Ferrous sulphate – 300 grams, Manganese sulphate – 300 grams, Boric acid – 200 grams. Mix all the ingredients and grind finely. Store in airtight container. 10 grams of this mixture dissolved in 5 litres of water and spray on all parts of the plants; particularly undersides of the leaves.

Method of finding the required quantity of NPK : If a tree needs 250 grams of nitrogen, 100 grams of phosphorus and 100 grams of potassium, quantity of each chemical can be worked out as follows :

- 543 grams of urea (46% nitrogen) will give 250 grams of nitrogen ($250 \times 100 \div 46 = 543$)
- 625 grams of single super phospahte (16% phosphorus) will give 100 grams of phosphorus ($100 \times 100 \div 16 = 625$)
- 166 grams of muriate of potash (60% potassium) will give 100 grams of potash ($100 \times 100 \div 60 = 166$)

16

Structure and Function and Cell Organelles

PLANT CELL STRUCTURE

Plants are unique among the eukaryotes, organisms whose cells have membrane-enclosed nuclei and organelles, because they can manufacture their own food. Chlorophyll, which gives plants their green color, enables them to use sunlight to convert water and carbon dioxide into sugars and carbohydrates, chemicals the cell uses for fuel.

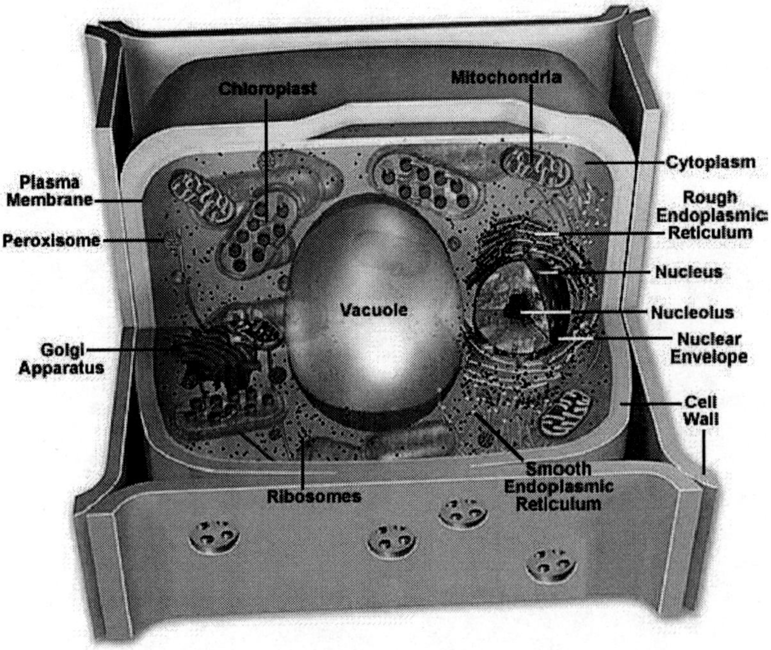

Anatomy of the Plant Cell

Like the fungi, another kingdom of eukaryotes, plant cells have retained the protective cell wall structure of their prokaryotic ancestors. The basic plant cell shares a similar construction motif with the typical eukaryote cell, but does not have centrioles, lysosomes, intermediate filaments, cilia, or flagella, as does the animal cell. Plant cells do, however, have a number of other specialized structures, including a rigid cell wall, central vacuole, plasmodesmata, and chloroplasts. Although plants (and their typical cells) are non-motile, some species produce gametes that do exhibit flagella and are, therefore, able to move about.

Plants can be broadly categorized into two basic types: vascular and nonvascular. Vascular plants are considered to be more advanced than nonvascular plants because they have evolved specialized tissues, namely xylem, which is involved in structural support and water conduction, and phloem, which functions in food conduction. Consequently, they also possess roots, stems, and leaves, representing a higher form of organization that is characteristically absent in plants lacking vascular tissues. The nonvascular plants, members of the division Bryophyta, are usually no more than an inch or two in height because they do not have adequate support, which is provided by vascular tissues to other plants, to grow bigger. They also are more dependent on the environment that surrounds them to maintain appropriate amounts of moisture and, therefore, tend to inhabit damp, shady areas.

It is estimated that there are at least 260,000 species of plants in the world today. They range in size and complexity from small, nonvascular mosses to giant sequoia trees, the largest living organisms, growing as tall as 330 feet (100 meters). Only a tiny percentage of those species are directly used by people for food, shelter, fiber, and medicine. Nonetheless, plants are the basis for the Earth's ecosystem and food web, and without them complex animal life forms (such as humans) could never have evolved. Indeed, all living organisms are dependent either directly or indirectly on the energy produced by photosynthesis, and the byproduct of this process, oxygen, is essential to animals. Plants also reduce the amount of carbon dioxide present in the atmosphere, hinder soil erosion, and influence water levels and quality.

Plants exhibit life cycles that involve alternating generations of diploid forms, which contain paired chromosome sets in their cell nuclei, and haploid forms, which only possess a single set. Generally these two forms of a plant are very dissimilar in appearance. In higher plants, the diploid generation, the members of which are known as sporophytes due to their ability to produce spores, is usually dominant and more recognizable than the haploid gametophyte generation. In Bryophytes, however, the gametophyte form is dominant and physiologically necessary to the sporophyte form.

Animals are required to consume protein in order to obtain nitrogen, but plants are able to utilize inorganic forms of the element and, therefore, do not need an outside source of protein. Plants do, however, usually require significant amounts of water, which is needed for the photosynthetic process, to maintain cell structure and facilitate growth, and as a means of bringing nutrients to plant cells. The amount of nutrients needed by plant species varies significantly, but nine elements are generally considered to be necessary in relatively large amounts. Termed macroelements, these nutrients include calcium, carbon, hydrogen, magnesium, nitrogen, oxygen, phosphorus, potassium, and sulfur. Seven microelements, which are required by plants in smaller quantities, have also been identified: boron, chlorine, copper, iron, manganese, molybdenum, and zinc.

Thought to have evolved from the green algae, plants have been around since the early Paleozoic era, more than 500 million years ago. The earliest fossil evidence of land plants dates to the Ordovician Period (505 to 438 million years ago). By the Carboniferous Period, about 355 million years ago, most of the Earth was covered by forests of primitive vascular plants, such as lycopods (scale trees) and gymnosperms (pine trees, ginkgos). Angiosperms, the flowering plants, didn't develop until the end of the Cretaceous Period, about 65 million years ago—just as the dinosaurs became extinct.

- **Cell Wall** - Like their prokaryotic ancestors, plant cells have a rigid wall surrounding the plasma membrane. It is a far more complex structure, however, and serves a variety of functions, from protecting the cell to regulating the life cycle of the plant organism.
- **Chloroplasts** - The most important characteristic of plants is their ability to photosynthesize, in effect, to make their own food by converting light energy into chemical energy. This process is carried out in specialized organelles called chloroplasts.
- **Endoplasmic Reticulum** - The endoplasmic reticulum is a network of sacs that manufactures, processes, and transports chemical compounds for use inside and outside of the cell. It is connected to the double-layered nuclear envelope, providing a pipeline between the nucleus and the cytoplasm. In plants, the endoplasmic reticulum also connects between cells via the plasmodesmata.
- **Golgi Apparatus** - The Golgi apparatus is the distribution and shipping department for the cell's chemical products. It modifies proteins and fats built in the endoplasmic reticulum and prepares them for export as outside of the cell.
- **Microfilaments** - Microfilaments are solid rods made of globular proteins called actin. These filaments are primarily structural in function and are an important component of the cytoskeleton.
- **Microtubules** - These straight, hollow cylinders are found throughout the cytoplasm of all eukaryotic cells (prokaryotes don't have them) and carry out a variety of functions, ranging from transport to structural support.
- **Mitochondria** - Mitochondria are oblong shaped organelles found in the cytoplasm of all eukaryotic cells. In plant cells, they break down carbohydrate and sugar molecules to provide energy, particularly when light isn't available for the chloroplasts to produce energy.

- **Nucleus** - The nucleus is a highly specialized organelle that serves as the information processing and administrative center of the cell. This organelle has two major functions: it stores the cell's hereditary material, or DNA, and it coordinates the cell's activities, which include growth, intermediary metabolism, protein synthesis, and reproduction (cell division).
- **Peroxisomes** - Microbodies are a diverse group of organelles that are found in the cytoplasm, roughly spherical and bound by a single membrane. There are several types of microbodies but peroxisomes are the most common.
- **Plasmodesmata** - Plasmodesmata are small tubes that connect plant cells to each other, providing living bridges between cells.
- **Plasma Membrane** - All living cells have a plasma membrane that encloses their contents. In prokaryotes and plants, the membrane is the inner layer of protection surrounded by a rigid cell wall. These membranes also regulate the passage of molecules in and out of the cells.
- **Ribosomes** - All living cells contain ribosomes, tiny organelles composed of approximately 60 percent RNA and 40 percent protein. In eukaryotes, ribosomes are made of four strands of RNA. In prokaryotes, they consist of three strands of RNA.
- **Vacuole** - Each plant cell has a large, single vacuole that stores compounds, helps in plant growth, and plays an important structural role for the plant.
- **Leaf Tissue Organization** - The plant body is divided into several organs: roots, stems, and leaves. The leaves are the primary photosynthetic organs of plants, serving as key sites where energy from light is converted into chemical energy. Similar to the other organs of a plant, a leaf is comprised of three basic tissue systems, including the dermal, vascular, and ground tissue systems. These three motifs are continuous throughout an entire plant, but their properties vary significantly based upon the organ type in which they are located. All three tissue systems are discussed in this section.

MITOSIS AND MEIOSIS

Mitosis

Organisms must be able to grow and reproduce. Prokaryotes, such as bacteria, duplicate deoxyribonucleic acid (DNA) and divide by splitting in two, a process called binary fission. Cells of eukaryotes, including those of animals, plants, fungi, and protists, divide by one of two methods: mitosis or meiosis.

Mitosis produces two cells, called daughter cells, with the same number of chromosomes as the parent cell, and is used to produce new somatic (body) cells in multicellular eukaryotes or new individuals in single-celled eukaryotes. In sexually reproducing organisms, cells that produce gametes (eggs or sperm) divide by meiosis, producing four cells, each with half the number of chromosomes possessed by the parent cell.

Chromosome Replication

All eukaryotic organisms are composed of cells containing chromosomes in the nucleus. Chromosomes are made of DNA and proteins. Most cells have two complete sets of chromosomes,which occur in pairs. The two chromosomes that make up a pair are homologous, and contain all the same loci (genes controlling the production of a specific type of product).

These chromosome pairs are usually referred to as homologous pairs. An individual chromosome from a homologous pair is sometimes called a homolog. For example, typical lily cells contain twelve pairs of homologous chromosomes, for a total of twenty-four chromosomes.

Cells that have two homologous chromosomes of each type are called diploid. Some cells, such as eggs and sperm, contain half the normal number of chromosomes (only one of each homolog) and are called haploid. Lily egg and sperm cells each contain twelve chromosomes.

Mitosis

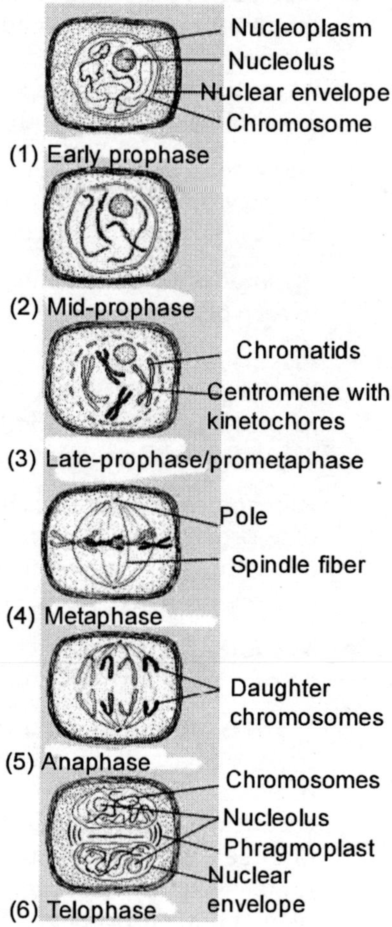

DNA must replicate before mitosis or meiosis can occur. If daughter cells are to receive a full set of genetic information, a duplicate copy of DNA must be available. Before DNA replication occurs, each chromosome consists of a single long strand of DNA called a chromatid. After DNA replication, each chromosome consists of two chromatids, called sister chromatids.

The original chromatid acts as a template for making the second chromatid; the two are therefore identical. Sister chromatids are attached at a special region of the chromosome called the centro mere. When mitosis or meiosis starts, each chromosome in the cell consists of two sister chromatids.

Mitosis andmeiosis produce daughter cells with different characteristics. When a diploid cell undergoes mitosis, two identical diploid daughter cells are produced.

When a diploid cell undergoes meiosis, four unique haploid daughter cells are produced. It is important for gametes to be haploid, so that when an egg and sperm fuse, the diploid condition of the mature organism is restored.

Cellular Life Cycles

Mitosis and meiosis occur in the nuclear region of the cell, where all the cell's chromosomes are found. Nuclear control mechanisms begin cell division at the appropriate time.

Some cells rarely divide bymitosis in adult organisms, while other cells divide constantly, replacing old cells with new. Meiosis occurs in the nuclei of cells that produce gametes. These specialized cells occur in reproductive organs, such as flower parts in higher plants.

Cells, like organisms, are governed by life cycles. The life cycle of a cell is called the cell cycle. Cells spend most of their time in interphase. Interphase is divided into three stages: first gap (G1), synthesis (S), and second gap (G2).

During G1, the cell performs its normal functions and often grows in size. During the S stage, DNA replicates in preparation for cell division.During theG2 stage, the cell makes materials needed to produce the mitotic apparatus and for division of the cytoplasmic components of the cell.

At the end of interphase, the cell is ready to divide. Although each chromosome now consists of two sister chromatids, this is not apparent when viewed through a microscope. This is because all the chromosomes are in a highly relaxed state and simply appear as a diffuse material called chromatin.

MEIOSIS

Meiosis is the mechanism behind sexual reproduction. In meiosis, four gametes are produced from a single cell. Gametes are specialized sex cells, the microspore (sperm) and the megaspore (egg). An egg fertilized by a sperm is a zygote. The significance of meiosis is that genetic material is recombined during the process. All offspring differ genetically from all others. Chromosomes normally exist in pairs. Each set of two chromosomes is called homologous chromosomes.

Homologous chromosomes share a similar size, shape, and position of the centromeres. When a cell contains the normal two sets of two chromosomes, it is said to have a diploid (2n) number of chromosomes. A haploid (n) cell has a single set of chromosomes. Gametes contain a haploid number of chromosomes. Many grasses and flowering plants have three or more sets of chromosomes. They are called polyploid. Plants with extra sets of chromosomes are typically larger and more vigorous than diploid members of the same species. Bread wheat is a good example of a polyploid plant used in agriculture. Some varieties are hexaploid. Meiosis differs from mitosis in some important ways. Meiosis involves two cell divisions that result in four cells. Each of the four cells produced has a haploid number of chromosomes.

During meiosis the genetic information from each parent is rearranged so that the resulting gametes have a unique combination of genes. The two nuclear and cytoplasmic divisions of meiosis are named meiosis I and meiosis II. Each division includes a prophase, meta-phase, anaphase, and telo-phase. During the S phase of interphase, the chromosomes duplicate just before meiosis I. The chromosome pairs join at their centromeres. Since a diploid number is duplicated, there are four chromatids, or two homologous pairs of chromosomes.

The four chromatids are referred to as a tetrad. In prophase I, these chromosomes lay side by side, a process called synapsis. At this time genetic material may be exchanged between the homologous chromatids in a process called crossing over. Enzymes cut each chromatid, sections are switched, and then the sections are fused together. In this way, genetic material is altered, leading to greater genetic variation among the offspring. Also, at this time the nuclear envelope, or membrane, vanishes. Metaphase I begins with the tetrads aligned along the equatorial plane. Spindle fibers attach to homologous chromosomes. In anaphase I, the homologous chromosomes of each pair sepa rate and are pulled toward the opposite poles. In telophase I, the nuclear envelope reappears and cytokinesis takes place.

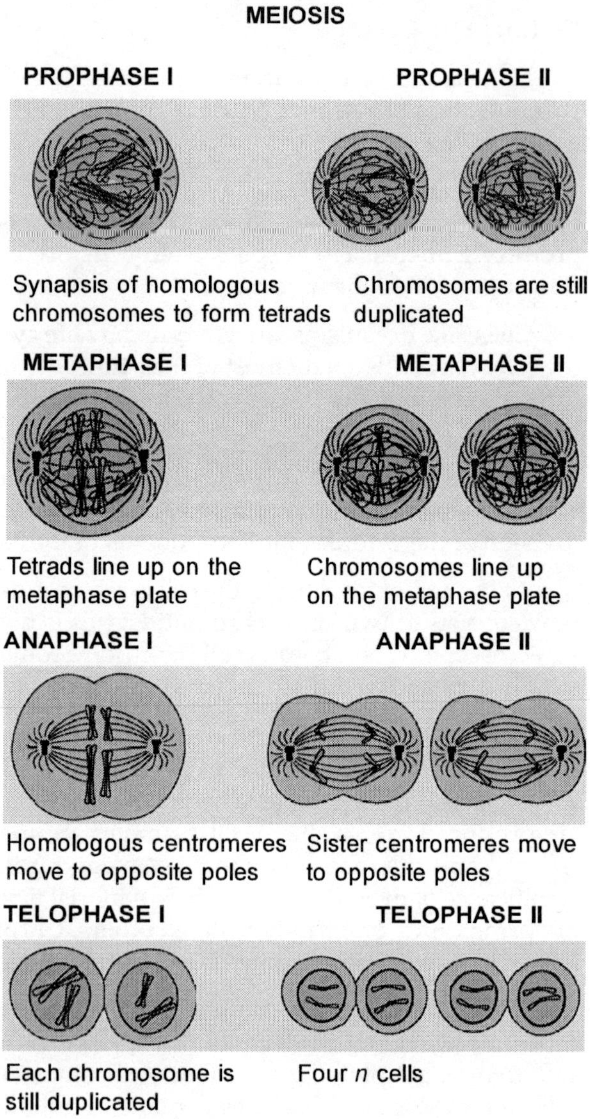

Meiosis II begins with a diploid number of chromosomes in each of the two cells. No further duplication of genetic material takes place prior to meiosis II. Prophase II is brief, since the chromatids are already condensed. Spindle fibers form, and the nuclear envelope breaks down. In metaphase II, the chromosomes line up along the equator. Anaphase II sees the chromatids pulled to opposite poles by spindle fibers. The nuclear envelope reforms, and the cytoplasm divides.

The two divisions of meiosis result at telephase II in four haploid cells, each with a different genetic make up. When fertilization takes place during sexual reproduction, the haploid gametes fuse to form a diploid cell called the zygote. The zygote develops into the embryo. It inherits a single set of chromosomes from the female parent and a single set from the male parent.

NUCLEAR DIVISION AND CYTOKINESIS

Mitosis and meiosis result in the division of the nucleus. Nuclear division is nearly always coordinated with division of the cytoplasm. Cleaving of the cytoplasmto form new cells is called cytokinesis. Cytokinesis begins toward the middle or end of nuclear division and involves not just the division of the cytoplasm but also the organelles.

In plants, after nuclear division ends, a new cell wall must be formed between the daughter nuclei. The new cell wall begins when vesicles filled with cell wall material congregate where the metaphase plate was located, producing a structure called the cell plate.

When the cell plate is fully formed, cytokinesis is complete. Following cytokinesis, the cell returns to interphase. Mitotic daughter cells enlarge, reproduce organelles, and resume regular activities. Following meiosis, gametes may be modified or transported in the reproductive system.

ALTERNATION OF GENERATIONS

Meiotic daughter cells continue development only if they fuse during fertilization. Mitosis and meiosis alternate during the life cycles of sexually reproducing organisms. The life-cycle stage following mitosis is diploid, and the stage following meiosis is haploid. This process is called alternation of generations.

In plants, the diploid state is referred to as the sporophyte generation, and the haploid stage as the gametophyte generation. In nonvascular plants, the gametophyte generation dominates the life cycle. In otherwords, the plants normally seen on the forest floor are made of haploid cells.

The sporophytes, which have diploid cells, are small and attached to the body of the gametophyte. In vascular plants, sporophytes are the large, multicellular individuals (such as trees and ferns), whereas gametophytes are very small and either are embedded in the sporophyte or are free-living, as are ferns.

The genetic variation introduced by sexual reproduction has a significant impact on the ability of species to survive and adapt to the environment. Alternation of generations allows sexual reproduction to occur, without changing the chromosome number characterizing the species

GAMETOGENESIS, FERTILIZATION AND EARLY EMBRYOGENESIS

Introduction

In vitro Embryo Production (IVEP) or ***in vitro*** Production (IVP) technique is currently in the central focus among all the Assisted Reproductive Technologies

(ARTs) in human as well as in animals. Therefore, the physiology of normal fertilization should be considered as a must for the development of any IVEP or IVP protocols especially for *in vitro* Fertilization (IVF) or Intracytoplasmic Sperm Injection (ICSI) techniques. Gametogenesis, fertilization and early embryogenesis or pre-implantation embryo development are crucial periods for normal development of an embryo afterwards. Until now researches in mammalian gametogenesis, fertilization and early embryogenesis mainly based on the laboratory animals and human. Compared with laboratory and farm animals like cattle, sheep and pig, studies in goat are scarce. Therefore, the current paper will briefly review some aspects of gametogenesis, fertilization and early embryogenesis in mammals with special reference to goat.

Gametogenesis

Genetically and functionally competent gametes are a prerequisite for normal fertilization and early embryo development. The first phase in the sexual reproduction of an organism is gametogenesis, a process of formation of gametes from the germ cells in the testes and ovaries. This process is termed as spermatogenesis in the male and oogenesis in the female. It is the fundamental biological process in both the sexes and the key event of gametogenesis is the halving of the number of chromosomes to produce haploid germ cells (sperm and oocyte) through meiosis. Thus, in goat, where the chromosome number of somatic cells is 60, each sperm and each oocyte has only 30 chromosomes. However, until this point spermatogenesis and oogenesis resume their similarity. After this, in the male, each primary spermatocyte divides meiotically and produces four spermatids, each destined to become a functional sperm. In the female, on the other hand, of the four cells produced from each primary oocyte only one finally becomes a functional oocyte. A schematic diagram of gametogenesis in mammals has been illustrated in the figure below.

In mammals, the male and female gametes originate from the embryonic yolk sac. The gametes initially colonize in the primitive gonadal ridge at the early stage of pregnancy by migration through the developing mesentery of the embryo, where germ cells associate with somatic cells; it continues with their multiplication, growth and maturation. Finally, migrate to the pelvic and inguinal regions to form the ovary or testis, respectively and ends at fertilization. Mammalian spermatogenesis and oogenesis are briefly described below:

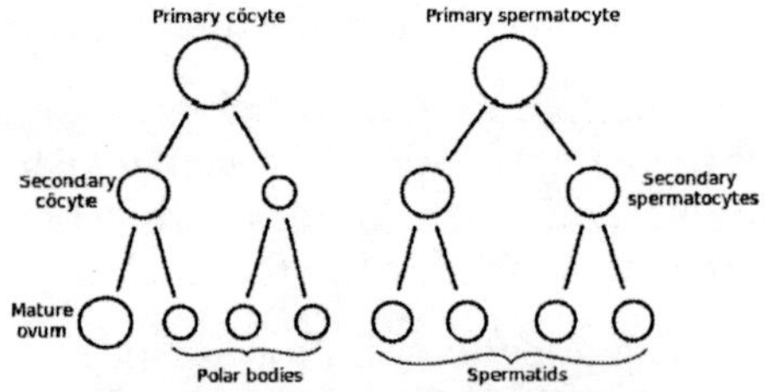

Scheme showing analogies in the process of maturation of the ovum and the development of the spermatids, following their individual pathways. The oocytes and spermatocytes are both gametocytes.

Spermatogenesis: Competent sperm are required for the successful contribution of the paternal genotype to embryo development. The process of spermatogenesis results in the formation of the haploid male gamete required for fertilization of an oocyte. Spermatogenesis is a continual and complex process that involves three major steps:

(a) **proliferation** - multiplication of spermatogonia by the process of mitosis (spermatocytogenesis);

(b) **meiosis (spermiogenesis)** - meiotic divisions whereby the chromosome number is reduced from diploid to haploid and

(c) **differentiation** - transformation of the round spermatid into the complex structure of the spermatozoon.

Spermatogenesis in buck and other male mammals begins at puberty through the proliferation of interphase germ cells, continues throughout adult life and takes place inside the seminiferous tubules of the testes. The age of puberty for male goat or buck ranged between 4 and 6 months. The walls of the seminiferous tubules contain the differentiating sex cells arranged in a stratified layer, 5 to 8 cells deep. The outermost layers contain spermatogonia, which have increased in number by spemtocytogenesis. The spemtocytogenesis begins with mitosis of the diploid A spematogonia in the basal compartment of the Sertoli cells. The A spematogonia differentiate into B spermatogonia which enter their final mitotic division prior to their entrance into the pre-leptotene phase of first meiosis (meiosis 1).

Meiosis occurs in the adluminal compartment of the Sertoli cell and results in the formation of primary spermatocytes. Condensation of chromosomes occurs during the leptotene phase followed by the zygotene phase. The long pachytene phase involves the crossing over of chromosomal material and is most susceptible to damage. Meiosis progresses through the diplotene phase, diakinesis, Metaphase I (MI) and anaphase, finally resulting in secondary spermatocytes (2c, 1n). Each secondary spermatocyte then enters the second meiotic division (meiosis 2), without the intervention of a resting period, resulting in spermatids with a haploid number of chromosomes and DNA content (1c, 1n), required for fertilization. The round-shaped spermatids proceed through spermiogenesis and metamorphically changed into highly specialized motile cells. Spermiogenesis consists of the Golgi phase, the acrosomal cap phase, the acrosomal phase and the complex maturation stage involves development of the sperm tail.

Deviations from the process of normal spermatogenesis result in abnormal morphology or dysfunction of the sperm cell. The progression from spermatogonia to mature spermatozoa in mammals require approximately 60 to 70 days, with at least three mitotic and two meiotic divisions during spermatogenesis. Finally, the newly formed sperm are released into the lumen of the seminiferous tubules. These sperm are immotile and still immature in terms of fertilizing capability. Therefore, to acquire motility as well as maturation they need to pass down the epididymis to the ejaculatory duct, which is known as epididymal maturation.

During epididymal maturation, the sperm shed the cytoplasmic droplet, undergo modifications in the protein, carbohydrate and glycoprotein composition of the plasma membrane and acquire a net negative charge (Yanagimachi, 1994; Harrison, 1996). Sperm motility and capacitation are suppressed during storage in the cauda epididymis, which is characterized by low pH, low Ca^{2+}, low Na^{+} and increased K^{+}. Disruptions in the epididymal environment may result in abnormalities of sperm function. Immediately after ejaculation, the sperm are incapable of fertilizing the oocyte and, therefore, to acquire fertilization potential, they need to undergo functional changes (or capacitation), which occur inside the female reproductive tract.

Although in comparison with the oocytes, the spermatozoa are very small, however, they are essentially very long and compact cells with a few highly specialized cytoplasmic structures, the flagellum for motility and the acrosome, which is instrumental in sperm-oocyte binding and fusion. Morphologically and functionally, a goat spermatozoon is composed of four regions:

(a) the head containing nucleus and the acrosome,

(b) the neck containing centrioles,

(c) the middle piece containing mitochondria and d) the tail piece or flagellum. A goat spermatozoon is approximately 60 μm long of which head and tail piece are 7.69 and 52 μm long, respectively. Frozen-thawed goat spermatozoa from proven quality Jermasia buck.

OOGENESIS

The maternal contribution to the development of the embryo is determined during formation and maturation of the female gamete, the oocyte. The ability of the oocyte to achieve sperm-oocyte fusion is acquired early in oogenesis or the process of oocyte formation. The oogenetic products synthesized during oocyte growth must also be sufficient to support embryonic development from fertilization until the activation of the embryonic genome. Ultimately, the nuclear and ooplasmic maturity of the oocyte influences the success of fertilization and embryo development. In mammals, oogenesis commences during early fetal development, stops at birth and continues during puberty throughout the reproductive life of the female. After continuation of meiosis, the oogenesis process until completion is very fast. Oogenesis in mammals includes seven steps:

(a) generation of primordial germ cells (PGCs),

(b) migration of PGCs to the prospective gonads,

(c) colonization of the gonads by PGCs,

(d) differentiation of PGCs to oogonia,

(e) proliferation of oogonia,

(f) initiation of meiosis and

(g) arrest at the diplotene stage of first meiotic prophase or prophase 1.

Oogonia are the early germ cells in the ovary, which increase in number by mitosis. Oogonial multiplication begins during early fetal development and ends months to years later in the sexually mature adult. Once mitosis ceases, the oogonia then grow in size and enter the prophase of the first meiotic division at approximately day 55 of gestation in the ewe and are then referred to as primary oocytes. Each oogonium or primary oocyte contains the diploid number of chromosome. The primary oocyte which is transformed from each oogonium is a cell which becomes enclosed in a follicle, known as primordial follicle. In goat, sheep and cow, large population (approximately 100,000) of primordial or pre-antral follicles with meiotically incompetent oocytes are present in the ovaries.

Most of them are lost at various stages of development owing to atresia and only a very minority of oocytes becomes available for ovulation. In contrast, researchers found in their histological study that one pair of ovaries of Batu goat (a Sri Lankan goat breed) aged between 18 to 36 months contained 35,092 primordial follicles (which are 90% of total ovarian follicle population), 10.67 normal and 20.42 atretic vesicular (antral) follicles (1-6 mm diameter). At birth, all oocytes from growing and dominant follicles are arrested at the diplotene stage of prophase 1. This dictyate stage is characterized by the enclosure of the chromosomes within the large nucleus, also known as the Germinal Vesicle (GV).

The oocytes remain in the arrested state until a few hours before ovulation. Surprisingly, the oocytes may stay at this arrested stage for a longer period of time depending on the species, waiting for the signal to resume growth and subsequent development occurs at puberty. The age of puberty for female goat or doe is ranged between 5 and 7 months. The reason for storing the oocytes in this remarkable frozen meiotic state is unknown.

Oocyte growth and development

The growth and development of an oocyte occurs inside an ovarian follicle and oocyte undergoes a progressive series of morphological modifications as it grows and proceeds through the different stages of development. Although data are lacking for doe, researchers indicated from their study that follicular morphology and activity are similar in does and ewes. In the ewe, primordial, primary and secondary follicles, respectively, appear in the fetal ovary at days 75, 100 and 120. Once a primordial follicle oocyte is activated to grow, it embarks on a complex journey that involves numerous molecular and morphological changes to both the oocyte and the follicle. The modifications are carefully orchestrated and require sensitive communication between the oocyte and surrounding Granulosa Cells or GCs.

These structural rearrangements facilitate the increasing energy and nucleic acid synthesis requirements of the developing oocyte and are a prerequisite to the oocyte achieving meiotic competence and embryo developmental potential. The first sign of morphological change when the oocyte begins to grow is turning of the flat GCs to cuboidal which is known as primary follicle. After completion of the morphological change, the GCs proliferate actively, which cause the follicles to develop and increase in size. Through a series of mitotic division of GCs, unilaminar primary follicles are converted to multilaminar secondary follicles, followed by the antral or tertiary follicles.

The antral follicle is a highly complex unit consisting of several layers of GC surrounding a fluid-filled cavity or 'antrum` in which the oocyte surrounded by somatic cells is bathed. In the doe, antrum formation began when the GCs are about six cell layers in thickness and the Zona Pellucida (ZP) is visible at this stage. The fluid found in the 'antrum` is known as Follicular Fluid (FF). During this growth phase there is a major increase in ooplasmic organelles. The follicle provides a microenvironment for oocyte growth, development and is responsible for the production of hormones. The walls of mature preovulatory follicles consist of membrana granulosa (mural granulosa), theca interna and theca externa. The GCs are cells of epithelial origin essential for the growth and survival of the oocyte. The GCs consist of the corona radiata; Cumulus Cells (CCs), membrana granulosa and antral granulosa cells. The CCs surround the oocyte, which nourish the oocyte, are involved in oocyte growth, maturation and participate in the formation of the ZP (made of a translucent acellular layer of glycoprotein). In addition, these cells have also been implicated in the modulation or generation of oocyte maturation inhibitors.

The CCs in close contact with the oocyte are known as corona radiata. They are in close contact with the oocyte through ooplasmic extensions or processes across the ZP (De Loos *et al.*, 1991), which are known as gap junctions. The heterologous gap junctions provide the basis for extensive network of intracellular communication among GCs. Normally CCs or corona cells surrounding the goat oocyte shed e"30 h after ovulation (Harper, 1982).

Oocyte maturation

As mentioned earlier that oocytes are arrested at the diplotene stage of the prophase 1 at birth, they resume meiosis after a long quiescent phase at puberty which involve sequential sub-cellular and molecular transformations by various components of the follicle. During postnatal life, starting from puberty, ovarian follicles continue to grow, mature and either ovulate or regress. Follicles are recruited continuously until the original store is exhausted. Reinitiation of meiosis in the fully-grown oocyte is the first sign of oocyte maturation, which involves condensation of interphase chromatin, breakdown of nuclear membrane (germinal vesicle breakdown: GVBD), spindle formation and chromosome segregation. *In vivo*, resumption of meiosis is initiated by a preovulatory LH surge and only occurs in fully grown, meiotically competent oocytes from dominant follicles. Small oocytes in primordial and primary follicles have no ability to resume meiosis.

Oocytes acquire the competence to resume meiosis when their size exceeds 80% of their final diameter; they then become gradually competent to progress to metaphase 2 (MII) as the diameter increases to over 90% of the maximum. The diameter of mature goat oocytes excluding ZP (ooplasm) ranged from 119-146 μm.

During this follicle and oocyte growth phase, oocytes not only acquire competency to resume meiosis, but also acquire ooplasmic maturity, also known as oocyte capacitation, both of which are required to ensure normal fertilization and embryo development. From *in vitro* studies, it is found that goat oocytes acquired the ability to initiate meiotic resumption in early antral follicles of 0.5 to 0.8 mm in diameter and to reach MI in follicles of 1.0 to 1.8 mm in diameter.

Although 86% of goat oocytes from follicles larger than 2 mm progress to MII, only a small proportion of them can support embryonic development. In cattle, oocytes originating from follicles larger than 6 mm in diameter yield a significantly higher percentage of blastocyst than the smaller follicles. In an ***in vitro*** study, a significantly higher oocyte maturation, morula and blastocyst development rates were achieved with goat oocytes originating from larger than 5 mm follicles compared with medium (>3-5) and smaller (2-3) follicles. To reach the maturity, goat oocytes (ooplasm) grow from 29.6 μm in primordial follicles to 119 to 146 μm in antral follicles (>2 mm in diameter). The ZP of a goat oocyte from antral follicle bigger than 2 mm is about 3.2 μm thick.

Before and at the time of LH surge, the oocyte is surrounded by a compact CCs investment. The oocyte undergoes a series of changes in its nucleus, ooplasm and organization of the plasma membrane (oolemma) during the period between the LH surge and ovulation, which is known as oocyte maturation. Completion of the meiosis 1 takes place when oocytes have undergone extensive growth in cellular interaction with GCs and theca cells. The oocyte undergoes asymmetric cytokinesis and extrudes the first polar body (PB-1) containing a haploid chromosome complement. Immediately after the meiosis 1 is completed, the meiosis 2 is initiated and the oocytes are again arrested at MII stage until fertilization, when an activation stimulus provided by sperm penetration triggers the completion of the meiotic cycle and initiates embryonic development.

Ooplasmic maturation is required to acquire to the conditions to block polyspermy in case of fertilization, to decondense penetrated spermatozoon and to form pronucleus (PN). It includes redistribution of cell organelles, migration of mitochondria to perinuclear position and accumulation of granules along the oolemma. The endpoint of this, *in vivo*, is the ovulation and release from the follicle of a MII oocyte with potential to support normal embryonic development. However, the doe ovulates two to three mature oocytes in each estrous cycle. Compared with human or mouse, goat oocyte is dark in opacity due to very dense ooplasm consisted of concentrated lipid materials.($p<0.05$)

ACTIVATION OF SPERM AND SPERM-OOCYTE INTERACTION

Fertilization encompasses a series of different steps which have to be performed in a well orchestrated way to create a new individual. These include sperm capacitation, sperm binding and penetration of the ZP, traversing the perivitelline space (PVS), binding and fusion with oolemma, activation of the oocytes and decondensation of the sperm head to form the Male PN (MPN). In mammals, fertilization process is internal and the male gametes (spermatozoa) must be introduced into the female reproductive tract at coitus or artificially. As already mentioned, when the ejaculated spermatozoa are deposited into the female reproductive tract at that time they have no fertilizing capability. Therefore, the spermatozoa need to gain this ability, or in other word, need to be activated or made in ready state first before they can interact with oocyte to ensure fertilization success. The known physiological events occurring during sperm activation and sperm-oocyte interaction have been reviewed mainly based on mice models.

Activation of Spermatozoa

In mammalian species, activation of spermatozoa follows several physiological and structural changes upon exposure to environmental signals in the female reproductive tract before they interact with the oocytes towards a successful fertilization. These include various alterations in the plasma membrane and intracellular components and changes in motility pattern and metabolism of the spermatozoa. Two main processes, namely capacitation and acrosome reaction, must occur to activate the spermatozoa before the sperm interact with the oocyte.

Capacitation

The spermatozoa must reside a minimum period in the female reproductive tract before gaining the ability to fertilize oocytes. It is speculated that during this time, glycoproteins from the sperm surface are removed, thus exposing receptor sites that can respond to oocyte signals and lead to acrosome reaction. This process allows the spermatozoa to bind to the ZP, which subsequently leads to the Acrosome Reaction (AR), penetration of the ZP and fertilization of the oocyte. In another word, the spermatozoa gains the capacity to fertilize oocyte and, therefore, is termed as capacitation. This phenomenon is first noted by Chang (1951) and Austin (1951) and the term 'capacitation' was referred by Austin (1951). The time required for sperm capacitation varies among different species of animals and ranges from less than one hour in male mouse to 6 h in man. The changes that occur during capacitation in the sperm plasma membrane include modification of ion channels, increased adenylate cyclase and cyclic adenosine monophosphate (cAMP), changes in surface glycoprotein moieties that lead to changes in lectin binding patterns and also enzymatic modification of surface proteins such as sugar transferases. Metabolic changes include increased glycolytic activity and oxygen consumption, hyperactivation associated with activation of adenylate cyclase system and loss of Zn^{+2} ions that lead to increased nuclear stability. A number of enzymes and factors that present in the female reproductive tract have been implicated to affect sperm capacitation, such as arylsulphatase, fucosidase and taurine. However, till to date, the exact mechanism on how these enzymes and factors capacitate sperm remains unknown.

During capacitation, sperm motility is apparently regulated by changes in the intracellular concentration of calcium ions through a calcium channel (named CatSper) that is only expressed in the tail of mature sperm (Ren *et al.*, 2001). It is thought that the capacitation phenomenon is necessary for spermatozoon to fuse with the oolemma, but not for subsequent steps of fertilization such as DNA decondensation and PN formation. This is supported by ***in vitro*** experiments in *Xenopus laevis*, an amphibian species, mouse and human in which injection of intact sperm into the ooplasm resulted in development of normal offspring. However, discrepancies also exists, for example, the capacitation step appears to be critical in cattle, goat and in other farm animals where ICSI is problematic.

The failure of ICSI in some farm animals may be due to the failure of removal of the perinuclear theca, a cytoskeletal capsule present between the sperm membrane and the nuclear envelope. This structure could block the access of cytoplasmic factors involved in decondensation of the sperm nucleus. This is supported by results where artificially capacitated bull spermatozoa resulted in PN formation and production of a normal calf after ICSI. Capacitation may be attained *in vivo* or *in vitro*. Different ***in vitro*** conditions are used to capacitate spermatozoa from various species. Capacitation is temperature-dependant and only occurs at 37° to 39°C.

Acrosome reaction

The first interaction between the spermatozoon and the oocyte is at the ZP, an extracellular coat that surrounds all mammalian oocytes. The sperm nucleus is covered by membrane bound secretory vesicle known as the acrosome which is a large, Golgi-derived lysosome-like organelle that overlies the nucleus in the apical region of the sperm head. The acrosome or its surrounding membranes contains a large array of hydrolytic enzymes including hyaluronidase, acrosin, serine protease, proacroson, phosphatase, arylsulphatase, colagenase, phospholipase C and β-galactosidase. The spermatozoon interacts with the ZP by the plasma membrane overlying the acrosome. The specific binding of the spermatozoon to the ZP induces in the acrosome a calcium-mediated **signal transduction** process that leads to AR.

The AR brings exposure of the inner acrosomal membrane to the outside by breaking the organelle and involves fusion of the outer acrosomal membrane with the overlying plasma membrane allowing the acrosomal content to be released. This process is necessary for the spermatozoon to acquire fusibility with the oolemma. The AR is accompanied by modifications in the sperm plasma membrane, which exposes receptors for ZP binding and possibly factors exposed on the equatorial segment in preparation for sperm-oocyte fusion. The acrosomal enzymes react with the extracellular matrix (or ZP) of oocyte and digest the ZP at the point of spermatozoon contact. After losing its acrosomal content the spermatozoon retains only the inner acrosomal membrane that makes direct contact with the ZP during penetration. Following fusion, the sperm plasma membrane remains in the ooplasm that indicate the point of fusion.

In mammals, researchers described the AR. Although, AR is now considered as a separate process, which triggers after capacitation, however, discrepancies exists as some authors believe that it was a part of the capacitation process and others considered AR as the final phase of capacitation. The AR is considered as the final prerequisite step in the sperm activation process before it gets the ability to fuse with the oocyte. It is obligatory that this reaction only occur in the presence of a rise in the intracellular calcium (Ca^{2+}) level. This increase of intracellular calcium can be achieved *in vitro* by exposing sperm to Ca^{2+} ionophores or phosphodiesterase inhibitors. An artificially high pH of 9.0-9.5 could also induce AR. Although, it is not clear whether the AR is initiated whilst the sperm is interacting with the cumulus mass, however, it is speculated that the reaction may be started in the CCs as a major component of the cumulus matrix is hyaluronic acid and the acrosome contains hyaluronidase. The AR is relatively rapid once the correct trigger signals have been received and may take 2 to 15 min *in vitro*.

Sperm-oocyte Interaction

As mentioned earlier, sperm-oocyte interaction is the earliest step towards the fertilization process, which involves the contact between the acrosome of the sperm and the ZP of the oocyte. The acrosome is membrane-bound and contains lytic agents such as proteases, sulphatases and glycosidases. On the other hand, the ZP of the oocyte is made up of protein and carbohydrates in the form of glycoprotein units that are probably stabilized by disulphide bonds. The principal types of carbohydrate found are fucose and glycoprotein units, which are synthesized by the oocyte itself.

After completion of AR, the sperm penetrate the ZP. Following penetration, the acrosome-reacted sperm passes through PVS and interacts with the sperm plasma membrane of the oocyte (oolemma). This initial interaction involves specific recognition, binding and then fusion between the sperm plasma membrane in the region of the equatorial segment and the oolemma. The fusion site on the equatorial segment may be excluded from the acrosome reaction and the sperm plasma membrane is still intact on the apical part of the postacrosomal sheath and the equatorial segment. The sperm tail is still beating outside the ZP after its head and mid-piece have entered the PVS and the equatorial segment has made an initial contact with the oolemma. The sperm head fuses with microvilli on the oolemma. The attachment of the sperm head to the ZP inevitably alters the permeability of the sperm plasma membrane, causing a transient change in the concentration of several intracellular ions.

Once fusion has occurred, the microvilli retract and draw most or the entire spermatozoon into the ooplasm. As it is incorporated into oocyte, the spermatozoon becomes immotile. Subsequently the entire spermatozoon including the tail is drawn into the ooplasm. This initiates syngamy and further development of the zygote. The exact mechanism of sperm penetration of the ZP and the complementary molecules that initiate penetration of the ZP by the sperm are not yet known. However, it is generally believed that the process involves receptor-ligand interaction between sperm-surface proteins and ZP glycoproteins. In rodents, these consist of sperm membrane galactosyltransferase and N-acetylglucosamine residues of the ZP. The receptor-ligand interaction induces the AR leading to exocytosis and release of acrosomal enzymes from the acrosomal cap. The specific sperm protein(s) responsible for sperm-oocyte interaction are yet to be fully characterized. However, four ZP proteins with variable roles in sperm-oocyte interaction have been isolated in mammals. In the mouse, ZP3 plays the primary role, while ZP1 is the primary sperm receptor in pig, rabbit and non-human primates. It is not known yet whether such a characterization is available for the goat. It is thought that the penetration of the ZP by the sperm is mediated by lytic acrosomal enzymes or by the mechanical action of the sperm itself. The latter author argues that available evidence is in favor of mechanical instead of lytic penetration.

FERTILIZATION AND EARLY EMBRYOGENESIS

Fertilization in mammals is one of the most carefully regulated cell-cell interactions in the animal body, involving two morphologically disparate cells that must recognize, bind and fuse with each other in a very specific way. It can be defined as the process of union of two germ cells, namely spermatozoon and oocyte, whereby the somatic chromosome number is restored and the development of a new and unique individual exhibiting characteristic of the same species is initiated. By transferring genetic information from one generation to the next, it ensures the immortality of an individual and by creating variation it allows evolutionary forces to operate.

As already mentioned earlier, before penetrating into the oocyte, various biochemical changes occur in the spermatozoon including capacitation, AR and sperm oocyte interaction. Following ZP penetration, a series of events take place leading to syngamy and the production of the zygote. These steps have been summarized previously. In the following three sub-sections oocyte activation, PN formation and cleavage as well as early embryonic development or embryogenesis in mammals with special reference to goat is briefly discussed.

Activation of Oocyte

Oocyte activation is the restoration of metabolic activity in the quiescent oocyte, in other word; it is the process of releasing the oocyte from the second meiotic arrest when the spermatozoon fertilizes it. It is a cell signaling event that results in events including the cortical granule reaction or Cortical Reaction (CR), decondensation of the sperm nucleus, maternal RNA recruitment, resumption of meiosis as evidenced by the extrusion of second polar body (PB-2) and later events such as PN formation and initiation of DNA synthesis and cleavage (Yanagimachi, 1994). The very early cellular event observed in all activated mammalian oocytes is an intracellular rise in Ca^{2+} concentration. In human, this increase occurs within 1 to 3 min of sperm-oocyte fusion and takes the form of a wave originating at the point of spermatozoon entry. The site of Ca^{2+} release and sequestration is thought to be the endoplasmic reticulum, where inositol 1, 4, 5-triphosphate (IP_3) receptors are present. The first Ca^{2+} transient is followed by a series of shorter Ca^{2+} transients of high amplitude (Ca^{2+} oscillations). In IVF studies, Ca^{2+} oscillations were observed in all mammalian species including goat, although their frequency is species specific. As fertilization progresses, the amplitude and frequency of the Ca^{2+} transients decrease, while the duration increases until an absolute cessation of Ca^{2+}

oscillations during entry into interphase and PN formation, several hours after sperm entry. Calcium oscillations require a continuous Ca^{2+} influx to refill endoplasmic reticulum stores. It was suggested that although a single rise is sufficient to produce activation, oscillations might be required for additional developmental events.

There are two postulated hypotheses of oocyte activation mechanism, namely 'receptor hypothesis' and sperm factor hypothesis, which describe the contribution of the spermatozoa to successful oocyte activation. In the receptor hypothesis, it is the spermatozoon interacting with the oolemma that results in oocyte activation. In this model, an oocyte surface receptor is coupled to a G-protein or a tyrosine-kinase-mediated signaling pathway and when activated by a sperm, activates phospholipase C that results in the formation of IP_3 and hence intracellular Ca^{2+} is released. The second hypothesis, which is called the sperm factor hypothesis, suggests that the release of intracellular Ca^{2+} is triggered by diffusible messenger(s) in sperm cytoplasm which enters the ooplasm following sperm-oocyte fusion. This hypothesis gained support with the development of ICSI technique where initial Ca^{2+} rise, Ca^{2+} oscillations and full oocyte activation occur after injecting sperm or sperm extract into the ooplasm.

Formation of Pronuclei

Soon after oocyte activation through sperm entry the PB-2 extrudes. The PB-2 is generally extrudes immediately adjacent to the PB-1. The mammalian sperm nucleus is packed with distinct protamines. When sperm enters the ooplasm, the sperm nuclear envelope breaks down, the protamines are lost, the sperm head enlarges in the ooplasm and chromosome or nuclear decondensation takes place a few hours by reduction of disulphide bonds between protamines by the action of glutathione. Protamines are replaced by the histones generated by the oocyte. Formation of MPN takes place simultaneously with disappearance of the nuclear membrane, decondensation of the chromosomes and reformation of the pronuclear membrane that is supported by action of growth factors. This coincides with decondensation of maternal chromatin and formation of the female PN (FPN). Usually, but not always, the MPN appears near the site of sperm entry whereas the FPN forms close to the PB-2. At this stage (pronuclear development), DNA synthesis and RNA transcription begin. The MPN and FPN then merge (syngamy) to form the zygote. This marks the end of the fertilization process and the beginning of embryonic development.

Cleavage and Early Embryogenesis

After the zygote stage, embryo enters into several mitotic divisions. The zygote or one-cell stage embryo is comparatively large, having a low nuclear to ooplasmic ratio. DNA replication and cell divisions occur without an increase in cell mass to attain a ratio similar to somatic cells. This process is referred to as cleavage. Once the diploid constitution of the species has been restored by fertilization then the cleavage commences. Cleavage of the zygote occurs by vertical division through the main axis of the oocyte from the animal to vegetal pole (animal pole refers to the site of PB extrusion and vegetal pole refers to the site of yolk reserve). The cleavage furrow often goes through the region where the PN resided at the initiation of syngamy. The resulting daughter cells are known as blastomeres. The plane of second division is also vertical and passes through the main axis but at a right angle to the initial plane of cleavage, resulting in 4 blastomeres. The third cleavage division occurs approximately at a right angle to the second, resulting in 8 blastomeres. This doubling sequence is followed on through the remainder of early cleavage.

Cleavage divisions are always mitotic and each blastomere receives full assortment of chromosomes. Although the blastomeres undergo mitosis like adult somatic cells and their number increases, however, unlike somatic cells they do not retain the size of the parent cell. The blastomeres resulting from each division are always approximately half the size of the parent blastomere. Thus, the size of a pre-implantation embryo remains the same even though the number of blastomeres increases. The embryo undergoes polarization and differences arise between the blastomeres as cleavage stage progresses. This may be due to the unequal distribution of ooplasmic components already laid down in the oocyte during oogenesis, or due to new embryonic gene transcription that results in changes to blastomeres. This way, each blastomere sets off on its own particular program of development to give rise to specific cell lines, for example, epithelium, muscle, nerve or other connective tissue.

During cleavage stage, individual blastomeres can be clearly detected when viewed under the microscope. It is important to note that the precise cleavage of zygotes and blastomeres into two equally sized daughter cells relies upon the position of the spindle and the functional activity of cytoskeletal elements. Slight variations in blastomere sizes within the same embryo are probably unimportant, but major differences may indicate defects in underlying cellular processes. Although oocyte size (diameter of ooplasm) was measured in most of the species, there was paucity of information on blastomeres size. A search of available literature revealed one paper where morphometric measurements of human ICSI-derived cleaved embryos were performed up to 4-cell stage. Using computer-controlled morphometric analysis of blastomere size, it was found that average diameter of blastomeres of 2-, 3-and 4-cell stage embryos were 80.1, 68.7 and 64.9 μm, respectively.

The diameter of ooplasm of a fully grown human oocyte or 1-cell embryo is 135 to 160 μm which is about the size of a mature goat oocyte (119-146 μm). It was found from their study that blastomere size significantly affected by degree of fragmentation and multinuclearity and that computer-assisted, multilevel analysis of blastomere size may function as a biomarker for embryo quality. The chronology of embryo development from 2-cell stage to blastocyst hatching in different species of farm animals including goat, rabbit, mouse and human has been presented in Table 3. In goat, initial and principal activations of embryonic genome (cell stage) are reported to be occurring at 2-cell and 8-cell stage, respectively.

After the embryo reaches to the morula stage it is very difficult to discern the boundaries between blastomeres as the embryo undergoes compaction in which the blastomeres flatten against each other to form intercellular junctions between them. Depending upon the species, there is a great deal of variation of the beginning of embryo compaction stage. In goat, compaction of the embryo begins at 8-cell stage. As the morula progresses to further embryonic development, some morphological change occurs and the morula progresses to blastocyst stage. The blastocyst is characterized by the formation of an outer layer of trophectoderm cells, Inner Cell Mass (ICM) and a fluid-filled cavity, known as blastocoel. In goat, the blastocoel appears at 120 h post-fertilization.

17

Plant Growth Regulators and Biotechnology

Plant growth regulators (also called plant hormones) are numerous chemical substances that profoundly influence the growth and differentiation of plant cells, tissues and organs. Plant growth regulators function as chemical messengers for intercellular communication . There are currently five recognized groups of plant hormones: auxins, gibberellins, cytokinins, abscisic acid (ABA) and ethylene. They work together coordinating the growth and development of cells. Ethylene is mainly involved in abscission and flower secscence in plants and is rarely used in plant tissue culture. In addition to the five principal growth regulators, two other groups sometimes appear to be active in regulating plant growth, the brassinosteroids and polyamines.

Plant hormones (also known as phytohormones) are chemicals that regulate plant growth, which, iare termed 'plant growth substances'.

Plant hormones are signal molecules produced within the plant, and occur in extremely low concentrations. Hormones regulate cellular processes in targeted cells locally and, moved to other locations, in other functional parts of the plant. Hormones also determine the formation of flowers, stems,leaves, the shedding of leaves, and the development and ripening of fruit. Plants, unlike animals, lack glands that produce and secrete hormones. Instead, each cell is capable of producing hormones. Plant hormones shape the plant, affecting seed growth, time of flowering, the sex of flowers,senescence of leaves, and fruits. They affect which tissues grow upward and which grow downward, leaf formation and stem growth, fruit development and ripening, plant longevity, and even plant death. Hormones are vital to plant growth, and, lacking them, plants would be mostly a mass of undifferentiated cells. So they are also known as growth factors or growth hormones. The term 'Phytohormone' was coined by Thimann in 1948.

Phytohormones are found not only in higher plants, but in algae too, showing similar functions, and in microorganisms, like fungi and bacteria, but, in this case, they play no hormonal or other immediate physiological role in the producing organism and can, thus, be regarded as secondary metabolites.

The word hormone is derived from Greek, meaning *set in motion*. Plant hormones affect gene expression and transcription levels, cellular division, and growth. They are naturally produced within plants, though very similar chemicals are produced by fungi and bacteria that can also affect plant growth. A large number of related chemical compounds are synthesized by humans. They are used to regulate the growth of cultivated plants, weeds, and in vitro-grown plants and plant cells; these manmade compounds are called Plant Growth Regulators or PGRs for short. Early in the study of plant hormones, "phytohormone" was the commonly used term, but its use is less widely applied now.

Plant hormones are not nutrients, but chemicals that in small amounts promote and influence the growth, development, and differentiation of cells and tissues. The biosynthesis of plant hormones within plant tissues is often diffuse and not always localized. Plants lack glands to produce and store hormones, because, unlike animals - which have two circulatory systems (lymphatic andcardiovascular) powered by a heart that moves fluids around the body - plants use more passive means to move chemicals around the plant. Plants utilize simple chemicals as hormones, which move more easily through the plant's tissues. They are often produced and used on a local basis within the plant body. Plant cells produce hormones that affect even different regions of the cell producing the hormone.

Hormones are transported within the plant by utilizing four types of movements. For localized movement, cytoplasmic streaming within cells and slow diffusion of ions and molecules between cells are utilized. Vascular tissues are used to move hormones from one part of the plant to another; these include sieve tubes or phloem that move sugars from the leaves to the roots and flowers, and xylem that moves water and mineral solutes from the roots to the foliage.

Not all plant cells respond to hormones, but those cells that do are programmed to respond at specific points in their growth cycle. The greatest effects occur at specific stages during the cell's life, with diminished effects occurring before or after this period. Plants need hormones at very specific times during plant growth and at specific locations. They also need to disengage the effects that hormones have when they are no longer needed. The production of hormones occurs very often at sites of active growth within the meristems, before cells have fully differentiated. After production, they are sometimes moved to other parts of the plant, where they cause an immediate effect; or they can be stored in cells to be released later. Plants use different pathways to regulate internal hormone quantities and moderate their effects; they can regulate the amount of chemicals used to biosynthesize hormones. They can store them in cells, inactivate them, or cannibalise already-formed hormones by conjugating them with carbohydrates, amino acids, or peptides. Plants can also break down hormones chemically, effectively destroying them. Plant hormones frequently regulate the concentrations of other plant hormones. Plants also move hormones around the plant diluting their concentrations.

The concentration of hormones required for plant responses are very low (10^{-6} to 10^{-5} mol/L). Because of these low concentrations, it has been very difficult to study plant hormones, and only since the late 1970s have scientists been able to start piecing together their effects and relationships to plant physiology. Much of the early work on plant hormones involved studying plants that were genetically deficient in one or involved the use of tissue-cultured plants grown *in vitro* that were subjected to differing ratios of hormones, and the resultant growth compared. The earliest scientific observation and study dates to the 1880s; the determination and observation of plant hormones and their identification was spread-out over the next 70 years.

CLASSES OF PLANT HORMONES

In general, it is accepted that there are five major classes of plant hormones, some of which are made up of many different chemicals that can vary in structure from one plant to the next. The chemicals are each grouped together into one of these classes based on their structural similarities and on their effects on plant physiology. Other plant hormones and growth regulators are not easily grouped into these classes; they exist naturally or are synthesized by humans or other organisms, including chemicals that inhibit plant growth or interrupt the physiological processes within plants. Each class has positive as well as inhibitory functions, and most often work in tandem with each other, with varying ratios of one or more interplaying to affect growth regulation.

The five major classes are:

Auxins

Auxins stimulate cell elongation and influence a host of other developmental responses, such as root initiation, vascular differentiation, tropic responses, apical dominance and the development of auxiliary buds, flowers and fruits. Auxins are synthesized in the stem and root apices and transported through the plant axis. The principal auxin in plants is indole-3-acetic acid (IAA). Several other indole derivatives, all as precursors to IAA, are known to express auxin activity, probably by converting to IAA in the tissue. Auxins in plant tissue culture are used to induce callus from explants , and cause root and shoot morphogenesis . Auxins are often most effective in eliciting their effects when combined with cytokinins.

Cytokinins

Cytokinins are able to stimulate cell division and induce shoot bud formation in tissue culture. They usually act as antagonists to auxins. (Cytokinins are N6 substituted derivatives of the nitrogenous purine base adenine.) Cytokinins most used in tissue culture include zeatin, adenine, 6-(g,g-dimethylallylamino) purine (2 iP) and kinetin. Cytoknins often inhibit embryogenesis and root induction.

Gibberellins

The main effect of gibberellins in plants is to cause stem elongation and flowering. They are also prominently involved in mobilization of endosperm reserves during early embryo growth and seed germination. Gibberellins are an extensive chemical family based on the ent-gibberellane structure. There exit over 80 different gibberellin compounds in plants but only giberrellic acid (GA3) and GA4+7 are often used in plant tissue culture. In tissue culture, gibberellins are used to induce organogenesis, particularly adventitious root formation.

Abscisic Acid

Abscisic acid (ABA) in plants is a terpenoid involved primarily in regulating seed germination, inducing storage protein synthesis and modulating water stress. In plant tissue culture, it is used to help somatic embryogenesis, particularly during maturation and germination.

Ethylene

Ethylene is a simple gaseous hydrocarbon with the chemical structure $H_2C{=}CH_2$. Ethylene is apparently not required for normal vegetative growth. However, it can have a significant impact on development of root and shoots. Usually, ethylene is not used in plant tissue culture.

PLANT GROWTH REGULATORS AND BIOTECHNOLOGY

Introduction

A plant growth regulator is an organic compound, either natural or synthetic, that modifies or controls one or more specific physiological processes within a plant. If the compound is produced within the plant it is called a plant hormone. A plant regulator is defined by the Environmental Protection Agency as "any substance or mixture of substances intended, through physiological action, to accelerate or retard the rate of growth or maturation, or otherwise alter the behavior of plants or their produce. Additionally, plant regulators are characterized by their low rates of application; high application rates of the same compounds often are considered herbicidal". Upon reading these descriptions, it strikes me that the definition is likely to be broadened, particularly as it relates to the EPA, as we consider changes that can be made through the modern methods of genetic engineering.

Exactly how do changes made through genetic engineering compare to classical methods of genetic manipulation? An example that contrasts the two approaches is helpful in understanding the differences and similarities between these two methods. Both classical and molecular approaches were used to increase the sugar content of the commercially available tomato. This work was made possible because certain wild tomato relatives, although unlike commercial varieties in appearance, have a higher sugar content. The plan was to transfer the higher sugar content of the wild tomato to the domesticated tomato and leave behind its smaller size, lower yield and bitter taste.

The classical breeding approach accomplished this goal through the mixing of genetic information from the two parents upon sexual exchange. After many cycles of backcrossing to the parental commercial variety, most information from the wild parent was eliminated but still some remained. In that uncharacterized bit of genetic material was the information for the sweetness characteristic, but also the information for an unexpected characteristic.

The newly developed variety had lowered fertility. This is because the breeder did not have total control over exactly what information was retained in the new tomatoes. They tried to minimize the unwanted information from the wild species, but despite this effort they were unable to eliminate everything but the sweetness characteristic. They ended up with a new variety that still had a substantial input from the wild species and in that information was the sweetness characteristic and something that caused lower fertility.

In the genetic engineering approach, the researchers found a single piece of genetic information that when removed would slow the breakdown of sugar. Through genetic engineering technologies, they were able to build that characteristic into the commercial variety and stop sugar degradation in the commercial tomato. They did this by making a very specific change in a single gene. They changed nothing else about the tomato. Additionally, in contrast to classical breeding, they knew precisely what information they were adding.

Another difference with this approach is that, although in this case the changed information came from the tomato species itself, it would have been possible to take that new genetic information from another plant species, a microbe or any other organism for that matter. In addition with this approach it is possible to "define" precisely when and where this newly acquired information will be made by using characterized regulatory regions that function when and where they are need

How is Biotechnology impacting agriculture?

What is being done with the new technology of biotechnology in the arena of plants. Today, there are products in the field and the marketplace. The new technologies of genetic engineering can result in more environmentally friendly plant pest-protection, foods with enhanced nutrition, more accurate and sensitive diagnostics, foods with improved processing and marketing characteristics, better and more efficient medical delivery, new methods for removing contaminants from soils and waters, and creation of products that are presently being made from nonrenewable resources. Many of these changes might be considered under the broad definition of a "plant growth regulator".

While products of this technology once were confined to the research laboratory, this is no longer the case. These and other new crops represent a substantial percentage of actual production acreage in the U.S. In 1998 50% of the cotton acreage, 30% of the soybean and 20% of the maize acreage in the U.S. were genetically engineered. In the U.S. some 60 million acres of G.E. crops were planted in 1998 and the projections for 1999 are that this number will increase, with a wider variety of products available to farmers and present in the marketplace..

In the short term and long term, what might some of these products be?

Pest Control

Herbicide tolerance. A major agricultural advance occurred with the identification of selective herbicides that can be used to eliminate weeds without affecting the crop plant. But achieving complete selectivity has been problematic for many crops. An alternative to finding new selective herbicides is to genetically engineer the crop to resist existing herbicides. The engineered mechanisms can include modifications in the site of action of the herbicide, in its detoxification or in the uptake and translocation of the herbicide to its site of action.

Such crops represent the first and most frequent application of biotechnology to agriculture. Of the total of 5900 permits and notifications issued through the end of 1998 by the USDA Animal and Plant Health Inspection Service (APHIS), 27% or 1569 permits were for herbicide-tolerant crop. In many cases, the herbicide tolerance is based on a modified site of action through the use of mutant or altered forms of the target protein. In these instances, the altered enzyme must be properly compartmentalized (chloroplast, cytoplasm, nucleus) and it must be assembled in a metabolically active form at its target location.

This is the case with glyphosate where the herbicide blocks a pathway that leads to the synthesis of several amino acids; blockage of this pathway leads to starvation for amino acids. Genetic engineering strategies have focused mainly on using mutant target enzymes that are resistant to glyphosate. A similar type of strategy is used with another group of herbicides, the imadazolinones and sulfonylureas, which also inhibit a key step in the biosynthesis of a different set of amino acids. Other approaches to engineering herbicide resistance involve the introduction of genes for enzymes that degrade and detoxify the herbicides.

One example in this category is bromoxynil in which resistance was engineered through the introduction of a bacterial gene that codes for an enzyme that converts bromoxynil to an inactive metabolite. Another example is glufosinate. Resistance to this herbicide can be engineered using a bacterial gene that acetylates and inactivates the herbicide. The last example is 2,4-D, a plant hormone that causes arrested development. Again, genetic engineering strategies employ a bacterial gene that encodes an enzyme that degrades 2,4-D. Cotton has been engineered to be resistant to this herbicide in order to prevent crop loss due to spray drift.

Although progress in engineering herbicide-resistant crops has been rapid, there are some problems with this approach. Technical problems include finding an effective strategy for engineering resistance and identifying the target site of the herbicide or a degradative or inactivating factor. In addition the resistance factor must be engineered to be expressed in the proper place and in sufficient levels. The herbicides for which tolerance is being engineered are generally low-use rate, low-toxicity, rapid-turnover herbicides.

Despite this, there are some environmental issues which, although not unique to genetically engineered varieties, must be taken into consideration.

- Generation of herbicide-tolerant weeds due to monoherbicide application. Frequent and long-term application of a single herbicide becomes more likely because of the use of specific herbicide-tolerant varieties. The tendency of the industry to engineer a large number of crop species with tolerance to a single herbicide will create pressure for this to occur.

- Transfer of resistance genes to related weeds. Many crops in which tolerance is being developed do not have weedy relatives here; exceptions are sugarbeet, certain cucurbits, radish, canola, oats, and carrots. As seed is moved internationally, however, the possibility of outcrossing with wild relatives in centers of diversity will increase; control measures should be instituted. In general, however, unless pollen travels over long distances to pollinate weeds located far away, this problem will be minimal.
- Encroachment of weeds not affected by the herbicide, i.e. weed shift. Development of elite germplasm resistant to a single herbicide, without comparable varieties resistant to other herbicides with dissimilar modes of action, could lead to an exacerbation of the weed shift problem.

Insect Resistance

A now standard method for engineering insect resistance in crop species is the use of the toxin genes from Bacillus thuringiensis; this is the basis for Bollgard cotton and the commercially available maize that is corn borer-resistant. These toxins are activated by cleavage in the midgut of insects; however, making engineered toxins that are effective against certain insects has not been straightforward. For example for a certain insect pest of alfalfa, Spodoptera armyworm, the situation was not straightforward. It required some extensive in vitro testing of synthetic toxins. In the end a specific synthetic delta-endotoxin gene was identified, which when expressed in optimum amounts in alfalfa, shows evidence of protection against the Egyptian cotton leafworm (*Spodoptera littoralis*) and the beet armyworm (Spodoptera exigua). In other cases new types of Bt's are being discovered and also some insecticidal compounds from other microbial species.

Viral Resistance

Infection with viruses is a problem with many crop species; however the sources of natural resistance are limited and chemical protection is not effective in many instances. A standard method for engineering viral resistance is the use of the coat protein gene. This approach has been used successfully for many viruses in many different plant species and the Freedom II squash was released in the marketplace last year. In the coming year genetically engineered papaya will enter the marketplace. This crop results from efforts to protect it against papaya ringspot virus, which had devastated certain production areas. Because there are limitations to the coat protein approach in terms of uniform applicability and broad protection to related viruses, it is necessary to develop alternative strategies that complement or replace the coat protein strategy.

Fungal and Bacterial Resistance

Methods for protecting against fungal pathogens involve the identification of natural plant protection compounds that, when expressed in higher amounts in appropriate tissues of the host plant, can lessen fungal damage. These are sometimes compounds deriving from secondary metabolic pathways. Work on compounds, such as these, can lead to approaches where increased or broader-spectrum disease resistance can result from modifying expression levels or timing of unmodified secondary metabolite (e.g. phytoalexin) or modifying the phytoalexins themselves to create new phytoalexins with novel activities.

In addition natural defense genes have been isolated for resistance to various pathogens in different plant species Of the first three such genes that were isolated, it was discovered that they share common domains. Understanding these domains and their function, it will be possible to devise plant protection strategies using these genes that provides broad spectrum resistance against a variety of pathogens.

Nematode resistance

A variety of approaches have been utilized to protect against damage from nematodes. Regulatory regions have been identified which are uniquely engaged when the nematode burrows into the root; simple physical damage of the root is not sufficient to turn on the promoter. This regulatory region can then be hooked to nematicidal proteins, which can then be delivered to the nematode at its precise site of attack. Such nematicidal proteins include several different proteinase inhibitors and lectins, which act in some cases synergitically to interfere with the sexual development of the nematode.

In addition, recently a natural resistance gene was isolated from tomato and found to provide protection in engineered plants to not only nematodes but also aphids, which have an entirely different mode of attack and damage pathway. It was found, after comparison of the gene to other natural resistance genes (fungal, viral and bacterial) from other species, that the nematode resistance gene shared common domains with these other genes, again pointing to the potential universality of these mechanisms and opening the door for creating some engineered proteins with widespread efficacy.

Harvest and Post-harvest Characteristics

Another arena in which we have seen product enter the marketplace and in which much research is being conducted relates to harvest and post-harvest characteristics. Two different approaches to delayed ripening have been commercialized. The approach of the Flavr Savr tomato utilized a technique allowing growers and producers extra time to pick and deliver tomatoes to the marketplace by interfering with polygalacturonase synthesis, an enzyme involved in pectin deposition. In this case the ripening process was delayed by several days but was not halted. In another approach to interfering with the ripening process, researchers stopped the ripening process completely by interfering with the production of ethylene, which is essential to ripening. By this process it is possible to leave a tomato on the vine for up to 100 days past the time when it would ordinarily be ripe and, once it is picked, to ripen the tomato on demand by exposure to ethylene.

Another post-harvest characteristic, which is the focus of genetic engineering technologies is the achievement of more uniform ripening. This was first accomplished with the cherry tomato, but the basic approach is also being attempted with processing tomatoes in order to achieve less waste and aid harvesting. This approach involves the manipulation of genes involved in slowing the degradation of ethylene.

Agronomic Traits

Nitrogen fixation and utilization. Fundamental work on the process of nitrogen fixation has been pursued for decades. With the advent of molecular techniques, pace of that research has increased and has broadened to include fundamental studies on the nature of the plant-microbe interaction necessary for nodule formation and nitrogen fixation. Work on the bacterium itself has resulted in engineered Rhizobium strains that have increased rates of nitrogen fixation in limited field trials, but those strains have not yet been released for widespread use by the EPA. Studies focused on understanding and manipulating the host range of nitrogen-fixing bacteria are also underway with the expectation of being able to extend the range of crop species that can have productive commensal relationships with bacterial nitrogen fixers.

In addition to looking at improving the efficiency of nitrogen fixation, fundamental work aimed at understanding nitrogen fertilizer use efficiency is also underway. This work hopes to lead to engineered plants, e.g. wheat and corn, that more efficiently use applied fertilizers.

Male Sterility

The development of hybrid varieties that result in increased yields of crop species has been a tedious process, requiring in many cases the manual detasseling of the male parent to prevent self-fertilization. Large scale production of hybrid seed, however, required more efficient mechanisms to suppress pollen production. Classical geneticists have identified naturally occurring male-sterile lines of some crops that were used for commercial seed production. Such strategies also required the identification of "restorer lines" that could restore male fertility by counteracting the genes that cause male-sterility. This is more easily accomplished with some crops than with others.

With the advent of genetic engineering, it became possible to develop strategies to create male sterile plants. These strategies made use of the fact that one could identify regulatory sequences that would lead to very specific tissue expression. In one strategy a promoter was identified that only drove expression in the inner layer of the pollen sac, the tapetum. Linked to this promoter was a bacterial enzyme, which degrades RNA, thereby interrupting the development pollen grains. A restorer of fertility was also identified; this protein is a chemical coupler of the RNA-degrading enzyme; the tight coupling of these two proteins inactivates the RNA-degrading enzyme, thus restoring fertility. This approach was used in canola first and is now being attempted in a variety of different crop and vegetable species.

Technology Protection System or "Terminator Technology"

This approach is a relatively new one patented by a small cotton company, Delta and Pine Land, and the USDA; the Monsanto Corporation has made a bid to buy DP&L, but that deal is still awaiting approval by the Department of Justice. The fundamental idea with this technology is to prevent a plant from reproducing itself by interfering with seed development, thus insuring that the user of the seed cannot replant a field without repurchasing the seed, thereby protecting the company's investment in developing the variety.

The system works through the interplay of three introduced genes. One of these genes leads to the production of a toxin that kills the seed in the final stage of development. This gene is initially interrupted by a stretch of DNA between the toxin gene itself and the regulatory region or promoter that is responsible for its synthesis. This gene configuration can then be transplanted or crossed with another genetically engineered plant that produces a scissor-like enzyme, capable of removing the segment in the toxin gene, thereby activating it and causing the seed to die. The third component of the system is a repressor gene that prevents the synthesis of the scissor-like enzyme. If all three components are present, the terminator technology is dormant and the seed is fertile. If the seeds are then treated with a stimulator, in one case an antibiotic called tetracycline, this compound can then block repressor of the scissor-like protein and this gene product can then snip out the DNA that is preventing the syn

Value-added Products

There is another area that does not involve plant growth regulators but is being intensely pursued by both the public and private sectors. This relates to the improvement of existing plant products, ones that already exist but for which new or improved functions can be identified that increase the value of the product.

An example would be specialty oils from rape or soybean, which are designed to have improved heat stability. Another example would be the genetic engineering of sugarbeet to produce fructans, a sweet, no-calorie sugar substitute.

An intriguing application is in the area of functional foods or neutriceuticals. This line of foods is based on the fact that we can now identify in many cases natural products in foods that can either cause adverse human condition or prevent disease. Examples of those products focused on factors in foods that cause disease or undesirable pharmacological effects include ameliorating the allergenic potential of foods, such as wheat, milk and peanut or removing caffeine from coffee.

In the category of natural products that prevent disease, there are many examples. Transgenic potatoes are being created which produce high quantities of

GAD, an enzyme believed to be involved in the prevention of type II juvenile diabetes. Researchers have identified an element in grapes that increases blood flow in blood vessels; grapes could be engineered to increase the level of such an element. Several groups are coming up with margarine and oils, based on natural plant sterols and stanols, that are not only "low in choles

18

Photosynthesis, Respiration and Transpiration

The three major functions that are basic to plant growth and development are:

- **Photosynthesis** – The process of capturing light energy and converting it to sugar energy, in the presence of chlorophyll using carbon dioxide (CO_2) and water (H_2O).
- **Respiration** – The process of metabolizing (burning) sugars to yield energy for growth, reproduction, and other life processes.
- **Transpiration** – The loss of water vapor through the stomata of leaves .

PHOTOSYNTHESIS

A primary difference between plants and animals is the plant's ability to manufacture its own food. In ***photosynthesis,*** carbon dioxide from the air and water from the soil react with the sun's energy to form ***photosynthates*** (sugars, starches, carbohydrates, and proteins) and release oxygen as a byproduct [Fig. 18.1]

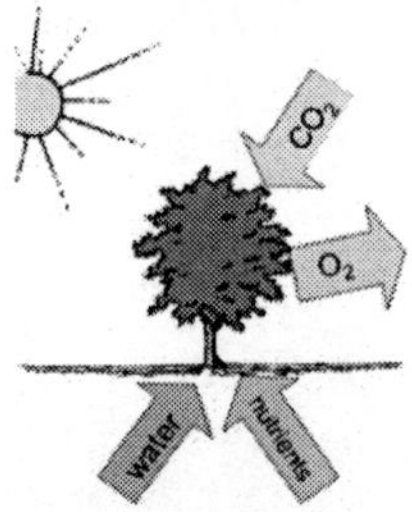

Fig. 18.1. In photosynthesis, the plant uses water and nutrients from the soil, and carbon dioxide from the air, with the sun's energy to create photosynthates. Oxygen is releases as a byproduct.

Photosynthesisliterally means *to put together with light.* It occurs only in the ***chloroplasts,*** tiny sub-cellular structures contained in the cells of leaves and green stems. A simple chemical equation for photosynthesis is given as follows:

carbon dioxide + water + light energy = glucose + oxygen

$$6CO_2 + 6H_2O + \text{light energy} = C_6H_{12}O_6 + 6O_2$$

This process is directly dependent on the supply of water, light, and carbon dioxide. Limiting any **one** of the factors on the left side of the equation (carbon dioxide, water, or light) can limit photosynthesis regardless of the availability of the other factors. An implication of drought or severe restrictions on landscape irrigation is a reduction in photosynthesis and thus a decrease in plant vigor and growth.

In a tightly closed greenhouse there can be very little fresh air infiltration and carbon dioxide levels can become limiting, thus limiting plant growth. In the winter, many large commercial greenhouses provide supplemental carbon dioxide to stimulate plant growth.

The rate of photosynthesis is somewhat temperature dependent. For example, in tomatoes, when temperatures rise above 96°F the rate of food used by respiration rises above the rate of which food is manufactured by photosynthesis. Plant growth comes to a stop and produce loses its sweetness. Most other plants are similar.

RESPIRATION

In ***respiration***, plants (and animals) convert the sugars (photosynthates) back into energy for growth and other life processes (metabolic processes). The chemical equation for respiration shows that the photosynthates are combined with oxygen releasing energy, carbon dioxide, and water. A simple chemical equation for respiration is given below. Notice that the equation for respiration is the opposite of that for photosynthesis.

glucose + oxygen = energy + carbon dioxide + water

$C_6H_{12}O_6 + 6O_2 = \text{energy} + 6CO_2 + 6H_2O$

Chemically speaking, the process is similar to the **oxidation** that occurs as wood is burned, producing heat. When compounds combine with oxygen, the process is often referred to as "burning", for example, athlete's "burn" energy (sugars) as they exercise. The harder they exercise, the more sugars they burn so the more oxygen they need. That is why at full speed, they are breathing very fast. Athletes take up oxygen through their lungs. Plants take up oxygen through the stomata in their leaves and through their roots.

Again, respiration is the burning of photosynthates for energy to grow and to do the internal "work" of living. It is very important to understand that both plants and animals (including microorganisms) need oxygen for respiration. This is why overly wet or saturated soils are detrimental to root growth and function, as well as the decomposition processes carried out by microorganisms in the soil.

The same principles regarding limiting factors are valid for both photosynthesis and respiration.

Comparison of photosynthesis and respiration

Photosynthesis	Respiration
Produces sugars from light energy	Burns sugars for energy
Stores energy	Energy is released
Occurs only in cells with chloroplasts	Occurs in most cells

Photosynthesis	Respiration
Oxygen is produced	Oxygen is used
Water is used	Water is produced
Carbon dioxide is used	Carbon dioxide is produced
Requires light	Occurs in dark and light

TRANSPIRATION

Water in the roots is pulled through the plant by **transpiration** (loss of water vapor through the stomata of the leaves). Transpiration uses about 90% of the water that enters the plant. The other 10% is an ingredient in photosynthesis and cell growth.

Transpiration serves three essential roles:

- **Movement of minerals** up from the root (in the xylem) and sugars (products of photosynthesis) throughout the plant (in the phloem). Water serves as both the solvent and the avenue of transport.
- **Cooling** - 80% of the cooling effect of a shade tree is from the evaporative cooling effects of transpiration. This benefits both plants and humans.
- **Turgor pressure** – Water maintains the turgor pressure in cells much like air inflates a balloon, giving the non-woody plant parts form. Turgidity is important so the plant can remain stiff and upright and gain a competitive advantage when it comes to light. Turgidity is also important for the functioning of the guard cells, which surround the stomata and regulate water loss and carbon dioxide uptake. Turgidity also is the force that pushes roots through the soill.

Water movement in plants is also a factor of osmotic pressure and capillary action. **Osmotic pressure** is defined as water flowing through a permeable membrane in the direction of higher salt concentrations. Water will continue to flow in the direction of the highest salt concentration until the salts have been diluted to the point that the concentrations on both sides of the membrane are equal.

A classic example is pouring salt on a slug. Because the salt concentration outside the slug is highest, the water from inside the slug's body crosses the membrane that is his "skin". The slug becomes dehydrated and dies. Envision this same scenario the next time you gargle with salt water to kill the bacteria that are causing your sore throat.

Fertilizer burn and dog urine spots in a lawn are examples of salt problems. The salt level in the soil's water becomes higher than in the roots, and water flows from the roots into the soil's water in an effort to dilute the concentration. So what should you do if you accidentally apply too much fertilizer to your lawn?

Capillary action refers to the chemical forces that move water as a continuous film rather than as individual molecules. Water molecules in the soil and in the plant cling to one another and are reluctant to let go. You have observed this as water forms a meniscus on a coin or the lip of a glass. Thus when one molecule is drawn up the plant stem, it pulls another one along with it. These forces that link water molecules together can be overcome by gravity.

19

Isomerism, Titrimetry and Volumetry

Isomerism, the existence of molecules that have the same numbers of the same kinds of atoms (and hence the same formula) but differ in chemical and physical properties. The roots of the word *isomer* are Greek - *isos* plus *meros*, or "equal parts". Stated colloquially, isomers are chemical compounds that have the same parts but are nonetheless not the same. To make a crude analogy, two bracelets, each consisting of five red and five green beads, could be arranged in many different isomeric forms, depending on the order of the colours. Each bracelet would have the same parts - that is, the five red and five green beads - but each variation would be different. One could also imagine combinations of those same beads in which pendant chains were attached to a bracelet in a variety of ways. One might imagine two bracelets of the same red-green order but with identical chains attached in different orientations. Such structures also would be analogous to isomers. In a more subtle analogy, one's hands can be seen as isomeric. Each hand possesses the same kinds of fingers, but a right hand can never be superimposed perfectly on a left hand; they are different.

Timing and energy are also factors in isomerism. Molecules are mobile entities, undergoing all sorts of rotational motions that change their shapes, and those motions require energy. Thus, some molecules can be the same on one timescale or set of energy conditions but different, or isomeric, on others. Finally, an isomer must be an energy minimum; it must lie in an energy well.

There are two general types of isomers. Constitutional isomers are molecules of different connectivity - analogous to simple bracelets in which the order of red and green beads is different. The second type is stereoisomers. In stereoisomers the connectivity is the same, but the parts are oriented differently in space.

CONSTITUTIONAL ISOMERS

Isomers that differ in connectivity are called constitutional (sometimes structural) isomers. They have the same parts, but those parts are attached to each other differently. The bracelets of red and green beads mentioned above are analogous to constitutional isomers. The simplest hydrocarbons - methane (CH_4), ethane (CH_3CH_3), and propane ($CH_3CH_2CH_3$) - have no constitutional isomers, as there is no other way to connect the carbons and hydrogens of these molecules consistent with the tetravalency of carbon and the univalency of hydrogen.

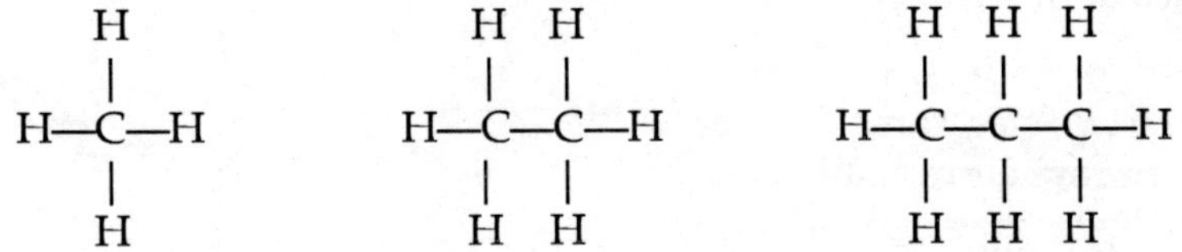

methane (CH_4) ethane (C_2H_6) propane (C_3H_8)

However, there are two different butanes, C_4H_{10}, and these two molecules, called butane and isobutane, are constitutional isomers. They are different molecules with different chemical and physical properties. Butane has its four carbon atoms bonded in a continuous chain.

The number of possible constitutional isomers increases greatly with the number of available atoms. There are only two butanes, but there are three pentanes (C_5H_{12}), 18 octanes (C_8H_{18}), and no fewer than 366,319 constitutional isomers of the hydrocarbon containing 20 carbon atoms and 42 hydrogens.

STEREOISOMERS

Generally defined, stereoisomers are isomers that have the same composition (that is, the same parts) but that differ in the orientation of those parts in space. There are two kinds of stereoisomers: enantiomers and diastereomers. Enantiomers are mirror images, like one's hands, and diastereomers are everything else. However, as is stated above, timescale and energy are important. In order to understand these considerations, it is helpful first to consider a special kind of stereoisomer, the conformational isomer.

CONFORMATIONAL ISOMERS

Methane (CH_4) is a molecule that is a perfect tetrahedron, and so it is commonly said that no isomerism is possible with methane. However, thecarbon-hydrogen bonds of methane constantly vibrate and bend, so that on very short timescales an apparent isomerism can be said to exist. But these structures are not energy minima, and so they do not qualify as isomers.

As complexity increases, isomerism induced by rotations about bonds becomes a bigger factor. In ethane (CH_3CH_3), for example, both carbons are approximately tetrahedral. Thus, there are two limiting structures—staggered ethane, in which the carbon-hydrogen bonds are as far apart as possible, and eclipsed ethane, in which the bonds are as close as possible. These two structures are certainly not the same. Perhaps the best view in which to see the difference is a "Newman projection" (named after American chemist Melvin Newman) in which one sights down the carbon-carbon bond and focuses on the positions of the six hydrogens. In a

Newman projection, the front carbon is located at the intersection of the bonds to the three attached hydrogen atoms, and the back carbon is an exploded circle, with the attached bonds emanating from the circumference of the circle.

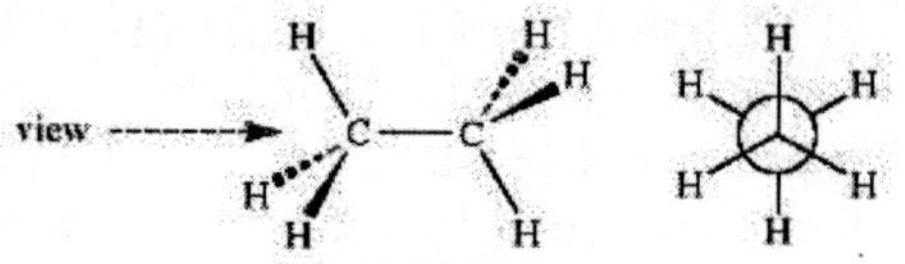

staggered ethane

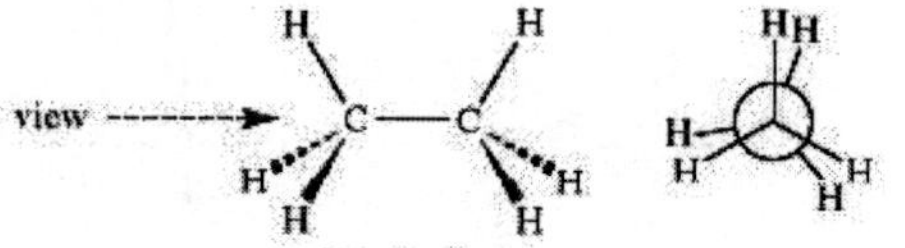

eclipsed ethane

Immediately, questions of energy arise: Which of the two structures is lower in energy and therefore more stable? The staggered form is lower in energy because in the eclipsed form electrons in carbon-hydrogen bonds on the opposite side of the carbon-carbon bond repel each other. The strain that this repulsion creates increases the potential energy of the eclipsed form. The energy difference is not large, about 3 kilocalories per mole (kcal/mol).

If one plots the energy change as ethane rotates around the carbon-carbon bond, another difficulty is revealed. Like the vibrational and rotational "isomers" of methane mentioned above, eclipsed ethane (E) is not even an energy minimum; it is an energy maximum, a transition state between two staggered ethanes (S). Therefore, ethane, like methane, really has only one form.

If substitutions are made in the ethane molecule—for instance, exchanging some of the hydrogen atoms for deuterium atoms to make 1,2-dideuterioethane—isomeric staggered forms become possible. These staggered forms, called "anti" and "gauche," of 1,2-dideuterioethane are different but are interconverted through rotations around the central carbon-carbon bond and are called "conformational isomers."

Whether these different ethanes can be separated depends only on the amount of energy necessary to convert one into the other—that is, to rotate the molecule about the carbon-carbon bond. In the case of 1,2-dideuterioethane, the energy barrier separating the conformational isomers is only 3 kcal/mol, far too low to make them separable under normal conditions.

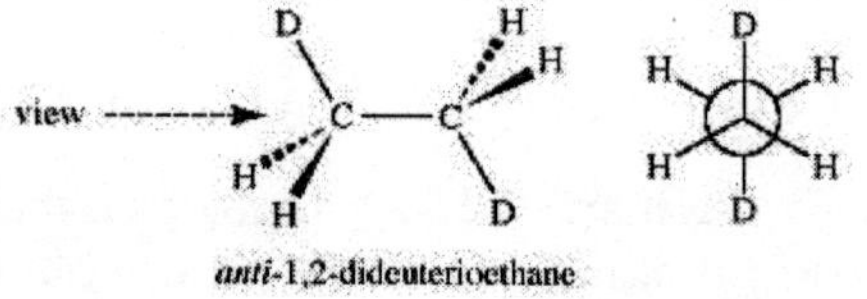

anti-1,2-dideuterioethane

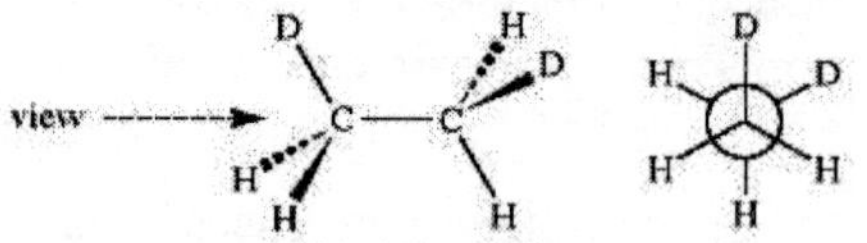

gauche-1,2-dideuterioethane

Isobutane has no conformational isomers, but butane is closely analogous to 1,2-dideuterioethane, in that a pair of anti and gauche conformational isomers is possible for that molecule. Because a methyl group (CH_3) is much larger than hydrogen or deuterium, the plot of energy versus rotational angle is more complex for butane than it is for ethane or 1,2-dideuterioethane.

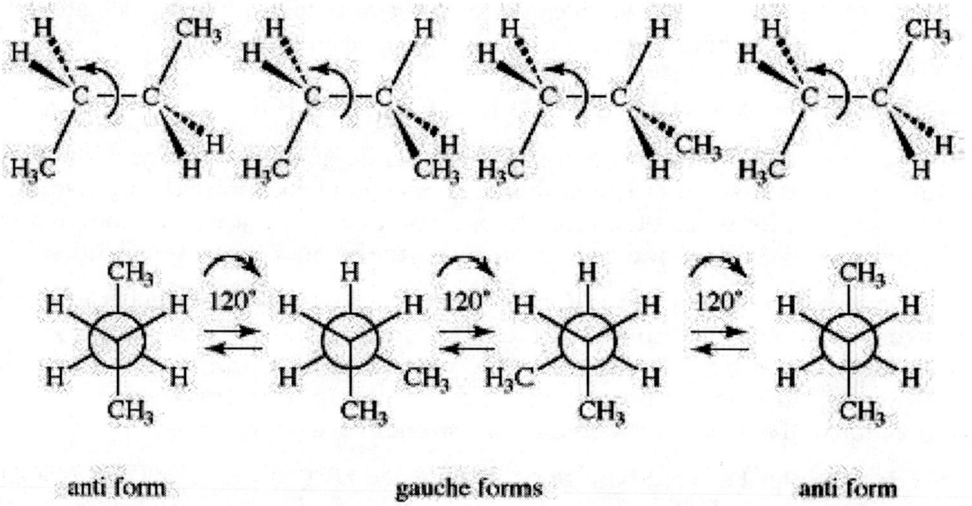

VOLUMETRIC ANALYSIS

Volumetric analysis is a quantitative analytical method. Volumetric analysis is a method in which the amount of a substance is determined by measuring the volume that it occupies and the volume of a second substance that combines with the first in known proportions. This is also called titrimetric analysis or titration because volume is an important factor in titration.It's a laboratory method of quantitative chemical analysis which is used to determine the unknown concentration of an analyte. Titration is a volumetric analysis because it's based on the measurement of volumes.

One standard solution is used which is solution of a reagent, also called titrent or titrator. A known volume of titrent reacts with a solution of analyte or titrand to determine its concentration. Thus, the process involves measuring the volumes of two solutions which react to each other.**The basic principles of volumetric analysis are given as below:**

1. The one solution to be analyzed contains an unknown amount of chemicals.
2. The reagent of known concentration reacts with chemical of unknown amount in the presence of an indicator to show the end-point. This is the point which shows the completion of the reaction.
3. The volumes are measured by a titration which completes the reaction between reagent and solution.
4. The volume and concentration of reagent used in the titration give the amount of reagent in moles.
5. The amount of unknown chemical in the measured volume of solution is calculated by using the mole ratio of the equation.

6. The amount of unknown chemical in the original sample is calculated by the amount of unknown chemical in the measured volume.

VOLUMETRIC ANALYSIS ACID-BASE TITRATION

The organic compounds containing the acidic group are analyzed by this titration. This is based on the neutralization reaction between acid and base. An acid-base indicator is used to detect the end point which indicates the completion of reaction between acid and base by changing the color of the mixed solution.

The selection of indicator is very important in acid-base titration because the equivalence point is determined by the stoichiometric of the reaction whereas the endpoint is measured by changing the color from indicator. The reaction is neutralized but it is not necessary to come to the **end point at pH = 7**. The completion of the reaction depends on the strength of acid and base.

For example: The acid-base titration between HCl (strong acid) and NaOH (strong base) in which phenolphthalein indicator is used.

Chemical reaction - $HCl + NaOH \rightarrow NaCl + H_2O$

Similar titration between NH_4OH (weak base) and HCl (strong acid) in which methyl orange is used as indicator.

$NH_4OH + HCl \rightarrow NH_4Cl + H_2O$

Steps for Acid base Titration

To determine the concentration of HCl, we take 20 ml of HCl and neutralize it with 0.150M of NaOH.

The steps for titration process are given below:

1. The titrant, NaOH solution of known concentration, is added from the burette.
2. 20ml HCl is taken in volumetric flask with the help of pipette and 2-3 drop of phenolphthalein indicator is added.
3. The solution is color less due to the acidic medium.
4. The solution of NaOH is added to the HCl drop by drop. As it comes in the contact with HCl acid, the color of solution becomes pink which quickly disappears. This is due to the formation of OH- ions from NaOH which reacts with indicator and changes the color. The solution becomes color less again due to the neutralization of OH^- ions with H^+ ions (from HCl).
5. After adding more NaOH, the equivalence point of titration is reached when the equal number of OH^- ions and H^+ ions react. At this point the pH of the solution in the flask is equal to 7 and the indicator is colorless.
6. After this, adding more NaOH drop by drop in the solution makes the solution pink from color less as the solution becomes basic now. So,

indicator changes its color in basic medium. This permanent change shows the end point of titration. Note this reading which is the volume of base required to neutralize 20 ml of HCl acid. If 50ml is the volume of NaOH (end point reading from burette).

Now to calculate the concentration of HCl ;

$HCl + NaOH \rightarrow NaCl + H_2O$

the molar ratio is 1:1 for this reaction

So mole of HCl = moles of NaOH

(molarity = moles/ volume)

[Molarity × Volume] of acid = [Molarity × Volume] of base

$M \times 20 = 0.150 \times 50$ ml

M = 0.150 x 50 /20 = 0.375M is the concentration of acid HCl.

INDICATORS USED FOR VARIOUS TITRATION

Strong Acid Against a Strong Base

For example, titration of HCl and NaOH. At the initial stage of titration, the pH changes very slowly and increases up to pH= 4. But with addition of small amount of alkali like 0.01 mL approx., pH value reaches to about 7. This shows the neutralization of acid. Further addition of small amount of alkali increases the concentration of hydrogen ions and the pH value rises to about 9. There is a rapid increase of pH from about 4 to 9 when the end point approaches. Indicators like methyl orange, methyl red and phenolphthalein could be used for these kind of neutralization reactions which show the color change within the pH range of 4 to 10.

Weak Acid against Strong Base

For example, titration of acetic acid against NaOH. The end point of this titration lies between pH 8 and 10 due to the formation of sodium acetate and water. So, phenolphthalein is a good indicator for this.

Strong Acid against Weak Base

For example, the titration of ammonium hydroxide with HCl. The end point is in the range of 6 to 4 which shows the acidic pH of solution. Methyl orange is a good indicator for this titration.

Indicator	Color change on acidic side	Range of color change	Color change on basic side
Methyl Violet	Yellow	0.0 - 1.6	Violet
Bromophenol Blue	Yellow	3.0 - 4.6	Blue

Indicator	Color change on acidic side	Range of color change	Color change on basic side
Methyl Orange	Red	3.1 - 4.4	Yellow
Methyl Red	Red	4.4 - 6.3	Yellow
Litmus	Red	5.0 - 8.0	Blue
Bromo thymol Blue	Yellow	6.0 - 7.6	Blue
Phenolphthalein	Colorless	8.3 - 10.0	Pink
Alizarin Yellow	Yellow	10.1 - 12.0	Red

Methods to Determine the Endpoint

1. **pH indicator** - This is a substance which shows the chemical change by changing the color.
2. **A potentiometer** - This is used to measure the electrode potential of the solution. These are used for redox titration. They show the end point with changing potential of the working electrode.
3. **pH meter** - It is a ion-selective electrode. In pH meter the potential of electrode depends on the amount of H+ ion present in the solution. The pH of the solution can be measured in the whole titration. This gives more correct result than indicators.
4. **Conductance** - The conductivity of solutions is also changed in titration and it depends on the ions present in the solution, mobility of ions and ions concentration.
5. **Color change** - In the redox reactions, the color of solution changes without use of indicator. This is due to different oxidation states of the product.

The volumetric analysis can be categorized into four types which are based on the type of reaction involved in the process.

Some important points should be remembered in doing volumetric analysis to get the accurate results.

1. All the equipments like burette, beaker, pipette and volumetric flask should be washed properly with distilled water before taking them in use as the presence of any other chemical can be the reason for wrong measurement.
2. The process of filling the pipette should be accurate to avoid excess addition of solutions.
3. The flask should be shaking well after adding the indicator and also the titration flask with addition of each drop of solution from burette.
4. The addition of acid should be drop wise.
5. Contamination should be avoided.

6. The indicator should not be used in excess.
7. The flask should be removed as the indicator changes color.
8. Sometimes, an air bubble in the nozzle of the burette can be the reason for altering the readings, so, it must be removed before taking the initial reading.
9. The burette should not be leaked during titration.
10. Keep eyes in the level of the liquid surface during the time of taking the burette reading or measuring flask and pipette etc.
11. Lower meniscus and upper meniscus are always read in case of color less and colored solutions respectively.
12. Do not blow through the pipette to expel the last drop of solution from it; simply touch the inner surface of the titration flask with the nozzle of the pipette for this purpose.
13. Index finger should be used for pi-petting the solution.

20

Functions of Carbohydrates, Proteins, Nucleic Acids, Enzymes and Vitamins

Carbohydrates are nutrients, along with proteins and other types of chemical compounds, but they are much more than that. In addition to sugars, of which there are many more varieties than ordinary sucrose, or table sugar, carbohydrates appear in the form of starches and cellulose. As such, they are the structural materials of which plants are made. Carbohydrates are produced by one of the most complex, vital, and amazing processes in the physical world: photosynthesis. Because they are an integral part of plant life, it is no wonder that carbohydrates are in most fruits and vegetables. And though they are not a dietary requirement in the way that vitamins or essential amino acids are, it is difficult to eat without ingesting some carbohydrates, which are excellent sources of quick-burning energy. Not all carbohydrates are of equal nutritional value, however: in general, the ones created by nature are good for the body, whereas those produced by human intervention - some forms of pasta and most varieties of bread, white rice, crackers, cookies, and so forth - are much less beneficial.

WHAT CARBOHYDRATES ARE

Carbohydrates are naturally occurring compounds that consist of carbon, hydrogen, and oxygen, and are produced by green plants in the process of undergoing photosynthesis. In simple terms, photosynthesis is the biological conversion of light energy (that is, electromagnetic energy) from the Sun to chemical energy in plants. It is an extremely complex process, and a thorough treatment of it involves a great deal of technical terminology. Although we discuss the fundamentals of photosynthesis later in this essay, we do so only in the most cursory fashion.

Photosynthesis involves the conversion of carbon dioxide and water to sugars, which, along with starches and cellulose, are some of the more well known varieties of carbohydrate. Sugars can be defined as any of a number of water-soluble compounds, of varying sweetness. (What we think of as sugar - that is, table sugar - is actually sucrose, discussed later.) Starches are complex carbohydrates without taste or odor, which are granular or powdery in physical form. Cellulose is a polysaccharide, made from units of glucose, that constitutes the principal part of the cell walls of plants and is found naturally in fibrous materials, such as cotton. Commercially, it is a raw material for such manufactured goods as paper, cellophane, and rayon.

MONOSACCHARIDES

The preceding definitions contain several words that also must be defined. Carbohydrates are made up of building blocks called monosaccharides, the simplest type of carbohydrate. Found in grapes and other fruits and also in honey, they can be broken down chemically into their constituent elements, but there is no carbohydrate more chemically simple than a monosaccharide. Hence, they are also known as simple sugars or simple carbohydrates.

Examples of simple sugars include glucose, which is sweet, colorless, and water-soluble and appears widely in nature. Glucose, also known as dextrose, grape sugar, and corn sugar, is the principal form in which carbohydrates are assimilated, or taken in, by animals. Other monosaccharides include fructose, or fruit sugar, and galactose, which is less soluble and sweet than glucose and usually appears in combination with other simple sugars rather than by itself. Glucose, fructose, and galactose are isomers, meaning that they have the same chemical formula ($C_6H_{12}O_6$), but different chemical structures and therefore different chemical properties.

PROTEINS

There are many stages of growth and development which take place throughout a plant's life. If the particular plant is a crop, then producers want these stages to occur efficiently to obtain high yields. If the plant is a weed, reducing the crop's yield potential, then producers look for ways to inhibit these cellular processes.

Herbicide proteins are the critical factors in both of these scenerios. They are important macro-molecules that participate in every aspect of plant growth and development. Proteins are involved in processes such as catalyzing chemical reactions (enzymes), facilitating membrane transport, intracellular structure and energy generating reactions involving electron transport, just to name a few. Compared to animals, plants contain low levels of protein due to the large amount of structural carbohydrate (cellulose) that compose most of a plant's structure.

To better understand plant growth and development we need to take a closer look at these protein molecules. Proteins are constructed from even smaller molecules called amino acids. In Figure 1, the general molecular structure of amino acids is illustrated. Notice that all amino acids contain both an amino group and a carboxyl group; however, individual amino acids differ at the 'R' group.

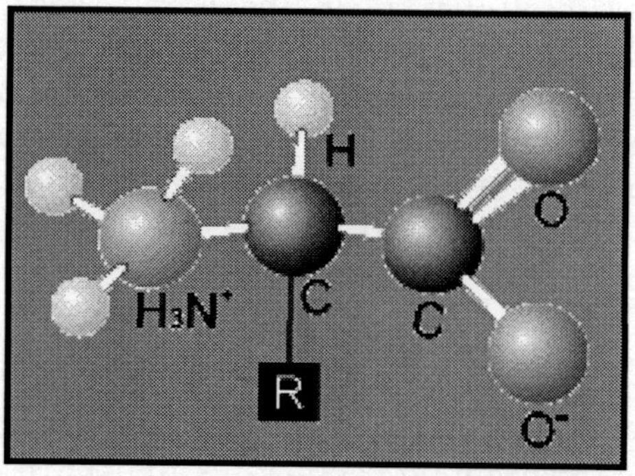

Fig. 20.1: All amino acids contain 3 parts, an amino group NH_3^+),a carboxyl group (COO^-)and an 'R' group. The 'R' group varies among amino acids.

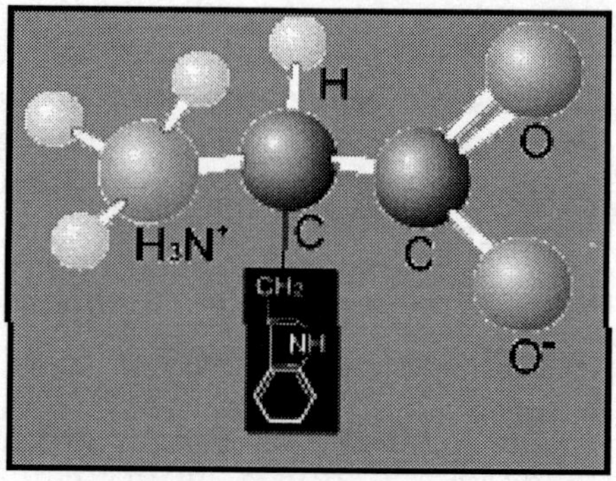

Fig. 20.2: Structure for a specific amino acid, tryptophan.

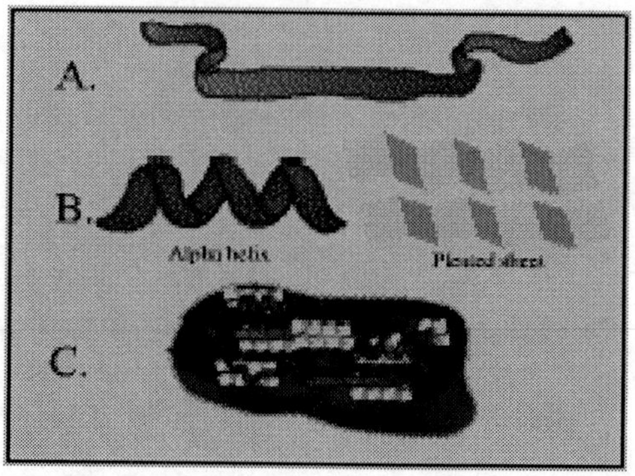

Fig. 20.3: Three structures of proteins are illustrated (A) primary structure, its amino acid sequence; (B) secondary structure, polypeptide coiling or folding; (C) tertiary structure, the overall shape of the polypeptide.

Unlike animals, plants do not derive amino acids by consuming other organisms. Therefore, all 20 of these amino acids must be synthesized by the plant. A challenge lies in the fact that proteins have a finite life span and must be constantly translated from m-RNA in order for plant growth and development to continue. This means that there must be a ready supply of all 20 amino acids for protein synthesis and ultimately plant growth and development occur.

A protein is created when a series of amino acids are bound together. The arrangement of the amino acids can be described at 3 different levels: primary structure, secondary structure and tertiary structure (Fig. 20.3). The primary structure is simply the order in which the amino acids are bound together. This specific order is initially encoded in the DNA sequence of the gene that provides the blueprint for the protein (Fig. 20.3-A).

The secondary structure of a protein describes the way the string of amino acids fold (Fig. 20.3-B). The specific bonding interactions among amino acids will determine if it is a coil or folding arrangement for these interactions to take place based on the primary structure.

Finally, the tertiary structure of a protein describes the overall shape of the protein. It is a protein's shape which ultimately determines a protein's function (Fig. 20.3-C).

Therefore, changing a gene's sequence can change the primary structure of a protein, the amino acid sequence. This in turn may change a protein's secondary structure and then it's shape, or tertiary structure. With an altered shape, the protein may function differently or may not function at all.

For example, plant's resistant to glyphosate have EPSP synthase enzymes with sightly different amino acid sequence than susceptible plants. This is due to a simple DNA mutation. The details will be explained later.

NUCLEIC ACIDS

Nucleic acids were discovered in the mid-nineteenth century, but their role as genetic material was not substantiated until the mid twentieth century. When chromosomes were discovered at the beginning of the twentieth century, they were quickly identified as the genetic material of the cell. Chromosomes were found to be composed of nucleic acids and proteins.

Through the experiments of Fred Griffith on transformation in pneumonia bacteria and the work of Alfred Hershey and Martha Chase on bacteriophages, by 1952 most biologists recognized deoxyribonucleic acid (DNA) as containing the genes. James Watson and Francis Crick provided the capstone to science's initial understanding of nucleic acids when they determined the double helix structure of DNA in 1953.

Heredity is the process by which the physical traits of an organism are passed on to its offspring. At the molecular level, DNA contains the information necessary for the transmission of genetic characteristics from one generation to the next, as well as the information required for the new organisms to growand to live. DNA is the chemical basis of heredity and provides the synthesis of new proteins, such as enzymes.

DNA and RNA

There are two types of nucleic acids within cells, the single-stranded ribonucleic acid (RNA) and the double-stranded DNA. Each kind has specific roles. DNA was isolated in 1869 by German chemist Friedrich Miescher.

The substance that Miescher found was white, sugary, and slightly acidic, and it contained phosphorus. Because it occurred only within the nuclei of cells, he called it "nuclein." The name was later changed to deoxyribonucleic acid, to distinguish it from ribonucleic acid, which is also found in cells.

In eukaryotic cells, DNA is present in the chromosomes of the nucleus and within the mitochondria and chloroplasts. Bacteria, yeasts, and molds, in addition to the chromosomes, contain circular strands of DNA, called plasmids, within the cytoplasm of their cells.

Plasmids are relatively small, circular strands of DNA that exist independently of thechromosome. Plasmids typically have only twenty-five or thirty genes, which are not essential to the host cell but often confer antibiotic resistance, the ability to pass DNA to other bacterial cells, and other useful functions.

Some plasmids are only found as single copies, whereas others occur as many copies. The mitochondria and chloroplasts of eukaryotic cells are self-replicating and contain a tiny circular chromosome (DNA) resembling a plasmid of a bacterium.

Viruses (minute parasites that infect specific hosts) contain only one type of nucleic acid—either DNA or RNA, never both, and the DNA or RNA can be single- or double-stranded. The DNA of some viruses can integrate into the DNA of the host cell. In this state, the viral DNA replicates as the host DNA replicates.

The genetic apparatus of a virus, whether RNA or DNA, is much the same as that of bacteria but is far less complex. Even large viruses (such as the pox virus) have only a few hundred genes. Smaller viruses (such as the polio virus) have considerably fewer.

Chemical Structure

Both DNA and RNA are long-chained polymers made up of nucleotides. The nucleotides, in turn, are made up of a nitrogenous base, a ribose or deoxyribose sugar, and a phosphate. All the bases of DNA and RNA are heterocyclic amines.

Two, adenine and guanine, are called purines; the other three, cytosine, thymine, and uracil, are called pyrimidines. The two purines and one of the pyrimidines, cytosine, occur in both RNA and DNA. Uracil is found only in RNA, while thymine occurs only in DNA.

The purines are nine-membered heterocyclic rings with nitrogen occurring in place of carbon at several positions. Adenine and guanine differ in the functional groups attached to them.

The pyrimidines are six-membered heterocyclic rings,with nitrogen in place of two of the carbon atoms. Like the purines, the three pyrimidines also differ in the specific functional groups attached to them.

The ribose sugars are made up of a five-membered heterocyclic ring containing one oxygen atom between carbons one and four. A fifth carbon (number five) is not part of the ring and is bonded to carbon number four.

Along with hydrogen atoms attached to each carbon, there is one hydroxyl group (OH) attached to each of the four heterocyclic carbon atoms in the ribose sugar of RNA. (The fifth carbon has a phosphate group attached to it.) The sugar of DNA is called D-deoxyribose because a hydroxyl group is missing from the second carbon, having been replaced by a hydrogen atom—thus the name deoxyribonucleic acid.

The sugar-base combination is called a nucleoside. The purines are linked to carbon one of the sugars with the nitrogen at position one. The nucleoside of guanine and ribose is guanosine; it is adenosine for adenine and D-ribose.

The pyrimidines of RNA, when attached to ribose, are uridine and cytosine. In DNA the nucleoside names are deoxyadenine, deoxyguanosine, deoxythymidine, and deoxycytidine.

Nucleotides are phosphate esters of nucleosides. In thesemolecules, a phosphate group (phosphoric acid) is attached to carbon five (called the 52 carbon) of the sugar (ribose or deoxyribose) in the nucleoside.

Nucleotides are named by combining the name of their nucleoside with a word describing the numbers of phosphates attached to it. Guanosinemonophosphate, for example, is the name of the phosphate ester of guanosine, which is often abbreviated as GMP.

Individual nucleotides also occur in cells. These free nucleotides usually exist as diphosphates or triphosphates. Examples of these are adenosine diphosphate (ADP) and adenosine triphosphate (ATP). ATP is the universal energy source for the anabolic processes of all cells, including the formation of the DNA and RNA.

DNA Structure and Function

DNA can be an extremely long molecule that is tightly wound within the nuclei of eukaryotic cells and within the cytoplasm of prokaryotic cells. Nuclear DNA is linear, whereas prokaryotic DNA is circular. (If the DNA in a human cell could be stretched out, it would measure roughly 2 meters, or 6 feet long; bacterial DNA would be about 1.5 millimeters long, or just over 0.5 inch.)

Using a typical lily as a point of reference, DNA is packaged into twenty-four chromosomes, twelve of which are contributed by the pollen and twelve by the egg. Every cell derived from the fertilized egg (zygote) will have exactly the same amount of DNA containing exactly the same genetic information.

Within the cytoplasm, several mitochondria (the sites of respiration) and chloroplasts (the sites of photosynthesis) are found, both of which contain their own DNA, which iscircular and resembles prokaryotic DNA in many respects.

DNA is a double-stranded spiral; its shape is called the double helix. Structurally, it may be compared to a ladder, with the rails or sides of the ladder consisting of alternating deoxyribose sugar and phosphate molecules connected by phosphodiester bonds between the 52 carbon of one sugar and the 32 carbon of the other.

The rungs of the ladder consist of purine (adenine and guanine, often abbreviated as Aand G, respectively) and pyrimidine (cytosine and thymine, often abbreviated as C and T, respectively) building blocks from the opposite strands, held together by hydrogen bonds.

The building blocks pair with each other consistently in what are called complementary pairs: Adenine always pairs with thymine with two hydrogen bonds, and cytosine always pairs with guanine with three hydrogen bonds. Consequently, the attraction between cytosine and guanine is stronger than that between adenine and thymine.

Because of this arrangement, the sequence of the purine and pyrimidine building blocks on one strand is complemented by the sequence of building blocks on the other strand.

The specificity of the base pairing between the two strands allows strands to fit neatly together only when such pairing exists. Each DNA strand has a 52 end with a hydroxyl group attached to the 32 carbon of a deoxyribose sugar.

When connected, the two strands are actually in an opposite orientation and are referred to as being anti parallel. This is best observed by looking at one end of the double-stranded molecule. One strand terminates with a 52 phosphate group and the other with a 32 hydroxyl group.

The specific nucleotide composition in a species is essentially constant but can vary considerably among organisms. Regardless, the amounts of adenine and thymine are always the same, as are the amounts of guanine and cytosine because of the required complementary pairing.

Due to the greater strength of G-C bonds, organisms with a high GC content have DNA that must be heated to a higher temperature to denature, or separate, the strands. Some bacteria that live in hot springs have an especially high GC content.

The instructions contained within the DNA molecules occur in segments called genes. Most genes instruct the cell about what kind of polypeptide (molecule composed of amino acids used to make functional proteins) to manufacture.

These polypeptides lead to the formation of enzymes and other proteins necessary for survival of the cell. Other genes are important in coding for the production of antibodies, RNA, and hormones.

RNA Types

The DNA acts as a template to make three kinds of RNA: messenger RNA (mRNA), transfer RNA (tRNA), and ribosomal RNA (rRNA). Each kind of RNA has a specific function. RNA is not found in chromosomes and is located elsewhere in the nucleus and in the cytoplasm.

The largest and most abundant RNA is rRNA. Between 60 and 80 percent of the total RNA in cells is rRNA, and it has a molecular weight of several million atomic mass units. The rRNA combines with proteins to form ribosomes, which are the sites for the synthesis of new protein molecules. About 60 percent of the ribosome is rRNA, and the rest is protein.

Although single-stranded, rRNA molecules fold into specific functional shapes that involve the pairing of portions of the molecule to form double stranded regions. The precise shape of rRNAs is important for their function, and some of them actually have catalytic properties, just as enzymes do. RNAs of this type are sometimes calledribozymes.

Molecules of mRNA carry the genetic information from DNA to the ribosomes. The process of converting the DNA code of a gene into an mRNA is called transcription. When attached to the ribosomes, mRNAs direct protein synthesis in a process called translation.

The size of the mRNA molecule depends upon the size of the protein molecule to be made. In prokaryotes (such as bacterial cells), as well as in mitochondria and chloroplasts, mRNAs are ready to take part in translation even while transcription of the remainder of the mRNA is taking place.

In eukaryotes (cells of most other forms of life), them RNAs transcribed from nuclear DNA are initially much larger than they are later, when they participate in translation. These mRNAs must be processed to removed large pieces of noncoding RNA, called introns, and to modify both ends of the mRNA in specificways.

After introns are removed, the remaining codon regions, called exons, are spliced together by splicesomes (a complex system composed of proteins and small RNAs). Once all the modifications are complete, them RNA is ready to be translated. A small number of mRNAs are translated in the nucleus, but most are transported to the cytoplasm first.

The smallest of the three main kinds of RNA is tRNA. Each of the tRNA molecules consists of about one hundred nucleotides in a single chain that loops back upon itself in three places, forming double-stranded regions that result in a structure that, when viewed in two dimensions, could be compared to a cross or clover leaf.

The function of tRNA is to bring amino acids to the ribosomes to be used in the formation of new proteins. Each of the twenty amino acids found in proteins has at least one particular tRNA molecule to carry it to the site of protein synthesis.

The cloverleaf shape of the tRNA molecule is maintained by hydrogen bonds between base pairs. The other parts of the molecule that do not have hydrogen-bonded base pairs exist as loops. Two parts of every tRNA molecule have significant biological functions. The first is the place where the specific amino acid to be transferred is attached.

This is located at the longest free end of the three-looped structure, often called the stem, where it is specifically attached to an adenine of an adenine monophosphate nucleotide. The second important site is the loop at the opposite end of the molecule from the stem.

This loop contains a specific three-base sequence that represents a code for the amino acid that is being transferred by the tRNA. This three-base sequence is called an anticodon and plays an important role in helping place the amino acid in the correct position in the protein molecule under construction.

ENZYMES IN PLANT GROWTH

Introduction

Plants are sessile organisms that became adapted to different environments by developing appropriate mechanisms for the use of natural resources in order to sustain growth and reproduction. Cultivated crops have been developed considering an unlimited supply of nutrients and water; nowadays limitation in nutrient availability, environmental concerns and climate change ask for the adoption of sustainable agricultural managements of cultivated land.

As autotroph organisms, plants acquire water and mineral nutrients (generally in ionic forms) from the soil, while oxygen and carbon dioxide come from the atmosphere. Generally essential elements need to be accumulated in plant tissues at concentrations higher than those found in the external media (e.g. due to soil constraints) or the concentration in the environment may be not suitable for optimal use efficiency by internal mechanisms (CO_2 vs. O_2 concentration in the air). These factors can limit plant growth and crop yield; furthermore, this situation might become even worse due to intensive agriculture and global warming. This implies a profound knowledge of mechanisms that plants evolved to acquire water and nutrients and to build up their structural and functional biomolecules; understanding how these mechanisms are regulated by internal and exogenous (environmental) factors is also crucial for the development of new efficient crops genotypes.

Nutrients' uptake from the soil solution, translocation and transport of solutes to different organs and cells within the plant are processes that need specific protein structures located at the cell plasma membranes allowing the passage of uncharged solutes and ions and, especially, capable to generate an electric potential favorable for trans membrane transport. The plasma membrane (PM) H^+-pumping ATPase has a unique role in solute transport in plant cells. On the other hand, ATP used in metabolic processes needs to be previously synthesized by photophosphorylation in the chloroplast or oxidative phosphorylation in the mitochondrion via the ATP synthase proteins.

Fixation of CO_2 is the key step in the photosynthetic biomass accumulation in higher plants. This task is accomplished by Rubisco (Ribulose-1,5-bisphosphate carboxylase/oxygenase), a chloroplast-located enzyme that maintained highly conserved function during evolution; although partly inefficient due to the double catalytic function (carboxylase/oxygenase); this enzyme play a central role in carbon fixation even in plants that developed variants to this mechanism. Ammonia assimilation into glutamine allows the formation of glutamate and further synthesis of plant amino acids. This reaction is catalyzed by glutamine synthase, an enzyme with different isoforms localized in plastids/chloroplasts and in the cytosol. Structural and functional features of these enzymes will be described and discussed in relation to their role in plant growth and response to environmental conditions.

Plasma Membrane H^+-ATPase: A Master Enzyme for Plant Nutrition

Movement of uncharged solutes and ions across biological membrane is essential to ensure metabolic reactions. This movement can be a passive as well an active process and involves the operation of channels and carriers. Both passive and active transport of ions across biological membranes need that a transmembrane electric potential is generated and maintained. In plants, this task is accomplished by the plasma membrane (PM) H^+-ATPase that is an electrogenic enzyme coupling the hydrolysis of ATP to the transport of H+ from the cytosol into the apoplast. This activity creates a transmembrane gradient of electric potential (negative inside) and pH (more acidic outside), which can be exploited in a variety of physiological processes such as the transport of nutrients and metabolites, preservation of intra- and extra-cellular pH, cell turgor and related processes [1]. In roots, that are exposed to changing external conditions, such as pH, concentration of nutrients and toxic elements and rhizosphere signals, the PM H^+-ATPase plays a pivotal role for mineral nutrition and the response to abiotic stress.

The plasma membrane H^+-ATPase belongs to the family of P-type ATPases, which use ATP and form a phosphorylated aspartyl intermediate during the reaction cycle. It is a single subunit protein with molecular mass of about 100 KDa containing ten trans membrane helices and four cytoplasmic domains (Fig. 20.4): the nucleotide binding domain (N-domain), the phosphorylation domain (P-domain), the phosphatase domain (A-domain) and the regulatory domain (R-domain, consisting of the C-terminal of the protein).

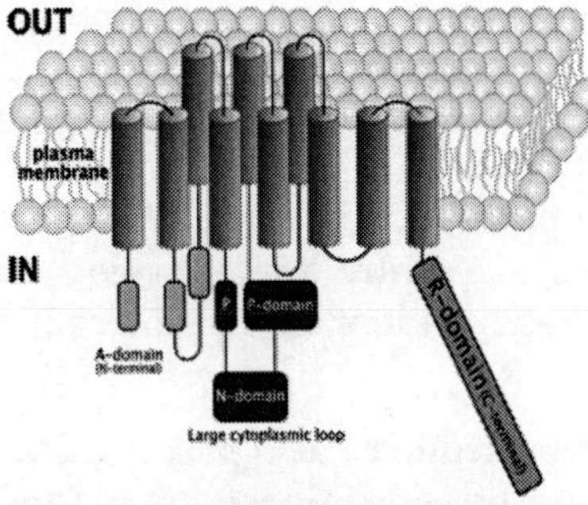

Fig. 20.1: Structure of PM H^+-ATPase.

The N-terminal end is directly involved in controlling the pump activity state interacting with the C-terminal end. The C-terminal region exerts a self-inhibiting function on the enzyme activity by binding to the large cytoplasmic domain. This inhibition is removed by binding of 14-3-3 proteins, that is dependent on the phosphorylation of the penultimate Thr residue. The fungal phytotoxin, fusicoccin stimulates H^+ pumping by blocking the complex of 14-3-3 proteins and the PM H^+-ATPase.

In several plant species, it has been found that the PM H^+-ATPase is encoded by a multigene family (about 10 genes) belonging to 5 sub-families. It has been suggested that the heterogeneity of isoforms can be linked to the multicellular nature of plants and the need for a fine regulation of the enzymatic activity. Analysis of expression patterns based on available micro array data show that most of the H^+-ATPase isoforms are expressed at a relative constant level and expression level does not change when a related isoform is deleted or reduced. Regulatory events involving modifications of activity, amount and gene expression have been reported in response to change in the concentration of ionic nutrients in the root external solution.

A close relationship between the activity of the PM proton pump of the root cells and transmembrane transport of anionic nutrients has been demonstrated in the case of NO_3^-. Nitrate uptake is an energy-dependent proton-coupled process. Exposure of maize roots to nitrate can cause the induction of the high-affinity transport system; this behavior is paralleled by a concomitant increase in activity and amount of the PM H^+-ATPase and by the preferential expression of the genes

MHA3 and MH4, belonging to sub-family II of the PM H+-ATPase in maize [11]. Spatial and temporal expression patterns of the two genes were also observed along primary maize roots that paralleled changes in enzyme activity and anion transport rates [12]. Other isoforms of the proton pump (MHA1, belonging to sub-family I) have been suggested to be involved in nitrate transport in maize.

Another example of regulation of the PM H^+-ATPase has been described in response to limited amounts of phosphate. When grown at low available phosphate white lupin (*Lupinus albus*, L.) release substantial amounts of carboxylates from specialized root structure, called cluster roots, and concomitantly acidify the rhizosphere. The burst of citrate exudation is accompanied by a strong acidification of the external medium and alkalization of the cytosol. The increase in proton secretion is due to both an increased transcription level of one of the two PM H^+-ATPase genes found in white lupin (LHA1 and LHA2) and a post-translational modification of H^+-ATPase protein involving binding of activating 14-3-3 protein. More recently, an RNA-Seq study showed that six H^+-ATPase transcripts exhibited Pi -dependent expression changes in white lupin roots.

Rhizosphere acidification mediated by the activity of PM H^+-ATPase has been reported to be also part of the response to limited iron availability in roots of dicots and non-graminaceous plants. It has been shown that under conditions of Fe deficiency, the activity and the quantity of the PM H^+-ATPase increase, with the enzyme, which appears to be, concentrated particularly in the rhizodermal and root hair cells of the sub-apical root area. It has also been found that in cucumber plants the expression of the PM H^+-ATPase CsHA2 gene, found both in roots and leaves, was not influenced by the Fe nutritional status of the plant, while the CsHA1 gene, expressed exclusively in the roots, was up-regulated by Fe deprivation.

Increases in PM H^+-ATPase enzyme activity have also been observed in the roots of plants adapted to acidic soils and, particularly in response to Al toxicity, a condition which often occurs in that kind of soils. It has been shown that resistant plants release a high amount of organic acid anions from the sub-apical regions of the roots and that the PM H^+-ATPase could be involved in this process. The observed activation of the enzyme due to the presence of Al, has been ascribed to an increased phosphorylation of a threonine residue localized in the auto inhibitory (C-terminal) domain of the PM H^+-ATPase, suggesting an involvement of 14-3-3 proteins. However, it is worth to note that citrate exudation in P-deficient white lupin plants exposed to Al was suggested to be uncoupled from PM H^+-ATPase activity and linked to K^+ rather than to H^+ extrusion; furthermore, a poor relationship between Al-induced oxalate exudation and PM H^+-ATPase activity was reported in tomato roots.

There is a number of reports indicating that PM H^+-ATPase could be involved in cell elongation; this function would imply a direct action of auxin on activity and, possibly, synthesis of the proton pump or an indirect one through induced changes in cytoplasmic pH or altered ion fluxes across plasma membrane. Whatever the mechanism, other signal compounds, like those present in the soil solution (e.g. humic molecules or hormone-like compounds released by rhizosphere microorganisms) have been shown to affect enzyme activity with different mechanisms and, in some cases, acting on the amount of the protein and of gene transcripts; these effects have been related to root growth, apoplast acidification and nutrient uptake.

ATP Synthase: An Extraordinary Nano-Engine

To directly sustain the energy necessary for growth and metabolism, living organisms use mainly that trapped in the phosphoranhydride bound contained in ATP molecules. The majority of ATP is regenerated from ADP and inorganic phosphate (Pi) by the ATP synthase complex. In plants, ATP is mainly produced via two mechanisms: the photophosphorylation in chloroplasts and oxidative phosphorylation in mitochondria. In chloroplasts, plants use the photosynthetic reaction centers to transport protons from the stroma into the lumen and create an electrochemical potential through the membrane of the thylakoids. In mitochondria, a series of complexes present in the respiration chain pumps protons and charge the inner mitochondrial membrane. Nevertheless in both organelles, the final step is catalyzed by the same type of enzyme, the ATP synthase, which transforms the energy of the electrochemical gradient across the membrane of the thylakoid or across the internal membrane of the mitochondrion into the chemical bound contained in the ATP molecule.

The structure of the ATP synthase is a complex of two main subunits, F_0 and F_1. The complex (F_0, F_1) forms a rotary engine that is able to convert the transport of protons, or sodium ions in bacteria, into chemical energy and this complex can also work in reverse mode as an H^+(or Na^+)-ATPase. F_0 is embedded in the membrane and consists of at least 1 a, 1 b2 and 10-15 c subunits; the c subunits form a ring in the membrane which spins with the passage of protons. The F_1 part is a water-soluble complex of proteins, which binds ADP and Pi, catalyze the synthesis of ATP and by conformational changes induced by the rotation of the F_0 counterpart release ATP.

Due to the dual activity of the ATP synthase a complex regulation mechanism controls its activity. In mitochondria, when the availability of oxygen drops, the electrochemical gradient of protons across the inner mitochondrial membrane decreases and the ATP synthase starts to consume ATP to reestablish the gradient. Under these conditions, the ATP production is sustain by the glycolysis and the factor regulating the ATP synthase, natural inhibitor protein IF1, binds to the ATP synthase due to the drop of pH in the mitochondria matrix.

In chloroplast, where no IF1 protein has been identified, the ATPase activity of the ATP synthase is repressed in the dark to prevent wasteful consumption of ATP. Under these conditions, accumulation of Mg_2^+-ADP and different modifications on the F1 subunits, including a disulfide bound, inhibit the ATPasic activity. Reversely when plants are exposed back to light, photosynthesis centers acidify the stroma, which induce the removal of the inhibiting ADP and the disulfide bound is reduced. Moreover the C-terminal domain of the Epsilon subunit, within the F_1 part, seems to act similarly to the auto inhibitory (C-terminal) domain of the PM H^+-ATPase (see above), inhibiting the ATP hydrolyzing activity the chloroplastic ATP synthase [33]. To sum up, the ATP synthase regulation is just starting to be revealed, but still needs further research.

Another interesting aspect about the functionality of the ATP synthase is the relative importance of the pH gradient and of the electrical potential across the membrane. It is a common believe that it is the pH gradient, which is the main driven force for the synthesis of ATP; however, it depends on the organelles considered. For example, in chloroplast, the electrical potential across the membrane is small but the pH gradient is high. In these conditions, chloroplastic ATP synthase has a large c ring (14 units), as each c unit transport one proton, this enzyme needs many protons for each ATP synthetize but less electrical potential per protons. On the other hand, mitochondrial one has a smaller c ring (10), thus a better proton per ATP ratio, due to the high electrical potential maintained by the respiratory chain for a similar, in comparison to chloroplast, pH gradient across the membrane. Therefore in mitochondria, the electrical potential is the main driving force and in chloroplast is the pH gradient.

Rubisco: An Old Enzyme for Future Challenges

Biomass accumulation and crop yield is strictly related to photosynthetic rate and efficiency. Plants have been grouped depending on the first compound that is generated upon incorporation of CO_2 in a pre-existing carbon skeleton.

C3 plants fix carbon of CO2 into ribulose 1,5-bisphosphate (RuBP) generating primarily two molecules of 3-phosphoglycerate (PGA, a 3-carbon compound). Other variants of photosynthetic carbon assimilation are represented by C4 (the first compounds has 4 C atoms) and Crassulacean acid metabolism (CAM) plants, which rely on CO2-concentrating mechanisms. Notwithstanding these differences Rubisco (ribulose-1,5 bisphosphate carboxylase/oxygenase) plays a central role in CO_2 fixation.

Rubisco of higher plants belongs to the form I of the enzyme, found also in algae and in most photosynthetic bacteria. It is a complex protein, with eight large subunits (four large subunit mass of about 50-52 kDa) and eight small subunits (mass of about 14-15 kDa) arranged in a L8S8 structure (four large subunit dimers along with eight non-catalytic small subunits capping the large ones).

The large subunits have the catalytic sites. Each subunit comprise an N-terminal domain and a larger C-terminal domain that forms a α/β-barrel; L2 dimers, formed by head-tail arrangement, have two active sites located at the L-L interface. The small subunits consist of four stranded antiparallel β-sheets with two α-helices; they are not essential for catalysis but provide structural stability to the Rubisco complex. L-subunits are synthesized from the single rbcL gene of the plastid genome; nucleus-encoded factors, chaperones and post-translational modification of N-terminal domain would help avoiding misfolding and protect the newly forming protein from proteolytic degradation.

Multiple copies of the rbcS gene, coding for the S-subunit, are located in the nucleus. An N-terminal transit peptide allows transfer of the S-subunits synthesized in the cytosol through the chloroplast envelope translocon complexes into the plastid. Within the stroma, the S-subunits undergo further posttranslational modification (transit peptide cleavage, Met-1 aN- methylation) prior to assembly into L8S8 complexes.

The activity of Rubisco is highly regulated. The enzyme is inactive in the dark and is converted to an active form upon illumination. Activation is mediated by several environmental and systemic factors, including temperature, pH, light, heavy metal concentrations, natural inhibitors, and by the activity of an ancillary protein: Rubisco activase.

Prior to catalysis, Rubisco needs to be preactivated; activation is the result of the binding of CO_2 to the 201-lysine residue near the catalytic site (position may slightly change depending on the species). The carbamate that is formed is then stabilized by Mg_2^+ binding. Carbamylation changes the conformation of the large subunit activating the enzyme that can bind RuBP and catalyzes a complex five-step reaction involving a CO_2 and a water molecule before the release of two 3-phosphoglycerate (3PGA) molecules. Carbamylation is essential for Rubisco activation, as the non-carbamylated Rubisco binds RuBP too tightly to allow catalysis. The first, rate-limiting, step in carboxylation is the enolization of RuBP via the carbamate side chain; pH values lower than 8.0 may lead to the generation of Xylulose-1,5-bisphosphate that inhibit the enzyme activity (see below).

Another protein, Rubisco activase, is also involved in mediating the light activation of Rubisco. This nucleus-encoded protein uses the energy of ATP to remove active-site bound sugar-phosphate inhibitors, such as 2 carboxyarabinitol 1-phosphate (CA1P) or xyulose-1,5-bisphosphate (XuBP), d-glycero-2,3-pentodiulose-1,5-bisphosphate (PDBP) and, under some conditions, RuBP itself. While XuBP and PDBP can be by-products of reaction intermediates, CA1P occurs naturally in the leaves of several plants and is a strong inhibitor of Rubisco. The affinity of Rubisco for CA1P is much stronger than that for RuBP, the substrate. As a result, CA1P, which accumulates in leaves during the night, inactivates Rubisco by blocking the binding sites. During the day (or on illumination), the bound CA1P is released from Rubisco by the concerted action of Rubisco activase and CA1P phosphatase.

The action of Rubisco activase may be crucial for maintaining Rubisco activity under low CO_2 supply and the sensitivity of Rubisco activase to high temperature might explain the decrease in Rubisco efficiency under these environmental conditions (Fig. 20.5).

Besides the carboxylation reaction, Rubisco reacts with oxygen to form one molecule of 2-phosphoglycolate and one of PGA; this reaction is the first step of the photorespiration pathway that leads to the release of previously fixed CO_2, NH_3 and energy. Due to photorespiration, C-fixing reaction has a reduced efficiency and a large amount of protein is needed to support adequate photosynthetic rates

(Rubisco accounts for an average of 50% of leaf protein). Photorespiration if favoured by prolonged drought stress conditions and high temperature.

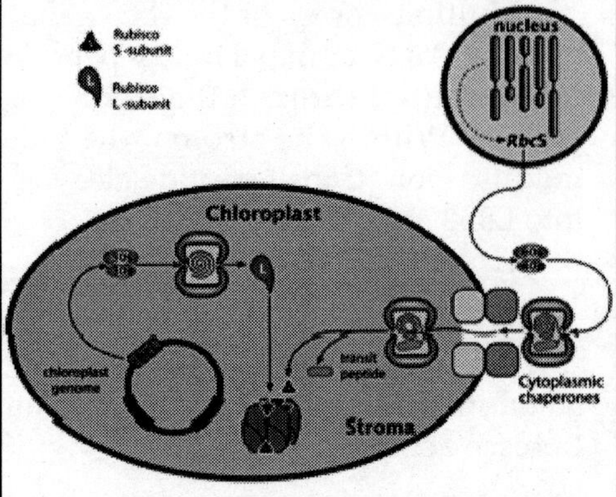

Fig. 20.5: Assembly of large (L) and small (S) subunits of Rubisco.

C4 plants have evolved biochemical mechanisms to elevate levels of CO2 that rely on spatial separation of the initial fixation of atmospheric CO_2 from the Calvin cycle. Phosphoenolpyruvate carboxylase (PEPC) catalyzes CO2 fixation to PEP in mesophyll cells producing oxaloacetate. Four-C acids (malate and aspartate) are then transported to bundle sheath cells, where they provide CO_2 to Rubisco, after undergoing decarboxylation. A pyruvate, phosphate dikinase (PPDK) catalyses the regeneration of PEP from pyruvate in mesophyll cells.

As compared to C3 plants, in C4 plants Rubisco shows lower affinity for CO_2 but higher carboxylation rates with minimal photorespiration; this would in turn lead to a higher biomass accumulation for a given amount of energy derived from sunlight. C4 plants can sustain high photosynthetic rates with a lower level of Rubisco; this implies that a lower amount of nitrogen is needed (higher nitrogen use efficiency). C4 plants can operate efficiently under low CO_2 levels, alleviating the need for wide stomata apertures, thereby reducing water loss.

Increasing CO_2 concentration associated with global warming might render C3 plants more efficient with respect to their Rubisco activity, although this might require increasing nitrogen supplies. Due to the low efficiency of Rubisco in C3 plants and the huge demand of Nitrogen to sustain the enzyme, strategies to improve Rubisco activity have received much attention in the last years.

Indeed it has been demonstrated that a high variability exists among vascular plant with respect to the catalytic properties of Rubisco; for example plants adapted to dryer environments showed a higher selectivity between CO_2 and O_2. On the other hand, it has also been noted that an increased specificity for the substrate may be accompanied by a decrease in the catalytic rate. Indeed, Rubisco of C4 plants show lower affinity than in C3 plants, as they are adapted to a relative high CO_2 concentration.

The possibility to introduce new Rubiscos in crops by conventional breeding has been exploited; furthermore biotechnological approaches have been tempted to modify Rubisco content and performance. Plastome transformation has evidenced that changes in L-subunit determine changes in photosynthetic rate; although not directly involved in catalysis, transformation of the nucleus-encoded S-subunits are also attractive. Another possible way to increase Rubisco efficiency is through introduction of CO_2-concentrating mechanisms (or C4-like features) in

C3 plants. Bioengineering plants for improved thermal tolerance of Rubisco activase, and a limited abundance of naturally occurring Rubisco inhibitors may represent indirect targets for improving Rubisco performance.

Glutamine Synthetase: The Eye of the Needle in Nitrogen Assimilation

Plant nitrogenous compounds, including proteins, are all virtually built up starting from glutamine that is the product of the ATP-dependent ammonia addition to a glutamate molecule. This reaction is catalyzed by glutamine synthetase (GS), the first enzyme of nitrogen assimilation (and re-assimilation), which plays a key role in plant growth and productivity as well as in nitrogen use efficiency (NUE).

In higher plants, with the exception of conifers, the enzyme is present as plastidial (GS1) and cytolsolic (GS2) isoforms encoded by a multigene family. The presence of isoenzymes in different plant organs has been referred to specific functions. Due to its abundance, this protein can be also used as nitrogen storage in plants.

Ammonia for GS activity derives from a wide variety of primary and secondary metabolic processes, including nitrate and ammonium uptake, N_2 fixation, photorespiration, protein and amino acid catabolism and phenylpropanoid biosynthetic pathway. This implies that different isoenzymes are involved in production of organic nitrogen in source tissues and the subsequent N assimilation in sink tissues.

Plant GS has been categorized as the type II commonly occurring in prokaryotes. Using X-ray crystallography it has demonstrated that the enzyme has a decameric structure composed of two face-to-face pentameric rings and possesses 10 active sites, each localized at the interface between the N-terminal and C-terminal domains of two neighbouring subunits. The subunit of cytosolic GS1 has a molecular mass of 38-40 kDa, while the plastid GS2 form range from 42 to 45 kDa. Glutamine synthesis is a two-step reaction involving the production of the activated intermediate ?-glutamyl phosphate from ATP and glutamate and the deprotonation of a bound ammonium ion to form ammonia, which attacks the carbonyl C to form glutamine.

Using different plant species, a number of 3 to 5 genes encoding for the cytosolic GS1 has been generally identified; on the other hand, a single gene encodes the chloroplastic GS2. Each of the GS genes appears to participate in different metabolic processes, based on where and how they are expressed [60]. The expression of GS1 genes and the presence of the enzyme differ considerably at the tissue and cellular levels. The GS2 gene is of nuclear origin and is targeted to the plastid; it is highly expressed in the mesophyll of leaves and other photosynthetic tissues. Expression is influenced by developmental and environmental cues, such as soil N availability, plant N status, external and internal C status, as well as changes in plant hormones.

A cytosolic gene has been shown to be highly expressed in infected cells of leguminous root nodules where ammonium produced by N_2 fixation has to be assimilated. The localization of a specific cytosolic GS isoenzyme in the vascular tissues has been reported for several species and related to N transport function. The plastidic GS2, besides its major role in ammonia assimilation for amino acid synthesis, is involved in re-assimilation of ammonium released by photorespiration in photosynthetic tissues.

GS1 has been implicated in assimilation of nitrogen in sink tissues. Increasing importance of GS1 relative to GS2 in senescing leaves suggests a role for the former in the mobilization of N to be delivered to different sinks (e.g. developing seeds). QTL analyses have shown that cytosolic GS is necessary for grain filling. It has also been shown that cytosolic GS protein can accumulate in mesophyll cells of plants in response to stress, such as pathogen attack [69], suggesting a role for this isoform in the re-assimilation of the nitrogen released during the disassembly of the photosynthetic apparatus.

Conifers do not possess GS2 gene, but rather they show two GS1 genes (GS1a and GS1b); based on light stimulation and parallelism between GS1a expression and chloroplast development it has been proposed that this gene might act similarly to GS2 in angiosperms. Interestingly the overexpression of cytosolic GS1a resulted in improved chemical characteristics of field grown hybrid poplars.

Understanding the role for the cytosolic GS1 and plastidic GS2 isoforms are being elucidated, mainly using mutant plants. This task is particularly difficult for GS1, due to the variable number of genes found in different plant species. Experiments using model and cultivated plants point to a non-redundancy of the different proteins, rather to a specific role for each of them. These aspects still deserve further research efforts.

Different kinds of post-translational modifications have been reported, involving Ca_2^+-dependent kinases and phosphorylation or binding of 14-3-3 proteins; furthermore selective phosphorylation of Ser97 residue and subsequent binding to 14-3-3 proteins, which causes proteolytic breakdown to an inactive product has been reported for plastidic GS2. Recently, ubiquitination of GS polypeptides has also been proposed as a reversible post-translational regulatory mechanism.

The possibility to alter the expression of either GS1 or GS2 and the enzyme activity has attracted attention of researcher due to the possible effects on N metabolism and NUE. Several transgenic approaches have been used, mainly based on overexpression or knockdown mutants.

Several studies have reported increased biomass and yield when GS genes are over-expressed in greenhouse and hydroponics experiments. Although the outcomes of these studies have been variable, they have clearly indicated that cytosolic GS1 can be important for efficient nitrogen assimilation, plant growth and biomass accumulation. As compared to GS2, GS1 might be a key component of plant NUE.

However it has also been evidenced that post-translational modification of GS might significantly affects the over-expression of this enzyme, thereby influencing its ability to increase NUE in the field. Further research is needed on these aspects; moreover, it has been proposed that gene stacking experiments utilizing GS along with other genes of interest for N metabolism might be a suitable strategy to get a clear effect on NUE. The variable effects of environmental conditions, especially N supply, observed in gene expression experiments [60] should be taken also into account when designing for transgenic approaches to evaluating NUE.

Concluding Remarks

Adaptation of plants to different environments and an efficient use of natural resources to sustain adequate crop productivity are strictly related to the coordinated action of metabolic processes within the plant. Several enzymes play crucial roles in this framework guaranteeing the basis for autotrophic behavior of higher plants. The enzymes analyzed in this chapter amply demonstrate this feature, as they catalyze key reactions in nutrient acquisition, energy production, carbon and nitrogen assimilation. Advances in protein structure definition, genomic approaches and identification of regulatory routes have made it possible to better understand the function of these enzymes, paving the way for designing plants adapted to changing environment and able to respond to new challenges of modern agriculture. Further improvement of our knowledge could conceivably derive from exploiting natural variation and by using transgenic approaches.

VITAMINS

Vitamins are a class of organic compounds. They are absolutely required for the maintenance of healthy life processes. Though they are required in small amounts, their capability of sustenance and their ability to perform biochemical functions is remarkable. The history of vitamins is one of the most important chapters in the field of medicine. People in olden days, knew that night blindness can be overcome or cured buy eating liver or using liver extracts. It is not until the British sailors on seven seas suffered from scurvy, that people realized the requirement of lime juice as a supplement in their diet. In fact, it was Casimir Funk who demonstrated that the extracts from rice husk, was able to cure the disease of Beriberi prevalent in human beings. Realizing the importance of some compounds which had amines so vital to the human body they were called as 'Vitamins'. Since then, remarkable progress has been made in this field. A large number of vitamins have been discovered, their structure and functions have been elucidated. It is paradoxical that the highly evolved human being is incapable of synthesizing the required vitamins, it is by the quirk of nature, the plants are endowed with the ability to synthesize all the required vitamins and also capable of supplying to other animals. Because of plants capacity to synthesize almost all vitamins in its body, it is difficult to obtain data on the symptoms due to deficiency of vitamins. However, the knowledge about vitamins deficiency in plants has come from the invitro studies of root cultures where roots don't grow without the addition of some vitamins this indicates that roots cannot synthesize some vitamins that are needed for their growth. Nonetheless, the knowledge about vitamins role in cellular metabolism has come mostly from animal studies. In this text a brief account of the source, structure and function of vitamins has been discussed. The study of vitamins is very important in understanding the biological processes. Based on the solubility, vitamins have been grouped into water soluble vitamins and fat soluble vitamins. Fat soluble vitamins are A, D.E & K and the rest are water soluble. Most of the vitamins have been found to act as coenzymes and some act as growth regulators.

Vitamin B Groups

Thiamine (Vitamin B1): Deficiency of this causes beriberi in human beings. In plants this vitamin is found in large quantities in actively growing regions and also in the husks of cereal grains. It is synthesized in leaves in the presence of light and then translocates to other regions preferably to growing regions. Thiamine consists of a substituted pyrimidine ring. It forms a bridge with another substituted thiozole by a methyl bridge. It exists as a free from and also as bound form called thiamine pyrophosphates. Thiamine pyrophosphate acts as the coenzyme for enzymes such as pyruvate decarboxylase and keto gluteraldehyde decarboxylase reactions where CO2 is removed.

Riboflavin (Vitamin B2): The deficiency of this vitamin causes a disease in human beings called. This vitamin is synthesized in plant leaves. Even micro organisms produce them. This yellow pigment is derived from isoalloxanthine. There are two types of riboflavins called riboflavin mononucleotide and riboflavin dinucleotide. They act as the prosthetic group of some important respiratory enzymes, ex., succinic dehydrogenase and NADPH dehydrogenase etc. They are involved in electron transport and transfer of hydrogen groups. It is suspected that this compound is involved in absorbing light at 445 mm and cause destruction of IAA and brings about phototropic curvature in stem tips. Delbruck calls this pigment as 'Cryptochromes'.

Nicotinic acid (Niacin): In human beings, the deficiency of this vitamin causes a disease called pellagra and black tongue in dogs. In plants, it is found in leaves and green stems. It requires light for its synthesis. For the development of roots this compound is absolutely required. As roots cannot synthesize niacin and its derivates, it is imported from aerial leaves. It is believed that it is synthesized from a precursor called tryptophan, which is also a precursor for IAA.

The term nicotinic acid is used because it is a component of a toxic alkaloid called nicotine found in tobacco leaves. It also exists as an amide called nicotinamide which is linked to a ribose sugar; hence it is called as the derivative of a ribose pyrimidine. There are two important complexes called nicotinamide dinucleotide (NAD) and nicotinamide dinucleotide phosphate (NADP).

These pyrimidine nucleotides function as coenzymes for many oxido-reductases which are involved in respiration, fatty acid metabolism, glucose monophosphate shunt, photosynthesis, amino acid synthesis and other such reactions. It is loosely bound to the apoenzyme part and involved in the transfer of hydrogen group and electrons.

Pentothenic Acid: It is found in significant quantities in aleurone layers of rice, wheat and other cereals. Synthesis of this component takes place in all parts of the plant body. It is a nine carbon amino carboxyl compound. Always it is linked to ribosyl adenine diphosphate at one end and to B mercaptoethylamine at the other. This complex is called coenzyme. This vitamin is involved in trans-acetylation reaction of pyruvate dehydrogenase and keto-glyceraldehyde dehydrogenase reactions. It is also involved in the synthesis of acetyl choline and citrate. Pentothenic acid has been implicated in photoperiodic reactions in plants. It plays an important role in the synthesis and oxidation of fatty acids.

Biotin: This vitamin is distributed in all parts of the plant body. Biotin consists of imidazole ring fused with thiophene inactivated by a protein called avidin, found in the white of the egg (raw). Heating destroys this inhibitor. Again this vitamin acts as the coenzyme covalently bound to some carboxylase enzymes involved in gluconeogenesis.

Vitamin B6 complex: This is made up of a group of pyridoxine and pyridoxal compounds like pyridoxine, pyridoxal, pyridoxal amine, pyridoxal phosphate and pyridoxal amine phosphate. They are distributed in all parts of the plant body like leaves, stem, roots, seeds, fruits, etc. The active part B6 co enzymes are pyridoxal phosphate and pyridoxalamine phosphate. They are involved in amino acid synthesis by transamination reactions. This is also an important growth factor in plants particularly for tissue cultures for rooting.

Folic Acid: As this acidic compound is derived from the leaves, it is called folic acid. First, it was isolated from spinach leaves and now it is known that it is found distributed in all parts of the plant body. Its deficiency causes various kinds of anemia in human beings. It is made up of substituted pteridine p-amino benzoic acid and glutamic acid, all together called pteroglutamic acid. The coenzyme form of folic acid is the reduced folate called tetrahdrofolate. Folic acid is involved in the transfer of hydroxy-methyl group of one amino acid to the other. It actually acts as a kind of shuttle between compounds. This is a very important coenzyme in amino acid metabolism, and also in the synthesis of nitrogen bases required for the nucleotides. In humans it cause tongue boils and blisters.

Lipoic Acid: This vitamin is also called as thio-acetic acid. Again it is found distributed in all the parts of the plant holds. This combines with lysine to form dihydrolipoic acid. As it has two sulphide groups, it is involved in oxidation reduction reactions. This is a very important coenzyme and it is responsible for oxidative decarboxylation reactions of pyruvate and other ketoacids.

Vitamin B_{12}: Vitamin B_{12} is used to cure pernicious anemia. This is also found in the plants; particularly leguminous root nodules. Structurally, it is very complex and contains cobalt in the middle of coring a ring and it is called Cyanacobalamin; because it contains cyanide group. It acts as coenzyme. This coenzyme is synthesized in symbiotic Rhizobium bacteria. It plays an important role in nitrogenase enzymatic reaction in fixing inorganic N_2 into NH_3.

Vitamin C (Ascorbic Acid): It is found in all the parts of the plant body but lemon, capsicum and other citrus fruits contain large amounts. The deficiency of this vitamin causes scurvey disease in human beings. Vitamin C acts as a strong reducing agent. It is involved in enzymatic hydroxylation of proline to hydroxyproline which is an important component of extension found in cell walls. It is also involved in cyclic oxidation reduction reactions.

Myo-inositol: A cyclic sugar alcohol called Myo-inositol is an important component of the plant body. It acts as a growth factor in plants and used in plant tissue cultures. Myo-inositol is an important component of membrane Phosphoglycerides. It is also involved signal transduction pathway.

Fat Soluble Vitamins

Vitamin A: Deficiency of vitamin A causes night blindness in human beings. Though it is synthesized as carotenes in the plant body, particularly in green leaves its role is not known in plant metabolism. From animal experiments, it is now known that it plays an important role in the eyes as an important component of Rhodopsin. In some bacteria like halo-bacteria, this vitamin plays an important role in hydrogen production. It is also known to be involved in growth, spermatogenesis and oogenesis.

Vitamin K: This fat soluble vitamin is found in plant leaves and other photosynthetic structures, particularly, in chloroplasts. It is involved in cyclic and non cyclic electron transport system. Nothing is known about its other functions in plants. It is also involved in antiport transport of Na ions. But in animals, it is very important in blood clotting. However, the role of other vitamins or such compounds is not clearly known in plants.

21

Major Pests and Diseases of Rice

DESCRIPTION

There are only two species of cultivated rice in the world, *Oryza sativa* (Asian rice) and *Oryza glaberrima* (African rice). Both species are annual grasses (except in the tropics, where the plant can be perennial) belonging to the family Poaceae which are cultivated for their grain which is considered a staple food in most parts of the world. Asian and African rice plants are morphologically very similar and can be difficult to tell apart. They have rounded stems (called culms) which are divided into nodes and internodes. The plant leaves are borne on the nodes of the stem and are long and slender with a pronounced midrib. The plant produces three flowers, two of which are reduced, on a spikelet on the terminal (last) internode of the stem. The rice grain is formed by the ripened ovary of the flower and is between 5 and 12 mm in length. Rice is an annual plant, harvested after one growing season and can reach a height of between 1 and 1.8 m (3.3–5.9 ft) depending on variety. Generally, African rice tends to form smaller, pear shaped grains with a red bran and olive to black seed coat and has several disadvantages compared with its Asian counterpart e.g. seed is easily scattered, the grain is difficult to mill and the crop gives a lower yield. The growing of Asian rice has therefore begun to supercede that of African rice in West Africa. Asian rice originates from China and African rice is believed to have been domesticated in areas around the Niger river in Africa.

Asian "basmati" rice`

Asian rice field

Asian rice with panicles

Mature Asian rice panicles

Rice growing terraces in the Philippines

Rice terraces in Vietnam

USES

After removal of the rice grain from the chaff, the rice can be used as brown rice or further processed to remove the bran to produce white rice. Brown and white rice may be consumed after cooking or may be ground into rice flour. Rice can be puffed under low pressure to produce puffed rice that is commonly used as a breakfast cereal. Rice bran oil can be produced from the inner husk and can be used as a cooking oil. Rice starch can be extracted and fermented to produce rice wine or brewed to produce sake.

PROPAGATION

Basic Requirements

Rice is mainly grown in warmer regions as the plants will not grow at temperatures below 10°C. Rice is considered to be a semi-aquatic annual grass and is commonly grown in paddies in wetlands or under shallow water. Several new methods of propagating rice have been developed which allow rice to be cultivated in less conventional areas e.g. drought resistant varieties are grown in upland areas.

Propagation

Rice is propagated directly from seed and sown on wet or dry seed beds or used to grow transplants in a nursery bed. Transplants produced in a nursery are always planted in dry seed beds when they are transferred to the field. Seeds may be sown in the field by broadcasting or by mechanical drilling. Three main methods are used for direct seeding rice in lowland areas: dry seedbeds, wet seedbeds and dapog. Dry seedbeds are prepared in close proximity to a water source. Each bed is generally 1.5 m (4.9 ft) in width and is seeded at a rate of 10 kg of seed for every 10 square meters. The seeds are covered with a light layer of soil and the bed is saturated with water until the seeds germinate. Wet seedbeds are raised nursery beds in which pre-germinated seeds are sown. The bed is puddled or wet with water and the germinated seeds are spread out uniformly and kept wet. When the seedling reach 2-3 cm (0.8–1.2 in) in height, shallow irrigation is used and the water levels in the bed are increased as the plants grow. Dapod is a method of producing transplants on a mat made of banana leaves of plastic sheeting which is used in some areas of the Philippines. Pre-germinated seeds are spread out on cement of wet soil and covered with the leaves or plastic sheeting. The cover is pushed down onto the seeds and continuously watered. After 11 days, the mat is rolled up and transferred to to the field.

Cropping Systems

Rice can be be grown in an irrigated system, as a rainfed crop or in an upland systems in managed fields known as paddies. In irrigated systems, supplemental water is provided during the dry season alone or in both the dry and wet seasons depending on the amount of local rainfall. Irrigated systems are required in areas where rainfall is very low. Irrigated fields are bunded and the water levels are carefully managed prior to harvest. Rainfed systems are generally a poorer alternative to irrigated systems as they are unstable and prone to drought or floods. Rainfed fields are also bunded but are only flooded for short periods and water depths never exceed 50 cm (20 in). In some parts of Asia, Africa and Latin America, rice is grown in upland areas in acidic and nutrient depleted soils. Fields are either planted on flat land in valleys or on mountainside terraces where the land is sharply sloping. Fields in upland systems are generally unbunded and surface water does not usually accumulate as in the other growing systems.

Harvesting

In many areas of the world rice is still harvested using the traditional method of cutting by hand. Rice should be cut when 80–85% of the panicles have turned from green to straw colored. When harvested by hand, the rice is cut using sharp knives or sickles. In some areas, rice is mechanically harvested using threshers or combines.

PHYSIOLOGICAL DISORDERS

Physiological disorders are quite common in rice crops grown under different conditions of soil. It is also called physiological diseases. It is frequently occurs in field with poor drainage and accumulation of toxic products from anaerobic decomposition due to reductive soil conditions.

Important physiological disorders are:

Deficiency of major or minor nutrients like N, P, K, Fe, Mn, Zn, Si etc.

Toxicity of elements like Fe, Mn, B, Al, etc.

Accumulation of toxic substances due to poor soil conditions like sulfide, organic acids, carbon dioxide etc.

Injury due to excess salt like Na salts etc.

Main Disorders

Nitrogen Deficiency

It is one of the common disorder found in rice and usually occurs at tillering and panicle initiation stage. The symptoms occur in older leaves (sometimes in younger leaves also) where we will see appearance of light green to chlorotic tip. The leaves may die out under sever condition, where as the deficient young leaves are narrow, short, erect, and lemon yellowish. Some times the whole field look yellowish.

Zinc Deficiency

Symptoms occurs on young or middle-aged leaves. The plants are stunted in growth with bronzing upper leaves and chlorotic basal leaves. Stacking of leaf sheath or joints are also common.

Boron Deficiency

Symptoms usually appear first on young leaves. Tips of emerging leaves are white and rolled. In severe conditions, growing points can die, but new tillers continue to emerge. Plants shows reduced height. When infected at panicle initiation stage, plants won't produce panicles.

Phosphorus Deficiency

The main symptoms are stunted dark green plants with erect leaves, thin stem and with few tillers. The infected leaves are narrow, short, very erect, and 'dirty' dark green. Some time you will see red and purple colors on leaves if variety produce anthocyanin.

Potassium Deficiency

Symptom first appears on older leaves where you can see tips showing yellowish brown margin or dark brown necrotic spots. Symptom occur from tip, then along leaf edges and spreads to leaf base. Younger leaves are droopy, short and dirty green color, whereas older leaves show yellowish to brown discoloration along intervenes. Some time this symptom is mistaken with tungro virus.

Calcium Deficiency

The symptoms are chlorotic white discoloration at tips of youngest leaves. Deficient plants are weak rooted. Necrotic tissue may develop along the lateral margin of the leaves. In acidic soils we can see premature leaf senescence.

Magnesium Deficiency

The older leaves shows pale discoloration with interveinal chlorosis. Green coloring appears as string of beads. The leaves are wavey and droopy.

MAJOR INSECT PESTS OF RICE

On the basis of the extent and severity of the damage, the following insects are considered as major pests of rice in Sri Lanka (RRDI, 1996).

Rice Thrips (RTH): *Stenchaetothrips biformis* (Bagnall) (Thysanoptera: Thripidae)

A pest of young rice seedlings. Adult and larvae suck the cell sap from the leaf tissues. Damaged leaves roll inwards along the margins, feeding causes leaf drying resulting poor crop growth. The damage is severe under water stress conditions. Late planted crops are more prone for damage. Short duration traditional rice varieties like Dahanala, Kaluheenati, Kalubalawee are resistant to thrips. Higher trichome density on leaf surface found to be responsible for thrips resistance in rice. Effective control methods available:

1. Submerge infested crops intermittently for 1-2 days.
2. Drag a wet cloth on the seedlings
3. Apply recommended insecticides if difficult to control
4. For endemic areas use a recommended seed-dressing formulation

Brown Plant Hopper (BPH): *Nilapavata lugens* (Stal) (Homoptera: Delphacidae)

Heavy infestations produce symptoms of hopper burn. Leaves dry and turn brown after insect feeding, and patches of burned plants are often lodged. A vector of grassy stunt and ragged stunt virus diseases. The rice plant is most sensitive to attack at late vegetative and reproductive stages.

The economic threshold for BPH at booting stage is 2 per hill and at heading 5 per hill. Since spiders are considered major predator of BPH, the economic threshold levels are adjusted according to the number of spiders present. Number of effective predators and parasites are known.

Ptb 33, a variety with a high level of resistance to BPH, is extensively used in the breeding program. A number of varieties with moderate level of resistance to BPH have been developed: Bg 379-2, Bg 300, Bg 403, Bg 304, Bg 357, Bg 358, Bg 360.

Effective control methods available

1. Cultivate resistant varieties.
2. Draining the paddy field to reduce moisture help prevent BPH multiplication.
3. Iindiscriminate use of insecticides during vegetative stage known to cause BPH outbreaks. Use insecticides only when and where needed during vegetative stage especially for the control of leaf eating caterpillars.
4. Monitor crop regularly for signs of early BPH infestations.
5. Select a safer insecticide if required.

Safer and effective insecticides are available for use during epidemics

Yellow Stem Borer (YSB): *Scirpophaga incertulas* (Lepidoptera: Pyralidae)

The caterpillars bore into the rice stem and hollow out the stem completely. Attacked young plant shows dead heart and older plants show white heads. Often plants break where the stem is hollowed out causing lodging.

Serious out breaks of YSB are very rare. Resistant varieties are not available. Effective insecticides are available for YSB control.

Rice Leaffolders (RLF): *Cnaphalocrocis medinalis; Marasmia* spp. (Lepidoptera: Pyralidae)

The caterpillars infest the leaves and feed on the mesophyll. They fasten the edges of a leaf together and live inside the rolled leaf. Feeding reduces productive leaf area that affects plant growth. Cloudy and humid weather, shady locations and high N-fertilizer favor pest build up.

Control measures available

1. Establish crop at recommended plant spacing
2. Use recommended dose of N-fertilizer
3. Monitor crop regularly. ELT
4. ETL 25% of leaves showing > 50% damage
5. Use safer IGR for control

Rice Gall Midge (RGM) *Orselia oryzae* (Diptera: Cecidomyiidae)

Coleoptern predatory beetle have been identified.

Severity of damage is related to the crop growth stage of attack. The larvae more down between the leaf sheaths until they reach the apical bud or one of the lateral buds. They lacerate the tissues of the bud and feed until pupation. The feeding causes formation of a gall called a "Silver" or "Onion" shoot.Galls terminate the tiller development and hence affect rice yield.

Gall midge damage is high in wet humid weather. As such gall midge infestation is high in dry and intermediate zones in maha and in the wet zone during yala.

Resistance available in varieties like Ptb 18/ Ptb 21 and Eswarakora has been used to develop a number of improved varieties with resistance to gall midge. Since biotype development on resistant varieties is common breeding for resistance is difficult. The gall midge biotype detected after 1986 is termed as biotype II. Varieties resistant to biotype II are: Bg 304, Bg 357, Bg 359, Bg 360.

Control methods:

1. Granular insecticides are recommended for gall midge control. Since farmers use granules after observing damage symptoms it is difficult to obtain a good control with granules.
2. Cultivation of resistant varieties in endemic areas is the most economical method.

Paddy bug (PB) L*eptocorisa oratorius* (Hemiptera: Alydidae)

Sucks the developing grains causing empty or partially filled grains. Both nymphs and adults damage the grains. Damage estimated to reduce 3-5% rice yield in the country.

Paddy can feed and reproduce only on rice. Adults and mature nymphs can feed and survive on alternate weed hosts.

A number of predators and egg parasitoids have been identified. Gryon nixoni is the most commonest egg parasitoid found in Sri Lanka.

Grain Moth - ***Sitotroge cerealella***

Infestation of grain moth starts in the field and may reach serious levels in the store. The damage is done by larvae which are elongated, dirty white about 8 mm long. The pupa is dark brown. The adult is a small, straw colored moth about 7 mm long; the wings are 15 mm across when open.Infestation of grain moth could be minimized by sun drying of seeds to minimize moisture content down to 8.0% and pack in polythene or paper bags.

Grain weevil - ***Sitophilus granarius***

Two species of stored product pests belongs to genus Sitophilus are found in rice in Sri Lanka. They are Sitophilus granerius and S. oryzae. Infestation of these two species starts in the field. Eggs laid on rice seeds, hatch into tiny grubs which feed the grain. Mature larvae are legless and dirty white about 4 mm long. Pupation takes place in the grain. Adult beetles are small brown weevils. They are about 3.5-4.0 mm long with rostrum.This pest could be controlled by spraying the store with pirimiphos-methyl at the rate of 27 ml per 9 liters of water. Sspray gunny bags with the same insecticide and sundry them before use.

Red flour beetle - ***Tribolium cestaneum***

Red flour beetle is a secondary pest and their damage is extensive in previously holed or broken grains. Both larvae and adults damage the seeds.

The larvae are yellowish white. The head is pale brown. They are about 6 mm long when fully grown. Pupae are yellowish white at the early stages and become brown in colour later. The adult is flat and reddish brown in colour.

DISEASES

Bacterial blight - ***Xanthomonas campestris***

Symptoms

Water-soaked stripes on leaf blades; yellow or white stripes on leaf blades; leaves appear grayish in color; plants wilting and rolling up; leaves turning yellow; stunted plants; plant death; youngest leaf on plant turning yellow

Comments

One of the most important diseases of rice; disease found in tropical and temperate regions; greatest economic impact in Asia.

Bacterial blight infected leaf

Management

Bacterial blight can be effectively controlled by planting resistant rice varieties; avoid excessive nitrogen fertilization; plow stubble and straw into soil after harvest

Bacterial leaf streak - *Anthomonas oryzae*

Symptoms

Bacterial leaf streak

Small, water-soaked streaks between leaf veins which are initially dark green and then turn translucent; streaks grow larger, coalesce and turn light brown in color; tiny beads of yellow colored bacterial exudate are common on the surface of the streaks; leaves turn brown and then gray-white in color before they die

Comments

Bacteria survive on infected seed and straw; bacteria may enter the plant through wounds; bacterial exudate can be spread in irrigation water; emergence of the disease is favored by high humidity and high temperatures; bacterial leaf streak is widespread in tropical Asia and West Africa

Management

Control of bacterial leaf streak is dependent on the use of resistant rice varieties and on planting of treated seed

Bakanae - *Fusarium moniliforme* Fungus

Symptoms

Bakanae infected plant in rice field

Seedlings are elongated, slender and pale; seedlings are stunted and chlorotic; death of seedlings; abnormal elongation of older plants which often makes them visible as they grow taller than uninfected plants in the field; sterile plants which do not produce panicles or produce empty panicles

Comments

Disease transmitted through infected seed; disease emergence favored by high temperatures

Management

Treating seeds with appropriate fungicides prior to planting can be very effective at controlling the disease; less susceptible rice varieties should be grown in areas where fungicide-treated seed is not available.

Brown spot* - Cochliobolus miyabeanus *Fungus

Symptoms

Circular, brown lesions on seedling; distorted primary and/or secondary leaves on seedlings; black discoloration of roots; death of seedlings; circular or oval lesions with gray center and reddish-brown margin on older plants; death of large areas of leaves; brown or black spots on grain; reduced number of grains; reduced kernel weight

Comments

Occurs wherever rice is grown; fungus overwinters on plant debris; disease emergence favored by water on surfaces of plant

Management

Ensure plants are provided with correct nutrients and avoid water stress; chemical seed treatments are effective at reducing the incidence of the disease

False smut* - Ustilaginoidea virens *Fungus

Symptoms

False Smut

The pathogen infect the rice plant during flowering stage and causes chalkiness of grain. The individual grains were covered with orange fungal mass in the beginning, later turns into greenish velvet color during sporulation stage and finally into charcoal black during spore maturation stage. It infect only few grains in spikelet. Recorded disease loss up to 75% in severe incidence. It also reduces market value of rice.

Comments

It is seed born disease and may also affect seed germination.

Management

Treat seeds with hot water (52° C) for 10 min. Roughing the infected plants from field and from harvested grains. Keep the rice field and surrounding clean. Use resistant varieties. Maintain humidity in field by alternate wetting and drying.

Leaf scald* - Microdochium oryzae *(Fungus)

Symptoms

As name suggest we will see scalded appearance on leaves. The lesion is marked with different zone from alternating light tan and dark brown from leaf tips or edges. As the leaves mature the lesion is with light brown halos. Margins and leaf tips are translucent.

Comments

The symptoms may vary depends on cultivar, growth stage and plant density. The disease is severe in Latin America and West Africa.

Management

Grow resistant varieties. Treat the seeds with suitable fungicide. Apply only recommended quantity of nitrogen fertilizer in split dose.

Narrow leaf spot (Cercospora leaf spot) - *Cercospora oryzae* (Fungus)

Symptoms

Short, elliptical or linear brown lesions on leaves; necrosis of leaves; blotchy pattern on leaves; premature ripening of kernels

Comments

Disease occurs in major rice growing regions in tropical and sub-tropical Asia, Africa, Australia, North America, South America and Central America

Management

There are no chemical controls currently recommended for the treatment of the disease; treating seeds with hot water or appropriate fungicides prior to planting can reduce the incidence of the disease

Rice blast - *Magnaporthe grisea* (Fungus)

Symptoms

Lesions on all parts of shoot; white to green or gray diamond-shaped lesions with dark green borders; death of leaf blades; black necrotic patches on culm; rotting panicles

Comments

Most important disease of rice worldwide; causes most damage in areas of intense cultivation; disease emergence favors high soil nitrogen content

Management

If disease is not endemic to the region, blast can be controlled by planting resistant rice varieties; avoid over-fertilizing crop with nitrogen as this increases the plant's susceptibility to the disease; utilize good water management to ensure plants do not suffer from drought stress; disease can be effectively controlled by the application of appropriate systemic fungicides, where available.

Grassy stunt - Rice grassy stunt virus (RGSV) Virus

Symptoms

Stunted plants; short, narrow pale green or yellow leaves; mottled or striped pattern on newly unfolded leaves; irregular dark brown spots on leaves; few or no panicles produced.

Comments

Transmitted by leaf hoppers; disease widespread in rice growing regions of South and Southeast Asia, southern China, southern Japan and Taiwan

Management

Several varieties of rice resistant to the leaf hopper vectors have been developed but the insects have overcome the resistance in several countries; applications of appropriate insecticides can help to reduce populations of vectors in temperate regions

Leafhoppers and planthoppers - *Nephotettix* spp. (insect)

Symptoms

Plants may show no symptoms of leafhopper of planthopper damage; feeding punctures can leave the plants susceptible to bacterial or fungal infections; insects transmit many rice viruses; if infestations is severe, insects may cause plant to completely dry out; adults insects are pale green or brown winged insects with piercing-sucking mouthparts

Comments

Leaf and planthoppers transmit many rice viruses, including grassy stunt and tungro virus

Management

Rotating crop for a period of one year is an effective and economical method of controlling hopper numbers; natural enemies and predators are often very successful at controlling hoppers and should be conserved by avoiding inappropriate use of insecticides which can damage their populations; planting resistant varieties is a very effective control method; chemical control with an appropriate insecticide may be necessary but should only be applied if the insects have reached an economic threshold

Mole cricket - *Gryllotalpa orientalis* (insect)

Symptoms

The insect is very destructive because it feeds on seeds, tillers of mature plants and roots. It mainly cut the tillers at ground level and causes gap in rice field. Usually the symptoms appear in patches.

Comments

We can see burrows of insect at sides of rice field and usually burrows will have heap of soil at entrance.

Mole cricket

Management

Use resistant varieties. Level the field properly and irrigate every 3-4 days after planting. Collect and kill the insects during land preparation. Avoid nurseries with raised bed to reduce cricket infestation during seedling stage. Improve biocontrol agents in field. If damage is large use food bait (commonly rice bran) mixed with insecticide and place along borders.

Rice bug - *Leptocorisa oratorius F. and Leptocorisa acuta Thunberg* (insect)

Symptoms

The insect attacks during spikelet stage of rice crop. Both nymphs and adults suck the content out of grains from pre-flowering spikelets to soft dough stage. This leads to unfilled, empty and discolored grains.

Rice bug

Comments

If the infestation is severe it may cause yield loss up to 30%.

Management

Keep the field and surrounding area free from weeds which serves as alternative host for insect during non cropping season. Equal distribution of fertilizers and water in rice field to encourage even crop growth. Collect and kill insects manually by using net during early morning and late after noon. Encourage biological control agents.

Rice case worm - *Paraponyx stagnalis Stagnalis* (Lepidoptera: Pyralidae)*Nymphula depunctalis (Guenee)* (insect)

Symptoms

Case worm larvae scraps chlorophyll from leaves. Another important symptom is the larvae cuts off leaf tips and make cylindrical tubes around them. In infected field you can see cylindrical tubes attached to plants or floating on water surface.

Nymphula depunctalis

Comments

The damaged leaf tissue looks like ladder.

Management

Drain water to remove floating larvae from field. Follow proper cultivation practices like nitrogen application and spacing. Encourage biological control agents like snails, spiders, lady bird beetles, dragon flies in rice field.

Rice gall midge - *Orseolia oryzae* (insect)

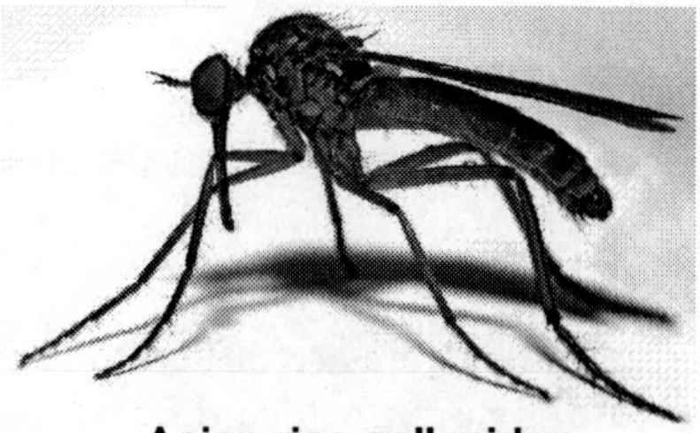

Asian rice gall midge

Symptoms

Gall midge maggot bore into bud or stalk of rice plant and feeds on internal content which leads to formation of tubular gall at the base of the tillers. This leads to elongation of leaf sheath which is commonly called as silver shoot or onion shoot. The leaves will be wilted, deformed and curled up.

Comments

It is common during tillering stage of rice crop.

Management

Grow available gall midge resistant cultivars. Follow proper cultural practices like crop rotation, ploughing the ratoon crop and other alternative hosts, planting early etc. Use light traps to attract adult flies and kill them. Conserve biocontrol agents in rice field.

Rice mealy bugs - *Brevennia rehi* (insect)

Rice mealy bugs

Symptoms

Both adult and nymphs feed on rice plant by sucking sap. The main symptoms are stunting and wilting of plants, yellowing and curling of leaves.

Comments

We can see white wax covered eggs, nymphs and adults on infected plants. The insects are common in field with well drained soil.

Management

Augment biocontrol agents (like lady bird beetles, chloropid flies, spiders, small encyrtid wasps) in rice fields.

Stem borers (Yellow stem borer, Striped stem borer, White stem borer, etc.) - *Scirpophaga incertulas* (insect)

Symptoms

Longitudinal white patches on leaf sheaths; central leaf whorl drying out and turning brown; tillers drying out without producing panicles; panicles may dry out or may produce no grain; adult insects are nocturnal moths which lay their eggs on the leaves or leaf sheaths of the rice plants; larvae are legless grubs which feed on leaf sheaths before entering the stem of the pant

Comments

Stem borers are generally considered to be the most damaging insect pest of rice

Management

Stem borers are difficult to control with insecticides as once they bore inside the stem they are protected from chemical sprays; in order for chemical control to be successful, repeated applications of appropriate insecticide must be made to the foliage; granular formulations give better control than sprays; clipping seedling prior to transplanting can successfully reduce moth numbers as eggs are laid at leaf tips; harvesting plants at ground level can remove the majority of larvae from the field; plowing or flooding the remaining stubble will kill off most of the remainder of the larvae in the field

Sheath blight - *Rhizoctonia solani* (Fungus)

Symptoms

Circular, oblong or elliptical, green to gray water-soaked spots on leaf sheaths; lesions with pale green or white center and purple-brown margin; lesions covering leaf sheaths and stems; poorly filled grains

Sheath blight

Comments

Occurs in all areas where rice is grown; second only importance to rice blast; most damaging in intensive rice production; spreads rapidly via irrigation

Management

Avoid overfertilizing plants as excessive nitrogen application has been shown to increase susceptibility to the disease; applications of foliar fungicides may be required; two applications are recommended and should be timed so that the first application is made between the early internode elongation and the second application made on emerging panicles 10-14 days later

Stem rot - *Magnaporthe salvinii* (Fungus)

Symptoms

Symptoms generally begin to appear after the mid tillering stage; black lesions appear on outer leaf sheath at the water-line; lesions expand and begin to infect inner leaf sheaths and culm begins to rot; infections which reach the culm can leaf to lodging of plants, unfilled panicles and death of tillers

Comments

Fungus survives in crop debris in soil after harvest; fruiting bodies are carried to the surface when fields are flooded where they then infect leaf sheaths at the water line

Management

Bury crop residue deeply in the soil after harvest; avoid excessive nitrogen fertilization; plant less susceptible rice varieties

Tungro - Rice tungro bacilliform virus (RTBV) (virus)

Symptoms

Plants are stunted with a yellow-orange discoloration; plants may have a reduced number of tillers and rust colored spots on leaves; leaves may be mottled, striped or exhibit interveinal necrosis

Comments

Disease is the most severely damaging virus of rice in South and Southeast Asia; virus is transmitted by leafhoppers

Management

Rice varieties resistant to tungro virus have been developed and control the disease successfully; intense cultivation has led to the breakdown of the resistance by some virulent leafhopper strains; in Indonesia, the disease is successfully controlled by scheduling planting to obtain synchronous development and practicing crop rotation with resistant varieties

22

Major Pests and Diseases of Maize

DESCRIPTION

Corn, *Zea mays*, is an annual grass in the family Poaceae and is a staple food crop grown all over the world. The corn plant possesses a simple stem of nodes and internodes. A pair of large leaves extends off of each internode and the leaves total 8–21 per plant. The leaves are linear or lanceolate (lance-like) with an obvious midrib and can grow from 30 to 100 cm (11.8–39.4 in) in length. The male and female inflorescences (flower bearing region of the plant) are positioned separately on the plant. The male inflorescence is known as the 'tassel' while the female inflorescence is the 'ear'. The ear of the corn is a modified spike and there may be 1–3 per plant. The corn grains, or 'kernels', are encased in husks and total 30–1000 per ear. The kernels can be white, yellow, red, purple or black in color. Corn is an annual plant, surviving for only one growing season prior to harvest and can reach 2–3 m (7–10 ft) in height. Corn may also be referred to as maize or Indian corn and is believed to originate from Mexico and Central America.

Corn tassel

Corn foliage

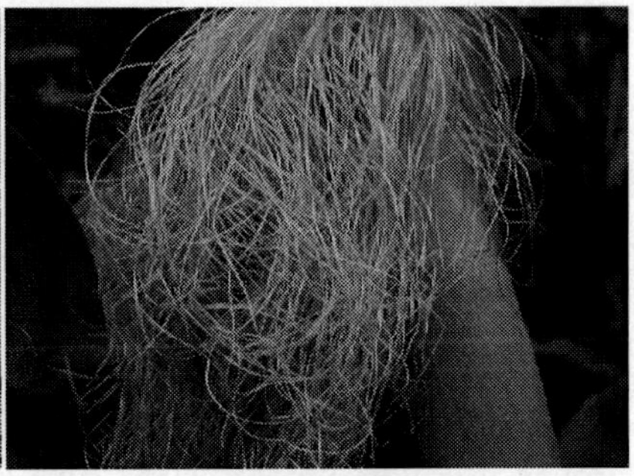

Corn silks

USES

Corn and cornmeal (dried, ground corn) are staple foods in countries all over the world. The ears can be cooked and eaten from the cob as a vegetable or the kernels can be removed and either eaten as is or used to produce a wide variety of foodstuffs including cereals and flour. Corn is also a major source of starch and the starch can be processed into oils and high fructose corn syrup. Corn is also commonly grown as a feed for livestock.

PROPAGATION

Basic requirements

Corn is best grown in warm, tropical and sub-tropical regions as it requires warm soils to develop optimally. One of the most important requirements for growing corn is a high quality soil which is deep, fertile and well-draining with a pH between 6.0 and 6.8. Corn plants are very heavy feeders and even the most fertile of soils may need to supplemented with nutrients as the plants develop, particularly nitrogen. Corn also requires ample space as it grows large in size and is pollinated by wind. It should be planted where it will receive full sunlight for most of the day and provided with ample moisture.

Planting

Planting dates for corn depend on the variety being grown. Standard varieties should be planted when the soil has warmed to at least 12.7°C (55°F) and supersweet varieties when the soil reaches 18.3°C (65°F). Soil can be brought up to temperature faster by laying black plastic mulches approximately 1 week prior to planting. Seeds should be sown about 2.5 cm (1 in) deep and 10–15 cm (~3–4 in) apart allowing 76–91 cm (~30–36 in) between rows. Corn should be planted in blocks (numerous rows) rather than in a single long row as it is wind pollinated and pollen can transfer between plants much more efficiently. Seedlings should be thinned to a final spacing 20–30 cm (8–12 in) when they are approximately 7.5–10.0 cm (3–4 in) in height. It is common to stagger corn plantings to ensure a continuous harvest over the summer months.

General Care and Maintenance

Corn plants are heavy feeders, particularly of nitrogen (N) and care should be taken to provide them with adequate nutrients by applying side dressings of fertilizer. Corn undergoes a rapid growth period between 30 and 40 days after planting and should be fertilized just prior to this. All fertilizer applications should be made before the tasseling period to ensure the plant maximizes N use. Be vigilant regarding signs of nutrient deficiency, plants should be a deep green color. Purple tinged leaves indicate that the plants are suffering from a lack of phosphorous whereas light green leaves indicate a lack of nitrogen. Apply fertilizer. Plants also require adequate soil moisture throughout the growing period in order to tassel and form silks. Soaker hoses can be used to great effect in small to mid-size plantings. Pollination occurs when pollen is transferred from the male tassel to the female silk by the wind. Each silk produced a single kernel of corn and partially filled ears are usually a result of poor pollination.

Harvesting

Each corn stalk should produce 1 large ear of corn. Under ideal conditions, the stalk will often produce a second, slightly smaller ear which reaches maturity slightly later than the first. Corn ears should be harvested at the "milk stage" of development when when the kernels within the husk are well packed and produce a milky substance when the kernel is punctured. Check ears for ripeness by gently peeling back a small portion of the husk. Be sure to check the ears frequently for ripeness and harvest as required as ears can quickly become over-ripe and lose their sweetness. Remove the ears from the stalk by pulling quickly downward while twisting and then refrigerate until consumption.

PHYSIOLOGICAL DISEASES

Nitrogen Deficiency

The typical symptom of nitrogen deficiency is the plant turns pale green; a 'V' shaped yellow coloration on leaves. This pattern starts from leaf end to leaf collar. The symptom begin from lower to upper leaves.

Nitrogen Deficiency

Phosphorous Deficiency

The deficient plants are dark green and lower leaves show reddish-purple discoloration.

Phosphorous Deficiency

Potassium Deficiency

The leaf margins turn yellow and brown coloration which appears like firing or drying. The symptoms progress from lower leaves to upper leaves.

Sulfur Deficiency

Symptom appears on younger leaves where we will see yellow color striping or interveinal chlorosis.

Zinc deficiency

Upper leaves shows broad bands of yellow coloration and later turn pale brown or gray necrosis. The symptom first appears in the middle of leaves and progress outward.

Potassium Deficiency

Sulfur Deficiency

Zinc deficiency

INSECT PEST MANAGEMENT IN MAIZE

Helicoverpa armigera (Corn Earworm)

Helicoverpa armigera is major, widespread, regular pest. Female moths lay eggs on the stem, leaves (both sides) tassels, silks and husks on the upper two-thirds of plants. Caterpillars hatching prior to silking cause little damage to tassels but may cause damage when migrating to cobs. Larvae from eggs laid on silks or husks may cause significant damage. Silk damage reduces pollination and grain-set. Feeding damage also occurs on the top 1-3 cm of the cob, and may result in the presence of mycotoxins.

Leaf damage can indicate pest presence. Parallel rows of holes are signs of feeding on unopened leaves. Helicoverpa are usually not considered

Maize pests by crop stage
Pests can occur at one or more growth stages (Insects that can potentially be a major pest are indicated in bold):

Germination	Growth	Silking-tasselling	Seed-filling -maturity
black field earwig	locusts	corn earworm	twospotted mite green
vegetable bug			
true wireworms	whitegrubs		redbanded shield bug
maize leafhopper			
maize thrips	whitefringed weevil		yellow peach moth
false wireworms	swarming leaf beetles		
cutworms	dayfeeding armyworm corn aphid		
	green vegetable bug		
	redshouldered leaf beetle		
	common armyworm		

economical to control, except in high value seed maize. Note that helicoverpa larvae may be confused with armyworms or cutworms.

Maize varieties with husks extending 50-80 mm beyond the top of the cob and closing tightly around the silks restrict the entry of larvae into the cob. Watering during dry weather prevents the husks from loosening.

Maize crops often have high levels of beneficial insects (predators and parasitoids) that may be harmed by insecticide applications. The combined action of natural enemies (including predators of eggs, larvae and pupae, parasites of eggs and larvae, and caterpillar diseases) can have a significant impact. Cultivation to a dept of 100 mm destroys overwintering pupae.

Chemical control should target small caterpillars (up to 5 mm) and be directed at tassels and emerging silks. The best product to use in an integrated pest management system is a naturally occurring nucleopolyhedovirus (NPV). There are a number of commercially formulated NPV products on the market for the control of helicoverpa.

Soil Insects

Soil-dwelling insect pests can seriously reduce plant establishment, plant populations, plant growth, and subsequent yield potential, and should be monitored for prior to plating. Seed treatments help deter feeding. In-furrow spraying helps protect young roots and shoots. Press wheels can reduce damage from false wireworm larvae and earwigs by encouraging plant emergence and firming the soil to reduce insects' ability to move through it. Soil baiting may reduce damage by black field earwigs and crickets that attack the tips of developing prop-roots (secondary roots). Shallow planting in warm moist soil will encourage rapid crop emergence and growth, thus reducing the impact of insects

Black Field Earwig

is a sporadic and potentially major pest of maize, black earwigs eat newly sown and germinating seed and the roots of crops resulting in poor establishment. Feeding on secondary roots may cause the plants to fall over as they get larger. Serious damage is usually confined to soils that retain moisture well, and earwigs prefer cultivated soils to undisturbed soil (zero till). Note: predatory earwigs are usually larger and light brown in colour.

Monitor crops after planting until establishment. Dig and sieve soil to detect adults and nymphs prior to planting. Use germinating seed baits and control if more than 50 earwigs in 20 germinating seed baits. Grain baits containing insecticide applied at sowing offer best protection. Insecticide seed dressings provide some protection. In-furrow sprays are not effective in protecting against dense populations. Use press wheels at sowing.

True Wireworm

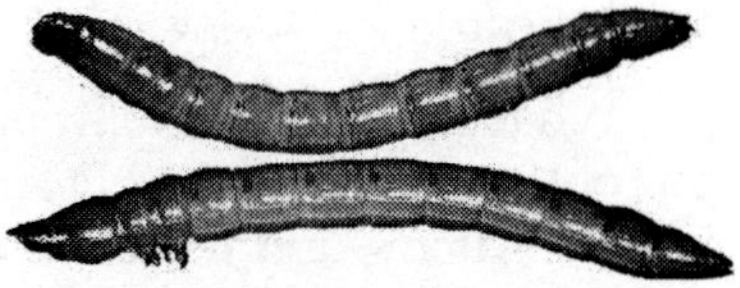

True wireworm larvae bore into germinating seed and chew on seedling roots and shoots resulting in reduced vigour, wilting or seedling death. Damage is worse when crop growth is retarded by dry, wet or cool conditions. Wireworms generally favour moist areas. True wireworm larvae may also feed on helicoverpa pupae.

Use germinating seed baits or soil sampling to detect larvae prior to sowing. Monitor crops after sowing until establishment. One larvae/germinating seed bait warrants control. Seed dressings, in-furrow sprays and granular insecticides offer some control.

False Wireworm

False wireworm larvae attack germinating seeds and seedling roots and shoots in spring, resulting in patchy stands. Damage is most common in early planted crops with low crop residue (e.g. cultivated paddocks). Adults may damage summer seedlings by chewing at or above ground level and replanting may be required.

To detect, either hand sift 10 soil samples (30 × 30 cm) or place 10 germinating seed baits throughout the paddock. One larva per sample warrants control. Prepare ground for even and rapid germination. Use of press wheels at planting provides some control. For larvae, use seed treatments or in-furrow sprays. For adults, use cracked grain baits. Natural enemies provide little control. Infestationsdtected after crop emergence cannot be controlled.

Cutworm

Cutworm larvae feed on leaves and stems of young plants, and ´cut´ down plants to eat the leaves. Partial damage to stems may cause the plant to wilt. Larvae typically shelter in the soil during the day and curl into a ´C´ shape when disturbed. Cutworms may be found in any soil type and often move into the crop from adjoining fence lines, pastures or weedy fallows. Crop areas attacked by cutworms tend to be patchy and the highest risk period is during summer and spring.

Inspect emerging seedlings twice per week. Treat seedlings when there is a rapidly increasing area of infestation or proportion of crop damage (>10% seedling loss). Treat older plants if more than 90% of plants are infested or more than 50% of plants have 75% or more leaf tissue loss. Spot treatments (e.g. along field edges) may be successful. Spray when caterpillars are feeding (dusk-night). Keep fallows clean and eliminate weeds from paddock perimeters for at least one month before planting. Severe damage to emerging crop can occur when large larvae are forced to move from weed hosts into the crop following spraying of the weeds. Cutworms are attacked by a range of natural enemies such as parasitoids, predators and diseases.

Whitegrub

Whitegrub larvae (*Heteronyx* spp., *Sericesthis* spp., and *Pseudoheteronyx* spp) feed on roots causing loss of vigour and lodging. Adults may feed on leaves. Damage is often patchy, and there are no effective controls, although a

*Metarhizium*fungus and entomopathogenic nematodes have been reported to occasionally cause high larval mortality. Avoid sowing new ground with maize after pasture in areas that have a known history of white grubs.

OTHER PESTS

Sucking pests

Maize leafhoppers and **maize thrips** are widespread but irregular in Queensland, and can rapidly re-infest crops after spraying meaning more than one spray may be required.

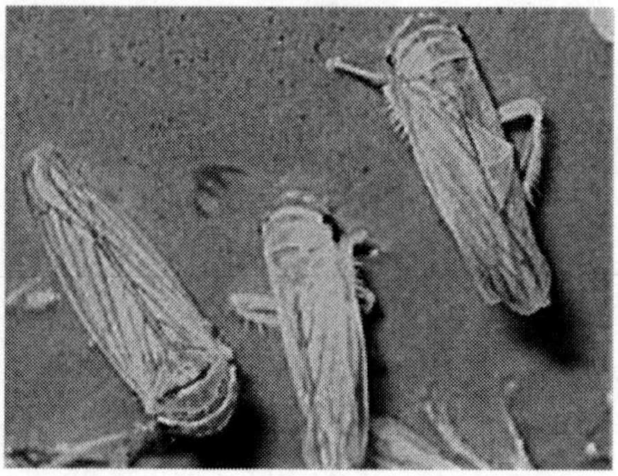

- **Maize leafhoppers** are a pest of germinating maize. Most common during late summer, they suck sap and high populations (>15/plant) can transmit wallaby ear mycoplasma. Mycoplasma-infected plants are dark green colour with thickened veins on the underside of leaves. Hybrid varieties offer some resistance to wallaby ear. Inspect crops weekly during the vegetative stage, and control if more than 10 leafhoppers/plant and wallaby ear symptoms are present.

- **Maize thrips** attack seedling and vegetative growth stages. Thrips in the whorl can stop the growth of small plants. Infected plants may have a yellow or silvery patches on the leaves and a desiccated or wilted appearance. Damage is more severe if plants are stressed by drought or water logging. Inspect weekly during seedling and vegetative stages, and control if thrips are found in the throat combined with yellowing of the throat or necrotic stripes on young leaves.

Corn aphid is the most common aphid species on maize and can affect any crop stage. Adults and nymphs suck sap and produce honeydew. High numbers can cause plants to turn yellow and appear unthrifty. Yield loss may occur on water stressed plants. The incidence of damage is generally too low to warrant control. Chemical control options are generally not cost effective and the insecticides that control aphids may negatively impact natural enemies. Inspect at weekly intervals. Predators of aphids include ladybird larvae, damsel bugs, bigeyed bugs, larvae of green lacewings and larvae of hoverflies. Wasp parasitoids mummify and kill aphids.

Green vegetable bugs (GVB) are widespread but irregular pests of maize during summer. Adults and nymphs feed by piercing and sucking on developing cobs, and may severely deform cobs. Although chemical control may be cost effective, there are currently no threshold levels for GVB in maize.

Green vegetable bugs

Two-spotted mite is a widespread but irregular pest of maize during seed fill to maturity. Mites are usually present towards the end of the crop cycle during late summer/autumn and are favoured by hot, dry weather. Adults and nymphs pierce and suck on lower leaf surfaces, causing yellowing on the upper leaf surfaces. Fine webbing on the lower leaf surface indicates their presence, and heavy infestations will result in leaf desiccation, leaf drop and yield loss. Initial infestations can be patchy. No thresholds are available for mites in maize and control is not cost effective. Conserve natural enemies through reduction of broad-spectrum insecticides against other pests as the disruption of natural enemies can flare mite outbreaks.

Redbanded shield bug

Redbanded shield bug is a widespread but minor summer/autumn pest that can be confused with green vegetable bug. Adults and nymphs feed by piercing and sucking on developing cobs, causing deformities, similar to green vegetable bug damage.

Chewing pests

Locusts are sporadic and potentially major pests of maize. Adults and hoppers chew irregular pieces from leaves and stems and can cause complete defoliation overnight if populations are high enough. Species found in Queensland include: Australian plague locusts, Migratory locusts, and Spur-throated locusts. The Australian Plague Locust Commission provides details of hopper migrations.

Whitefringed weevil larvae chew into lateral roots causing death and reduced vigour. Infestations are usually patchy. Mass emergence of adults occurs after rain in November-January, and damage is often worse when two host crops (e.g. maize, peanuts, chickpea, lucerne) are grown in sequence.

Leaf beetles are an irregular pest of maize:

- The redshouldered leaf beetle is restricted to coastal areas and can infest at any stage of crop growth. Swarms of adult beetles move into a crop and feed on foliage, tassels, silks and the husk at the top of the cob. Injury to silks may reduce seed set. Feeding exposes the cobs to other insects and diseases. Infestations tend to be patchy so thorough weekly checking is required. Control is warranted if 95% of plants in an area are infested and 70% of flag leaves are eaten. Chemical control is cost effective at high infestations.
- Swarming leaf beetles are a minor, irregular pest in Queensland. The black leaf beetle can be a major pest in northern areas. Leaf beetles are likely to be present during the seedling stage. Larvae feed on roots causing up to 40% seedling death. There are currently no recommended methods of monitoring and economic injury levels have not yet been established. Avoid planting maize immediately after grass pasture.

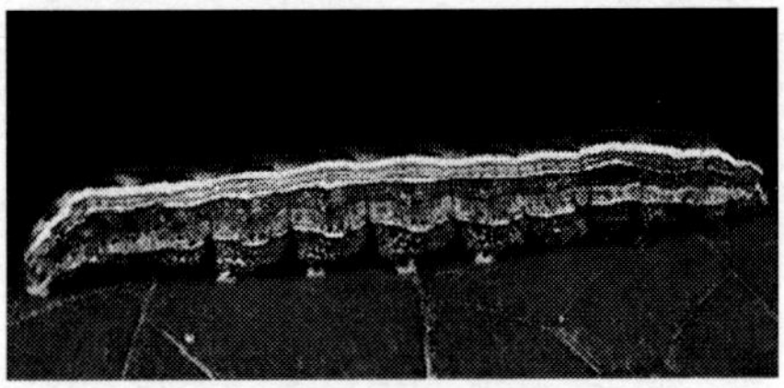
Armyworms

Armyworms can occur in large numbers especially when good rain follows a dry period. During the day the common armyworm shelters in the throats of plants or in the soil and emerge after sunset to feed. Dayfeeding armyworm are active during the day. Young plants may be defoliated or killed. Older plants can outgrow damage but seed yield may be reduced. Signs of damage include chewed leaf margins and faecal pellets at the base of young plants or in the throats of older plants. Monitor during seedling and vegetative stages. Egg lays are often associated with heavy rainfall so check for larvae several weeks after rainfall events. Look for larvae under clods of soil, under vegetation and at the base of plants. As a guide, control is warranted if out of a count of 30 plants, 27 are infested, and more than 21 have at least 75% flag leaf loss.

Many chemicals will control armyworms but their effectiveness is often dependent on good penetration and control may be more difficult in high-yielding thick canopy crops, particularly when larvae are resting under leaf litter at the base of plants. As larvae are most active at night, spraying in the afternoon or evening may produce the best results. Armyworm larvae are attacked by a number of parasitoids that may assist in reducing the intensity of outbreaks, although are unlikely to give timely control if armyworm numbers are high. Predators include green carab beetles, predatory shield bugs and perhaps common brown earwigs. Viral and fungal diseases are recorded as causing mortality of armyworms.

Yellow peach moth is a minor and irregular pest of maize in Queensland. Larvae tunnel into stems or cobs producing masses of webbing and excreta at the tunnel entrance. There are no chemical controls available. The habit of mining into stems and cobs makes spray application ineffective as larvae are not exposed to insecticide. They are similar in appearance to pink-spotted bollworm larvae.

Yellow peach moth

DISEASES

Anthracnose - *Colletotrichum graminicola* (Fungus)

Symptoms

Anthracnose symptoms vary widely depending on numerous factors such as genotype, age of plant and environmental conditions; small oval or elongated water-soaked spots which enlarge up to 15 mm long appear on leaves; lesions develop a tan center and red-brown or orange border; lesions may coalesce to form large necrotic patches; severely infected leaves on susceptible hybrids may wither and die; fungal fruiting bodies develop on dead tissues and may produce pink or orange spore masses; the fungus may also cause top dieback and stalk rot

Comments

Fungus overwinters on crop debris; emergence of disease is favored by high temperatures and extended periods of wet and cloudy weather; seedlings and mature plants are most susceptible to the disease

Management

Plant hybrids resistant to anthracnose; rotating crops and plowing crop debris into soil may help reduce incidence of early season infections

Aphids (Corn leaf aphid, Peach Aphid) *Rhopalosiphum maidis* (Insect)

Symptoms

Heavy infestations can result in curled leaves and stunted plants; honeydew secretions promote growth of sooty mold; corn leaf aphids are blue-green in color, peach aphids are green-yellow in color; aphids may transmit viruses when feeding

Comments

Grassy weeds also serve as hosts for corn-leaf aphids; peach aphids have a wide host range

Management

It is rare for aphids to reach levels that are damaging to the plant and no control is generally warranted as insecticide sprays will not prevent transmission of viruses

Armyworms (Corn armyworm, Beet armyworm) - *Mythimna unipuncta, Spodoptera exigua* (Insect)

Symptoms

Singular, or closely grouped circular to irregularly shaped holes in foliage; heavy feeding by young larvae leads to skeletonized leaves; shallow, dry wounds on fruit; egg clusters of 50-150 eggs may be present on the leaves; egg clusters are covered in a whitish scale which gives the cluster a cottony or fuzzy appearance; young larvae are pale green to yellow in color while older larvae are generally darker green with a dark and light line running along the side of their body and a pink or yellow underside

Comments

Insect can go through 3–5 generations a year

Management

Organic methods of controlling the armyworm include biological control by natural enemies which parasitize the larvae and the application of *Bacillus thuringiensis*; there are chemicals available for commercial control but many that are available for the home garden do not provide adequate control of the larvae

Bacterial leaf blight - *Pseudomonas avenae* (Bacterium)

Symptoms

Water-soaked linear lesions on leaves as they emerge; lesions turn brown and may subsequently turn gray or white; lesions may have a red border; after the leaves are mature, lesions do not tend to extend any further; no new lesions tend to appear after tasseling; if corn variety is susceptible, mature leaves may shred after maturity

Comments

Bacteria can also cause disease in oats, barley, wheat, some millets and sorghum

Management

Resistant hybrids should be planted in areas where the disease is prevalent; plowing crop debris into soil and rotating crop may not be effective at controlling the disease due to its extensive host range

Bacterial stalk rot - *Erwinia chrysanthemi* (Bacterium)

Symptoms

Plants suddenly beginning to lodge (bend to lie along the ground) midway through season; one or more internodes above soil line turning brown, water-soaked, soft and slimy; tissue has fould odor and mushy appearance;

Comments

Disease is most commonly found in plantations which have overhead irrigation systems or in areas with high rainfall; disease emergence is favored by high temperatures and high humidity

Management

Plow all crop debris into soil in Fall; plant corn in well-draining soil to prevent waterlogged plants

Cercospora leaf spot (Gray leaf spot) - *Cercospora zeae-maydis* (Fungus)

Symptoms

Small necrotic spots with chlorotic halos on leaves which expand to rectangular lesions 1-6 cm in length and 2-4 mm wide; as the lesions mature they turn tan in color and finally gray; lesions have sharp, parallel edges and are opaque; disease can develop quickly causing complete blighting of leaves and plant death

Comments

Disease emergence is favored in areas where a corn crop is followed by more corn with no rotastion; severity and incidence of disease is likely die to continuous corn culture with minimum tillage and the use of susceptible hybrids in in the midwestern corn belt of the USA; prolonged periods of foggy or cloudy weather can cause severe Cercopora epidemics

Management

Plant corn hybrids with resistance to the disease; crop rotation and plowing debris into soil may reduce levels of inoculum in the soil but may not provide control in areas where the disease is prevalent; foliar fungicides may be economically viable for some high yeilding susceptible hybrids

Charcoal rot - *Macrophomina phaseolina* (Fungus)

Symptoms

Symptoms are usually first apparent at the tasseling stage; plant stalks become shredded and pith is completely rotted with stringy strands of vascular tissue left intact; small, black fungal fruiting bodies are visible in the vascular strands and give the tissue a gray coloration; fungus grows into internodes of the stalk causing the plant to ripen early and causing the stalk to weaken; plant may break

Comments

Emergence of the disease is favored by warm soils with a low moisture content; fungus overwinters in the soil and can also survive on other host plants which include sorghum and soybean

Management

There are currently no available fungicides to treat the disease; avoid stressing plants by practicing good water management; rotating crops with small grains may help reduce disease incidence

Common rust - *Puccinia sorghi* (Fungus)

Symptoms

Oval or elongated cinnamon brown pustules on upper and lower surfaces of leaves; pustules rupture and release powdery red spores; pustules turn dark brown-black as they mature and release dark brown powdery spores; if infection is severe, pustules may appear on tassels and ears and leaves may begin to yellow; in partially resistant corn hybrids, symptoms appear as chlorotic or necrotic flecks on the leaves which release little or no spore

Comments

Disease is spread by wind-borne spores; some of the most popularly grown sweet corn varieties have little or no resistance to the disease

Management

The most effective method of controlling the disease is to plant resistant hybrids; application of appropriate fungicides may provide some degree on control and reduce disease severity; fungicides are most effective when the amount of secondary inoculum is still low, generally when plants only have a few rust pustules per leaf

Common smut (Boil smut, Blister smut) - *Ustilago zeae* (Fungus)

Symptoms

Tumor-like galls on plant tissues which are initially green-white or silvery white in color; interior of galls darken and turn into masses of powdery dark brown or black spores (with the exception of galls on leaves which remain greenish in color); galls may reach up to 15 cm in diameter and are common on ears, tassels, shoots or midrib of leaves; galls on leaves remain small and do not burst open

Comments

Fungus overwinters on crop debris or in the soil and can survive for several years; fungus usually enters the plant through wounds; application of nitrogen fertilizer increases incidence of disease, while application of phosphorous fertilizer decreases infection

Management

Although many practices may be recommended for the control of common smut, the only method that is completely effective is to grow resistant corn hybrids

Corn earworm - *Helicoverpa zea* (Insect)

Symptoms

Feeding damage to leaves, tassel and leaf whorls; preferred feeding site is the ear and insect produces extensive excrement at the tip of the ear; younger larvae feed on silks, severing them from the plant; young caterpillars are cream-white in color with a black head and black hairs; older larvae may be yellow-green to almost black in color with fine white lines along their body and black spots at the base of hairs; eggs are laid singly on both upper and lower leaf surfaces and are initially creamy white but develop a brown-red ring after 24 hours and darken prior to hatching

Comments

Adult insect is a pale green to tan, medium sized moth; can be a very damaging pests ofcorn; insect overwinters as pupae in the soil

Management

Corn earworms are most problematic on sweet corn varieties and treatment should be applied at egg hatch; monitor plants for eggs and young larvae and also natural enemies that could be damaged by chemicals; *Bacillus thuringiensis* or Entrust SC may be applied to control insects on organically grown plants; appropriate chemical treatment may be required for control in commercial plantations

Cutworms (Black cutworm, Variegated cutworm) *Agrotis ipsilon, Peridroma saucia* (Insect)

Symptoms

Stems of young transplants or seedlings may be severed at soil line; if infection occurs later, irregular holes are eaten into the surface of fruits; larvae causing the damage are usually active at night and hide during the day in the soil at the base of the plants or in plant debris of toppled plant; larvae are 2.5–5.0 cm (1–2 in) in length; larvae may exhibit a variety of patterns and coloration but will usually curl up into a C-shape when disturbed

Comments

Cutworms have a wide host range and attack vegetables including asparagus, bean, cabbage and other crucifers, carrot, celery, corn, lettuce, pea, pepper, potato and tomato

Management

Remove all plant residue from soil after harvest or at least two weeks before planting, this is especially important if the previous crop was another host such as alfalfa, beans or a leguminous cover crop; plastic or foil collars fitted around plant stems to cover the bottom 3 inches above the soil line and extending a couple of inches into the soil can prevent larvae severing plants; hand-pick larvae after dark; spread diatomaceous earth around the base of the plants (this creates a sharp barrier that will cut the insects if they try and crawl over it); apply appropriate insecticides to infested areas of garden or field if not growing organically

Downy Mildew disease *Peronosclerospora sorghi (Sorghum downy mildew)*

Symptoms

Symptoms of all maize downy mildew pathogens are similar although may vary depends on cultivar, age and climate. The disease appear as early from two weeks after sowing resulting in chlorosis and stunting. In older plants the leaves shows mottling, chlorotic streaking and lesions and white striped leaves. Usually the leaves are narrower and more erect when compare to healthy plants and are covered with a white, downy growth on both surfaces.

Comments

The disease is both air and seed born. The pathogen have several alternative hosts.

Management

Grow available resistant varieties and hybrids. Follow crop rotation with non host crops. Use suitable systemic fungicide for both seed treatment and foliar spray. Keep the fields free from weeds. Drying seeds before sowing reduces the disease incidence.

Flea beetles (Various spp.) - Various (Insect)

Symptoms

Small holes or pits in leaves that give the foliage a characteristic "shothole" appearance; young plants and seedlings are particularly susceptible; plant growth may be reduced; if damage is severe the plant may be killed; the pest responsible for the damage is a small (1.5–3.0 mm) dark colored beetle which jumps when disturbed; the beetles are often shiny in appearance

Comments

Flea beetles may overwinter on nearby weed species, in plant debris or in the soil; insects may go through a second or third generation in one year

Management

In areas where flea beetles are a problem, floating row covers may have to be used prior to the emergence of the beetles to provide a physical barrier to protect young plants; plant seeds early to allow establishment before the beetles become a problem - mature plants are less susceptible to damage; trap crops may provide a measure of control - cruciferous plants are best; application of a thick layer of mulch may help prevent beetles reaching surface; application on diamotecoeus earth or oils such as neem oil are effective control methods for organic growers; application of insecticides containing carbaryl, spinosad, bifenthrin and permethrin can provide adequate control of beetles for up to a week but will need reapplied

Giberrella stalk and ear rot - *Giberella zeae* (Fungus)

Symptoms

Plants wilting and leaves changing color from light to dull green; lower stalk turns straw yellow; internal stalk tissue breaks down; interior of stalk has a red discoloration; black fungal fruiting bodies may be visible on the stalk, often at internodes, and can be easily scraped off; if fungal infection affects the ears, it produces a red mold at the tips of the ear which spreads down; early infection may result in the ear being covered in pink mycelium which causes the corn husk to adhere to the ear

Comments

Fungus can enter through wounds to stalk or ear; ear rot is caused by the fungus infecting silks and moving down through the ear; fungus survives on corn debris in soil and on debris of other host plants such as wheat

Management

Stressed plants are more susceptible to Gibberella - providing adequate fertilization and irrigation can help reduce incidence of disease; control insects, especially stem and ear borers; hybrids differ in their susceptibility to the disease and further information is required in order to develop specific control measures

Goss's bacterial blight - *Clavibacter michiganensis* (Bacteria)

Symptoms

Gray or yellow stripes with irregular margins on leaf surfaces; stripes follow leaf veins and contain characteristic dark green to black water-soaked spots; if infection occurs early then plant may become wilted or withered; it is common to find a crystalline residue on leaves caused by dried bacterial exudate

Comments

Disease overwinters in diseased crop debris on, or close to, the soil surface; temperatures below 12°C (53.6°F) and above 40°C (104°F) bacterium grows more slowly and may even be killed off

Management

Plant resistant sweetcorn hybrids; rotate crop; plow crop debris into soil immediately after harvest

Holcus spot - *Pseudomonas syringae* (Bacteria)

Symptoms

Circular or elliptical spots 2-10 mm across near the tips of lower leaves which are dark green and water soaked initially but become cream to tan before turning dry and brown; lesions may have red-brown margins; large lesions may have a yellow halo

Comments

Disease can occur anywhere where corn is grown but is not usually very damaging

Management

Disease is usually not severe but if it does become a problem crops should be rotated and any debris should be plowed into the soil after harvest

Maize dwarf mosaic - Maize dwarf mosaic virus (MDMV) (Virus)

Symptoms

Chlorotic spots and streaks on leaves which develop into a mottled or mosaic pattern; susceptible plants may be stunted; ear formation and development cease; mosaic and mottling with no red discoloration are characteristic symptoms of the disease

Comments

Virus is transmitted by more than 15 different species of aphid and is passed to the plant from the insect in seconds to minutes of feeding; sorghum is also a major host of the virus

Management

Many commercial corn hybrids are highly tolerant of the disease and no control is needed; control aphid populations on plants and remove any Johnson grass growing in the vicinity as it can act as a reservoir for the virus

Northern Leaf Blight - *Exserohilum turcicum* (Fungus)

Symptoms

In the beginning we will notice elliptical gray-green lesions on leaves. As the disease process this lesions become pale gray to tan color. Later stage the lesions looks dirty due to dark gray spores particularly under lower leaf surface. The disease can be easily identified in the field due to its long, narrow lesions which are unrestricted by veins.

Comments

The disease mainly spread through rain splash and wind.

Management

Follow proper tillage to reduce fungus inoculum from crop debris. Follow crop rotation with non host crop. Grow available resistant varieties. In severe case of disease incidence apply suitable fungicide.

Pythium root rot - *Pythium* spp. (Fungus)

Symptoms

Above-ground, plants may be yellow and stunted; roots have obvious lesions and roots are discolored; root cortex will come away when pulled gently, exposing the white stele; can also cause damping-off of seedlings

Comments

Fungus overwinters in soil and crop debris; disease emergence is favored by high soil moisture and low temperatures leading to low soil oxygen levels

Management

Control of the disease relies on improving soil drainage or planting corn in areas where the soil is well-draining; systemic fungicides can be used to treat seed prior to planting to protect seedlings from disease

Root knot nematode - *Meloidogyne incognita*

Symptoms

Below ground we can see galls on the roots due to female nematode feeding. Above ground the plants are stunted, yellow and patchy in growth. Severely infested plant may die before harvest.

Comments

The galls are formed by female nematode feeding resulting in formation of giant cells.

Management

Deep summer ploughing helps in reducing nematode population. Follow crop rotation with nematode antagonistic plants. Grow resistant varieties. In severely infected field follow soil fumigation with suitable nematicide.

Slugs (Mollusc)

Symptoms

Irregularly shaped holes in leaves and stems; leaves may be shredded; slime trails present on rocks, walkways, soil and plant foliage; several slug species are common garden and field pests; slugs are dark gray to black in color and can range in size from 2.5 to 10 cm (1-4 in)

Comments

Slugs prefer moist, shaded habitats and will shelter in weeds or organic trash; adults may deposit eggs in the soil throughout the season; damage to plants can be extensive

Management

Practice good garden sanitation by removing garden trash, weeds and plant debris to promote good air circulation and reduce moist habitat for slugs and snails; handpick slugs at night to decrease population; spread wood ashes or eggshells around plants; attract molluscs by leaving out organic matter such as lettuce or grapefruit skins, destroy any found feeding on lure; sink shallow dishes filled with beer into the soil to attract and drown the molluscs; chemical controls include ferrous phosphate for organic gardens and metaldehyde (e.g. Buggeta) and carbaryl (e.g Sevin bait) for non-organic growers

Southern corn leaf blight - *Bipolaris maydis* (Fungus)

Symptoms

Foliar symptoms vary with hybrid and different fungal isolate; lesions on leaves may be tan and elongated and run between leaf veins; lesions may have a buff or brown colored margin; another race of the fungus causes tan, spindle shaped or elliptical lesions with a water-soaked margin that turns into a yellow halo

Comments

Fungus overwinters in corn debris in soil; disease occurs worldwide but is emergence favors areas with a warm, damp climate

Management

The most effective method of controlling the disease is to plant resistant hybrids; cultural control methods include plowing crop debris into soil after harvest and rotating crops

Spider mites (Various spp.) Arachnid

Symptoms

Leaves stippled with yellow; leaves may appear bronzed; webbing on underside of leaves; small kernel size; mites may be visible as tiny moving dots on the webs or underside of leaves, best viewed using a hand lens; usually not spotted until there are visible symptoms on the plant; leaves turn yellow and may drop from plant;

Comments

Spider mites thrive in dusty conditions; water-stressed plants are more susceptible to attack

Management

In the home garden, spraying plants with a strong jet of water can help reduce buildup of spider mite populations; if mites become problematic apply insecticidal soap to plants; certain chemical insecticides may actually increase mite populations by killing off natural enemies and promoting mite reproduction

Thrips (Various spp.) Insects

Symptoms

If population is high leaves and may be distorted and curl upwards; edges of leaves may dry up and are speckled with black feces; insects are small (1.5 mm) and slender and best viewed using a hand lens; adult thrips are pale yellow to light brown and the nymphs are smaller and lighter in color

Comments

May be found on corn at any time during the growing season

Management

Avoid planting next to onions, garlic where very large numbers of thrips can build up; use reflective mulches early in growing season to deter thrips; apply appropriate insecticide if thrips become problematic; young plants will recover from damage and treatment is not often necessary as the thrips are beneficial for controlling mites

23

Major Pests and Diseases of Pulses

CHICKPEA (GRAM PEA) (*Cicer arietinum*)

Purple chickpea flower

White chickpea flower

Chickpea plant

Description

The chickpea, *Cicer arietinum*, is a leguminous annual plant in the family Fabaceae grown for its edible seeds. The plant has a branched, straight or bending stem with small feathery leaves arranged alternately on the stem. The leaves are composed of 11–15 individual leaflets which are oval in shape. The flowers are produced singly or in pairs and can be white, pink, purple or blue in color. The seed pod is rhomboid or ellipsoid and contains 1–4 cream, brown, green or black seeds. The chickpea plant can range in height from 20 cm (7.9 in) up to 100 cm (39.4 in) and as an annual, grows over only one growing season. Chickpea may also be referred to as gram pea, garbanzo bean or ceci bean and originate from south-eastern Turkey.

USES

Chickpea is primarily consumed as a dry pulse. The shelled peas are eaten as snack or vegetable. The seed husks can be used as a feed for animals. Chickpeas are also commonly cooked and ground into a paste to produce the popular dish, hummus.

PROPAGATION

General requirements

Commercially grown chickpea

Chickpeas are cool-season legumes which are best grown as a winter crop in the tropics or as a spring or summer crop in temperate regions. Chickpeas are classified into two distinct types based on seed characteristics. Desi chickpeas have a thick, colored seed coat and the surface of the seed is rough and angular whereas the Kabuli type have white or beige seeds with a smooth surface. Kabuli chickpeas are best grown in temperate areas whereas Desi chickpeas are best suited to semi-arid areas of the tropics. Chickpeas will grow optimally at temperatures between 15 and 29°C (59–84.2°F) with extremes of temperature above 35°C (95°F) and below 15°C (59°F) causing flowers to drop, reducing production. Plants will perform best when planted in well-draining sandy loam soils with a pH between 5.0 and 7.0 in areas where the annual rainfall is between 600 and 1000 mm.

Planting

Chickpeas are propagated directly from seed with timing of planting depending on the variety being grown and geographic location. Spring crops should be planted when the soil has warmed to at least 5°C (41°F). Chickpeas are leguminous and when planting in a site which has not previously been used for chickpea cultivation, seed should be inoculated with an appropriate type of Rhizobacteria prior to planting. Seed is usually spread by broadcasting or by drilling in rows. Desi types require a seed rate of 30 to 40 kg per hectare whereas Kabuli types require 80 to 100 kg per hectare. The seed should be planted 2 to 12 cm (0.8–4.7 in) deep and when planting in rows, seed should be spaced 10 cm (4 in) apart allowing 25 to 60 cm (9.8 to 23.6 in) between rows. Seedlings usually emerge between 7 and 15 days after sowing depending on temperature.

General care

In the home garden, chickpea seedlings will benefit from the addition of a layer of mulch after they have emerged to suppress weeds and conserve soil moisture. Plants should be provided with additional irrigation during periods of dry weather but care should be taken not to overwater as this can cause the plants to drop their flowers and/or pods. Application of fertilizer is generally not necessary as chickpeas are leguminous and fix their own nitrogen with the aid of micro-organisms but requirements vary from field to field and management should be based on the results of a soil test. Like other pulses, chickpeas require phosphorus, potassium and micronutrients for growth and application should be based on the results of soil testing. Suppression of weeds in commercial fields is important as chickpeas do not compete well and weed will reduce productivity. Pre- and postemergence herbicide applications can be helpful for managing weed. If a field has a history of weed problems then it is not suitable for chickpea production.

Harvesting

Chickpeas are ready to harvest approximately 100 days after planting. in the home garden, chickpeas can be collected and eaten when green but for dried seeds, the leaves should be allowed to turn brown before collecting the pods. The pods should be allowed to dry and split open before collecting seeds. In commercial production, chickpeas can be harvested by swathing and/or combine.

DISEASES

Ascochyta blight - *Ascochyta rabiei*

Symptoms

Water-soaked pale spots on young leaves which enlarge rapidly under cool, wet conditions and coalesce to cause blighting of leaves; elongated lesions often cause girdling of the stems which break off; new shoots may form at the breakage points; if pods become infected it can lead to reduced seed set; if infected seeds are planted, the seedlings will develop dark brown lesions at the base of the stem and may dry up and die

Comments

Disease emergence if favored by wet weather; spores are carried to new plants by wind and water splash

Management

Grow more resistant varieties such as PBA Slasher or Genesis™ 090; even resistant varieties require fungicide application at early podding to ensure high quality seed; more susceptible varieties may require a first fungicide application approximately 4-6 weeks after sowing

Beet armyworm - *Spodoptera exigua*

Symptoms

Singular, or closely grouped circular to irregularly shaped holes in foliage; heavy feeding by young larvae leads to skeletonized leaves; larvae are dark green to brown caterpillars with banding patterns

Comments

Beet armyworm is a serious pest of chickpea in India and Mexico; Insect can go through 3–5 generations a year

Management

Organic methods of controlling armyworms include biological control by natural enemies which parasitize the larvae and the application of *Bacillus thuringiensis*; there are chemicals available for commercial control but many that are available for the home garden do not provide adequate control of the larvae.

Chickpea leafminer - *Liriomyza cicerina*

Symptoms

Leaves may have a stippled appearance from females puncturing leaf with ovipositor to feed on exudate; female lays eggs under leaf surface and newly hatched larvae damage the leaf by feeding on the inner tissues; feeding damage from larvae causes the development of winding white trails of the leaf surface; if feeding damage is extensive, the entire leaf may dry out and drop from the plant; damage to young seedlings may result in the death of the plant; crop yield may be reduced.

Comments

Chickpea leafminers can cause heavy losses in North Africa, West Asia and Northern Europe

Management

Cultural control methods include planting chickpeas in early winter instead of Spring when the populations of the insects are at less damaging levels; crop debris should be plowed deeply into the soil to destroy overwintering pupae; chickpea cultivars with smaller leaf sizes are less attractive to leafminers; insects may be controlled through the application of appropriate chemical insecticides.

Cowpea aphid (Black aphid) - *Aphis craccivora*

Symptoms

Deformed leaves and shoots; curled leaves; if infestation is severe then plants may be killed; seed fill and yield may be reduced; aphids secrete a sticky, sugary substance called honeydew which encourages the growth of sooty mold on the plants; adult insect is small and soft bodied and is easily distinguished from other aphids by its shiny-black color.

Comments

Black aphids can cause severe damage when infestation is high but more commonly cause problems in chickpea crops through the transmission of several plant viruses.

Management

Plants should be monitored for signs of aphids; if insects are present then control measures should be implemented; some chickpea cultivars are more susceptible to aphid infestation than others - cultivars with a low density of trichomes (leaf hairs) are more susceptible than others; chemical control may be warranted although aphids have developed resistance to several insecticides in India; cultural control methods include early planting which promotes early closure of the plant canopy and reduced the spread of viruses; aphid infestations tend to be worse when broad plant spacing is employed.

Cutworms (Black cutworm, Winter cutworm) - *Agrotis ipsilon, Agrotis segetum*

Symptoms

Stems of young transplants or seedlings may be severed at soil line; if infection occurs later, irregular holes are eaten into the surface of fruits; larvae causing the damage are usually active at night and hide during the day in the soil at the base of the plants or in plant debris of toppled plant; larvae are 2.5–5.0 cm (1–2 in) in length; larvae may exhibit a variety of patterns and coloration but will usually curl up into a C-shape when disturbed.

Comments

Favors late tillage and planting; major pest for corn and will start attacking everything else after corn is rotated out.

Management

Remove all plant residue from soil after harvest or at least two weeks before planting, this is especially important if the previous crop was another host such as alfalfa, beans or a leguminous cover crop; plastic or foil collars fitted around plant stems to cover the bottom 3 inches above the soil line and extending a couple of inches into the soil can prevent larvae severing plants; hand-pick larvae after dark; spread diatomaceous earth around the base of the plants (this creates a sharp barrier that will cut the insects if they try and crawl over it); apply appropriate insecticides to infested areas of garden or field if not growing organically.

Damping-off - *Pythium* spp.

Symptoms

Failure of seedling to emerge; light brown, seedlings with light brown to redwater-soaked roots and stems; collapse of plants; plant dry up and die; stunted plant growth; rotting taproot with few lateral roots.

Comments

Occurs more often in cold temperatures when growth of seedlings is slow and in moist soil.

Management

Treat seeds with fungicide prior to planting.

Dry root rot - *Macrophomina phaseolina*

Symptoms

Leaves and leaf stems wilting; dark, rotten tap roots; gray fibrous fungal threads on the tap root.

Comments

Favors high temperature and low moisture.

Management

No fungicides provide effective control of the disease and management therefore relies on cultural practices; utilize adequate plant spacing to avoid overcrowding and competition for water which can promote the disease; crop rotation to a non-host may help reduce the population in the soil.

***Fusarium wilt* - Fusarium oxysporum**

Symptoms

Weak and wilting leaf stems, leaves and flowers; lower leaves drying out and dying; leaves turning brown or pale yellow; splitting the stem reveals discoloration of the inner tissue; leaves turn dull yellow in color and collapse.

Comments

Disease emergence favors warm, moist soils; disease can be spread by water splash, movement of infected soil and plants and by infected seed.

Management

The primary method of controlling the disease is to use resistant varieties; damage can be reduced by application of appropriate fungicides; crop debris should be removed or plowed deeply into the soil after harvest; if disease is present in the soil then a rotation to a non-host for a period of three years can reduce the levels of inoculum in the soil.

***Phytophthora root rot* - Phytophthora megasperma**

Symptoms

Leaves of plants turning yellow and drying out; decaying roots; small brown lesions on roots which enlarge and create necrotic patches; lesions may girdle stem.

Comments

Favours warm, wet soil.

Management

Varieties with resistance to the disease are available in most areas where root rot is a problem.

Pod borers (*Cotton bollworm, Australian bollworm*) - *Helicoverpa armigera, Helicoverpa punctigera*

Symptoms

Young larvae feed on foliage initially; young chickpea plants may be completely destroyed; older larvae bore into seed pods and consume seeds; insect frass (feces) may be present outside the feeding holes.

Comments

Helicoverpa armigera is widely distributed in Asia, Africa, Australia, and the Mediterranean; also a pest of cotton, pigeonpea, sunflower, tomato, maize, sorghum, pearl millet, okra, beans, tobacco, linseed and a number of fruit trees; *Helicoverpa punctigera* is a major pest of chickpea in Australia.

Management

The insect can be very damaging in the areas where it occurs and plants should be monitored carefully for presence of larvae; identifying the species of Helicoverpa present can be important for management decisions as *H. armigera* is resistant to some insecticides (particularly synthetic pyrethroids), while *H. punctigera* is susceptible to all insecticides; small larvae should be distinguished with the use of a hand lens or microscope; young *H. armigera* larvae have a distinctive saddle on the fourth body segment which is absent from the larvae of *H. punctigera* (see image); older larvae can be distinguished by the color of the hairs behind the head - *H. armigera* possess white hairs, while *H. punctigera* have black hairs; both types of larvae may also be controlled organically via release of natural enemies which parasitize the larvae and the application of *Bacillus thuringiensis.*

Sclerotinia stem rot (White mold) - *Sclerotinia sclerotiorum*

Symptoms

Plants rapidly wilting and dying, often without turning yellow; as plants dry out they may turn straw yellow in color; small black fungal bodies (sclerotia) may be present on the surface of the root just below the soil line together with white fluffy mycelium; water soaked lesions may be present on the stem in Spring; infected tissues dry out and may become covered in white mycelium.

Comments

Disease emergence favors very wet weather conditions; disease is usually introduced to non-infected areas by infected seed.

Management

Plant only certified seed; if disease is known to present rotate crops with non-hosts such as cereals; if problem is severe then a 4 year rotation away from susceptible plants may be required; there are no seed treatments or fungicides available to treat the disease

PIGEON PEA (*Cajanus cajan*)

Description

Pigeonpea, *Cajanus cajan*, is a perennial shrub in the family Fabaceae grown for its edible pods and seeds. Pigeonpea is a highly branched shrub with a woody base, slender stems and trifoliate leaves. The plant leaflets are oblong or elliptical in shape and the leaves are alternate and arranged spirally on the stems. The plant usually produces yellow flowers, but they can be yellow with streaks of purple or red. The flowers are produced on racemes of 5–10 flowers. The seed pods are flat and either straight or sickle shaped and measure 5–9 cm (2–3.5 in) in length. Each pod can contain between 2 and 9 seeds which can be white, cream, brown, yellow, purple or black or mottled with any combination of these colors. Pigeonpea can reach 0.5–4.0 m (1.6–13.1 ft) in height and is usually grown as an annual, harvested after one season. It may also be referred to as red gram or congo pea and originates from India.

USES

Pigeon pea is one of the most important legumes grown in semi-arid tropical regions and young seeds are consumed fresh as a vegetable or can be allowed to mature before drying and eating as a pulse. The seed pods are also edible and are eaten as a vegetable. The leaves and seed husks of the plant can be used as an animal feed.

PROPAGATION

Basic requirements

Pigeon pea grows best in hot humid climates where temperatures are between 18 and 38°C (64.4–100.4°F). The plants will grow in a wide range of soils, from sandy

Pigeon pea flower

Pigeon pea plant

soil to clay and also in soils with low fertility. Pigeon pea will grow optimally in a well drained soil with a pH between 5.0 and 7.0. Once established, pigeon pea is relatively tolerant to drought conditions and can survive for long periods with little irrigation.

Propagation

Pigeon pea is propagated directly from seed which should be sown in a prepared seed bed. Seeds should be planted to a depth of 2.5–10 cm (1–4 in) leaving 30–50 cm (12–20) between plants and 150 cm (60 in) between rows. Higher seeding rates should be used if the pant is being grown for use as a green manure. Pigeon pea is commonly intercropped with millets, cotton, sorghum or groundnut.

General care and maintenance

All weeds should be eliminated from the seed bed to prevent competition with the initially slow growing seedlings. Generally, pigeon pea does not require irrigation or fertilization. An application of phosphate at a rate of 20–100 kg per hectare is recommended and irrigation may be necessary if the plants are intensively grown.

Harvesting

Pigeon pea is commonly harvested by hand. Machine harvesting by combine is possible if a variety is grown where pods ripen uniformly. The plant is cut at the ground when the majority of pods have reached maturity. The plants are air dried and then threshed to remove the seeds.

DISEASES

Alternaria blight - *Alternaria alternata*

Symptoms

Small irregular brown lesions on leaves which expand and turn gray-brown or dark brown with concentric zones; older areas of lesions may dry out and drop from leaves causing shot hole; lesions coalesce to form large necrotic patches.

Comments

Disease emergence favored by high humidity and warm temperatures; plants grown in nitrogen and potassium deficient soils are more susceptible.

Management

Plant beans in fertile soil; foliar fungicide application may be required in order to control the disease.

Anthracnose - *Colletotrichum* spp.

Symptoms

Small, dark brown to black lesions on cotyledons; oval or eye-shaped lesions on stems which turn sunken and brown with purple to red margins; stems may break if cankers weaken stem; pods drying and shrinking above areas of visible symptoms; reddish brown spots on pods which become circular and sunken with rust colored margin

Comments

Disease transmitted through infected seed; fungus can survive in crop debris in soil and reinfect crop the following season.

Management

Plant resistant varieties; use certified disease free seed; avoid sprinkler irrigation, water plants at base; plow bean crop debris into soil.

Aphids (Cowpea aphid, Pea aphid, etc.) - *Aphis craccivora, Acyrthosiphon pisum*

Symptoms

Small soft bodied insects on underside of leaves and/or stems of plant; usually green or yellow in color, but may be pink, brown, red or black depending on species and host plant; if aphid infestation is heavy it may cause leaves to yellow and/or distorted, necrotic spots on leaves and/or stunted shoots; aphids secrete a sticky, sugary substance called honeydew which encourages the growth of sooty mold on the plants.

Comments

Distinguishing features include the presence of cornicles (tubular structures) which project backwards from the body of the aphid; will generally not move very quickly when disturbed.

Management

If aphid population is limited to just a few leaves or shoots then the infestation can be pruned out to provide control; check transplants for aphids before planting; use tolerant varieties if available; reflective mulches such as silver colored plastic can deter aphids from feeding on plants; sturdy plants can be sprayed with a strong jet of water to knock aphids from leaves; insecticides are generally only required to treat aphids if the infestation is very high - plants generally tolerate low and medium level infestation; insecticidal soaps or oils such as neem or canola oil are usually the best method of control; always check the labels of the products for specific usage guidelines prior to use.

Armyworms (Beet armyworm, Western striped armyworm) - *Spodoptera exigua, Spodoptera praefica*

Symptoms

Singular, or closely grouped circular to irregularly shaped holes in foliage; heavy feeding by young larvae leads to skeletonized leaves; shallow, dry wounds on fruit; egg clusters of 50-150 eggs may be present on the leaves; egg clusters are covered in a whitish scale which gives the cluster a cottony or fuzzy appearance; young larvae are pale green to yellow in color while older larvae are generally darker green with a dark and light line running along the side of their body and a pink or yellow underside

Comments

Insect can go through 3–5 generations a year

Management

Organic methods of controlling armyworms include biological control by natural enemies which parasitize the larvae and the application of *Bacillus thuringiensis*; there are chemicals available for commercial control but many that are available for the home garden do not provide adequate control of the larvae

Cercospora leaf spot - *Cercospora cajani*

Symptoms

Small light brown lesions on upper surfaces of leaves; angula brown spots on leaves; leaf death; lesions on stems and petioles

Corn earworm - *Helicoverpa zea*

Symptoms

Larvae damage leaves, buds, flowers, pods and beans; young caterpillars are cream-white in color with a black head and black hairs; older larvae may be yellow-green to almost black in color with fine white lines along their body and black spots at the base of hairs; eggs are laid singly on both upper and lower leaf surfaces and are initially creamy white but develop a brown-red ring after 24 hours and darken prior to hatching

Comments

Adult insect is a pale green to tan, medium sized moth; insect is also very damaging pests of corn; insect overwinters as pupae in the soil

Management

Monitor plants for eggs and young larvae and also natural enemies that could be damaged by chemicals; *Bacillus thuringiensis* or Entrust SC may be applied to control insects on organically grown plants; appropriate chemical treatment may be required for control in commercial plantations

Cutworms - *Agrotis* spp.

Symptoms

Stems of young transplants or seedlings may be severed at soil line; if infection occurs later, irregular holes are eaten into the surface of fruits; larvae causing the damage are usually active at night and hide during the day in the soil at the base of the plants or in plant debris of toppled plant; larvae are 2.5–5.0 cm (1–2 in) in length; larvae may exhibit a variety of patterns and coloration but will usually curl up into a C-shape when disturbed

Comments

Cutworms have a wide host range and attack vegetables including asparagus, bean, cabbage and other crucifers, carrot, celery, corn, lettuce, pea, pepper, potato and tomato

Management

Remove all plant residue from soil after harvest or at least two weeks before planting, this is especially important if the previous crop was another host such as alfalfa, beans or a leguminous cover crop; plastic or foil collars fitted around plant stems to cover the bottom 3 inches above the soil line and extending a couple of inches into the soil can prevent larvae severing plants; hand-pick larvae after dark; spread diatomaceous earth around the base of the plants (this creates a sharp barrier that will cut the insects if they try and crawl over it); apply appropriate insecticides to infested areas of garden or field if not growing organically

Leafminers - *Lyriomyza* spp

Symptoms

Thin, white, winding trails on leaves; heavy mining can result in white blotches on leaves and leaves dropping from the plant prematurely; early infestation can cause fruit yield to be reduced; adult leafminer is a small black and yellow fly which lays its eggs in the leaf; larvae hatch and feed on leaf interior

Comments

Mature larvae drop from leaves into soil to pupate; entire lifecycle can take as little as 2 weeks in warm weather; insect may go through 7 to 10 generations per year

Management

Check transplants for signs of leafminer damage prior to planting; remove plants from soil immediately after harvest; only use insecticides when leafminer damage has been identified as unnecessary spraying will also reduce populations of their natural enemies

White mold (Sclerotinia rot) - *Sclerotinia sclerotum*

Symptoms

Flowers covered in white, cottony fungal growth; small, circular, dark green, water-soaked lesions on pods leaves and branches which enlarge and become slimy; cottony white growth may be visible on lesions during periods of high humidity; death of branches and/or entire plant

Comments

Fungus can survive in soil for in excess of 5 years; disease can be spread by wind, contaminated irrigation water and by infected seeds

Management

Rotate crops with non-hosts like cereals and corn; plant rows parallel to direction of prevailing winds to prevent spread of disease from secondary hosts nearby; avoid excessive nitrogen fertilizer; use a wide row spacing

Wilt - *Fusarium udum*

Symptoms

Sudden yellowing of leaves; death of leaves; plant death; blackened tissue at base of stem; symptoms may be present on only one side of plant

Comments

Fungus can survive in soil for several years

Management

Practice long term crop rotation; avoid over or under watering plants

BEAN (*Phaseolus vulgaris*)

Description

The common bean, *Phaseolus vulgaris*, is an herbaceous annual plant in the family Fabaceae which is grown as a pulse and green vegetable. The common bean can be bushy, vine-like or climbing depending on the variety being grown. The leaves grow alternately on the stems, are green or purple in color and are divided into 3 oval leaflets with smooth edges. The leaves can grow 6–15 cm (2.4–5.9 in) long and 3–11 cm (1.2–4.3 in) wide. The common bean produces white, pink, lilac or purple flowers which are approximately 1 cm (0.4 in) in diameter, and bean pods 8–20 cm (3.1–7.9 in) long and 1–1.5 cm (0.4–0.6 in) wide which can range in color

Green beans

Runner bean flowers

Bush bean in flower

from green to yellow or black to purple. Each pod contains 4-6 smooth, kidney-shaped beans. Common bean plants are annual plants and last only one growing season and range greatly in size from the bushy varieties 20–60 cm (7.9–24 in) in height; to vines or runner beans which can reach 2–3 m (6 ft 7 in–9 ft 10 in) in length. The common bean includes many varieties and may be referred to as bush bean, dry bean, dwarf bean, field bean, French bean, snap bean, garden bean, haricot bean, kidney bean, pole bean or string bean. The plant originates from the Americas.

Uses

The common bean is used as a pulse and green vegetable eaten fresh or cooked. The beans can be dried, cooked in sauce and canned.

PROPAGATION

Basic requirements

Common beans are warm-season crops and should be planted after all danger of frost has passed and the soil has warmed. Beans will grow best at soil temperatures between 15.5 and 29°C (60–85°F) and are sensitive to cold temperatures and frosts. Beans will grow best in a fertile, well-draining soil with a pH between 6.0 and 6.75 Beans will perform best in full sunlight.

Varieties

Common beans can either be bush or pole varieties. Bush beans will grow erect without any support and require less care than pole varieties. Pole beans grow vertically on a support and are generally easier to harvest. Most type of bean are now available as both bush and pole varieties. Some green bean varieties may be referred to as "string" beans. This name is a reference to older varieties which produced a stringy fibre along the seam of the pod. Modern cultivars were bred which did not produce this substance and which are commonly referred to as "snap" beans due to the ease with which the green pods can be snapped in two.

Purple snap bean variety

Sowing Seeds

Beans should be direct seeded in the garden in when the soil has reached a temperature of at least 15.5°C (60°F), with the optimum temperature for germination being between 15.5 and 29°C (60–85°F). Planting at cooler temperatures leads to slow germination and promotes seed rotting. Seeds should be planted 2.5–3.5 cm (1–1.5 in) deep. Bush beans should be planted 5–10 cm (2–4 in) apart allowing 0.6–0.9 m (2–3 ft) between rows. Pole beans can be planted in both row and hills. In rows, seeds should be spaced 15–25 cm (6–10 in) apart allowing 0.9–1.2 m (3–4 ft) between rows. For a continuous harvest of beans over the summer months, make new plantings every 2–3 weeks.

Poles and Trellises

Pole beans should be provided with a pole or trellis to climb on to support the weight of the pods and allow light to penetrate to all parts of the plant, helping to prevent disease. Bean poles should have a rough surface to help the plant to grip and should be 1.8–2.1 m (6–7 ft) long. Three or four poles can be used to form a tripod onto which the plants can be trained. Bean trellises can be constructed easily using posts (or a tripod arrangement of poles), wire and twine. Position a post at either end of the area in which you wish to plant a row of beans and connect with two lengths of wire. The first wire should be approximately 13 cm (5 in) from the ground, and the second 1.5–1.8 m (5–6 ft) from the ground. Finally, use the twine to create a V-shaped trellis by tying the twine to the bottom wire, bringing it up to the top wire and looping it back down around the bottom wire. Continue to zigzag the string all the way along the wires to the second support before tying the twine off. A rough textured twine is best as it will encourage the plant to climb and twine around it. Pinch back the growing tips of the plants once they reach the top support to encourage the plant to branch.

Harvesting

Beans are generally ready for harvest approximately two weeks after bloom. The beans should be harvested just before the seeds are mature and before they form bumps on the pod. The pods should be firm and snap when they are bent. Pick beans every 2–3 days to ensure the plants remain productive. Pinch beans rather than pulling to avoid damaging the plant. Cut pole beans from the plant using scissors.

DISEASES

Alternaria leaf spot - *Alternaria alternata*

Symptoms of Alternaria leaf spot on bean leaves and pods

Small irregular brown lesions on leaves which expand and turn gray-brown or dark brown with concentric zones; older areas of lesions may dry out and drop from leaves causing shot hole; lesions coalesce to form large necrotic patches.

Comments

Disease emergence favored by high humidity and warm temperatures; plants grown in nitrogen and potassium deficient soils are more susceptible.

Management

Plant beans in fertile soil; foliar fungicide application may be required

Anthracnose - *Glomerella lindemuthiana*

Symptoms

Small, dark brown to black lesions on cotyledons; oval or eye-shaped lesions on stems which turn sunken and brown with purple to red margins; stems may break if cankers weaken stem; pods drying and shrinking above areas of visible symptoms; reddish brown spots on pods which become circular and sunken with rust colored margin.

Comments

Disease transmitted through infected seed; fungus can survive in crop debris in soil and reinfect crop the following season.

Management

Plant resistant varieties; use certified disease free seed; avoid sprinkler irrigation, water plants at base; plow bean crop debris into soil.

Aphids (Cowpea aphid, Pea aphid, etc.) - *Aphis craccivora, Acyrthosiphon pisum*

Symptoms

Small soft bodied insects on underside of leaves and/or stems of plant; usually green or yellow in color, but may be pink, brown, red or black depending on species and host plant; if aphid infestation is heavy it may cause leaves to yellow and/or distorted, necrotic spots on leaves and/or stunted shoots; aphids secrete a sticky, sugary substance called honeydew which encourages the growth of sooty mold on the plants.

Comments

Distinguishing features include the presence of cornicles (tubular structures) which project backwards from the body of the aphid; will generally not move very quickly when disturbed.

Management

If aphid population is limited to just a few leaves or shoots then the infestation can be pruned out to provide control; check transplants for aphids before planting; use tolerant varieties if available; reflective mulches such as silver colored plastic can deter aphids from feeding on plants; sturdy plants can be sprayed with a strong jet of water to knock aphids from leaves; insecticides are generally only required to treat aphids if the infestation is very high - plants generally tolerate low and medium level infestation; insecticidal soaps or oils such as neem or canola oil are usually the best method of control; always check the labels of the products for specific usage guidelines prior to use.

Armyworms (Beet armyworm, Western striped armyworm) - *Spodoptera exigua, Spodoptera praefica*

Symptoms

Singular, or closely grouped circular to irregularly shaped holes in foliage; heavy feeding by young larvae leads to skeletonized leaves; shallow, dry wounds on fruit; egg clusters of 50-150 eggs may be present on the leaves; egg clusters are covered in a whitish scale which gives the cluster a cottony or fuzzy appearance; young larvae are pale green to yellow in color while older larvae are generally darker green with a dark and light line running along the side of their body and a pink or yellow underside.

Comments

Insect can go through 3–5 generations a year.

Management

Organic methods of controlling armyworms include biological control by natural enemies which parasitize the larvae and the application of *Bacillus thuringiensis*; there are chemicals available for commercial control but many that are available for the home garden do not provide adequate control of the larvae.

Bacterial blight - *Xanthomonas campestris* syn. *Xanthomonas axonopodis*

Symptoms

Water-soaked spots on leaves which enlarge and become necrotic; spots may be surrounded by a zone of yellow discoloration; lesions coalesce and give plant a burned appearance; leaves that die remain attached to plant; circular, sunken, red-brown lesion may be present on pods; pod lesions may ooze during humid conditions.

Comments

Disease can be introduced by contaminated seed; bacteria overwinters in crop debris; disease emergence favored by warm temperatures; spread is greatest during humid, wet weather conditions.

Management

Plant only certified seed; plant resistant varieties; treat seeds with an appropriate antibiotic prior to planting to kill off bacteria; spray plants with an appropriate protective copper based fungicide before appearance of symptoms.

Bacterial brown spot - *Pseudomonas syringae*

Symptoms

Small, dark brown necrotic spots on leaves which may be surrounded by a zone of yellow tissue; water soaked spots on pods which turn brown and necrotic; pods may twist and distort in area of infection.

Comments

Bacterium overwinters in crop residue; disease more severe when foliage is wet for extended periods

Management

Plant only certified seed; rotate crops regularly; remove crop debris from field after harvest.

Black root rot - *Thielaviopsis basicola*

Symptoms

Elongated red-purple lesions on root tissue which turns dark gray to black; lesions coalesce to form large dark areas on roots and stems; deep lesions can cause stunted growth, wilting leaves, defoliation and plant death.

Comments

Fungus survive in plant debris in soil.

Management

Rotate crops with non-susceptible grasses; avoid excess irrigation or drought stress.

Corn earworm - *Helicoverpa zea*

Symptoms

Larvae damage leaves, buds, flowers, pods and beans; young caterpillars are cream-white in color with a black head and black hairs; older larvae may be yellow-green to almost black in color with fine white lines along their body and black spots at the base of hairs; eggs are laid singly on both upper and lower leaf surfaces and are initially creamy white but develop a brown-red ring after 24 hours and darken prior to hatching.

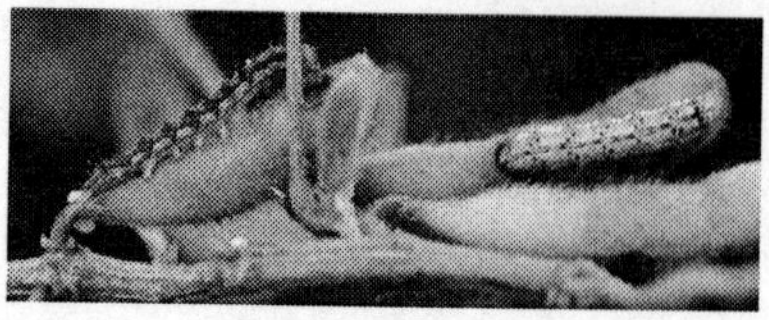

Corn earworm

Comments

Adult insect is a pale green to tan, medium sized moth; insect is also very damaging pests of corn; insect overwinters as pupae in the soil

Management

Monitor plants for eggs and young larvae and also natural enemies that could be damaged by chemicals; *Bacillus thuringiensis* or Entrust SC may be applied to control insects on organically grown plants; appropriate chemical treatment may be required for control in commercial plantations

Cutworms - *Agrotis* spp.

Symptoms

Stems of young transplants or seedlings may be severed at soil line; if infection occurs later, irregular holes are eaten into the surface of fruits; larvae causing the damage are usually active at night and hide during the day in the soil at the base of the plants or in plant debris of toppled plant; larvae are 2.5–5.0 cm (1–2 in) in length; larvae may exhibit a variety of patterns and coloration but will usually curl up into a C-shape when disturbed

Comments

Cutworms have a wide host range and attack vegetables including asparagus, bean, cabbage and other crucifers, carrot, celery, corn, lettuce, pea, pepper, potato and tomato

Management

Remove all plant residue from soil after harvest or at least two weeks before planting, this is especially important if the previous crop was another host such as alfalfa, beans or a leguminous cover crop; plastic or foil collars fitted around plant stems to cover the bottom 3 inches above the soil line and extending a couple of inches into the soil can prevent larvae severing plants; hand-pick larvae after dark; spread diatomaceous earth around the base of the plants (this creates a sharp barrier that will cut the insects if they try and crawl over it); apply appropriate insecticides to infested areas of garden or field if not growing organically

Fusarium root rot - *Fusarium solani*

Symptoms

Young plants stunted with chlorotic leaves; older plants with chlorotic leaves and some leaf drop; severely decayed roots which are hollow and dry.

Comments

Fungus can survive in soil for several years.

Management

Practice long term crop rotation; avoid over or under watering plants; some bean varieties exhibit some tolerance.

Halo blight - *Pseudomonas syringae*

Symptoms

Small water-soaked spots on underside of leaves which turn necrotic and become visible on upper surface; lesions may develop an area of chlorotic tissue around the spots; lesions on expanding leaves may cause distorted leaves; red-brown lesions may be visible on pods; pod lesions may ooze or may turn tan in color.

Comments

Bacterium survives in seeds and crop debris and enters plants through natural openings such as stomata and is spread by splashing water and soil movement.

Management

Plant disease free seed or treat seed with an antibiotic to reduce levels of bacterium; rotate crops to non-hosts every 2 years; plow bean debris deeply in soil after harvest.

Leafminers - *Lyriomyza* spp

Symptoms

Thin, white, winding trails on leaves; heavy mining can result in white blotches on leaves and leaves dropping from the plant prematurely; early infestation can cause fruit yield to be reduced; adult leafminer is a small black and yellow fly which lays its eggs in the leaf; larvae hatch and feed on leaf interior.

Comments

Mature larvae drop from leaves into soil to pupate; entire lifecycle can take as little as 2 weeks in warm weather; insect may go through 7 to 10 generations per year.

Management

Check transplants for signs of leafminer damage prior to planting; remove plants from soil immediately after harvest; only use insecticides when leafminer damage has been identified as unnecessary spraying will also reduce populations of their natural enemies

Loopers (Cabbage looper, Alfalfa looper) - *Trichoplusia ni*, Autographa californica

Symptoms

Large or small holes in leaves; damage often extensive; caterpillars are pale green with a white lines running down either side of their body; caterpillars are easily distinguished by the way they arch their body when moving; eggs are laid singly, usually on the lower leaf surface close to the leaf margin, and are white or pale green in color

Comments

Insects overwinter as pupae in crop debris in soil; adult insect id a dark colored moth; caterpillars have a wide host range

Management

Looper populations are usually held in check by natural enemies; if they do become problematic larvae can be hand-picked from the plants; an organically acceptable control method is the application of *Bacillus thuringiensis* which effectively kills younger larvae; chemical sprays may damage populations of natural enemies and should and should be selected carefully

Mexican bean beetle - *Epilachna varivestis*

Symptoms

Irregular patches of feeding damage on underside of leaves which causes the top surface of the leaf to dry out, giving the leaves a lacy appearance; insect will also damage flowers and small pods; pods may be damaged so badly that they drop from the plant; adult insect is an orange-brown beetle with black spots; larvae are fat-bodied grubs which taper at the end and are in rows of conspicuous spines

Comments

Beetles can decimate bean crops; beetles overwinter as adults and undergo 2-3 generations per year

Management

Some bean varieties may be less attractive hosts for the beetle, e.g. snapbeans are preferred hosts over lima beans; early varieties may escape damage form beetles beetle populations can be reduced by remove overwintering sites such as brush and leaves on the ground; handpick larvae and adults; brush eggs from leaves and destroy; apply insecticidal soap to leaf undersides if infestation is heavy

Mosaic - Bean common mosaic virus (BCMV)

Symptoms

Mottled dark and light green patterns on leaves; leaves may be distorted; yellow dots may be present on leaves; growth of plant may be reduced

Comments

BCMV can be transmitted by seed and has a worldwide distribution; BCMNV also transmitted through infected seed but geographic range more restricted

Management

Plant only virus-free seed; plant resistant varieties

Spider mites (Two-spotted spider mite) - *Tetranychus urticae*

Symptoms

Leaves stippled with yellow; leaves may appear bronzed; webbing covering leaves; mites may be visible as tiny moving dots on the webs or underside of leaves, best viewed using a hand lens; usually not spotted until there are visible symptoms on the plant; leaves turn yellow and may drop from plant

Comments

Spider mites thrive in dusty conditions; water-stressed plants are more susceptible to attack

Management

In the home garden, spraying plants with a strong jet of water can help reduce buildup of spider mite populations; if mites become problematic apply insecticidal soap to plants; certain chemical insecticides may actually increase mite populations by killing off natural enemies and promoting mite reproduction

Stinkbugs (Consperse stinkbug, etc.) - *Euschistus conspersus*

Symptoms

Dark colored pinpricks on fruit surrounded by a lighter area that turns yellow or remains light green; stink bugs often carry pathogens in their mouthparts which can cause secondary infections and decay of fruit; adult insect is shield-shaped and brown or green in color; may have pink, red or yellow markings; eggs are drum shaped and laid in clusters on the leaves; larvae resemble the adults but are smaller

Comments

Adult insects overwinter under leaves, on legumes, blackberries or on certain weeds such as mustard or Russian thistle.

Management

Remove weeds around crop which may act as overwintering sites for stink bugs and practice good weed Management throughout the year; organically accepted control methods include the use of insecticidal soaps, kaolin clay and preservation of natural enemies; chemical treatments are not recommended for tomatoes that are to be processed for paste or canning unless secondary infections with other pathogens are a concern.

White mold (Sclerotinia rot) - ***Sclerotinia sclerotum***

Symptoms

Flowers covered in white, cottony fungal growth; small, circular, dark green, water-soaked lesions on pods leaves and branches which enlarge and become slimy; cottony white growth may be visible on lesions during periods of high humidity; death of branches and/or entire plant.

Comments

Fungus can survive in soil for in excess of 5 years; disease can be spread by wind, contaminated irrigation water and by infected seeds.

Management

There is no true immunity to white mold in any bean varieties; rotate crops with non-hosts like cereals and corn; plant rows parallel to direction of prevailing winds to prevent spread of disease from secondary hosts nearby; avoid excessive nitrogen fertilizer; use a wide row spacing.

24

Major Pest and Diseases of Fruits and Vegetables

CURRANT LETTUCE APHID

Currant lettuce aphid, *Nasonovia ribis-nigri* (Mosey) [CLA] is primarily a contamination pest of lettuce, chicory, endive and radicchio. The aphids colonise lettuce hearts and rosettes, making them unsaleable. CLA can also vector cucumber and lettuce mosaic virus although this has not been observed in infested crops.

Currant lettuce aphids prefer to feed on new leaves. They can be found inside the wrapper leaves and hearts of iceberg lettuce varieties. In an open lettuce variety, they are found deep within the leaf rosette. CLA are often scattered, and do not tend to form dense colonies.

Description

Immature aphids are yellow-green and wingless. Adults can be winged or wingless and are 2.5 mm in length, greenish to yellow-green, with irregular narrow dark bands on the abdomen.

Hosts

Currant lettuce aphid has both wingless and winged forms. The primary host plants for this aphid species are gooseberry and red, black and white currants (*Ribes* spp.). To survive winter in cold temperate climates, the aphids lay eggs on gooseberries and currants (Figure 1).

Chicory and endive (*Cichorium* spp.), nipplewort (*Lampsana* spp.), hawksbeard (*Crepis capillaris*), hawksweed (*Hieracium* spp.), speedwell (*Veronica* spp.), artichoke, tobacco and petunia are also secondary hosts.

How do aphids spread?

Dispersal of aphids is mainly as winged adults. These winged adult aphids can be dispersed widely by wind currents. The potential for aphid spread is considered

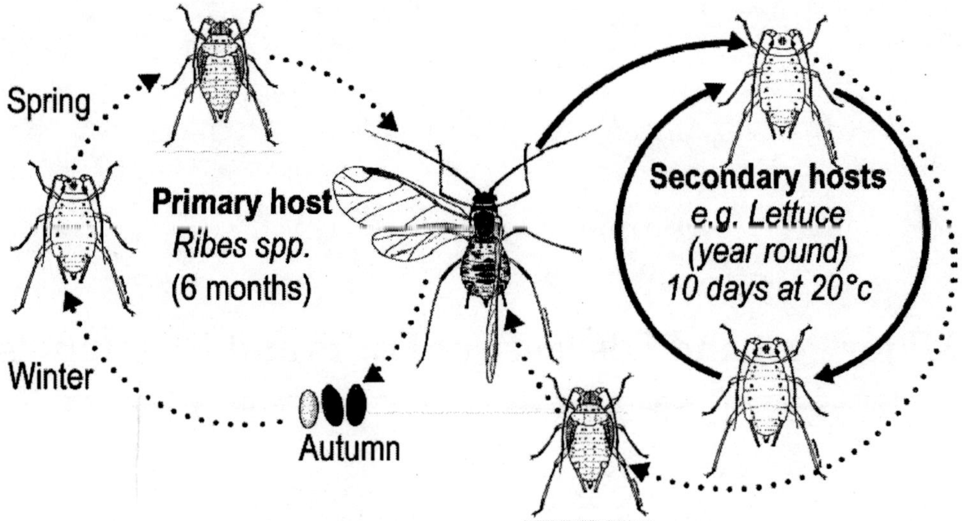

Fig. 24.1. The currant lettuce aphid life cycle

high, particularly when the proportion of winged adults increases within a colony. Currant lettuce aphids are small, and colonize the inner lettuce leaves. This means they can be spread unnoticed by the movement of infested produce or lettuce seedlings.

Management Options

After the first wave of CLA into lettuce production areas, CLA populations have not remained high. In all production areas the aphids have been hard to find for periods of the year.

- Source control (contaminated product or seedlings)
- *Nasonovia*-resistant lettuce varieties
- Monitoring lettuce
- Biologically based Integrated Pest Management
- Confidor® or Durivo® seedling treatments
- Durivo® furrow pre-plant plant hole drench
- Foliar insecticides sprays in open lettuce or prior to hearting
    - Pirimor® 2 Day WHP
    - Chess® 2 sprays per crop, 7 Day WHP
    - Movento® 2 sprays per crop, 3 Day WHP
    - Dimethoate® 7 Day WHP
- Sanitation (control weed hosts, bury infested lettuce)
- Post-harvest washing

Source control

Care should be taken that currant lettuce aphid is not introduced to your property via transplants or movement of other plant material. Ensure your nursery supplier has a management plan for aphids. Currant lettuce aphids are small, and can be easily spread in harvested produce and seedlings. The use of second-hand boxes for produce can spread aphids and other insects.

Nasonovia-resistant lettuce varieties

Seed companies are incorporating the 'Nas resistance' gene into most of their lettuce lines which prevents CLA from successfully feeding. Note other species of aphids can feed on Nas resistant varieties. In Europe in 2008 a new CLA biotype was found that overcame the Nas resistance gene and has subsequently spread over Europe. We do not have this CLA biotype but do need to monitor for it.

Varietal performance and yields differ between lettuce growing areas, so it is recommended that varieties be trialled and compared to your standard variety before doing commercial scale plantings.

Monitoring lettuce

Regular crop monitoring for insects is recommended, as it enables informed pest management decisions and if necessary timely insecticide applications. In lettuce seedlings and pre-heart lettuce, attention needs to be paid to the innermost leaves and in leaf folds, where the aphid prefers to live. Once the lettuce has hearted some destructive sampling is needed. Since CLA may occur non-uniformly across paddocks, a number of widely dispersed sites need to be sampled.

Biologically based Integrated Pest Management (IPM)

In all states biologically based IPM has been demonstrated as an effective management strategy. Beneficial insects, such as brown lacewings, ladybird beetles and hoverfly larvae (syrphids), are effective aphid predators. The use of broad-spectrum insecticides is likely to kill many beneficial insects. Growers using an IPM strategy with good beneficial populations are best placed to manage currant lettuce aphid for the long term. In the Sydney basin CLA was found difficult to manage over the winter period when beneficials were absent from late autumn. However in some years CLA populations have been virtually absent in unsprayed and susceptible lettuce varieties highlighting the need to monitor.

Seedling drenches

Imidacloprid (Confidor®) or thiomethoxam (aphid active component of Durivo®) have systemic activity and can be applied either as a seedling drench or as a furrow pre-plant spray. These treatments at label rates will prevent aphid infestations from occurring for at minimum 4 weeks and more typically for 6-10 weeks depending on rainfall. In very wet conditions activity decreases more quickly.

Imidacloprid and thiomethoxam (aphid active component of Durivo®) seedling drenches are not compatible with biological IPM, as the chemical treatment can indirectly kill beneficial insects, or interrupt their natural population growth.

Foliar insecticides

Foliar applied insecticides are only effective against CLA prior to hearting, or in open lettuce varieties. Pirimicarb (Pirimor®), Spirotetramat (Movento®) and Pymetrozine (Chess®) are IPM-compatible insecticides registered for use on aphids in lettuce. Pirimicarb resistance has been reported in Europe. New Zealand tests have shown that the strain of CLA in Australia is not resistant. Pymetrozine appears to work best when it can stay wet for as long as possible; hence, it is best applied after irrigation, in the evening or very early morning.

Broad spectrum insecticides with active ingredients such as dimethoate and maldison are registered in some states of Australia for controlling aphids in lettuce. Broad spectrum insecticides are undesirable in a biological IPM management strategy.

Sanitation

Controlling secondary host weeds on and around the farm is an important management strategy to reduce potential CLA pressure. Secondary host weeds worth controlling include prickly lettuce (*Lactuca serriola*), hawksbeard (*Crepis capillaris*), speedwell (Veronica), nipplewort (*Lampsana* spp.) and globe artichokes.

Heavily infested lettuce crops, where aphids cannot be controlled with insecticides, should be incorporated into the soil as soon as possible. Lettuce consignments that have been recalled due to CLA infestation should be buried rather than dumped.

Post-harvest washing

Washing lettuce will not disinfest lettuce hearts of aphids. Loose leaf lettuce washing processes with fine water filtration systems can reduce the number of aphids in packaged or processed lettuce products.

DIAMONDBACK MOTH CONTROL IN ASIAN LEAFY BRASSICA CROPS

The ***Key Pest*** of brassica crops is ***Diamondback moth*** (Cabbage moth), *Plutella xylostella* (Linnaeus). Feeding by the caterpillar stage of this insect can cause holes in leaves all over the plant making most of the leaves unmarketable.

The current practice of weekly spraying of insecticide is unnecessary and can contribute to the build up of resistance to insecticides in this pest, resulting in control failures. Asian leafy brassica growers need to adopt the 'Two Window' strategy developed by Avcare Insecticide Resistance Action Committee in order to prevent the build up of resistance.

Life history of the insect and damage caused

The adults are greyish brown moths about 9 millimetres long. When the wings are folded at rest, on the ridge formed by the folded wings a row of diamond-shaped yellow markings appear. The hind wings are fringed with long grey hairs. When the infestation is heavy, moths can be seen flying on slight disturbance of the leaves.

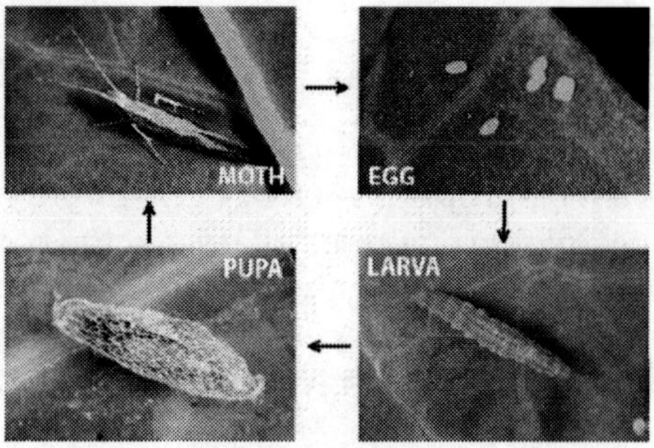

Life cycle

Adult females lay tiny yellow eggs on the undersides of leaves. Eggs hatch in a few days into colourless slender caterpillars. These caterpillars either feed on the surface tissues of the leaves or mine between the two surfaces of the leaf and leave clear window-like patches. As the caterpillars grow rapidly, they become green and at this stage they can perforate the older leaves by chewing large pieces out of them.

The larvae, if present in large numbers, eat holes in leaves all over the plant, giving the plant a lacy pattern and render it unmarketable.

Larvae when disturbed drop and hang by a silken thread. They feed for ten days to a month depending on the temperature. When fully grown they can reach up to 12 millimetres in length. When fully grown they stop feeding, spin flimsy, spindle shaped net-like cocoons on the under surface of the leaves and pupate in them. A brown pupa can be seen inside the cocoon. The adult moth emerges from this pupa after one to two weeks. The life cycle may be as short as sixteen days at warmer temperatures and therefore there are multiple generations per year on farms with brassicas present.

Preferred crop hosts and alternative weed hosts

The pest can also survive on alternative weed hosts such as wild radish, wild turnip and turnip weed.

Management of the pest

Presence of Diamondback moth can be detected by the moths flying away when the plants are disturbed in the field. If flying moths are seen, the crops should be examined carefully. Small green caterpillars could be seen feeding on the under surface of the leaves. When the caterpillars are disturbed, they will drop from the leaf and try to hang by a silken thread.

Choice of insecticides

A *Bt* (*Bacillus thurungiensis*) based product (e.g. Xentari®) should be tried first. This will allow the parasites and predators to attack the pest and reduce the number of sprays needed later. A week after the first spray, twenty plants should be randomly checked to decide whether to spray again or not. Our work in season showed that 1–3 sprays of Xentari® based on crop monitoring kept the Diamondback moth under control better than weekly sprays with other insecticides.

BANANA RUST THRIPS AND BANANA SILVERING THRIPS

Banana rust thrips, *Chaetanaphothrips signipennis*, and banana silvering thrips, *Hercinothrips bicinctus*, occasionally damage banana fruit. These thrips live in colonies in sheltered places on the banana plant, especially behind the bases of leaf stalks. When they infest flower or fruit bunches their feeding blemishes the fruit, sometimes very severely. Banana rust thrips has been the more important pest of the two. Banana silvering thrips damage has rearely occured in recent times.

Banana Rust Thrips

Description and life history

The adult thrips is yellow, about 1.3 mm long, and has narrow fringed wings. Each forewing has two dark areas. The females lay eggs in the plant tissue, under leaf sheaths and where fruits touch. These larvae hatch after about a week and are white to cream and, when fully developed after about another week, are about the same size and shape as the adults, but have no wings. The mature larvae enter the soil and form white pupae that look like mature larvae. Adult thrips emerge from the pupae 7 to 10 days later.

The thrips congregate in colonies on the pseudostems behind the bases of leaf sheaths, and their feeding there leaves the plant tissue blood red in colour. They congregate on fruit, mainly where the fruits touch each other. Both the adults and the larvae feed by puncturing plant surface cells and sucking up the sap. There are many generations per year but the greatest numbers of thrips occur from November to March. Although adult thrips can fly, major spread is far more likely by movement of infested planting material to new areas. Banana rust thrips only develops on a few plant species and banana plants are the only sources of infestation in the plantation. In affected plantations thrips damage develops mainly at the warmer sites.

Damage

Banana rust thrips may infest bunches at any time during their growth, but infestations that develop when the bunches emerge cause the most severe damage. Injured areas on young fruit first appear water soaked, then look discoloured and grey and later become rust coloured. With further growth of the fruit cracks may develop in the scarred areas. Injury to fruit is usually on the sides of fruits that are touching or are close together, but in severe infestations the whole fruit may be blemished. Sometimes the fruits split.

Banana Silvering Thrips

Description and life history

The adult is about 1.5 mm long, and yellow to brown with a darker abdomen and pale yellow hindwings, each with two broad, brownish bands. On the fruit, adults look dark with a pale yellow line along the body, formed by the folded yellow hindwings. The larvae are yellow white, often with a globule of black excrement at the tip of the abdomen. The life history is similar to banana rust thrips. Banana silvering thrips has also been recorded infesting passionfruit, choko and some weeds.

Damage

Fruit is attacked at all stages. The damaged areas develop a silvery blemish, spotted with the thrips' dark excreta. In severe infestations the blemish may be reddish brown, and deep longitudinal cracks may develop in the blemished skin.

Control

For new plantings, take planting material from plantations free of banana rust thrips, or far better, use tillue-cultured bananas. Discourage weed growth in plantations where banana silvering thrips attack is known to occur, as they breed on some weeds. In particular, ensure choko vines are removed.

Insecticides applied in spring to the bases of the plants and surrounding soil for banana weevil borer control, assist in preventing damage by banana rust thrips, but appropriate bunch treatments at the time of bunch pruning or covering are much more reliable.

ONION THRIPS IN ONION

Onion thrips (*Thrips tabaci*) is a tiny (<1.5 mm long), slender, free-moving insect that is often found in large numbers in onion. Adults are pale yellow to light brown

Fig.24.3. Onion thrips adult and nymph (inset).

and have a pair of wings fringed with long hairs (Fig. 24.3). The immature stages have the same body shape as adults but are lighter in colour and are wingless.

Damage caused by onion thrips

Both adults and nymphs feed by piercing and rasping the leaf surface and drinking the liquid. The feeding areas later appear as silvery patches on the leaves). When feeding areas are large, the plant's ability to photosynthesise and maintain water balance is greatly reduced, resulting in yield loss or reduced bulb size. Onion thrips may also enter harvested bulbs and breed there, thus reducing marketability of bulbs. Apart from direct damage, onion thrips is a vector of tomato spotted wilt virus (TSWV) and iris yellow spot virus (IYSV); the latter is a potentially destructive virus of onion.

Identification

Most (>90%) thrips found in onion are onion thrips. Occasionally a few plague thrips (*Thrips imaginis*) are also found, especially early in the crop season. Adults of the two species can be separated easily under the microscope by the presence (in plague thrips) or absence (in onion thrips) of red pigment in the ocelli on the head of freshly collected specimens.

Later in the crop season, some predatory desmothrips may also be present. These are large thrips, more than double the length of onion thrips and plague thrips. They have banded wings that are round at the tips.

Where are onion thrips found?

In a young onion plant, both adults and nymphs are found mostly in between the inner leaves. As plants mature, most adults disperse to other parts of the leaves. Nymphs also disperse but the majority remain in between the inner leaves. In a mature plant with fallen leaves, adults and nymphs are also found in clusters inside the leaf folds.

Monitoring

Onion thrips density can be assessed directly by on-site visual inspection or extraction and lab counting, or indirectly by trapping. In on-site visual inspection, make sure touching leaves are separated and fallen leaves are lifted to reveal hidden thrips. Extract thrips by immersing and shaking the plants in ethanol or water for a few minutes, and then filtering the liquid through fine mesh. You can then count the thrips on the mesh, using a microscope. Alternatively, cut leaves into pieces and place in a funnel connected to a collection vial. Place a few drops of turpentine on a cotton wick, and place that on top of the plant material to repel the thrips to the collection vial. For either visual inspection or extraction, a minimum of 10 plants should be checked from each monitoring block. Yellow sticky traps are used to trap onion thrips. A minimum of five sticky traps should be placed in each monitoring block. The traps are retrieved after a period of time and then examined under a microscope. In addition to onion thrips, flies, midges, bugs and other thrips species may also be trapped in the sticky trap. Other common thrips species found in sticky traps in onion fields are plague thrips, dandelion thrips (*Tenothrips frici*), haplothrips, and tomato thrips (*Frankliniella schultzei*). Onion thrips and plague thrips are generally paler than the other three species. In addition, onion thrips and plague thrips have seven antennal segments, while the others all have eight antennal segments.

WESTERN FLOWER THRIPS AND TOMATO SPOTTED WILT VIRUS

Western flower thrips

Western flower thrips (WFT), *Frankliniella occidentalis* is primarily a pest as a vector of tomato spotted wilt virus (TSWV) in tomatoes, lettuce, potatoes, and capsicum. Its feeding can cause scarring and deformations on leaves and fruit, with seedlings and soft tissue particularly prone to feeding damage. Capsicums, cucumbers and beans are susceptible to fruit scarring.

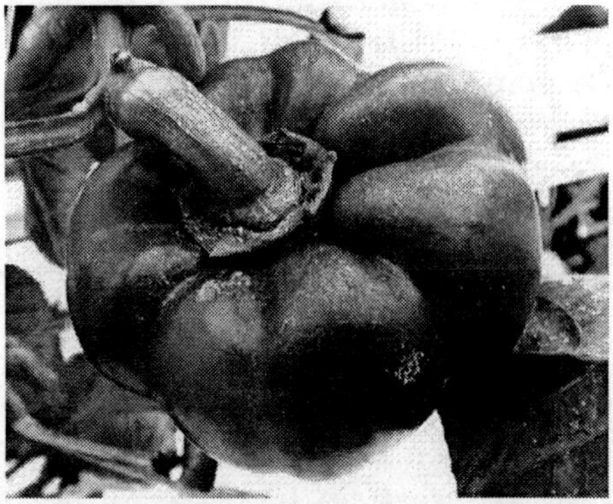

Fig. 24.4. WFT scarring on capsicums

WFT is more of a problem than other thrips species because it develops resistance to pesticides easily, hence there are few chemical options to control it.

WFT was first found in Western Australia in 1993 and has spread to all states and most production areas since.

WFT description

Immature thrips are pale yellow, thin, wingless and up to 1 mm in length. Adults are also thin, with yellowish head and darker abdomen. They are about 1.5-2 mm in length, with two feathery wings.

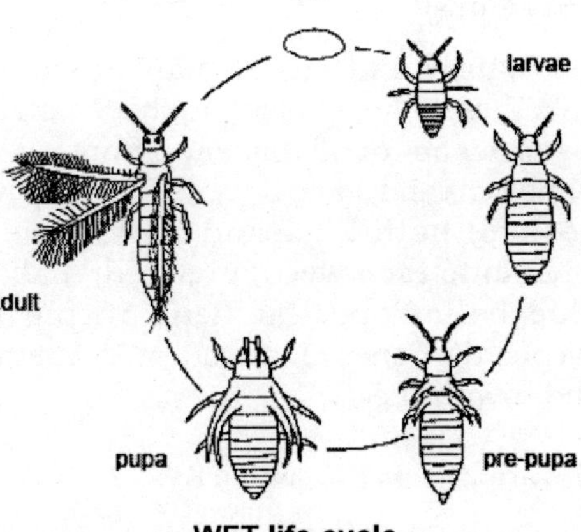

WFT life cycle

The life cycle of WFT is illustrated in Fig. 24.5. Eggs are laid into soft plant tissue. Within a few days eggs hatch into a wingless juvenile or larval stage. Thrips have two feeding larval stages followed by non-feeding pre-pupal and then pupal stages which tend to hide in soil crevices or within foliage. Winged adults emerge from the pupae to mate and feed. The length of the life cycle and life expectancy of the adults depend on temperature and food quality. At 30°C the life cycle is approximately 12 days while at 20°C it is 19 days.

WFT hosts

Western flower thrips breeds on a wide range of flowering plants including weeds, vegetable crops and fruit trees.

TOMATO SPOTTED WILT VIRUS

Tomato spotted wilt virus (TSWV) is a tospovirus transmitted by some species of thrips. WFT, tomato thrips (*Franklienella schultzei*) and onion thrips (*Thrips tabaci*) are common vectors for TSWV in vegetables. Melon thrips (*Thrips palmi*) is also a vector for TSWV but is not widespread in NSW. Once a plant is infected with TSWV it cannot be cured, so prevention or use of tolerant varieties, if available, are the only management options.

TSWV Description

Tomato spotted wilt virus is one of the most wide-spread and damaging viruses affecting vegetable crops in Australia. TSWV was first described in Australia in 1915 and has been a sporadic problem since then. The arrival of the very efficient vector WFT has seen an increase in the seriousness of the disease, particularly in hydroponic and covered systems. TSWV causes significant damage to solanaceous vegetables such as tomatoes, potatoes and capsicums, but also to lettuce and a wide range of herbs and ornamental crops. Cucumber infections are symptomless.

TSWV hosts

Many hundreds of plants (>900) are TSWV hosts, most being in the Solanaceae, Asteraceae or Fabaceae. Some show symptoms and some do not. Common weed hosts of both WFT and TSWV include amaranth, cape weed, pigweed, mallows, blue heliotrope, fat hen, purple top, shepherd's purse, nightshades, Scotch thistle and sow thistle.

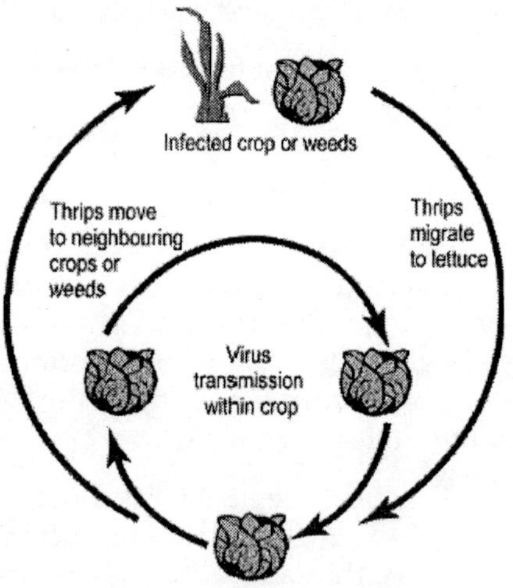

Diagram of thrips–TSWV transmission

How do thrips transmit TSWV?

Once the thrips larva has acquired the virus, it will multiply within the larva. When an infected larva reaches adulthood it can fly to a new plant, transmitting the virus as it pierces the plant cells and sucks the contents. The virus does not pass through the egg stage so each succeeding generation of thrips must re-acquire the virus as larvae feeding on TSWV-infected plants.

Management options

A TSWV-infected plant cannot be cured. Management options focus on preventing infection and minimising spread.

- Source control
  - avoiding contaminated or infected seedlings
  - weed management within and surrounding crops
  - roguing and destroying infected plants
  - removing or cultivating in crops after harvest
  - screening greenhouses with thrips-grade mesh
- TSWV resistant varieties (capsicums)
- Monitoring crops for WFT and TSWV
- Biologically based Integrated Pest Management
- Foliar insecticide sprays to control WFT.

Source control

The most important management option is to reduce the populations of WFT and TSWV. Avoid bringing in seedlings contaminated with WFT or already infected with TSWV. Sourcing seedlings from nurseries that are screened with thrips-grade mesh and actively monitoring for WFT and TSWV will greatly reduce your chances of bringing them onto your farm.

Given that both WFT and TSWV have very large host ranges, management of weeds within and surrounding your crops is essential. In areas where both WFT and TSWV populations are high, putting pressure on local councils and neighbours to also control roadside or paddock weeds, particularly broadleaf weeds, can greatly assist in reducing the overall regional pressure.

Trials in South Australia using native plants, particularly saltbushes and grasses that are poor hosts for WFT and TSWV, around greenhouses and along road verges can reduce the incidence of virus in nearby crops. The added benefit is that the plantings reduce the need for weed management around the structures.

If TSWV is noticed in crops, removing the plants showing symptoms will reduce the within-crop infection. Early detection and removal can greatly reduce final crop losses due to TSWV.

Chipping plants and leaving them on the ground is not sufficient; the infected plants must be removed completely from the farm, bagged or buried. If a planting is heavily infected with TSWV it may be much better to remove the whole crop to avoid infection of younger plantings.

Crops grown in greenhouses can be protected from WFT using thrips-grade mesh covering all openings and double doors to avoid thrips entering.

TSWV-tolerant Varieties

Some varieties of capsicums and tomatoes are resistant to TSWV although strains of TSWV that break the resistance can develop in areas of high TSWV pressure. Therefore, if you do use resistant varieties it is still important to reduce the virus pressure through weed management and other sanitation measures.

Monitoring WFT and TSWV

Sticky traps, visual monitoring and vacuum sampling are all used to monitor WFT. Blue traps may be preferable for monitoring WFT because they are less attractive to other non-thrips species. Tapping flowers over a white tray is recommended when susceptible crops are flowering. As part of monitoring the crop for a range of pests a small proportion of thrips will be picked up in a vacuum sample, although this method of sampling is not recommended if primarily assessing for thrips numbers.

Not all plants that are infected by TSWV will show symptoms. Crops that are susceptible will tend to show symptoms on the new developing foliage after infection. Test kits are available for testing for TSWV.

Alternatively, plant or thrips samples can be sent to state department diagnostic laboratories.

Biological Controls

Biological controls have not been considered important for WFT control in Australia until recently. Thrips are highly mobile and small and many of the common generalist predators do not feed on them. Predatory mites are common but rarely appear to adequately control WFT numbers. Predatory mites such as *Transieus (=Typhlodromips) montdorensis* and *Amblyseius cucumeris* are, however, proving to be effective in greenhouses that use only 'selective' chemistry and have adequate ventilation. Commercial rearing systems are being developed with existing commercial producers of beneficial organisms.

Some field trials are also assessing the potential for using soil amendments to raise soil organic carbon as a means of encouraging native predatory mites, particularly *Pergmasus* sp.

Another promising area is the use of entomopathogenic (insect infecting) fungi. Two groups have developed strains of *Beauvaria* and *Metarhizium* fungi that are effective against thrips and some other sap-sucking insects. They are currently working with a commercial producer and the APMVA on registration.

Chemical Controls

Insecticide applications targeting WFT can reduce WFT populations and reduce within-crop transmission of TSWV. Given that WFT is notoriously effective at developing resistance to chemicals used against it, is important to adhere to the recommended resistance management strategy.

Not all effective chemicals are available for all crops so it is similarly important to use only the chemicals specifically registered or available via Permit for your crop.

Correct chemical application can be extremely important for WFT; for example, make sure your spray equipment is properly calibrated, use insecticide rated nozzles, use the appropriate water rates, and spray only in suitable weather conditions. For more information pick up the Spray Sense information sheets from your nearest NSW DPI office or from the web site.

Integrated Pest Management

Integrated pest management (IPM) is a strategy that draws on a range of management tools with the goal of using the least ecologically disruptive techniques to manage pests to within economically acceptable levels. For TSWV and WFT management, an IPM approach concentrates on reducing the source of both WFT and TSWV. Where it is possible, the use of TSWV tolerant varieties are recommended. Monitor crops for both WFT and TSWV levels and when TSWV is observed rogue out and destroy the infected plants. If growing in a greenhouse use thrips-grade mesh on all openings and use double doors.

If WFT numbers are high enough to be causing physical damage at vulnerable stages or TSWV is present, then insecticide sprays may be needed. Use recommended rates, adhere to the resistance management strategy and apply sprays to maximise spray coverage.

Sending Samples for Identification

Management strategies are most effective when accurate identification of both thrips and viruses is made.

Adult thrips can be identified either from specimens collected into a vial or container, or from sticky traps. If it is likely to be some time before you can deliver or send the sample then, if possible, collect adults into a small quantity of rubbing alcohol (available at the chemist). Collect at least 10 specimens as handling and transportation may damage important diagnostic features used to identify the insects. Sticky traps can be covered in plastic cling wrap before removing from the field or greenhouse. Try to avoid squashing sticky traps as accurate identification is difficult if specimens are damaged.

For plants suspected of being infected with TSWV, collect a number of plants showing the range of symptoms. Wrap plant material in damp but not wet paper, place in a plastic bag, keep cool and send or deliver as quickly as possible.

25

Insect Pests of Crucifer Vegetables

The crucifer vegetables—cabbage, cauliflower, broccoli, Brussels sprouts, turnip and radish—may be attacked by a number of insects. Some of these, such as cabbage white butterfly, cabbage moth and cabbage aphid, feed only on crop and weed plants of the family Cruciferae. Others, such as Helicoverpa caterpillars and cutworms, feed on a wide range of plants.

CABBAGE WHITE BUTTERFLY (*Pieris rapae*)

The cabbage white butterfly, *Pieris rapae*, is the most common pest of crucifers in New South Wales. Its larvae feed voraciously, chewing large holes in the leaves and fouling the plants with excrement. Cabbage white butterfly is most active in the spring and autumn months.

The butterfly is cream to yellowish, with black-tipped forewings and central spots; the wingspan is 40 to 50 mm. The butterflies are often seen obtaining nectar from plants unrelated to crucifers; they are attracted to blue and yellow flowers. They place their pale yellow, spindle-shaped eggs singly, usually on the outer leaves. The younger caterpillars feed on the undersides of these leaves, and move towards the centre of the plant as they grow. Older caterpillars are usually on the upper surfaces of the central leaves. When fully grown the caterpillars are about 30 mm long and velvety green, with faint yellow stripes down the back and along each side. The pupae are about 18 mm long, greyish brown, yellow or green and are usually attached to the undersides of the older leaves of the host plant or to some nearby object. The life cycle under suitable conditions occupies about a month.

Cabbage White Butterfly

The cabbage white butterfly is parasitised by several species of wasps. Two of the most common parasitoids are *Cotesia rubecula* and *Cotesia glomerata* from the hymenopteran family Braconidae. They can be recognised by yellow silken cocoons beside the dead caterpillars. *C. rubecula* produces a single cocoon from each host whereas *C. glomerata* produces a mass of cocoons from each host.

CABBAGE MOTH (*Plutella xylostella*)

The cabbage moth, *Plutella xylostella,* is also a serious pest of crucifers. The youngest caterpillars are leaf miners. Older caterpillars feed in sheltered situations on the undersides of leaves or in the outer heart leaves, making many small holes that are often window pane-like because the upper epidermis has been left intact. The moths are about 9 mm long and greyish brown, with a series of diamond-shaped markings on the centre-line of the back when the moth is at rest. The moths are active at night, laying clusters of yellow eggs along the ribs and margins of the more sheltered leaves. The caterpillars are tapered at each end and when fully grown are green and about 12 mm long.

Cabbage Moth

When disturbed the caterpillars wriggle away and drop from the leaf, attached by silken threads. When fully grown they pupate in silken, net-like cocoons attached to the leaves. In warm conditions the life cycle takes about 3 weeks. Cabbage moth is more troublesome in dry weather.

Natural mortality is mainly caused by several imported parasitic wasps including *Diadegma semiclausum, Diadegma rapi, Diadromis collaris, Apanteles ippeus* and Cotesia *plutellae*. Rain or overhead irrigation can also cause high levels of mortality. Control of cabbage moth in commercial Brassica crops still relies heavily on insecticides. It needs to be noted however that cabbage moth is notorious for its rapid development of resistance to insecticides. Hence it is important to rotate insecticides of different groups. Spray decisions should be based on regular monitoring instead of calendar days.

HELICOVERPA CATERPILLARS

The caterpillars *Helicoverpa armigera* and *H. punctigera* damage a wide range of crops formerly known as Heliothis caterpillar. (Helicoverpa was formerly known as Heliothis caterpillar.). In some seasons, cabbages and cauliflowers are attacked. The caterpillars may feed on the outer leaves of young plants or burrow into the hearts of older plants. The moths have wingspans of 30 to 45 mm and are generally buff to reddish brown, with darker markings, and are often seen flying in crops at dusk. The females lay their dome shaped, yellowish white, 0.5 mm diameter eggs singly on the leaves. The caterpillars grow to 40 to 50 mm long. At this size they are green, yellow, pink, reddish brown or almost black, often with a broad yellowish white stripe along each side of the body and a dark-edged whitish line down the middle of the back. They have conspicuous body hairs on tubercles. When fully grown the caterpillars pupate in the soil.

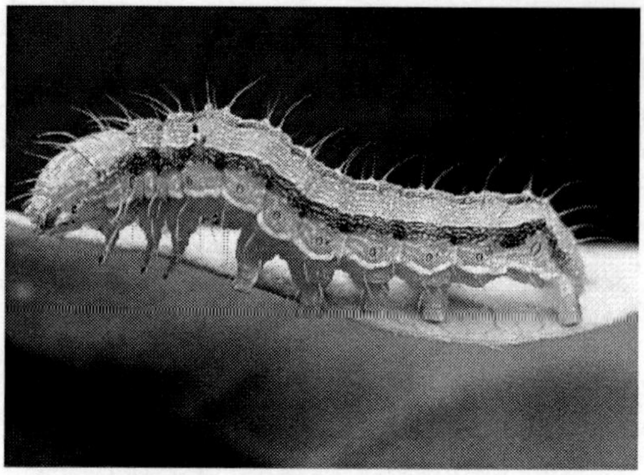

Helicoverpa **caterpillars**

Emergence of the moths from pupae in the soil depends on the soil moisture content. Thus crops are more likely to be attacked after a period of rain. Helicoverpa caterpillars have a very wide host range including lucerne, sweet corn, tomatoes and ornamental and weed species. They are most troublesome in late summer and autumn. Once they have penetrated cabbage hearts they are protected from insecticide sprays.

CABBAGE APHID (*Brevicoryne brassicae*)

Feeding by large numbers of cabbage aphid, *Brevicoryne brassicae*, a sap-sucking insect, causes wilting and stunting in young plants and yellowing, curling and leaf distortion in older plants. This pest is most prevalent in late summer and autumn. It is the most common pest of Brussels sprouts. The adult aphid is about 2.5 mm long, soft-bodied, greyish with a mealy covering, and may be winged or wingless. The immature stages resemble the wingless adults. This aphid clusters densely on the leaves.

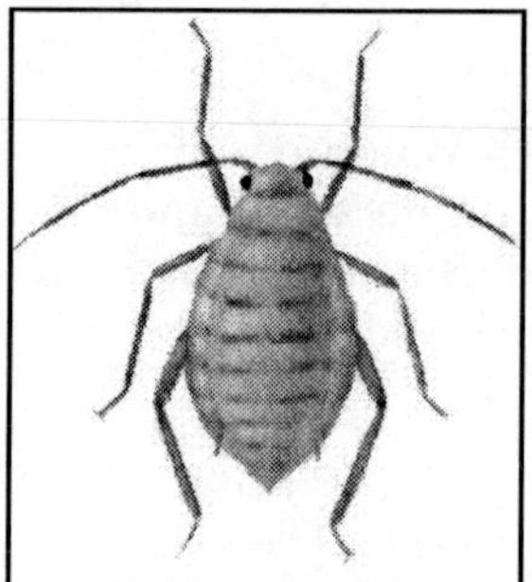

Cabbage aphid

Two other aphids are commonly associated with crucifers. Green peach aphid, *Myzus persicae*, is usually on the undersides of older leaves. It is about 2 mm long when adult and green to pale yellow or pink. This aphid, which has a very wide host range, is important only as a vector of virus diseases. Turnip aphid, *Lipaphis erysimi*, a greenish, wax-dusted aphid, about 2 mm long when adult, feeds only on cruciferous plants, but is found more commonly on cruciferous weedspthan on crop plants.

Aphids on crucifers are often kept under control bypnatural enemies-mainly tiny wasps that parasitise thepaphids, and ladybirds and their larvae and lacewing andphover fly larvae that eat the aphids.

CUTWORMS (*Agrotis* spp.)

Cutworms, *Agrotis* spp., are soil-inhabiting caterpillarspthat feed on stems and foliage near ground level,pusually at night, and destroy seedling plants. By day thepcaterpillars hide in the soil, 1 to 10 cm deep, usuallypnear damaged plants. They are smooth-bodiedpcaterpillars, 25 to 50 mm long when fully grown, andpgrey, grey-green, blackish, or brown with a pinkish redptinge. As some other caterpillars do, they coil up and remain green, still if picked up. The adults are stoutbodiedpmoths with pale brown, brownish grey,ppurplish brown or grey-black forewings andpwingspans of 30 to 55 mm. The females lay their eggspon the soil or on the lower parts of plants.

Cutworms

Ground that has been cultivated recently after rain or flooding, and weedy cultivated or uncultivated ground, is most likely to be infested.

CLUSTER CATERPILLAR (*Spodoptera litura*)

Cluster caterpillar, *Spodoptera litura*, is a leaf eating caterpillar that feeds in groups when young. As they grow older the caterpillars feed singly, spreading out to other parts of the plant or to neighbouring plants; they chew large holes in the leaves and may tunnel into cabbage hearts. The adults are stout-bodied moth with wingspans of 30 to 45 mm. The forewings are brownish with cream markings, and the hindwings are white. The females lay their eggs mainly on the undersides of leaves in clusters covered with brown scales from the moths' bodies. When fully grown the caterpillars are 40 to 50 mm long and are brown, black or grey, with a row of dark, rounded-triangular marks along each side of the back and two pairs of large yellowish or white spots near the head. This pest occurs most commonly in late summer and autumn.

Cluster caterpillar

CABBAGE CENTRE GRUB (*Hellula hydrates*)

Caterpillars of cabbage centre grub, *Hellula hydrates, tunnel* into the growing points of the plants, covering the entrances with webbing and excreta. Occasionally they feed within the leaves of older plants, forming blisters. The adult is a grey-brown moth with a wingspan of about 18 mm. It holds its wings horizontally when resting.

The females lay their eggs on young growth. When fully grown the caterpillars are about 12 mm long and creamish with brown longitudinal stripes.

This pest can be troublesome throughout summer and autumn, mainly in hot dry weather.

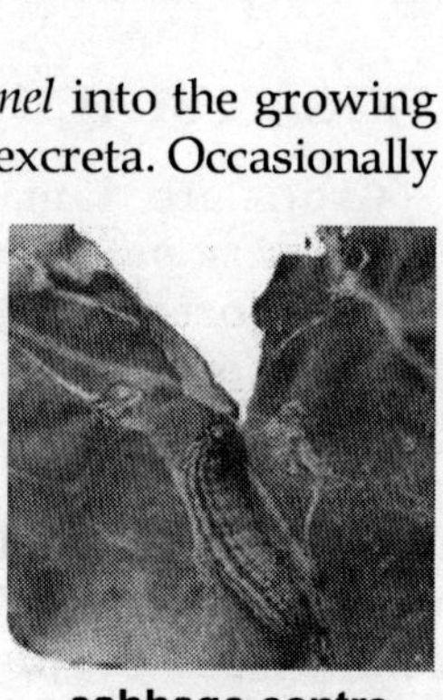

cabbage centre grub

CABBAGE CLUSTER CATERPILLAR (*Crocidolomia pavonana*)

Cabbage cluster caterpillar, *Crocidolomia pavonana, occurs* only very occasionally in New South Wales. The caterpillars feed in groups on the tops of the leaves and often produce a considerable amount of webbing. They are about 20 mm long when fully grown, and are green, or green with light brown backs, and have black spots and light longitudinal markings. The adults are light brown moths with a wingspan of about 25 mm. They lay their eggs in clusters.

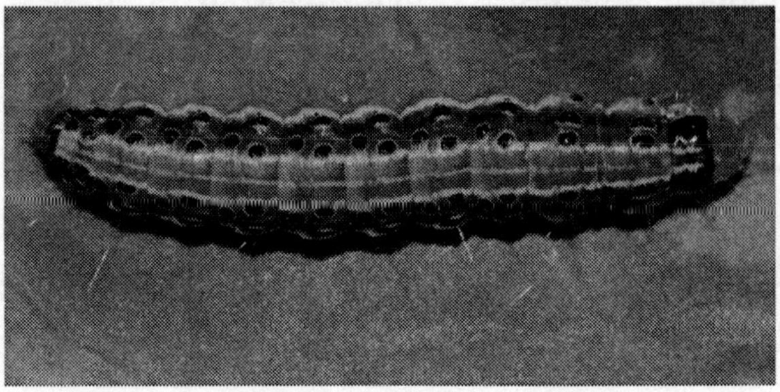

Cabbage cluster caterpillar

LOOPER CATERPILLARS (*Chrysodeixis* spp.)

Looper caterpillars, *Chrysodeixis* spp., move with a looping motion and feed mostly on the undersides of leaves. Young caterpillars eat through to the upper epidermis of the leaf, leaving window pane-like holes. Older caterpillars chew large, ragged holes. They are 30 to 40 mm long when fully grown, with green or blue-green, white-striped bodies that taper towards the head. The adults are dark brown moths with silver markings on the forewings and wingspans of 30 to 40 mm. The females lay whitish, 0.6 mm diameter, slightly flattened eggs singly, usually on the undersides of leaves.

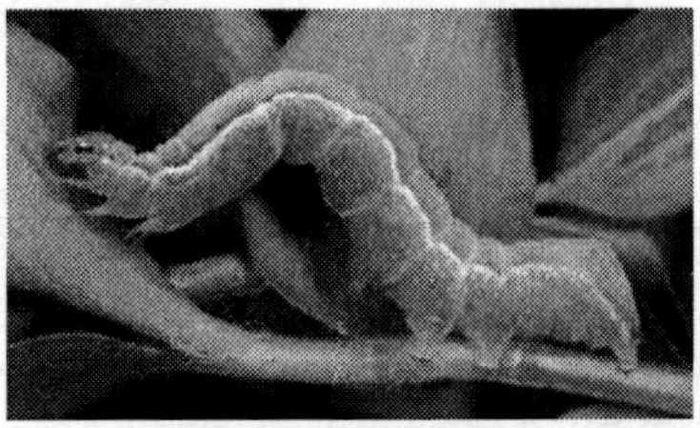

Looper caterpillars

Looper caterpillar infestations are often suppressed by natural enemies—parasites, predators and diseases.

AFRICAN BLACK BEETLE (*Heteronychus arator*)

Crops are damaged by African black beetle, *Heteronychus arator*, when they are planted into beetle infested former grassland, or alongside infested grassland, or when swarming beetles fly in. The beetles chew the stems of seedlings just below ground level, making a ragged injury, and the plants die. The beetle is about 12 mm long and shiny black and can usually be found in the soil near the damaged plants. African black beetle is a pest of coastal districts, and is troublesome from late August to November and again from January

African black beetle

to March. It breeds mainly in grassland, where the white, soft larvae ('curl grubs'), with hard brown heads, feed on organic matter and plant roots in the soil. Dry conditions during the spring and early summer favour its development.

RUTHERGLEN BUG (*Nysius vinitor*)

Rutherglen bug

Occasionally in hot, dry conditions in spring and early summer Rutherglen bug, *Nysius vinitor*, appears in plague numbers. It invades crops, usually as flying adults, but sometimes as crawling swarms of immature bugs. The bugs suck sap from stems and leaves. Severely attacked plants, particularly young plants, wilt and may die. The Rutherglen bug adult is about 5 mm long, narrow-bodied and greyish brown, with prominent black eyes and silvery wings. The immature bugs are reddish and pear-shaped.

Rutherglen bug breeds on weeds and moves into crops when the weeds dry off. When immature bugs are swarming into a crop they can be stopped by a furrow with the steep side nearest the crop. Rutherglen bug can be controlled by insecticide spraying, but repeated spraying is needed during plagues. Also spray infested weed growth around the crop.

CONTROL

Check crops frequently for pest development, especially when the plants are young. Cutworms and black beetle rapidly destroy young plants. Do not plant into land where black beetle is in evidence; this is usually land that has been growing grasses and has had only a short cultivation preparation. Do not plant alongside grassland, as the beetles may walk from there into the crop. Cabbage aphids can severely restrict growth of young plants, so take care that damaging populations do not develop.

Insect activity is largely governed by weather conditions. During the colder months in many districts the activity of insect pests of crucifers virtually ceases. At other times of the year insect activity may be so great that control sprays will be needed at 7 to 14 day intervals. Regular treatment at these intervals is much more efficient than spraying after damage develops. Small caterpillars of any species require less insecticide to kill them. Some insects such as cabbage moth and Helicoverpa caterpillars feed in sheltered positions, and controlling them adequately is very difficult if they have become well established in the crop.

Cabbage white butterfly, cabbage moth, cabbage centre grub, cabbage cluster caterpillar and cabbage and turnip aphids feed only on cruciferous plants. Abandoned crops are reservoirs of infestation for subsequent crops, so plough in old crop residues as soon as harvesting is finished.

26

Principles of Weed Science

INTRODUCTION TO WEEDS

Description of a Weed

There are numerous definitions of a weed, including:

- a plant out of place and not intentionally sown.
- a plant growing where it is not wanted.
- a plant whose virtues have not yet been discovered.
- plants that are competitive, persistent, pernicious, and interfere negatively with human activity.

No matter what definition is used, weeds are plants whose undesirable qualities outweigh their good points, according to man. Our human activities create weed problems since no plant is a "weed" in nature. Though we may try to manipulate nature for our own good, nature is persistent. Through the manipulation process, certain weeds are controlled, while, other more serious weeds may thrive because favorable growing conditions for them also have been meet. Weeds are naturally strong competitors and those weeds that can best compete always tend to dominate. Both humans and nature are involved in plant breeding programs. The main difference between the two programs is that man breeds plants for yield, while nature breeds plants for survival.

CHARACTERISTICS OF WEEDS

Certain characteristics are associated with and allow the survival of weeds. Weeds posses one or more of the following:

a) abundant seed production;

b) rapid population establishment;

c) seed dormancy;
d) long-term survival of buried seed;
e) adaptation for spread;
f) presence of vegetative reproductive structures; and
g) ability to occupy sites disturbed by human activities.

There are approximately 250,000 species of plants worldwide; of those, about 3% or 8000 species behave as weeds.

Weeds are troublesome in many ways. Primarily, they reduce crop yield by competing for water, light, soil nutrients, and space. Other problems associated with weeds in agriculture include:

a) reduced crop quality by contaminating the commodity;
b) interference with harvest;
c) serve as hosts for crop diseases or provide shelter for insects to overwinter;
d) limit the choice of crop rotation sequences and cultural practices; and
e) production of chemical substances which are toxic to crop plants (**allelopathy**), animals, or humans.

BENEFITS OF WEEDS

Despite the negative impacts of weeds, some plants usually thought of as weeds may actually provide some benefits. Some attributes include:

- soil stabilization;
- habitat and feed for wildlife,
- nectar for bees;
- aesthetic qualities;
- add organic matter;
- provide genetic reservoir;
- human consumption; and
- provide employment opportunities.

Weeds have a controversial nature. But to the agriculturist, they are plants that need to be controlled, in an economical and practical way, in order to produce food, feed, and fiber for humans and animals. In this context, the negative impacts of weeds indirectly affect all living beings.

WEED ECOLOGY AND BIOLOGY

Weed Ecology

Weed ecology might be described as the weed's lifestyle - where does it tend to thrive, what are its particular needs and adaptations to its environment? People have a major influence on weed ecology such as weed transport/spread and creating various cropping and management techniques that favor a particular weed species. Also, weedy plants have the capability to survive under adverse conditions and use adaptive mechanisms that enable them to thrive under conditions of extreme soil disturbance. Understanding weed ecology can help in designing management systems to minimize their impact.

Weed Biology

Effective weed management is dependent upon the biology of the weed including type and lifecycle. Weeds are more easily identified and/or managed at certain times during their lifecycle.

Life Cycles

Summer Annuals

Seeds germinate in spring, vegetative during spring/summer, and flowers and sets seed in mid to late summer, die in fall

Examples:

- common lambsquarters
- pigweed
- hairy galinsoga
- velvetleaf
- large crabgrass
- common ragweed
- giant foxtail
- common purslane
- smartweed

Winter annuals

Seeds germinate in fall and winter, vegetative during spring, and flowers and set seed in late spring/early summer before it dies

Examples:

- common chickweed
- downy brome
- shepherdspurse
- henbit

Biennials

Plants live more than one year over two growing seasons; seeds germinate and overwinter in a rosette stage, then complete life the following year

Examples:

- wild carrot
- common teasel
- bull thistle
- common burdock

Perennials

simple: generally spread by seed; large root but no spreading horizontal roots

Examples:

- dandelion
- common pokeweed
- dock
- plaintain

creeping: reproduce by rhizomes and stolons; some seed reproduction

Examples:

- Canada thistle
- poison ivy
- multiflora rose
- quackgrass
- ground ivy
- hemp dogbane
- yellow nutsedge
- Japanese knotweed
- groundcherry

Weed Identification

Effective weed management requires proper identification of weeds - otherwise tactics chosen may not work and end up costing money and frustration. Below are some of the key features to look at when identifying a plant accused of being a weed! Many good books, fact sheets and websites now feature photo galleries of weeds at various stages to help with identification (see end of section).

Botanical Review

Grassy weeds and sedges

- monocots, one cotyledon (coleoptile in seedling grasses)
- parallel veins
- grasses-round, oval, or flat stems with hollow internodes
- sedges-generally, triangular, solid stem

Broadleaf weeds

- dicots, two cotyledons (seed leaves)
- usually have wider leaves than grasses or sedges
- netted veins
- branched stem

Species	Distinguishing Features
smooth crabgrass	membranous ligule, no to few hairs around collar otherwise hairless, bluish color
large crabgrass	membranous ligule, hairy blade and sheath
barnyardgrass	no ligule, flat stem
goosegrass	membranous ligule, flat stem, few hairs near collar, distinct parallel veins, "flattened"
quackgrass	clasping auricles, white rhizomes
wirestem muhly	toothed membranous ligule, scaly rhizomes, bushy appearance
nimblewill	toothed membranous ligule, scaly rhizomes, bushy appearance
witchgrass	hairy ligule, very hairy sheath and blade (otherwise similar to fall panicum)
fall panicum	hairy ligule, prominent white mid-rib in blade
annual bluegrass	slightly pointed membranous ligule, light green, folded leaves, boat-shaped tips
giant foxtail	hairy ligule, fine hairs on upper blade
yellow foxtail	hairy ligule, long straggly hairs near collar, flat stem, purplish near base
green foxtail	hairy ligule, no hairs (smooth on blade)
shattercane	membranous ligule, prominent mid-rib, shiny black seed

Species	Distinguishing Features
johnsongrass	membranous ligule, prominent mid-rib, reddish-brown seed or rhizomes
yellow nutsedge	triangle stem, shiny, V-shaped leaves, rhizomes and tubers (nutlets)
prostrate knotweed	elliptic, dull blue-green, leaves, ochrea, flowers in leaf axils
wild buckwheat	rounded arrow shape leaves, ochrea at petiole base, triangular seeds
Pa. smartweed/ladysthumb	true leaves have purple blotches, stems are reddish-purple, ochrea has no hairs vs. ladysthumb ochrea which has hairs, otherwise smaller plant but similar
mile-a-minute	triangular leaves, waxy-look, prominent ochrea, recurved spines
red sorrel	arrow/spade shaped leaves with lobes at base, ochrea, long slender seed stalk, sour taste
curly/broadleaf dock	wavy leaf edge vs. broad, flat heart-shaped base on broadleaf dock, ochrea
common lambsquarters	greyish cast, frosted appearance (esp. on new leaves)
tumble pigweed	light green, bushy, small wavy leaves, flowers clusters in leaf axils
redroot/smooth pigweed	notch on end of first true leaves, reddish hue on under leaf, red stem, both can have hairs on stems, look similar until mature—rr pig. has long spike seed heads, sm. pig. has shorter spikes w/ finger-like projections
common pokeweed	reddish-purple stem, dark purple berry clusters, large poisonous taproot
common purslane	reddish-purple stem, dark purple berry clusters, large poisonous taproot
chickweedspp.	*common:* broadly ovate leaves, single row of hairs on stem, winter annual; mouse-ear: very hairy stems and leaves, perennial
mustard spp.	most have heart to kidney-shaped cotyledons, most have long narrow seed pods, variable features for each speciesyellow rocket-winter annual, smooth dark green leaves,lobes at basewild mustard-w.annual, may have hairs on leaf, wavy. lobyleavesshepherdspurse- w. annual, rosette at base, coarsely lobed leaves that clasp around stem, triangular, heart-shaped seed podf. pepperweed-finely toothy basal leaves, leaves up thesingle stalk, seed head branched with small boat shapedseed podsVa. pepperweed-similar to field pep. but smooth leaves and stem, branches lower on stemwild radish-deeply lobed/cut wavy leaves, coarse hairs onleavesf. pennycress-large flat round, notched seed pods, plant can look similar to pepperweed

Species	Distinguishing Features
multiflora rose	like garden rose, 5-9 leaflets of compound leaf, feathery stipules at base, white flowers
black medic	looks like spindly alfalfa, 3-leaflets, yellow flowers and black seed clusters
white clover	trifoliate leaves w/ V-shaped, greenish-white leaf blotch, white flowers
prostrate spurge	prostrate to ground, pink stems and green leaves with purple blotches, milky sap
velvetleaf	heart-shaped, toothed leaves and cotyledons, stem and trueleaves densely hairy
spurred anoda	3-lobed leaves, triangular-ovate w/purple veins, hairy, 6-pointed seed pods, in south
common mallow	round, wavy leaves w/base near center, white flowers, fruits like button or “cheese”
prickly sida	toothed oblong leaves, small spines at leaf base, yellow flowers, seedling-like velvetleaf
poison hemlock	lacy leaves, large plant, white flowers in umble, purple spots on hollow stalk, hairless
wid carrot	lacy leaves like garden carrot, white flowers clusters, biennial
hemp dogbane	elliptical leaves, purple stems, branchy, rhizomes, milky sap
common milkweed	oblong leaves with parallel veins that connect near the outer edge, hairy on under side of leaf, milky sap, larger in stature than dogbane
bindweed spp.	field: rounded tips and pointed lobes;hedge: arrow-shaped (triangular) and squared off lobes (i.e., hedge has edge), both have large trumpet-like white/pink flowers
morning glory spp.	tall: hairy heart-shaped leaves, butterfly shape cotyledons; ivyleaf: hairy, three-lobed leaves, butterfly shape cotyledons;pitted: smooth heart-shaped leaves, purple edges, deeply indented butterfly shaped cotyledons;all may have purple, white, pink flowers
ground ivy	creeping, square stem, toothed kidney/rounded leaves, common in lawns
henbit	round, hairy, toothed leaves, square, branched stem, flowers in whorl of upper leaves, winter annual
purple deadnettle	resembles henbit but leaves are more triangular and crowed at top, top leaves purple
jimsonweed	smooth leaves, prominent mid-rib, purple stem, unpleasantodor when crushed
smooth groundcherry	similar to EBNS but flower petals are fused, lantern-type seed pod and is perennial

Species	Distinguishing Features
horsenettle	toothed leaves, yellow spines on petiole, mid-rib and veins,grape sized fruits
eastern black nightshade	some hairs on stem and leaf margins, toothed edges, purplish color on under leaf, flowers star shaped with five petals, green berries turning black at maturity, annual
creeping speedwell	opposite, rounded/kidney shaped leaves w/ toothed edges, prostrate, stolons, in lawns
plantain spp.	buckhorn: long narrow leaves, tall, slender seed stalk,broadleaf: large oval leaves
wild cucumber	5-7 lobed leaves (star shape), large egg shaped seed pod
burcucumber	3-5 lobed leaves (pentagon shape), fruits in seed cluster
ragweed spp.	*common:* spoon-shaped cotyledons, finely lobed and hairy leaves;*giant:* large, spoon-shaped cotyledons, first leaves irregularly toothed or lobed, older leaves 3-5 lobed, 5-10+ft. tall
mayweed chamomile	lacy leaves, daisy like flower, strong unpleasant odor
common burdock	large, heart-shaped base leaves, stem and leaves w/ whitish hairs, spiny seed pod, biennial
musk thistle	lobey leaves and stems spiny, spiny "wings" down stalk, pretty, dense flower head
Canada thistle	crinkled leaf edges with spiny margins, horizontal roots, perennial
bull thistle	deeply cut, hairy leaves with large spines, biennial
horseweed (marestail)	many leaves (w/ scattered white bristles) around and up the stalk, branchy seed head
hairy galinsoga	leaves egg shaped to rounded triangle, hairy, yellow w/ white petal flowers, in gardens
common groundsel	irregular, long loby leaves, yellow flower clusters, in flower beds
dandelion	deeply toothed leaves, yellow flowers, milky sap
common cocklebur	smooth, waxy cotyledons, true leaves wavy, large triangle, rough, sandpaper feel, purple specks on stem, spiny seed pod

INTEGRATED WEED MANAGEMENT

Integrated weed management ideally involves the use of multiple strategies to manage weed populations in a manner that is economically and environmentally sound. Such strategies include cultural, mechanical, chemical, and biological methods.

Pear orchards may be infested with a variety of annual and perennial weeds, each competing with the trees for water and nutrients. Competition for these resources is of greater concern with young trees because weeds can delay production and reduce tree growth and vigor. Weeds cause problems in older orchards because they can increase the risk of frost damage early in the season, harbor pests and pathogens, and interfere with irrigation systems, and harvest.

Integrated weed management strategies vary from orchard to orchard and are influenced by location in the state, climatic conditions, soil texture and profile, irrigation practices, topography, cost, and grower preferences. There are several components to a good orchard weed management program. These include preventive strategies, orchard floor management, and weed monitoring. Further, proper use of preemergence and postemergence herbicides and timely cultivation are important factors in weed management.

Weeds are commonly controlled either chemically or mechanically in a 4- to 6-foot-wide strip in the tree row. Resident vegetation is generally permitted to grow in the areas between the tree rows but it must be managed through repeated mowing, tillage, or chemical treatment. Mulches, subsurface irrigation, flamers, and grazing by geese or other animals can also be used to control weeds in orchards.

Prevention

- Preventing weeds from producing seed and eliminating the establishment of new weeds into the orchard are the most cost-effective methods of weed management.
- Keep irrigation canals, ditch banks, and the irrigation systems free of weeds and weed seeds. Also keep the areas immediately around these areas weed-free.
- Eliminate low spots in the orchard and maintain drainage systems to prevent standing water. Fix leaking irrigation systems. Moist sites encourage weed emergence and growth.
- Pay attention to weeds growing on the orchard margins; they should be controlled before they produce seeds that can disperse into the orchard.
- Clean the undercarriage and tires of vehicles and equipment before they enter the orchard to prevent seeds and reproductive parts of weeds from being transported from infested sites.

Monitoring

Detecting new weeds and weeds that escaped previous control efforts is an important component of an effective weed management plan. Correctly identify the weed species present, especially in the seedling stage. Become familiar with each weed's growth and reproductive habits in order to choose the most effective management options.

Monitor regularly to help choose the proper timing and treatments; most herbicides are effective against many, but not all, weed species. After application, assess if treatments were successful. Weeds often grow in patches, making postemergence herbicide applications or mechanical control to the whole orchard unnecessary. Spot-treating may save time and money while achieving acceptable weed control.

How to monitor

- Survey the orchard for weeds in late fall and again in late spring.
- Keep records, including a map.
- Pay particular attention to perennial and other problem weed species. Note their location on the map.
- Record weeds found in rows and middles separately. Weeds in tree rows must be managed, but some low-growing, non-aggressive annual weeds in row middles may be beneficial as a cover crop.
- Also keep records of weed management actions including timing, rates and dates of herbicide applications and cultivations.

Survey information collected over a period of years indicates how weed populations may be changing and how effective your long-term management operations have been.

Orchard floor management

A well-managed orchard floor cover between the tree rows has several benefits. It provides a stable surface for machinery to operate under wet conditions that otherwise would prevent access to the orchard. The plants in the ground cover develop root channels that improve soil structure and water infiltration. Improved infiltration rates also reduce the risk of off-site movement of pesticides. Further, plant cover reduces soil compaction and the potential for erosion.

Resident vegetation

Resident orchard-floor vegetation has several benefits if it does not include species that invade the tree rows or are difficult to control with herbicides. An example of an unacceptable ground cover is hairy fleabane, a prolific, wind-borne seed producer that is susceptible to post-emergence herbicides only when small and is difficult to control with the pre-emergence herbicides registered for pear plantings.

Seeded cover crop

Planting a cover crop between the tree rows is an alternative to managing resident vegetation. Choose a cover crop mix with known properties such as mowing height and frequency, time to seed set, and time to senescence. (For information on choosing a cover crop. Properly managed cover crops can help prevent problem weed species from invading the orchard. Tall cover crops or weeds, however, increase the risk of frost damage and fruit russeting in spring and should be closely mowed in the Sacramento Valley or even eliminated using herbicides or discing on the North Coast.

Irrigation system considerations

Design weed management programs so that they fit the irrigation system. For example, the dissipation of pre-emergence herbicides is slow in furrow- and basin-flood systems with raised berms because the irrigation water does not come in contact with the herbicide-treated soil on the berm. However, in sprinkler, micro-sprinkler, and drip-irrigated orchards the irrigation water contacts the herbicide, thus increasing its dissipation rate.

Weed control provided by pre-emergence herbicides also breaks down faster around sprinkler heads or drip emitters than in the rest of the orchard. Areas around sprinkler heads and micro-sprinkler or drip emitters require additional weed-control measures, such as a post-emergence herbicide application or hand hoeing. A sensor-controlled sprayer that applies herbicides only to the areas where weeds are growing, similar to a spot treatment, can reduce herbicide use by 50% or more compared to a post-emergence treatment to the entire orchard floor.

Soil type considerations

Consider soil type when selecting a weed management strategy. Sandy loams to loamy sands require lower rates of pre-emergence herbicides for effective weed control compared to clay loam soils. Labels for many pre-emergence herbicides have specific application rates for specific soil textures. Applying the rate of herbicide suggested for a clay loam soil to loamy sand not only wastes herbicide but may also lead to crop injury and contamination of ground or surface water.

Timing of cultivation is more flexible on loams and loamy sands than on soils high in clay because equipment moves easily through soil. Lighter soils are generally easier to access for spraying and other field operations during wet conditions than heavier soils.

Weed management before planting

It is easier and cheaper to control perennial weeds before planting the orchard than after, because there is a better selection of treatment options available when the ground is fallow. Established weeds can be controlled either chemically or mechanically. Control annual weeds before they set seed by mowing, discing, or using herbicides. Depending on the species, perennial weeds can be controlled mechanically by discing repeatedly during the summer, using herbicides, or a combination of the two techniques.

The ideal time to control perennial grasses such as dallisgrass, bermudagrass, and johnsongrass is the summer before planting. Apply glyphosate when the grasses are actively growing, then cultivate 2 weeks later. If weeds resume growth after cultivation, consider a second broadcast or spot treatment with glyphosate or the grass-specific herbicides sethoxydim, fluazifop-p-butyl, or clethodim.

Cultivation alone can bring many underground plant structures to the surface and cause them to desiccate. For this method to kill the perennial plants, the soil must be dry for the root systems to completely desiccate and die. If the soil is not dry enough, cultivation can have the unintended effect of spreading perennial weeds, such as field bindweed. Many other perennial weeds, including nutsedge, can be effectively controlled by cultivating with a soil-inverting plow that buries the underground tubers or nutlets deep into the soil profile where they desiccate or rot.

Grading the orchard

Grade a new orchard site to ensure even drainage and to eliminate low spots that tend to promote perennial weed growth. Also, proper drainage prevents formation of wet areas within the tree row. Constant wetting accelerates the dissipation of herbicides, which leads to weed growth.

Preparing tree rows

Although a preemergence herbicide such as pendimethalin can be incorporated in the future tree row before planting, treated soil must not be placed around the roots at planting or tree injury may result. When planting the trees, place untreated soil directly around the roots and then cover them with a surface layer of treated soil. During the early years of tree establishment, maintain a weed-free strip that is at least 30 inches from the trunk on each side of the tree to prevent weeds from competing for water and nutrients with the developing tree. If planting holes are dug with an auger, use glyphosate before planting and then follow planting with an application of preemergence herbicide once the soil has settled around the trees.

Weed management in newly planted orchards

In orchards that have received an herbicide treatment prior to planting, disturb the soil as little as possible once the trees are planted. In orchards that are furrow-irrigated, establish one or two narrow furrows along the planted trees. Perennial grasses can be controlled with clethodim, fluazifop-p-butyl, or sethoxydim. Glyphosate can be used to suppress nutsedge and perennial broadleaf weeds. Avoid spraying pear foliage or trunks with glyphosate.

Plastic-coated wrappers may help to protect trunks from contact with herbicides. Care must be taken to prevent sunburn inside the wrappers, especially on trees from cold storage planted in late spring. If planting late, use tree wrappers designed to reduce the inside temperatures and paint the trunk all the way to the ground with white interior latex paint diluted with twice as much water (1:2 paint:water ratio).

Regular preemergence and postemergence treatments during the establishment years, especially during the active growing months between April and November, remove much of the competition from weeds and facilitate efficient irrigation and other cultural practices. Fabric mulches used in tree rows can eliminate the need to treat around young trees, thus reducing the risk of phytotoxicity.

Cross-discing (cultivation both within and across the tree row) is an alternative to herbicide use in some orchards. However, discing near trees can injure tree roots and lead to excessive suckering. Excessive suckers can result in phytotoxicity problems if systemic herbicides are applied to the tree row in the future. If mechanical control is used, additional control measures (hand hoeing or spot treatment with herbicides) will be needed for weeds growing adjacent to the trees.

Weed management in established orchards

Vegetation (either resident vegetation or cover crop) maintained in the orchard middles can be managed by mowing. Where there is risk of frost damage, closely mow cover crops or resident vegetation in early spring. An alternative to mowing is to let the cover crop grow until it is nearly mature and then roll it with a ringroller to press the vegetation down. This accelerates the senescence process but allows some seeds to mature. The intact mulch blocks light and may help prevent weed seeds from germinating. Vegetation can also be managed chemically by applying low rates of a postemergence herbicide to stunt the plants (chemical mowing). If not well managed, this practice can lead to an orchard with predominantly herbicide-resistant weeds.

It is easier to control annual weeds with chemical or mechanical tools when they are small and not yet established. Control perennial weeds that emerge from seed with timely cultivation or effective herbicides before they produce reproductive structures, which can occur in as little as one month under ideal growing conditions. Established perennial weeds such as field bindweed are generally most vulnerable to control during early flowering when they start storing carbohydrates in their roots or reproductive structures for next year's growth. Systemic herbicides applied at this stage are translocated to the roots or rhizomes to better kill the weed. It is also important to apply systemic herbicides to vigorously growing plants as herbicide uptake and translocation is reduced in stressed plants.

Preemergence and postemergence herbicides are common management tools used within the tree row. For best results, most preemergence herbicides need to be sprayed onto the soil just before irrigation or rainfall so that the water carries the chemical into the soil where the weed seeds are located. Apply when 0.25 to 0.5 inch of precipitation is expected; do not apply if 1 inch or more is expected in a short period because excessive leaching or runoff of the herbicide may occur. Check the pesticide label for specific application details. Preemergence herbicides can provide control for 6 to 9 months, depending on the solubility of the material, adsorption of the material to soil particles, the weed species present, dosage applied, and amount of rainfall or irrigation that occurs. Herbicide leaching is greater on sandy than clay soils. Prolonged moist conditions during winter, in furrow bottoms, or around low-volume emitters during irrigation favor the breakdown and leaching of herbicides.

Postemergence herbicides are used on established weeds. They can have either contact activity or be translocated throughout the plant. Contact herbicides, such as paraquat, kill those parts of the plant that are actually sprayed, making good coverage and wetting essential. A single application should kill susceptible annual weeds. Re-treatment may be necessary if coverage is poor, annual weeds reestablish, or for suppression of perennial weeds that regrow from roots or other underground reproductive structures.

Translocated herbicides, such as glyphosate, move into the plant and are translocated to the growing points, killing actively growing tissue above or below ground. Glyphosate, however, does not translocate into mature nutsedge tubers. Complete coverage with translocated herbicides is not essential but does improve control. Complete control of established perennial weeds is often difficult, because their root structures are often extensive compared to the top growth. Regular applications over several years may be needed to achieve satisfactory control.

27

Multi-choice Questions

Q. Which of the following is not a nitrogenous fertilizer?

1) Ammonium sulphate
2) Urea
3) Ammonium nitrate
4) Super phosphate

Ans: 4

Q. HD 2967 is the new high yielding variety of -

1) Rice
2) Maize
3) Mustered
4) Wheat

Ans: 4

Q. The scientific study of soil is -

1) Earth Study
2) Soil Science
3) Pedology
4) Soil Chemistry

Ans: 3

Q. Prabhat is an early short duration variety of -

1) Red gram
2) Wheat
3) Maize
4) Rice

Ans: 1

Q. The Minimum Support Price for Foodgrains was introduced in the year-

1) 1954
2) 1944
3) 1964
4) 1974

Ans: 3

Q. Soil factors are otherwise known as -

1) Climatic factors
2) Edaphic factors
3) Biotic factors
4) Physiographic factors

Ans: 2

Q. Which of the following is a commercial crop?

1) Cotton
2) Bajra
3) Jowar
4) Paddy

Ans: 1

Q. Triticum aestivum, the common bread wheat is -

1) Tetraploid
2) Hexaploid
3) Haploid
4) Diploid

Ans: 2

Q. Monoculture is a typical characteristics of -

1) Shifting cultivation
2) Subsitence farming
3) Specialized horticulture
4) Commercial grain farming

Ans: 4

Q. Which crop requires water-logging for its cultivation?

1) Tea
2) Coffee
3) Rice
4) Mustard

Ans: 3

Q. Agronomy is a branch of Agriculture that deals with -

1) Breeding of crop plants
2) Principles of field management

3) Principles and practice of crop production
4) Protection of crops from Diseases and Pests

Ans: 3

Q. Soils of Western Rajasthan have a high content of

1) Aluminium
2) Calcium
3) Nitrogen
4) Phosphorus

Ans: 2

Q. The Black rust of disease of wheat is caused by-

1) *Xanthomonas graminis*
2) *Puccinia graminis*
3) *Puccinia recondita*
4) None of these

Ans: 2

Q. A crop grown in zaid season is

1) Soyabean
2) Water melon
3) Jute
4) Maize

Ans: 2

Q. The adoption of High Yielding Variety Programme in Indian Agriculture started in -

1) 1966
2) 1965
3) 1968
4) 1967

Ans: 1

Q. Which of the following is a food crop?

1) Palm
2) Jute
3) Cotton
4) Maize

Ans: 4

Q. Which of the following is an oilseed ?

1) Cardamom
2) Garlic

3) Clove
4) Mustard

Ans: 4

Q. Which one of the following makes a case for intensive, modern farming?

1) Cropping pattern
2) Higher output using organic method
3) Remunerative price
4) None of these

Ans: 1

Q. Which of the following is not an agricultural product?

1) Alum
2) Cotton
3) Jute
4) Rice

Ans: 1

Q. Crop rotation helps to

1) lessen use of pesticides
2) yield more crops
3) produce a greater choice of plant products
4) eliminate parasites which have selective hosts

Ans: 4

Q. Potassium chloride contains K -

1) 18%
2) 48%
3) 44%
4) 60%

Ans: 4

Q. Plant micronutrient is -

1) Carbon
2) Boron
3) Magnesium
4) Sulphur

Ans: 2

Q. Which gas is released from paddy fields?

1) CO_2
2) H_2S
3) CH_4
4) NH_3

Ans: 3

Q. Which two crops of the following are responsible for almost 75% of pulse production in India?

1) Gram and pigeon pea
2) Gram and moong bean
3) Moong bean and lentil
4) Pigeon pea and moong bean

Ans: 1

Q. Fire curing is followed in -

1) Bidi tobacco
2) Hookah tobacco
3) Cheroot tobacco
4) Chewing type tobacco

Ans: 4

Q. Groundnut pegs when developed in the soil from -

1) Tubers
2) Fruits
3) Stems
4) Roots

Ans: 2

Q. In Jute growing areas the usual alternate crop is -

1) Cotton
2) Wheat
3) Sugarcane
4) Rice

Ans: 4

Q. Neelum is a variety of -

1) Grape
2) Papaya
3) Mango
4) Apple

Ans: 3

Q. The Commission of Agricultural Costs and Prices fixes the -

1) Support price
2) Wholesale price
3) Retail price
4) None of these

Ans: 1

Q. Vector of phyllody disease is -

1) Thrips
2) Mite
3) White fly
4) Jassid

Ans: 1

Q. Gynodioecious varieties of papaya produce -

1) Only male plants
2) Female and hermaphrodite
3) Male and hermaphrodite plants
4) Only female plants

Ans: 4

Q. Isolation distance for foundation seed of rice is -

1) 30 metre
2) 3 metre
3) 35 metre
4) 50 metre

Ans: 2

Q. Botanically pineapple is a -

1) Pome
2) Baluster
3) Berry
4) Sorosis

Ans: 4

Q. The basic unit of development under the Integrated Rural Development Programme is a -

1) District
2) Family
3) Village
4) Community Development Block

Ans: 3

Q. Ratna is a variety of-

1) Wheat
2) Barley
3) Maize
4) Rice

Ans: 4

Q. Seed rate of American cotton is-

1) 20 kg/ha
2) 30 kg/ha

3) 35 kg/ha
4) 12 kg/ha

Ans: 1

Q. Greening of potato results in-

1) Increase in nutritional quality
2) Increase in disease resistance
3) Decrease in disease resistance
4) Decrease in nutritional quality

Ans: 4

Q. Sugarbeet Nematode is -

1) *Heterodera avanae*
2) *Heterodera cajani*
3) *Heterodera jae*
4) *Heterodera schacti*

Ans: 4

Q. Which is the saturated fatty acid of the following -

1) Stearic acid
2) Arachidonic acid
3) Oleic acid
4) Linoleic acid

Ans: 1

Q. Iron is an important component of -

1) Siroheme
2) Ferredoxin
3) Cytochromes
4) All of these

Ans: 4

Q. The chemical, which is used for controlling the mites, is known as -

1) Fungicides
2) Mematicides
3) Acaricides
4) Insecticides

Ans: 2

Q. WP abbreviates as -

1) Wettable Paste
2) Wettable Powder
3) Water Paste
4) None of these

Ans: 2

Q. Which of the following elements is not essential element of plants but proves to be beneficial for some plants?

1) Boron
2) Sodium
3) Iodine
4) Copper

Ans: 2

Q. The pyrite is mostly found in-

1) Bihar
2) Rajasthan
3) Andhra Pradesh
4) Maharashtra

Ans: 4

Q. Parthenocarpy occurs in-

1) Peach
2) Mango
3) Jackfruit
4) Banana

Ans: 3

Q. Water use efficiency is the highest is case of-

1) Border irrigation
2) Drip irrigation
3) Sprinkler irrigation
4) Flood irrigation

Ans: 2

Q. Atmosphere is essential for-

1) Winds
2) Cloud formation
3) Weather phenomena
4) All of these

Ans: 3

Q. Which one of the following plants belongs to family Anacardiaceae?

1) Papaya
2) Orange
3) Cashewnut
4) None of these

Ans: 3

Q. In India post-harvest losses of fruit and vegetable is . . . per cent of the total production.

1) 15-20
2) 50-50
3) 40-45
4) 25-30

Ans: 4

Q. The animals produced by mating of two different breeds of the same species is known as -

1) Mixed breed
2) Cross breed
3) Exotic breed
4) Pure breed

Ans: 2

Q. Recording of milk production in dairy farm is done mainly for -

1) Selection of good producer
2) Increase in production of milk
3) Ensuring quality of milk
4) Quick selling of milk

Ans: 1

Q. The average gestation period in buffalo is of how many days?

1) 310
2) 210
3) 400
4) 345

Ans: 1

Q. *Citrus tristeza* virus is transmitted through -

1) Aphid
2) Thrips
3) Nematode
4) Plant hopper

Ans: 4

Q. Which one of the pathogens is monocylic?

1) Ustilago
2) Alternaria
3) Phytophthora
4) Puccinia

Ans: 1

Q. Caenocytic mycellium is found in -

1) Mastigomycotina
2) Deuteromycotina
3) Ascomycotina
4) None of these

Ans: 3

Q. Penicillin acts on-

1) Cell wall
2) RNA
3) Cell membrane
4) None of these

Ans: 1

Q. Blue colour tag is issued for -

1) Foundation seed
2) Certified seed
3) Nucleus seed
4) Foundation seed

Ans: 2

Q. Generally, cereals are deficient in -

1) Protein
2) Tryptophan
3) Methionine
4) Lysine

Ans: 1

Q. Each anther has how many pollen sacs?

1) Four
2) Two
3) One
4) Three

Ans: 2

Q. Rice and wheat has how many stamens?

1) 3,3
2) 6,3
3) 3,6
4) 6,6

Ans: 1

Q. The chemical, which attracts opposite sex insects of a species, is known as-

1) Hormones
2) Allomones

3) Kairomones
4) Pheromones

Ans: 4

Q. Damaging satge of potato tuber month is -

1) Adult
2) Pupa
3) Larva
4) All of these

Ans: 3

Q. Piercing and sucking type mouth-parts are present in the insect -

1) Hemiptera
2) Orthoptera
3) Lepidoptera
4) Isoptera

Ans: 1

Q. Classification of insects and rules of their nomenclature comes under the branch -

1) Morphology
2) Taxonomy
3) Ecology
4) Physiology

Ans: 2

Q. Beetles belong to order--

1) Lepidoptera
2) Isoptera
3) Coleoptera
4) Diptera

Ans: 3

Q. Bacteriophage virus is the-

1) Bacterial virus
2) Fungal Virus
3) Algal virus
4) Protozoal virus

Ans: 1

Q. Micro-organism,which can grow at higher temperature, is called

1) Thermophils
2) Mesophils
3) Phycrophils
4) None of these

Ans: 1

Q. Who has first time seen the micro-organism?

1) Robert Koch
2) John Tyndall
3) Antonie van Leeuwenhoek
4) Louis Pasteur

Ans: 4

Q. White colour of soil is due to the presence of -

1) Silica
2) Iron
3) Manganese oxide
4) All of these

Ans: 3

Q. Which of the 'complex fertilizer'?

1) Ammonium sulphate nitrate
2) Single superphosphate
3) Ammonium phosphate
4) Calcium ammonium nitrate

Ans: 3

Q. Drip irrigation is useful in which region?

1) Humid
2) Dry
3) High rainfall
4) None of these

Ans: 2

Q. Among the following crop rotations, which is good for in creasing soil Nutrient status?

1) Rice-Wheat
2) Groundnut-Wheat
3) Pearlmillet-Wheat
4) Sorghum-Wheat

Ans: 2

Q. For waterlogged rice cultivation, the fertilizer that may be avoided is -

1) Sodium nitrate
2) Urea
3) Ammonium chloride
4) None of these

Ans: 4

Q. The ratio between marketable crop yield and water used in evapotrans-piration is known as-

1) Field water use efficiency
2) Economic irrigation efficiency
3) Consumptive use efficiency
4) Water use efficiency

Ans: 1

Q. Sulphur, containing amino acid is -

1) Valine
2) Isolucine
3) Cystine
4) None of these

Ans: 3

Q. Glycolysis occurs only in the-

1) Absence of O_2
2) Presence of O_2
3) Both (A) and (B)
4) None of these

Ans: 1

Q. Photorespiration is inhibited by -

1) 2, 4-Dinitrophenol
2) α-hydroxy sulphonates
3) CMU and DCMU
4) None of these

Ans: 3

Q. Biofertilizers are -

1) Organic manures
2) Green manure
3) Culture of micro-organism
4) None of these

Ans: 3

Q. 'Chanchal' is a variety of -

1) Brinjal
2) Tomato
3) Chilli
4) Capcicum

Ans: 3

Q. Central Soil Salinity Research Institute is located at -

1) Karnal
2) Bihar
3) Dehradun
4) Jodhpur

Ans: 1

Q. Seed plant technique is followed in -

1) Wheat
2) Bajra
3) Potato
4) Paddy

Ans: 4

Q. For providing inputs like quality seeds, fertilizers and pesticides, the agency present at the Village Panchayat Samiti Level is -

1) Nationalised Banks
2) Cooperative Society
3) Insurance Companies
4) NABARD

Ans: 4

Q. Where do the female mango leaf hoppers lay their eggs?

1) Inside the tissue of leaf margin
2) On the dorsal surface of leaves
3) On the ventral surface of leaves
4) Inside the mid-rib of leaves

Ans: 3

Q. In H.T.S.T. pasteurization, which one of the following organisms is chosen as index organism for killing?

1) **S.thermophilus**
2) **S.lactis**
3) **B.subtilis**
4) **M.tuberculosis**

Ans: 1

Q. Thermophilic micro-organism grow well at temperature-

1) 10°C - 20°C
2) 20°C - 40°C
3) 50°C - 60°C
4) 5°C - 7°C

Ans: 3

Q. Pink bollworm is a pest of -

1) Gram
2) Okra
3) Mustard
4) Cotton

Ans: 4

Q. The croppping intensity of maize-potato-tobacco is -

1) 200%
2) 300%
3) 100%
4) None of these

Ans: 2

Q. National Sugar Institute (N.S.I.) is located at--

1) Kanpur
2) New Delhi
3) Varanasi
4) Lucknow

Ans: 1

Q. Khaira disease of rice can be controlled by spraying -

1) Copper sulphate
2) Calcium sulphate
3) Zinc sulphate
4) Borax

Ans: 3

Q. Which one of the following can be suitable for cropping as a wheat mixed crop?

1) Cabbage
2) Cotton
3) Mustard
4) Jowar

Ans: 3

Q. What culture should be given priority in groundnut cultivation?

1) Mycorrhiza
2) Rhizobium
3) Phosphobacteria
4) Azospirillum

Ans: 3

Q. Prabhat is an early short duration variety of -

1) Black gram
2) Red gram

3) Green gram
4) Gram

Ans: 2

Q. In maize plants -

1) Silk appear first
2) Both of these appear at same time
3) Tassels appear first
4) None of these

Ans: 3

Q. Blind hoeing is recommended for -

1) Wheat
2) Maize
3) Groundnut
4) Sugarcane

Ans: 4

Q. Kisan Mitra is an employee of -

1) Central Government
2) Corporation
3) None of these
4) State Government

Ans: 4

Q. Red Delicious is a variety of -

1) Mango
2) Papaya
3) Apple
4) Guava

Ans: 3

Q. The number of essential mineral elements of plant is -

1) 16
2) 21
3) 13
4) 20

Ans: 1

Q. Sulphur-coated Urea contains N -

1) 21%
2) 33%
3) 40%
4) 26%

Ans: 2

Q. Granite is a .... rock.

1) Metamorphic
2) Igneous
3) Sedimentary
4) None of these

Ans: 3

Q. Chemical formula of pyrite is--

1) FeS
2) CuS
3) MnS
4) FeS_2

Ans: 4

Q. Soil fertility is reduced due to -

1) Over irrigation
2) Poor drainage
3) Imbalanced use of fertilizers
4) Continuous cropping

Ans: 3

Q. Anemometer measures -

1) Wind direction
2) Relative humidity
3) Net radiation
4) Wind velocity

Ans: 4

Q. Damping-off disease of vegetable nursery can be controlled by-

1) Solarization
2) Mixing of fungicides in soil
3) Seed treatment
4) All of these

Ans: 4

Q. Whiptail is a disorder of cauliflower due to deficiency of -

1) Zinc
2) Boron
3) Potassium
4) Molybdenum

Ans: 4

Q. The colour of tomato is due to the presence of--

1) Carotene
2) Lycopin

3) Anthocyanin
4) Xanthomonas

Ans: 2

Q. Mastitis is a disease of which organ?

1) Uternus
2) Heart
3) Udder
4) Lung

Ans: 3

Q. Colostrum should be fed to newborn calves for -

1) ½ day
2) 1 day
3) 4 day
4) 10 day

Ans: 4

Q. Toda is breed of -

1) Cattle
2) Goat
3) Buffalo
4) Sheep

Ans: 3

Q. Mastitis in animals is due to -

1) Worms
2) Virus and Worms
3) Fungi and dry hand milking
4) Bacteria and Virus

Ans: 4

Q. Asexual reproduction includes -

1) Amphimixis
2) Apomixis
3) Allogamy
4) Autogamy

Ans: 3

Q. In India, gene bank of wheat is located at -

1) Kanpur
2) Ludhiana
3) Karnal
4) IARI, New Delhi

Ans: 3

Q. TPS technique is related to -

1) Tomato
2) Sugarcane
3) Potato
4) All of these

Ans: 3

Q. SRI is a techniqu used in -

1) Maize
2) Groundnut
3) Wheat
4) Rice

Ans: 4

Q. Numbers of agro-climate and ecological zones classified by ICAR respectively are -

1) 15, 131
2) 131, 8
3) 8, 131
4) 21, 15

Ans: 1

Q. The Green Revolution has mainly been successful for-

1) Wheat
2) Rice
3) Maize
4) Gram

Ans: 1

Q. Guttation occurs in plants through -

1) Stomata
2) Hydathodes
3) None of these
4) Both (A) and (B)

Ans: 4

Q. Stomata open at night in -

1) C4 plants
2) C3 plants
3) CAM plants
4) None of these

Ans: 3

Q. Living Cells are not essential for-

1) Transpiration

2) Evaporation
3) Guttation
4) All of these

Ans: 2

Q. α and β-tubulins are protein components of-

1) Actin filaments
2) Microtubules
3) Intermediate
4) All of these

Ans: 4

Q. 'First blight' of sugarcane is due to deficiency of nutrient -

1) Mn
2) Zn
3) P
4) Fe

Ans: 1

Q. Percentage of P_2O_5 in 'Pelofas' fertilizer is -

1) 12
2) 16
3) 11
4) 18

Ans: 3

Q. Which one of the following is not a primary nutrient?

1) S
2) N
3) K
4) P

Ans: 1

Q. Which group of plant nutrients involves in N_2 fixation?

1) P, S, Mo
2) P, S, Co
3) P, Mo, Co
4) All of these

Ans: 1

Q. Which one of the following fertilizers is known as 'Kisan Khad'?

1) Urea
2) Calcium Ammonium Nitrate
3) None of these
4) Ammonium Sulphate

Ans: 2

Q. Zoological name of white grub is-

1) *Holotrichia consanguinea*
2) *Helicoverpa armigera*
3) *Spodoptera litura*
4) *Bamisia tabaci*

Ans: 1

Q. Botanical name of nobel canes is-

1) *Saccharum officinarum*
2) *Saccharum barberi*
3) *Saccharum spontaneous*
4) *Saccharum sinensis*

Ans: 1

Q. Nullisomics produce which type of gametes?

1) n-1
2) n+1
3) n
4) n+1-1

Ans: 1

Q. The crossing over occurs during-

1) Diplotene
2) Zygotene
3) Leptotene
4) Pachytene

Ans: 4

Q. This is one of the best 'poultry feed stuff' and having good source of animal protein as it contains 34-55 percent protein-

1) Groundnut Cake
2) Fishmeal
3) Soyabean-meal
4) Linseed-meal

Ans: 2

Q. Which one of the following Indian breeds of sheep , you will suggest meat and carpet wool production?

1) Deccani
2) Nellore
3) Gaddi
4) Mandya

Ans: 4

Q. Which one of the following Rice varieties you will recommend for growing in saline areas of Haryana State?

1) Panvet-1
2) CSR 30
3) CST 7-1
4) HKR 126

Ans: 4

Q. The Shoot and fruit borers, jassids, spider mites and leaf rollers are the major pests of which of the following vegetable crops?

1) Tomato
2) Okra or Bhindi
3) Cucumber
4) Peas

Ans: 2

Q. The Larvae of which of the following Pests of Sorghum crop, cut growing points and cause dead-hearts ti the plant?

1) Aphids
2) Termites
3) Cutworms
4) Stem-Borer

Ans: 4

Q. Which is the most widely distributed and commercially reared honeybee species in the world?

1) Apis florea
2) Apis Dorsata
3) Apis Cerana
4) Apis Mellifera

Ans: 4

Q. Of the total area under chillies in India, the share of which state is about 27 to 28 percent?

1) Andhra Pradesh
2) Maharashtra
3) Karnataka
4) Tamil Nadu

Ans: 1

Q. Which one of the following states has the largest area under Kharif Maize?

1) Uttar Pradesh
2) Rajasthan

3) Madhya Pradesh
4) Bihar

Ans: 1

Q. Presently, which of the following chemical fertilizers is not Produced in India and is being imported?

1) Triple Superphosphate(TSP)
2) Potassium Sulphate
3) Ammonium Sulphate
4) All of these

Ans: 2

Q. Which is the most widely used green manuring crop in Assam, West Bengal, Bihar, Haryana, Punjab, TN and Uttar Pradesh (This crop does well on Alkaline and Waterlogged soils?

1) Sunnhemp
2) Dhaincha
3) Egyptian Clover
4) Senji (*Melilotus parviflora*)

Ans: 2

Q. Which of the following award is associated with Agriculture?

1) Bourlog Award
2) Shanti Swaroop Bhatnagar
3) Arjun Award
4) Vyasa Samman

Ans: 1

Q. Which material should be higher in the ratio of the pregnant cow?

1) Fat
2) Protein
3) Carbohydrates
4) Dry matter

Ans: 2

Q. In how many years does a bull get ready for insemination?

1) 2-2½ years
2) 3-3½ years
3) 1½-2 years
4) None of these

Ans: 1

Q. Which is not a hybrid variety of Mango?

1) Mallika
2) Ratna

3) Arka Puneet
4) Dashehari

Ans: 4

Q. What is place of India in the World in Tea production?

1) First
2) Second
3) Third
4) Fourth

Ans: 1

Q. Which fruit crop has the largest area in India?

1) Banana
2) Citrus
3) Mango
4) Guava

Ans: 3

Q. Which country is the Second highest producer of fruit and vegetables in the world?

1) Brazil
2) North America
3) China
4) India

Ans: 4

Q. Which crop is affected by Tobacco caterpillar?

1) Jute
2) Sugarcane
3) Lucerne
4) Sugarbeet

Ans: 1

Q. What optimum temperature is needed for the growth of Potato tuber?

1) 17°C to 19°C
2) 14°C to 16°C
3) 10°C to 12°C
4) 22°C to 25°C

Ans: 1

Q. Which variety of Groundnut is grown in summer?

1) Avtar
2) Chitra
3) Chandra
4) Amber

Ans: 1

Q. Which is not fodder variety of Cowpea?

1) Russian Giant
2) K-585
3) Sirsa-10
4) Azad-1

Ans: 4

Q. Which variety of Barley is not for Malt purpose?

1) Pragati (K-508)
2) Geetanjali (K-1149)
3) Ritambhara (K-557)
4) D.L.-88

Ans: 2

Q. Which is not true in case of lentil?

1) Chromosome-14
2) I.P.L.-High yield
3) Seed rate-35-40 kg
4) Quantity of proten in lentil seed-18%

Ans: 2

Q. Which is not a variety of Vegetable Pea?

1) Arkel
2) Azad Pea-3
3) Pant Matar-2
4) Aparna

Ans: 4

Q. How many days old paddy seedling is used for SRI technology?

1) 8-12 days
2) 12-15 days
3) 25-30 days
4) 30-35 days

Ans: 1

Q. How much nursery area is required for transplanting one hectare of paddy crop?

1) 1000 m^2
2) 750 m^2
3) 500 m^2
4) 250-400 m^2

Ans: 1

Q. Which variety is not susceptible to insects & disease?

1) Pant Dhan-10
2) Govind

3) Narenda Dhan-2
4) Saket-4

Ans: 4

Q. Which paddy variety is not suitable for upland situation?

1) Narendra Dhan-I
2) Renu
3) Saraju-52
4) Narendra Dhan-118

Ans: 1

Q. Which is the highest digestible protein fodder in the following?

1) Lucerne
2) Cowpea
3) Clusterbean
4) Berseem

Ans: 4

Q. How much biomass in quintal per hectare is obtained from green manure of the sunnhemp and dhaincha crops?

1) 300-325 quintals
2) 225-275 quntals
3) 200-225 quintals
4) 325-350 quintals

Ans: 1

Q. Which is not an organic matter in the following-

1) Crude protein
2) Carbohydrate
3) Vitamins
4) Hormones

Ans: 4

Q. Which herbicide resides for the longest period in the soil?

1) Chlorpropham
2) Linuron
3) Propachlor
4) Simazine

Ans: 2

Q. Which of the following is not a method of knowing seed life?

1) Respiration test
2) Embryo culture method
3) Seed dormancy method
4) Indigocarmine method

Ans: 4

Q. Which of the following is not a variety of seeds?

1) Hybrid seed
2) Composite seed
3) Breeder seed
4) Mutant seed

Ans: 4

Q. Opening and closing of stomata depends on-

1) Sunlight
2) Water pressure
3) Transpiration
4) Temperature

Ans: 3

Q. At what temperature does the wilt disease virus grow faster?

1) 40°C - 45°C
2) 35°C - 40°C
3) 24°C - 28°C
4) 22°C - 26°C

Ans: 3

Q. Evaporation is measured by which instrument?

1) Barometer
2) Psychrometer
3) Lysimeter
4) Hygrometer

Ans: 3

Q. 'Pheromone Trap' attracts-

1) male moths
2) female moths
3) caterpillar
4) female bugs

Ans: 1

Q. What is the average temperature of cow and buffalo?

1) -98.4°F
2) 100°F
3) 101.5°F
4) 102°F

Ans: 3

Q. Potato tuber growth is stopped at what temperature?

1) 40°C - 42°C
2) 30°C - 32°C

3) 35°C - 37°C
4) 38° - 40°C

Ans: 2

Q. Which is not prepared from patato?

1) Farina and Alcohol
2) Paper
3) Wine
4) Acetic acid

Ans: 2

Q. Soldier insect harms which crop more?

1) Urad
2) Arhar
3) Moong
4) Paddy

Ans: 4

Q. Which pH range is not suitable to grow the crop?

1) Oats - 5.0 - 7.5 pH
2) Cotton - 6.0 - 7.5 pH
3) Bean - 6.0 -8.0 pH
4) Potato - 4.5 - 6.5 pH

Ans: 4

Q. How much minimum temperature is essential for wheat germination and optimum temperature for crop growth in degree Celsius?

1) 3.5°C-5.5°C and 20°C-22°C
2) 5.6°C-7.5°C and 16°C-18°C
3) 8°C-10°C and 30°C-35°C
4) 10°C-12°C and 25°C-30°C

Ans: 4

Q. The ideal temperature for most of the cultivable crops is-

1) 30°C - 50°C
2) 15°C - 40°C
3) 35°C - 40°C
4) 45°C - 55°C

Ans: 2

Q. Growth of early emerging leaves becomes faster because of-

1) cell division and cell enlargement
2) stunt growth of plants
3) faster photosynthesis
4) low pressure of outer atmosphere

Ans: 1

Q. How much percentage dry weight of crops should be at physiological maturity?

1) 28%
2) 20%
3) 25%
4) 30%

Ans: 3

Q. To reduce the crop-weed competition, at what stage are the herbicides used?

1) At germination
2) At tillering
3) At ear emergence
4) After first irrigation

Ans: 4

Q. How does the supply of nitortgen in grains take place?

1) From old leaves
2) From plant roots
3) From stem
4) By photosynthesis

Ans: 1

Q. Inarching method is used for culture of which fruits?

1) Mango and Guava
2) Mango and Grapes
3) Guava and Litchi
4) Phalsa and Guava

Ans: 1

Q. Which disease is not related to Bajra?

1) Green Ear
2) Ergot
3) Wilt
4) Rust

Ans: 3

Q. What is the suitable Rabi maize variety?

1) Sharadmani
2) Azad Uttam
3) Naveen
4) Ganga -5

Ans: 1

Q. Which is not the symptom of Khaira disease?

1) Dark grey colour spots on leaves
2) Adverse effect on root growth

3) More diseases stop the crop growth
4) Stem of plants turn and fall down

Ans: 1

Q. At what stage are more nutrients essentially required in cereal crops?

1) Growth stage of plants
2) Formation of leaves
3) Panicle initiation
4) Maturity of crops

Ans: 1

Q. What is the order of c4 plants?

1) Sugarcane - Maize - Sudan grass - Bajra
2) Sugarcane - Cotton - Paddy - Maize
3) Sudan grass - Sugarcane - Paddy - Bajra
4) Cotton - Maize - Bajra - Sugarcane

Ans: 1

Q. Which is not natural factor affecting soil fertility?

1) Topography
2) Soil age
3) Air
4) Parent material

Ans: 3

Q. The leaching loss of Nitrogen (N) is more in the form of-

1) Ammonia
2) Nitrate
3) Nitrogen
4) Water solution

Ans: 2

Q. The major fungi that effect food-grains in storage are-

1) Mucor
2) Rhizopus
3) Candida
4) Aspergillus

Ans: 1

Q. Which species of honeybee is not Indian?

1) *Apis florea*
2) *Apis dorsata*
3) *Apis dorsata*
4) *Apis mellifera*

Ans: 4

Q. Which is not basic principle of Agronomy?

1) To select appropriate materials for seed & sowing
2) Management of soil and climate
3) Appropriate intercropping activities management for corp
4) Livestock management for Agriculture

Q. Which is not matched in relation to sugarcane?

1) Seed treatment - Aglol 3%
2) For seed - 6-7 month old crop
3) Sowing - Upper portion is more used
4) After flowering - Used for sowing

Ans: 4

Q. Which does not match in relation to Cotton?

1) C-520 - Diploid
2) G-27 - Diploid
3) Vikas - American
4) Ranivan - American

Ans: 4

Q. Which is not true in relation to Gram?

1) Subfamily -Papilionaceae
2) Chromosome NO.-22
3) Acid-Malic and Oxalic
4) Origin-North America

Ans: 4

Q. Which variety of Barley is huskless?

1) Pragati (K 508)
2) Ritambhara (K 551)
3) Geetanjali (K 1149)
4) Karan -3

Ans: 4

Q. Which disease occurs, when more sorghum is consumed?

1) Rickets
2) Scurvy
3) Nightblindness
4) Pellagra

Ans: 4

Q. Which is not true in relation to Bajra?

1) Pennisetum Typhoides
2) Graminae Family
3) Chromosome No - 20
4) Origin Africa

Ans: 4

Q. Which Sorghum variety is not multicut?

1) Pusa Chari-2
2) M. P. Chari -2
3) M. P Chari
4) U. P. Chari -1

Ans: 4

Q. Which is the highest digestible protein non-leguminous crop among the following?

1) Napier
2) Maize Silage
3) Maize
4) Jowar

Ans: 4

Q. Which is not an inorganic matter in the following?

1) Magnesium
2) Iron
3) Fat
4) Iodine

Ans: 3

Q. Dr. M.S. Swaminathan has distinguished himself in which of the following fields?

A. Nuclear Physics
B. Agriculture
C. Astrophysics
D. Medicine

Ans B (Agriculture)

Q. The Green Revolution in India was the outcome of the efforts of who amongst the following?

A. M.S. Swaminathan
B. C. Rangrajan
C. K.V. Kamath
D. Rakesh Mohan

Ans A (M.S. Swaminathan)

Q. The National Bank for Agriculture and Rural Development (NABARD) was established in the year?

A. 1970
B. 1975
C. 1977
D. 1980

Ans - D (1982)

Q. The head office of the NABARD is located in?

A. Lucknow
B. Hyderabad
C. New Delhi
D. Mumbai

Ans- D (Mumbai)

Q. Where is the Cenlial Rice Research Institute located?

A. Bangaluru
B. Kanpur
C. Coimbatore
D. Cuttack

Ans - D (Cuttack)

Q. NABARD was established in the?

A. Fourth Five Year plan
B. Fifth Five Year plan
C. Sixth Five Year plan
D. Eighth Five Year plan

Ans C (Sixth Five Year plan)

Q. Who is the present Chairman of Protection of Plant Varieties and Farmers' Right Authority (PPV&FRA)?

A. Dr. R.R. Hanchinal
B. Dr. P.L. Gautam
C. Dr. S. Nagarajan
D. Dr. Swapan K. Datta

Ans - A

Q. Which among the following is another name for vitamin B_{12}?

A. Niacin
B. Pyridoxal phosphate
C. Cobalamin
D. Riboflavin

Ans C

Q. The term 'Heterosis' was coined by

A) G.H. Shull
B) W. Bateson
C) T.H. Morgan
D) E.M. East

Ans - A

Bibliography

Akira Tanaka and Shouichi Yoshida. Nutritional Disorders of the rice plant in Asia. *Technical Bulletin* (1970). International Rice Research Institute.

Bockus, W., W., Bowden, R. L., Hunger, R. M., Morrill, W. L., Murray, T. D. and Smiley, R. W. (eds.) (2010). *Compendium of Wheat Diseases*. American Phytopathological Society Press.

CABI Crop Protection Compendium. (2008). *Cajanus cajan* (pigeon pea) datasheet.

CABI Crop Protection Compendium. (2008). *Cicer arietinum* datasheet.

CABI Crop Protection Compendium. (2008). *Daucus carota* datasheet.

CABI Crop Protection Compendium. (2008). *Phaseolus vulgaris* datasheet.

CABI Crop Protection Compendium. (2008). *Triticum aestivum* (wheat) datasheet.

CABI Crop Protection Compendium. (2012). *Zea mays* datasheet. .

CABI Crop Protection Compendium. (2014). *Oryza sativa* (rice) datasheet.

Drost, D. (2010). *Beans in the Garden* . Utah State University Cooperative Extension.

Duke, J.A. (1983). *Triticum aestivum L. Handbook of Energy crops*.

Espinoza, L. and Ross, J. (Eds.) *Corn Production Handbook*. University of Arkansas Division of Agriculture Cooperative Extension Service.

Gaur, P.M., Tripathi, S., Gowda, C.L.L., Ranga Rao, G.V., Sharma, H.C., Pande, S. and Sharma, M. (2010). *Chickpea Seed Production Manual*. International Crops Research Institute for the Semi-Arid Tropics.

Kirkpatrick, T.L. and Rothrock, C.S. (2001). *Compendium of Cotton Diseases*. American Phytopathological Society Press.

Lerner, B.R. (2001). *Growing Beans in the Home Vegetable Garden*. Purdue University Cooperative Extension Service.

Lisu Chen, Lin Lin, Guangzhe Cai, Yuanyuan Sun, Tao Huang, Ke Wang, Jinsong Deng (2014). *Identification of Nitrogen, Phosphorus, and Potassium Deficiencies in Rice Based on Static Scanning Technology and Hierarchical Identification Method*.

Nene, Y.L., Reddy, M.V., Haware, M.P., Ghanekar, A.M., Amin, K.S., Pande, S. and Sharma, M. (2012). *Field Diagnosis of Chickpea Diseases and their Control*. Information Bulletin No. 28 (revised).

Nutrition deficiency in rice. *Better Crops International*. Vol. 16, Special Supplement, May 2002.

Rice Knowledge Bank. International Rice Research Institute.

Ritchie, G.R., Bednarz, C.W., Jost, P.H. and Brown, S.M. (2004). *Cotton Growth and Development. Cooperative Extension Service*, University of Georgia College of Agricultural and Environmental Sciences.

Schwartz, H.F., Steadman, J.R., Hall, R. and Forster, R.L. (2005) *Compendium of Bean Diseases*.

Sheahan, C.M. (2012). *Plant guide for pigeonpea (Cajanus cajan)*. USDA-Natural Resources Conservation Service, Cape May Plant Materials Center. Cape May, NJ. 08210.

Singh, F. and Diwakar, B. *Chickpea Botany and Production Practices*. International Crops Research Institute for the Semi-Arid Tropics.

Valenzuela, H. and Smith, J. (2002). *Pigeonpea*. University of Hawaii Cooperative Extension Service.

Webster, R. K. and Gunnell, P. S. (Eds.) (1992). *Compendium of Rice Diseases*. American Phytopathological Society Press.

White, D. G. (1999). *Compendium of Corn Diseases*. American Phytopathological Society Press.

Index

❑❑❑